Valuing Clean Air

Valuing Clean Air

The EPA and the Economics of Environmental Protection

CHARLES HALVORSON

OXFORD
UNIVERSITY PRESS

OXFORD
UNIVERSITY PRESS

Oxford University Press is a department of the University of Oxford. It furthers
the University's objective of excellence in research, scholarship, and education
by publishing worldwide. Oxford is a registered trade mark of Oxford University
Press in the UK and certain other countries.

Published in the United States of America by Oxford University Press
198 Madison Avenue, New York, NY 10016, United States of America.

Library of Congress Cataloging-in-Publication Data
Names: Halvorson, Charles, author.
Title: Valuing clean air : the EPA and the economics of environmental protection /
Charles Halvorson.
Description: New York, NY, United States of America : Oxford University Press, [2021] |
Includes bibliographical references and index. |
Identifiers: LCCN 2020049830 (print) | LCCN 2020049831 (ebook) | ISBN 9780197538845 (hardback) |
ISBN 9780197538869 (epub) | ISBN 9780197538876 (electronic)
Subjects: LCSH: United States. Environmental Protection Agency—History. |
Environmental policy—United States—History. | Environmental protection—
Economic aspects—United States—History.
Classification: LCC TD171 .H34 2021 (print) | LCC TD171 (ebook) |
DDC 363.739/2560973—dc23
LC record available at https://lccn.loc.gov/2020049830
LC ebook record available at https://lccn.loc.gov/2020049831

DOI: 10.1093/oso/9780197538845.001.0001

1 3 5 7 9 8 6 4 2

Printed by Integrated Books International, United States of America

For Emma

Contents

Contents

Acknowledgments

This book exists because of the generosity of many people.

Thank you first and foremost to my family. My parents taught me to be curious about the world and sustained me in body and soul wherever I followed my interests. My mother, Mary Morrison, was my first writing teacher and remains my biggest champion. My father, George Halvorson, gave me a healthy sense of confidence as well as the wisdom to see life's good bounces as good fortune. Thank you to Lorie Halvorson and Clint Morrison, who saw this project all the way through as stepparents and the finest partners for my parents I could ever ask for. My in-laws, Amy and Peter Pulitzer, brought me hiking, biking, diving, and, best of all, deep into their amazing family. My grandparents showed me that the academic life was a worthy and deeply satisfying one. My grandmother, Jean Probst, was the first woman to teach math at Macalester College, and while I wish that she had passed on some of that felicity with numbers, she will forever be a model for me in the determination and the kindness with which she approached her work. My grandfather, Tom Probst, is a prankster of the first order, and he showed me how to live a purposeful life without giving up any mischief. My grandmother, Barbara Halvorson, was a teacher, a mayor, and a family anchor who lived with a fortitude I aspire to. I never got the chance to meet my grandfather, George Halvorson, but his lifelong dedication to education has clearly deepened this rich inheritance. My wonderful bunch of brothers, Jonathan Halvorson, Seth Halvorson, Derek Schaible, and Michael Halvorson, sisters, Anna Nelson and Calley Morrison, sister-in-law Charlotte Pulitzer, and all of their equally great partners enthusiastically cheered this project along. Jonathan laid out a path as the family's first PhD and bequeathed me his Harlem apartment. Seth kicked ass. More than once, Derek jumped in to dig me out of technological holes. With unflagging encouragement, Michael has helped me navigate academia and life beyond.

Before this project could begin, several teachers helped me learn to love learning. At Saint Paul Academy, Eric Severson first pushed me to see myself as a writer. Andrea Sachs sparked my interest in history, and then did me a great favor by hiring me for my first teaching position. At Lewis & Clark

College, Stephen Beckman taught me how to do the rigorous research that history requires. Andrew Bernstein introduced me to the joy of dissecting a book and the field of environmental history. Paul Powers and Robert Kugler demonstrated that the life of the mind was truly the most enjoyable. Reiko Hillyer showed me that history can be a radical act, inspiring me to go to graduate school. At Columbia University, I had the honor of being a student of Barbara Fields, whose history pulls no punches and yet is full of astonishing empathy for her fellow humans. With warmth and wit, Gergely Baics helped me learn to teach.

From the beginnings of this project, many people have poured in ideas and support. Thank you to the members of my dissertation committee. Karl Jacoby helped me to see the EPA as an important subject in its own right. Paul Sabin centered the 1970s as a critical point in the country's history and helped me connect environmental policy to the wider political transformations. Richard John showed me how to do rigorous policy and business history. Merlin Chowkwanyun helped me trace the intricate politics of environmental health and provided a jolt of confidence late in the dissertation process. Despite my always needing something at the last minute, Sharee Nash moved administrative mountains.

Underscoring the deep generosity of the historical profession, many other people have contributed to this project. David Rosner helped me to understand air pollution as first and foremost a problem of public health. Louis Hyman took me on as a participant in the first-ever History of Capitalism summer camp and provided advice and encouragement throughout the project. Brian Balogh lent his policy history brilliance to this project and connected me to Dan Carpenter, who provided an insightful reading as my mentor in the National Fellowship program. Neil Maher, Raechel Lutz, Gene Cittadino, Scot McFarlane, and the rest of the New York Metropolitan Seminar in Environmental History gave me a stimulating and supportive environmental history community throughout my time at Columbia. Though I wish we had had many more hours to discuss the subjects of this book, I am grateful for the enthusiasm and ideas that Marc Eisner shared with me as I began to work on it. Chris Sellers and Leif Frederickson broadened my understanding of environmental health and, with the rest of the Environmental Data and Governance Initiative, model the critical need for engaged historical scholarship today. At Oxford University Press, Susan Ferber has proven to be a dream editor, sharpening every idea and word in this book, and patiently adapting as the world and my timelines changed. Thank you also to

Jeremy Toynbee and the other editors at Newgen who prepared this book and the two anonymous reviewers who provided incisive critiques and generous advice for how to improve the argument and writing.

My research took me to archives across the country, where I was invariably met by able and patient staff who helped me find the material that this project is based on. Archivists at the National Archives and Records Administration in College Park, Boston, and San Bruno helped me find and pull hundreds of boxes of EPA files. Archivists at the Richard Nixon, Gerald Ford, Jimmy Carter, Ronald Reagan, and George H. W. Bush presidential libraries helped me navigate the idiosyncrasies of recordkeeping across those administrations. Archivists at Bates College, Stony Brook University, and Yale University assisted in my exploration of environmental advocates. Librarians at the Arthur W. Diamond Law Library at Columbia Law School retrieved countless issues of *Environment Reporter* from basement stacks, expressing only good humor as I slowly made my way through the many binders. The librarians of Butler Library evinced similar patience throughout six years of requests, including annual reports that occupied entire carts. Before she retired, Mary Cargill provided invaluable help in finding congressional material.

I had the great fortune to interview two dozen former EPA officials and other policymakers for this project. I am particularly indebted to Mike Levin, who sat with me for multiple interviews and shared his personal papers from his time as chief of the EPA's Regulatory Reform Staff. Thank you to Alan Loeb, the keeper of those papers and a historian himself, who ferried dozens of Mike's boxes to and from storage.

Many institutions made this project possible. The Graduate School of Arts and Sciences at Columbia University supported my graduate training and much of my research and writing. The Department of History sponsored research trips and conference papers, and bestowed upon me the honor of the Bancroft Dissertation Award, which helped to make possible the publication of this book. The Gerald R. Ford Presidential Library supported my research on the Ford administration and the American presidency with a substantial research grant and the generous Dissertation Award in Honor of Robert M. Teeter. The Miller Center of Public Affairs sponsored me as a National Fellow. The American Council of Learned Societies and the Mellon Foundation furnished a year that allowed me to complete my dissertation free of teaching responsibilities.

I have had the great fortune of superb colleagues at every stage of this project. At Columbia, Jason Resnikoff, Allison Powers Useche, Mookie Kideckel,

Mary Freeman, George Aumoithe, Manuel Bautista Gonzalez, Sam Daly, AJ Murphy, Emilie Connolly, and many others made the six years of graduate school a whirlwind of intellectual challenge and good times. I miss fiercely our post-seminar drinks at 1020. At Wesleyan University, Lori Flannigan, Ann Tanasi, Courtney Fullilove, Demetrius Eudell, Erik Grimmer-Solem, Victoria Smolkin, Laura Ann Twagira, Cecilia Miller, Paul Erickson, Ronald Schatz, Jennifer Tucker, Oliver Holmes, Jesse Nasta, Valeria López Fadul, Gary Shaw, and many others helped me realize my dream of being a professor and then cheered me on as I decided to try something different. At Gemic, my wonderful coworkers have taught me to think in new ways as I finished this book.

Throughout nearly a decade of study, research, and writing, an incredible set of friends have sustained me. When I moved to New York to go to graduate school, someone told me that the city would teach me as much as anything I learned in the classroom. That turned out to be true, but only for the friends I found there. Together with that Columbia cohort, Mary Kate Miranowski, Dave Miranowski, Kaitlin Bray, Scott Mikawa, Núria Forqués Puigcerver, Patrick Lamson-Hall, Kelly Britton, Stephan Alessi, Xan Kernan-Schloss, Colin Reilly, Danielle Kraus, Jessica Schramm, Erica Dube, Dave Adams, Thyra Heder, CJ Marsi, and many others kept me forever tired and happy. Likewise, Christov Churchward, Elise Maxwell, Martin Meyer, and Erik Huckle made trips back to Minnesota deeply grounding and full of adventure. While the Windigo is no more, we will always have the fish.

When I began graduate school, I also started out on a new path with an old friend who arrived in New York with a chihuahua named Frida and an unmatchable zest for life. Through unending support and the repeated injection of perspective, Emma Pulitzer helped me navigate the solitary and sometimes dispiriting work of writing a dissertation and then a book. More important, Emma helped me grow into the person I am today. I am more fortunate than I could ever say to have her as my partner.

Finally, this book owes its greatest debt to my graduate advisor, Elizabeth Blackmar. Simply put, Betsy is the smartest and the most generous person I have ever met. Many years ago, she saw the inklings of this project in my afternoon ramblings in her office and she patiently pulled those ideas forward into this book, along the way reading more drafts than I care to count. Wherever fortune takes me, having had the opportunity to be Betsy's student will always be one of the great privileges of my life.

Abbreviations

AEI	American Enterprise Institute
AEP	American Electric Power
API	American Petroleum Institute
BACT	best available control technology
CEQ	Council on Environmental Quality
COWPS	Council on Wage and Price Stability
EDF	Environmental Defense Fund
EDGI	Environmental Data and Governance Initiative
EPA	Environmental Protection Agency
LAER	lowest achievable emissions rate
NAAQS	National Ambient Air Quality Standards
NAPCA	National Air Pollution Control Administration
NIPCC	National Industrial Pollution Control Council
NRDC	Natural Resources Defense Council
NSPS	New Source Performance Standards
OIRA	Office of Information and Regulatory Analysis
OMB	Office of Management and Budget
PSD	Prevention of Significant Deterioration program
RACT	reasonably available control technology
RARG	Regulatory Analysis Review Group
RFF	Resources for the Future
SIP	State Implementation Plan

Valuing Clean Air

Introduction

Save EPA

In January 1982, the *Doonesbury* comic strip brought its readers to a window ledge high above the headquarters of the Environmental Protection Agency (EPA), where a demoralized enforcement attorney was contemplating suicide. As the popular political cartoon explained, the career EPA employee's desperation owed to the devastation unleashed by EPA administrator Anne Gorsuch and her boss, President Ronald Reagan. "Are you going or not?" taunted the cartoon Gorsuch, whose real-life counterpart was in the midst of deep budget and staffing cuts. Out on the ledge, the attorney explained to an anxious friend that Gorsuch and Reagan threatened to destroy everything the EPA had accomplished since its creation in 1970. Central to these accomplishments was a dramatic reduction in air pollution, which *Doonesbury*'s beleaguered enforcement attorney underscored by declaring that he could read the license plates of the cars far down below his perch. "It's the end of the dream," the attorney warned his friend and readers across the country.[1]

The *Doonesbury* series was the dark comedy of a media blitz put together by an organization called Save EPA. A volunteer network of former EPA employees and their allies, Save EPA came together in 1981 to defend the agency against the Reagan administration. With Gorsuch at the EPA's helm, the Reagan administration was in the midst of severely reducing the agency's capacity to govern. Making this threat more pernicious, Reagan and Gorsuch were waging this attack on the agency behind the scenes, through reorganization plans, budgetary maneuvers, and various other tactics that were hard for the general public to perceive. Recognizing that he did not have popular support to dismantle the agency outright, Reagan was betting that he could bleed the EPA to death before anyone realized what was happening. To counter this pernicious attack, Save EPA's volunteers set themselves up as a clearinghouse for information—leaking budget proposals, meeting notes, and anything else its volunteers and allies could lay hands on, and offering

Valuing Clean Air. Charles Halvorson, Oxford University Press (2021). © Oxford University Press.
DOI: 10.1093/oso/9780197538845.003.0001

their insider analysis to reporters, congressional allies, and others of the damage that these changes would have on the agency.

Save EPA succeeded. The threat to EPA eventually attracted the attention of the press, environmental advocates, Congress, and the general public, becoming a major thorn in the Reagan administration's side. Caught up in scandals that Save EPA helped to expose, Gorsuch resigned in 1983. As the EPA grew as a political liability, Reagan retreated from much of his deregulatory agenda. Back in January 1982, the attorney in the *Doonesbury* series had eventually turned away from the ledge, and while the comic strip Gorsuch promptly fired him after he clambered back inside his office, he presumably departed with another trove of information for Save EPA.

The story of Save EPA highlights the fact that environmental regulation is both vitally important and essentially opaque to the general public. The agency was established in 1970, part and parcel of a sweeping transformation in environmental politics. Over the preceding decade, environmental advocates had captured public attention and focused it on the damage that industrial society was inflicting on the environment—from rivers that had become little more than open sewers to cities choking in smog. In response, Congress passed a sweeping set of laws that empowered the federal government to make and implement regulations to address a host of environmental concerns. State and local governments had regulated pollution prior to the 1960s, but the new federal policies represented a revolution in the breadth and force of their intervention. In a few short years, a clean environment became a national birthright, to be attained and secured by strict, science-based standards that applied everywhere across the country. Charged with implementing and overseeing those standards, the EPA was the centerpiece of the bold assertion that the federal government had a responsibility to protect the environment, the authority to command private business to reduce their pollution, and the capacity to dictate how they did so.

But revolutions are always contested. Challenging the policy changes that accompanied the rise of modern environmentalism in the 1960s, regulated companies and their political allies argued that establishing a natural right to a clean environment was naïve and even socially hazardous. According to this narrative, pollution was the inevitable byproduct of an industrial economy that had brought unprecedented prosperity and physical health to the American people. While industrial voices admitted that there were problems associated with pollution, they were quick to point out that there were also problems associated with its control, as companies diverted capital from productivity-enhancing investments or shut down in the face of untenable mandates, cutting off the wages and spending that fueled America's economy. According to the business community, controlling pollution needed to be carefully weighed against other social priorities. Empowering the federal government to "command-and-control," as critics of strengthened regulation pejoratively described the EPA's direct mandate model, risked economic ruin.

As *Valuing Clean Air* shows, the contest over environmental protection came to orbit around the EPA. Charged with implementing much of the sweeping environmental legislation of the early 1970s, the EPA became the central space where thorny questions about public welfare were adjudicated. In setting and enforcing technical standards, the EPA determined what environmental protection looked like, how much it cost, and even how it felt, as the agency's rules literally changed the composition of the air across much of the country. While most Americans gave little thought to the intricacies of public policy when they took a breath, regulated industry, environmental advocates, presidential administrations, congressional representatives, and a host of other parties wasted little time in cutting channels into the EPA's policymaking.

The EPA's story and the contest over environmental protection unfolded as part of the convulsions that shook American politics in the second half of the twentieth century. From the early twentieth century, government regulation had been an important tenet of the liberal belief that private industry needed to be governed by an active state to protect the public from the excesses of capitalism. That philosophy gained widespread support in the wake of the Great Depression, informing the many commissions and other regulatory institutions that guided much of the country's economy through the postwar period.[2] In many industries, especially new ones such as nuclear power, regulators and the companies they oversaw built close working relationships. So close, in fact, that critics on both the left and the right eventually came to see regulatory governance as posing risks to the public welfare—from the left, by limiting accountability, and from the right, by stifling competition.[3] By the 1960s, neoclassical economic critiques of the supposed inefficiency of government regulation swirled in political discourse alongside libertarian philosophical arguments about the supposed risks of regulation to individual freedom and other cherished values, with regulated industry buoying both lines of challenge.[4] In demanding new federal intervention but also new powers of citizen oversight of that intervention, the environmental movement of the 1960s reflected this critical inflection point in liberal governance.[5] By the time of the EPA's formation, any consensus about the proper role of the state had disappeared and the growing contest over liberalism would shape the EPA—and vice versa, as environmental policy became a generative space for a shift away from direct mandate interventions to market-based models in public policy.

Central to this story is the emergence of economics as the chief arbiter of value in public policymaking. The same period that saw the EPA's creation also witnessed the rise of economics as the "language of public policy," as one new study puts it.[6] While that rise may seem inevitable from our contemporary vantage point, it was not a foregone conclusion in the 1970s. The notion that the value of the environment could be expressed monetarily cut to the core of popular understandings of public welfare and expectations for the state, and it was resisted accordingly. The ascent of economics in determining the value of clean air was long and not at all straightforward, driven by various forces for what were often antithetical reasons, as this book explores. In addition to challenging the inevitability of the triumph of economics, this history of the protection of clean air serves as a reminder that that triumph is in fact incomplete, with other understandings of value continuing to animate public policy into the present.

In connecting changing ideas about environmental value to the major political struggles of the last fifty years, this book partakes in a turn toward regulatory policy as a critical space in the evolution of the American state. Political scientists have led much of this turn, finding in regulation fruitful ground for the study of American political development.[7] Historians too have turned their attention to regulation, adding a richer understanding of how environmental standards and other interventions have textured ordinary life.[8] Some of the best of this scholarship has explored the EPA as a critical site where popular ideas about the environment were transformed into public policy.[9] But a more sustained examination of the EPA is needed to fully comprehend the politics of environmental value. While there are many excellent accounts of the environmental movement and the seismic shifts in law and culture that it produced, more is needed about what came next, when that starburst of environmental concern intersected with the convulsions of the liberal state. Historians have elsewhere shown the 1970s and 1980s to have been a pivotal period in the ascendance of a neoliberal politics that puts its faith in markets over expert governance when it comes to public welfare.[10]

As this book shows, environmental governance played a critical role in the neoliberal turn, sparking and refracting ideas about the responsibility, authority, and capacity of the state that would come to define the modern political imagination.

This book focuses on clean air policy because the regulation of air pollution has served as a key space for the development, debate, and deployment of critical technologies of governance and new approaches to environmental value over the past half century. It does not attempt an exhaustive history of air pollution policy or of the EPA. Rather, the EPA's administration of the Clean Air Act from 1970 to the 1990s serves as the narrative backbone for an exploration of how a popular consensus about the responsibility, authority, and capacity of the state to address a collective problem was translated into public policy, and how that consensus was then attacked, defended, and transformed as policy.

Through the EPA's governance of air pollution, this book traces four key themes animating modern environmental politics. The first is the shift among Republican voters and elected officials from supporting to opposing environmental protection. From the late 1960s to the early 1990s, a majority of Americans and their elected officials believed that the federal government had a responsibility to clean up and protect the environment. As Chapter 1 describes, in the late 1960s, this consensus shifted the locus of environmental politics from local and state authorities to the federal level, as Congress and the president responded to a surge in environmental concerns with legislation and executive action that gave the federal government the authority and capacity. As Chapters 2 and 3 explain, this bipartisan consensus was the most important factor behind the EPA's strength and success. But, as Chapters 4 and 5 describe, this consensus began to erode in the late 1970s in the face of economic stagnation, which fueled critiques of "over-regulation" rising up from a nascent neoliberalism among Democrats and a rising libertarianism within the Republican Party. The EPA endured with broad, if tempered, support. But as Chapter 6 shows, expansions of the mandate for federal action on the environment proved harder and harder to achieve. In the 1990s, the ascent of a potent anti-environmentalism within the Republican Party forestalled further expansion of environmental protections at the federal level.

The second theme, closely related to the first, is the politicization of science in policymaking. New, ecological awareness of the dangers of pollution helped to spur the environmental movement. The Clean Air Act and other resulting legislation tasked the EPA with basing its regulatory interventions on the latest scientific research. As both the proponents and opponents of stronger interventions quickly realized, the EPA's formation of that scientific basis proved to be a critical point in determining the strength of the resulting rules. The strengthening of protections under Democratic and Republican administrations resulting from advancements in scientific understanding of the risks of various pollutants underscores the power of scientific research in driving the EPA's agenda. By the 1990s, however, much of the Republican Party had grown comfortable with a crude approach to science couched in a bad faith representation of the uncertainty inherent to the scientific process. As the Epilogue explains with regard to climate change, the politicization of science has largely blocked the bipartisan cooperation that undergirded the remarkable environmental achievements of that earlier period.

The third theme is a growing faith in the efficiency of markets. Environmental policymakers in and outside the EPA responded to obstacles in expanding mandates by shifting toward market-based approaches to meeting environmental objectives. This shift encompassed a wide variety of policies and proponents, united by the belief that the costs to industry of complying with regulations represented an obstacle to achieving environmental goals and that those compliance costs would fall if the government transferred some authority over pollution control to industry. Undergirding that belief was the assumption that businesses knew best (and would always know best) how to reduce pollution and that the government could capture this efficiency with carefully designed policies that incentivized firms to achieve their full potential in pollution control. As the second half of the book explores, this shift grew from localized compliance alternatives in the late 1970s to the creation of the nation's first cap-and-trade program in the Clean Air Act Amendments of 1990. Throughout, the shift was contested by environmental advocates, who were concerned about losing power that they and the state had so recently won. Many of those advocates were also opposed to the very idea of granting businesses transactionable rights to pollute (a premise that market-oriented policies tended to require). But as continued progress on environmental goals was threatened by growing marginal costs, widening economic woes, and rising Republican hostility, this opposition faded. The eventual embrace of market-based strategies by most environmental advocates in the 1990s helped create a new environmentalism distinct in logic and language from what came before.

The fourth, final, and most important theme of this book is the rise of monetary approaches to environmental value. In many ways, the EPA's story is a story of how to value the environment. A rising appreciation among economists in the 1960s for the economic benefits of protecting environmental quality and a resulting effort to express those benefits in monetary terms intersected with the rise of popular ideas that valued aspects of the environment in the ethical language of rights, including a right to breathe clean air. These two perspectives were not necessarily antagonistic and, for a time, economists and environmentalists worked toward the same goal of persuading the federal government to take charge of environmental protection. But a growing reliance on economics among policymakers created more and more friction around techniques such as cost/benefit analysis, which environmentalists understood to inherently favor short-term costs to industry over long-term benefits to society. While sharing many of those concerns, EPA staff and officials embraced a monetary approach to environmental value in order to defend the agency's policies against concerted pressure from industry and its political allies. Environmental advocates slowly followed suit, becoming increasingly reliant on economics to make their case for strong environmental interventions. Here too, the 1990s can be seen as something of a culmination, though underlying questions about incommensurability and the ethics of the monetary framing of environmental value have returned to the fore in contemporary conversations about climate change, as explored in the Epilogue.

The EPA's adoption of market-oriented compliance models and a monetary approach to value were part and parcel of the agency's practice of a politics of the possible in service of a remarkable reduction in pollution. Over the past fifty years, EPA regulations sharply reduced emissions of nearly every major pollutant (the glaring outlier being carbon dioxide) despite significant increases in population and economic output. There are many ways to measure the social benefits of those improvements, from the millions of additional days of work gained by a decline in respiratory illnesses to a clear view across the Grand Canyon unobstructed by regional haze. A 2011 study estimated that the cumulative monetary benefits of the EPA's administration of the Clean Air Act would reach at least $50 trillion by 2020, with an extraordinary fifty to one ratio of benefits to costs.[11] As this book demonstrates, there was not one single path for the EPA to follow in attaining those benefits. Instead, EPA staff and officials learned to navigate powerful sets of competing interests, producing and adapting policies and practices that dramatically improved environmental quality.

Telling the Environmental Protection Agency's story requires a claim that is at once impossible and essential: that an institution can be imbued with a sense of agency by the people who make it up. To speak of the EPA's mission, indeed, to address the EPA in the singular, is to acknowledge the power of that ongoing communal investment. Describing the EPA as having purpose and volition does not preclude recognition of the many facets of the institution or the turmoil or contests that took place within it—this book is concerned with precisely those debates. Nor does it isolate the EPA from the constellation of outside actors who were often as important as those inside the agency in defining, challenging, and defending the EPA's mission. There are characters who pop up throughout this story who only briefly or never worked at the EPA, and that is part of the story. But no matter how varied or porous the EPA might appear under close examination, a shared set of values and sense of purpose animated the agency. Doug Costle, who helped to create the EPA, served as its third administrator, and contributed to its defense during the Reagan administration, later reflected on what he called the agency's "conscience": the belief among the EPA's staff and their allies that the government had an essential role to play in protecting clean air and water from the inevitable degradation of free enterprise left to its own devices.[12] More than anything else, the EPA's historical agency emanates from this shared commitment to the idea that the federal government has the responsibility, authority, and capacity to protect the environment.

1

The Costs of Pollution

Tom Crocker let his imagination run wild as he walked to work through the sticky Florida summer. A PhD candidate in economics at the University of Missouri, Crocker had been dispatched to central Florida in 1964 to study air pollution. In the rich agricultural country east of Tampa, ranchers and farmers were incensed about a rash of dead cattle and citrus trees, which they blamed on rising emissions from the local phosphate industry. Worried that the pollution might also threaten human health and finding local and state governments unequal to the challenge, these local complainants had managed to draw national attention to the problem, including the young Crocker, who arrived on a grant from the Public Health Service. All across the country, environmental activism was on the rise and would soon coalesce in a national environmental movement that eventually spurred Congress and the president to create national standards for clean air and a new agency to enforce them. But as Crocker walked back and forth from work, he was envisioning not new regulations but new markets.[1]

Rather than forcing phosphate producers to install expensive pollution controls or shut down, as seemed to be where public policy was headed, Crocker wondered if the flourishing industry could buy the right to pollute the air around their processing plants. The agriculturalists could move elsewhere and buy their own rights to keep that air free from pollutants. Such ideas were out of step with the vast regulatory expansion then getting under way at the state and federal level—an expansion that his own federal patron was helping to drive through the research that Crocker had been sent to do on the monetary damages of the air pollution. But the economist's ideas contained the seeds of something important to come.

The environmental movement spurred a legal revolution, institutionalizing the idea that the public had inalienable rights in the natural world. Environmental activists came from different backgrounds and responded to a range of factors that came together in the 1960s, including the unprecedented prosperity of the postwar period, the new threats of a nuclear and synthetic age, the successful modeling of federal intervention in the civil

Valuing Clean Air. Charles Halvorson, Oxford University Press (2021). © Oxford University Press.
DOI: 10.1093/oso/9780197538845.003.0002

rights movement and the Great Society, newly responsive courts, and a growing understanding of ecology. Republican and Democratic lawmakers responded with a flurry of legislation, including landmark protections for clean air and water. These laws laid out an expansive idea of the public interest, creating new regulatory agencies to protect the public from the potential dangers of the private sector and giving citizen groups a seat at the table from which to hold those new administrative bodies accountable.

A simultaneous environmental turn occurred among economists. Long attuned to the social costs of private enterprise, economists in the 1950s grew increasingly concerned that environmental degradation posed a significant threat to present and future prosperity. As economists tallied the monetary cost of various environmental problems, such as the rising health care costs associated with an increase of dangerous pollutants in the air, they offered alarming tabulations of the costs of unchecked pollution. By the 1960s, this environmental economics was paralleling the environmental movement in calling for federal intervention, albeit under the logic of addressing the inefficiencies that private enterprise had created.

While economists and environmental activists both called for the federal government to act to address pollution, they tended to have different understandings of what this response should look like. These differences were the result of fundamentally different approaches to the question of environmental value. Economists saw monetary costs and benefits as the best arbiters of value and approached pollution as an economic cost to society. Environmental activists, by contrast, valued clean air as a natural right. With a liberal faith in the government's capacity to direct private enterprise still dominant in the 1960s, economists were marginal to the national conversation about pollution and so the distance between their logic of costs and benefits and the activist notion of natural rights did not much matter. But economic upheaval in the 1970s would open a fervent debate about the monetary costs of protecting a natural right to clean air—a debate that economists eagerly stepped into.

Recasting the familiar history of the modern environmental movement, this chapter weaves together the creation of a national air pollution regime with the story of the economists who helped to establish the social costs of pollution. These economists were a diverse group, not least when it came to the question of the ideal role of the government in addressing pollution. Some of these economists, including the young Tom Crocker, saw growing public concerns about the environment as an opportunity to prove the efficiency of markets in allocating valuable goods, even air. Other economists held that there were critical aspects of the environment that could never be transacted for, blocked by physical realities that even the most inventive advocates of market approaches could not transcend. Yet in describing the underlying pollution problem and its mitigation in terms of costs and benefits, the economic profession as a whole put forward a monetary framing of environmental quality that implicitly challenged notions of inalienable environmental rights and eventually came to serve as a key logic for contesting the articulation of such rights in public policy.

The Environmental Movement and the Environmental Economist

At first, air pollution was a local problem. In the nineteenth century, the explosion of coal-powered manufacturing in cities like Pittsburgh and Chicago generated thick clouds of particulate matter that darkened the sky, choked lungs, blackened textiles, and blanketed cities in dust. Smog, a portmanteau of smoke and fog first used in London around the turn of the twentieth century, gave a name to this industrial atmosphere. Despite the obvious problems, puffing smokestacks signaled rising prosperity, and local leaders were hesitant to take aggressive measures to curtail air pollution, which posed the sort of acute health risks that had led to aggressive government responses to water pollution. But a rising middle class, especially the middle-class women who drove much of the activism of the Progressive Era, recast lingering coal smoke as part of the dirt and disorder of the industrial city. Black smoke and the resulting smog, were taken up in the larger Progressive campaign for cleanliness and order.[2] Building on the authority of local governments to regulate nuisances—the use of private property in ways that injured others—these reformers spurred the passage of preemptive laws that empowered local health officials to prohibit businesses from generating noxious smoke. But this authority proved difficult to enforce as the courts tended to reject blanket bans on pollution and accept polluters' arguments that they had made investments in more efficient boilers or other tweaks, even as they continued to emit dark smoke. Reformers pressed on, persuading state legislatures to grant new authority to regulate pollution.[3]

Economic estimates of the monetary damages caused by dirty smoke aided reformers in framing air pollution as a social cost. In Pittsburgh, where coal smoke was so dense that the city was forced to use streetlights during the day, the Mellon Institute of Industrial Research conducted a study in 1913 that estimated the annual cost of air pollution to the city to be nearly $10 million.[4] In addition to the costs of coping with the smoke—including all that artificial lighting—the Mellon study argued that smoke was retarding the development of a more diverse economy, as textile manufacturers and other businesses stayed clear of Pittsburgh. Studies in Cleveland and other cities found similar damages, lending ammunition to Progressive reformers in pushing local governments to act.[5] A theoretical understanding of the problem came in 1920, when English economist Alfred Pigou coined the term "externality" to describe the noxious byproducts that industrial producers freely dumped into rivers and air, to the detriment of the public welfare. Pigou recommended that polluting firms pay compensatory taxes according to the costs their externalities imposed on society.[6]

By the time of Pigou's writing, air pollution had largely become the domain of engineers, whose focus on the technical efficiency of individual systems pushed the larger critiques of Progressive reformers to the margins. In response to the implementation of local ordinances, businesses had hired engineers to study how pollution abatement might be achieved. By the 1910s, engineers across industry shared a consensus that large reductions in pollution were possible and that reducing pollution would be accomplished by improving the efficiency with which coal was burned, generating significant savings for industry in the process. As engineers established themselves more broadly in society as an expert class and as the technical discussion of pollution control grew too complicated for reformers to follow, Progressives found themselves increasingly sidelined in the control of air pollution. Conversations about pollution that had once orbited around the smokestack and its implications for the public welfare instead focused on the efficiency of each company's industrial boiler. Like economists, engineers were concerned about the monetary costs of pollution, but their interests lay in how pollution affected the balance sheets of the polluters.[7]

Air quality gradually improved in the 1920s and 1930s, although the principal reason for this success was not the efficiency gains made by industrial engineers but rather the adoption of cleaner energy sources. The expansion of oil and natural gas as well as the electrification of industrial manufacturing together dissipated the smoke in eastern industrial cities and allowed newer cities such as Los Angeles to grow without darkening their skies. Coal still powered eastern cities, but it was a smaller part of the fuel mix and was

increasingly used in central electric generating plants that were far more efficient in how much pollution they released relative to the energy they generated than the individual factory power plants they replaced.[8]

But even as coal smoke dissipated, the country faced new air pollution
concerns. The burning of oil and natural gas and the manufacture of increasingly complex chemicals emitted a slew of compounds into the air, many
of them dangerous to human health. In Los Angeles, suburban residents
confronted a new smog problem in the form of stinging mists that could not
be blamed on coal. This pushed the state to set up the country's first metropolitan area air pollution control authority in 1947. In the 1950s, the Los
Angeles Air Pollution Control District quickly became a leading site of air
pollution expertise in the country, identifying petroleum consumption as the
culprit behind the new "photochemical" smog. Burned as gasoline or other
fuels, petroleum released hydrocarbons and nitrogen oxides that combined
in the California sunshine to produce ozone, the highly reactive compound
that stung eyes, corroded surfaces, and clouded the view.[9]

While smog would become part of Los Angeles's unique mythos, communities across the country began suffering from new air pollution problems.
These new forms of air pollution could be frighteningly deadly, as a tragedy
in a small town near Pittsburgh revealed in 1948. That year, a strong temperature inversion trapped the nitrogen dioxide and other compounds released
by zinc and steel plants in Donora, Pennsylvania. Over the course of a few
days, the resulting smog killed twenty people and sickened thousands more.
This drew national attention to an air pollution problem that had evolved
from coal smoke into a more complex and more sinister problem. Where
engineers had more or less succeeded in making coal smoke the province of
individual firms, Donora helped to frame these new air pollution problems
as public concerns.[10]

Air pollution became an enduring national concern through the persistent agitation of activists around the country, who exposed first local and
then state responses as inadequate in the face of the growing problem. Much
of this activism took shape in major metropolitan areas such as Los Angeles
and New York, with their acute and well-publicized problems. But air pollution afflicted communities nationwide, smaller cities, and rural and suburban areas. Grassroots organizing in places such as Jacksonville and central
Florida called attention to the social costs of the environmental degradation
that accompanied the postwar economic boom and helped to lay the foundation on which the national movement to address air pollution would be built.

Polk Country, a rich agricultural area in the center of Florida, would seem like an unlikely space for air pollution. But in the 1950s, the expansion of phosphate refining set local cattle ranchers and citrus growers on a collision course with the phosphate industry. Phosphorous is a necessary component in plant growth, and land that is being intensely farmed typically requires the application of phosphorous to ensure the continued fertility of the soil. Central Florida happens to sit over one of the world's largest deposits of phosphate ore, which has been mined for use as fertilizer since the nineteenth century. In the postwar period, skyrocketing demand for fertilizer and new advances in chemical processing shifted Florida's phosphate production from mining operations with limited impact on their surroundings into a massive processing industry. In the 1960s, the industry employed more than 10,000 workers and supplied nearly 90 percent of the nation's phosphates and fully 30 percent of the global total. But the new techniques for separating the phosphorous molecules from the phosphate ore also unlocked fluorides, highly reactive compounds that in high concentrations present a serious threat to the health of humans, plants, and animals. In the early 1950s, citrus growers and cattle ranchers in central Florida began to notice that emissions from phosphate plants appeared to be killing their groves and herds—a poisoning confirmed by citrus experts and veterinary researchers.[11]

In a sequence that was being repeated across the country in the postwar period, growing awareness of the problem of phosphate pollution was met with local protests and escalating demands for government intervention. Women drove much of this activism, organizing early campaigns through the auspices of existing women's groups focused on quality of life concerns. In central Florida, Harriet Lightfoot faced the growing phosphate pollution problem from her position as chair of the Community Improvement committee in her local Women's Club. Together with citrus growers and cattle ranchers, she and other local activists formed the Citizen's Committee on Air Pollution, with Lightfoot responsible for the new body's Division of Health. The Citizen's Committee collected evidence to document the severity of the phosphate pollution, which they presented to the Florida state legislature in 1954. The legislature formed an interim committee of its own to study the problem, which recommended in 1957 that the state create a dedicated pollution control authority. Instead, the state legislature decided to create the Florida Air Pollution Control Commission to take action against individual complaints. Dissatisfied activists in Polk County forced the commission to establish the state's first pollution control district in Polk and Hillsborough

Counties in 1958; by 1960, the district had the authority to set and enforce standards that limited emissions of fluorine and other pollutants. But the new laws and institutions produced little relief, as state officials proved reluctant to enforce them against companies that were responsible for much of the local region's economic base. Even as phosphate plants invested in pollution controls, the industry was expanding production.[12]

Meanwhile, in the northwest corner of the state, residents of Jacksonville were discovering their own pollution problem. Like most cities around the country, Jacksonville's air pollution came from a variety of sources—phosphate refining, but also pulpwood production, chemical production, shipbuilding, electricity generation, petroleum storage, automobiles, and the incineration of the city's garbage. The risks posed by these various emission sources were not fully understood at the time, but residents could see and feel the effects of the growing pollutant load. Corrosive compounds discolored paint and stained clothes hung out to dry, and pollution damaged plant leaves and irritated the lungs and eyes of Jacksonville's residents, especially those who lived in poorer neighborhoods near the worst sources of pollution.[13]

In the 1950s, the rising social costs of pollution attracted the attention of a growing cohort of economists, who would help to articulate a case for government action. H. Scott Gordon was among the first to argue that rules or regulations were needed to restrain the selfish behavior of firms and individuals. In a 1954 article, Gordon laid out the case for protecting what he called "common-property resources." Hypothesizing a fishery with a limited supply of fish and no rules governing behavior, Gordon argued that the inherent self-interest of each fisherman would eventually drive the fishery to exhaustion. In Gordon's mind, the individual fisherman simply had no incentive to leave fish in the water to catch in the future since he knew that his fellow fishermen would expand their current haul to take any fish he did not take. In order to protect the fishery (or any common-property resource), binding rules limiting the behavior of the participants were required.[14]

Gordon's assumption that firms and humans naturally and singularly pursued their self-interest served as a key premise of both environmental and neoclassical economics. That assumption of inherent self-interest was not yet universally accepted among social theorists or even economists in the 1950s, but the intellectual work to apply microeconomic assumptions to macroeconomic policies had begun.[15] An allegorical fight over fish provided the perfect setting for this neoclassical revival, which had as its subject *homo economicus*, the intrinsically self-interested actor whose relationship to his peers was by nature one of competition over limited resources. While Gordon called for regulations to temper that instinctual acquisitiveness, the profit maximizing subject he and other economists helped to conjure later served to naturalize a political philosophy that erased any notion of responsibility for one's fellow humans.

The founding of the Washington, DC, think tank Resources for the Future (RFF) established a home for economists interested in environmental policy. As its name suggests, RFF encouraged federal policymakers to protect the country's natural resources for future use—a mission statement that placed it in line with business-supported conservationist efforts dating back a half a century to Gifford Pinchot and the creation of the Forest Service.[16] Whereas earlier conservationists had focused on minimizing waste in the extraction and processing of natural resources, RFF used economic analysis to evaluate possible resource uses on the basis of the monetary costs and benefits of the alternatives—one of which was to not use the resource at all.[17] Seeded by the Ford Foundation with nearly $3.5 million for its first five years of operation and connected to officials in the highest levels of government, RFF quickly became a powerful institutional base for economists who hoped to translate their ideas into federal policy. With the subsequent arrival of additional Ford funding for an urban economics program, RFF expanded its focus to include the economics of pollution.[18]

In the 1950s, more and more of those economists made a case for government regulation. Economists measured social cost against a standard of maximizing social wealth, and many came to believe that only the government had the power to address the environmental degradation that was producing a suboptimal outcome. In 1954, Paul Samuelson produced a mathematical proof of the inability of markets to protect what he called "public goods," which opened the theory up to mathematical testing and debate.[19] Four years later, John Kenneth Galbraith popularized the notion that a common wealth was being squandered by the individual pursuit of happiness, arguing in the widely read 1958 book *The Affluent Society* that government regulation was needed to protect the high quality of American life from the prosperity that fueled it.[20]

While federal policymakers heard this call to arms, they insisted that their role was to support the states in addressing the air pollution problem. From the 1950s to the late 1960s, elected officials offered steadily expanding funding to address the air pollution problem, while steadfastly resisting taking direct responsibility for curbing emissions. In 1955, Congress passed the Air Pollution Control Act, allocating $5 million per year to the Public Health Service (PHS) to determine the extent of the air pollution problem and provide technical assistance to the states to address it.[21] In 1958, the PHS sponsored the first national conference on air pollution, which laid out the myriad health risks posed by routine exposure to air pollution and the rise in pollutant emissions across the nation.[22] The 1958 conference also spotlighted the economic damage caused by pollution, with RFF's President Reuben Gustavson taking the stage to describe the social costs of pollution as a $7.5 billion annual scourge to the nation.[23]

Following the 1958 conference, the surgeon general convened an Ad Hoc Task Group of pollution control officials, public health researchers, and business leaders to establish priorities for PHS-funded research. In its 1960 report, the Task Group noted that research up until that point had primarily focused on health risks, while the full effects of air pollution were much broader, including "economic losses due to damage to vegetation and livestock, corrosion of materials, soiling of surfaces, and reduction in visibility." Citing Gustavson's 1958 speech, the report stated that the cost of those losses amounted to between $4 and $8 billion annually—an alarming estimate in both its magnitude and uncertainty. In response, the Task Group called for a tripling of the $500,000 that industry and government were currently spending on new research into the agricultural damage resulting from air pollution and a sixfold increase in the $100,000 being spent on research into damage in other sectors.[24]

In 1960, PHS created a Division of Air Pollution and, over the next few years, officials repeatedly cited the economic costs of air pollution to justify the division's expanding work.[25] At its 1962 National Conference on Air Pollution, for example, PHS dedicated an entire session to the subject of "agricultural, natural resource, and economic considerations." A summary of the proceedings made explicit what the *National Goals of Air Pollution Research* had intimated two years earlier: establishing the costs of air pollution would help convince the public that the pollution controls pursued by local, state, and federal governments would yield benefits that justified the upfront costs of those programs.[26]

Economists who studied the problem of pollution were not unified in supporting the expansion of regulatory controls. In 1960, Ronald Coase published a seminal essay, "The Problem of Social Cost," which argued that market transactions could be more effective than legal rules in directing competing users of environmental resources to a socially optimal allocation—defined as the maximization of production. Coase used a series of legal cases around nuisance claims to demonstrate that overall economic output would be raised if individuals and firms could bargain over the use of environmental inputs like unsullied air, since those resources would be put to their most efficient use by the party that was willing to pay the most for them. One example that Coase gave described a textile weaver whose products were being discolored by the emissions of a nearby chemical manufacturer. Rather than a court issuing an injunction against the manufacturer, Coase proposed that the two parties should bargain for the air. The manufacturer could install technology to control the harmful emissions, move away, or pay the textile weaver to suffer the damage. Since the manufacturer's and the weaver's choice from among those alternatives would be guided by the maximization of profits, the end result would be a more efficient use of the clean air in question than would be the case if the manufacturer was simply prohibited from operating. In practice, Coase warned that legal rights to the resource in question might be necessary where transaction costs (such as the gathering of information about the pollution, or the existence of multiple parties to the problem) were prohibitively high.[27] But Coase would become a lodestar for future economists who championed the efficiency of market-based solutions to environmental problems.

Comparing Coase's article to Rachel Carson's *Silent Spring*, published two years later, reveals the gulf between his conception of social costs from her articulation of what would soon become mainstream environmentalist thinking. Drawing attention to the dangers of mass chemical use on the natural world, Carson argued that policymakers had missed the side effects of miracle compounds such as the insecticide dichlorodiphenyltrichloroethane (better known as DDT) because they lacked a basic scientific understanding of ecosystems and the long timescale of industrial toxicity. While the benefits of DDT were immediately apparent in higher agricultural yields, such chemicals also damaged vital parts of the complex webs in which all life was embedded. These social costs tended to appear over a longer term and in forms that were hard to predict and perhaps impossible to fully measure. In her indelible explanation of one such chain of events, Carson wrote about a farming community that had accidentally poisoned its own land awakening to a spring without birdsong.[28] Introducing ecology into popular discourse, Carson helped to generate an argument for hesitation in the face of uncertainty (the roots of a precautionary approach to risk). With her appeal to the social loss of a spring, Carson also advanced the belief that the environment was worthy of being protected, even when the monetary value of such protection could not be established. Much of the ensuing tension around the application of economics in environmental policymaking that this book explores would be the result of trying to reconcile the Carsonian and Coasian understandings of public welfare.

Meanwhile, activists in Jacksonville and central Florida continued to press local and state authorities for relief from their pollution problems. Ann Belcher, a working-class woman in Jacksonville, emerged as a counterpart to Polk County's Harriet Lightfoot, rallying her neighbors to demand relief from the Jacksonville city council for problems that included the struggles of many residents with respiratory issues during periods of bad pollution and property destroyed by corrosion. Receiving a sympathetic response but no action from the council, Belcher turned to the state government, writing a letter to the governor in 1963 that enumerated the monetary damage that she had suffered. From Polk and Hillsborough counties, Lightfoot likewise complained to the governor of health risks and damage to local industries and revealed that she had told friends to cancel vacations to the state. When they failed to receive a satisfying reply, Belcher and Lightfoot joined with activists across the country in appealing to federal officials for help.[29]

Though these officials were not ready to establish federal authority over air pollution, a growing number were willing to take on additional federal responsibility. In 1963, Democratic leaders in the Senate created a new Subcommittee on Air and Water Pollution under the auspices of the Public Works Committee and appointed a young Democrat from Maine named Edmund Muskie to chair it. Later that year, Congress passed the Clean Air Act in 1963, which made permanent the federal air pollution control research program and vastly expanded the amount of funding available to local and state authorities to $95 million over three years. At the time of the legislation, only fourteen states had a dedicated pollution control office. They were also spotty at the local level. The Los Angeles County Air Pollution Control District had in 1963 over 400 employees—as many as worked in air pollution control in the entire federal government. Other cities with long histories of industrial manufacturing and attendant air pollution, such as Pittsburgh and New York, also had pollution control authorities. But having an office dedicated to pollution control was more indicative of a long-standing problem than an effective solution, as local authorities struggled to devise and implement solutions of adequate scale.[30] In addition to boosting those local and state efforts, the Clean Air Act of 1963 instructed federal officials to issue nonbinding air quality criteria to guide local and state improvement efforts and established a narrow set of conditions under which federal officials could intervene in issues of interstate pollution. Nonetheless, even as the legislation increased the federal role, the responsibility and authority for addressing air pollution remained with the states.[31]

From his position as chairman of the Senate's environmental subcommittee, Senator Muskie had established himself as an environmental champion on the national stage, holding hearings and commissioning reports on different pollution issues. It was through these efforts that federal attention finally homed in on Florida's air pollution problem. In 1964, Muskie's subcommittee arrived in Tampa as part of a dozen field hearings on air pollution they had organized around the country.[32] In keeping with the local jurisdiction over pollution in this period, the field hearings focused on the specific problems germane to each venue—smog from automobiles in Los Angeles and particulate matter emitted by industry in Chicago.[33]

In the Tampa hearings, local activists debated the scale of the problem with advocates of the phosphate industry. Paul Huff, chairman of Polk County Farm Bureau's Air Pollution Control Commission, joined representatives of the Florida Citrus Mutual and the Polk County Cattle's Association in testifying about the damages of phosphate mining and manufacturing to trees and cattle, and the Citizen's Committee on Air Pollution raised fears about the threat to public health. The phosphate industry, represented by the Florida Phosphate Council, argued that the problem was being overblown and reinforced the industry's importance to the local economy.[34] Eager to augment their testimony with real-life observation, the Florida Phosphate Council and the Citizen's Committee each organized tours of the phosphate operations for the senators and the subcommittee staff. The morning after a full day of hearings, the Senate party boarded a chartered bus with members of the Citizen's Committee to visit damaged citrus groves and meet with agricultural researchers who were studying the effect of fluorine on cattle and citrus trees. At lunchtime, the bus deposited the Senate party at the International Mines and Minerals Park for a meal organized by the Florida Phosphate Council, after which they toured several of the area's phosphate manufacturing plants with Florida Phosphate Council representatives.[35] With little pollution visible during the afternoon tour, Floyd Bowen, the manager of one plant and the chairman of the Florida Phosphate Council, felt confident enough to remark that his operation "was as clean as a Candy Factory." The clear, cool weather that Friday was a stroke of luck for the phosphate manufacturers. But according to the Citizen's Committee, the manufacturers had left little to chance, scaling back production ahead of the tour. Huff later wrote to Senator Muskie to insist that the subcommittee had witnessed deceptively high air quality, enclosing photographs taken less than a day later, when the humidity had returned "and the phosphate plants were back to full operation." On the back of each photograph, Huff described the contrast between the clean skies that the subcommittee had seen and the normal polluted conditions to which the photographs bore witness.[36]

In Tampa and elsewhere around the country, the subcommittee's field hearings raised unanswered questions about the federal government's responsibility to control air pollution.

Intended by Senator Muskie to generate information about the national scope of the problem as well as its local variations, the hearings created expectations that the federal government intended to do something to reduce that pollution. Following the hearings, Jane May of Hillsborough County

Figure 1.1 Central Florida's seemingly intransigent phosphate pollution problem, as depicted in a photograph sent by local activist Paul Huff to Senator Edmund Muskie, 1964. From Paul Huff to Senator Edmund Muskie, March 2, 1964, Subcommittee on Air and Water Pollution, Senate Office Staff and Committee Staff Files, Series V.C. US Senate, Box 58, Folder 1, EMP.

wrote Senator Muskie to inform him that she had watched as the subcommittee party toured her neighbor's damaged citrus groves, seated in the chair where she spent much of her time after health problems ended her career as a schoolteacher. May told Muskie that she had had no explanation for her own twenty-six acres of damaged trees or her ravaged lungs until the Farm Bureau's Paul Huff informed her that the nearby mines of the Smith Douglas Phosphate Company were to blame. She might have sold her land, May confided, but buyers knew it was worthless because of the mine. So, May "began conferences, phone calls, letters to the various authorities. All to no avail." May had sued Smith Douglas Company, but a decision had yet to be reached. Although Smith Douglas told May and other growers that they had installed "the most expensive equipment to prevent the escape of gases," May stated, "the local men tell us confidentially . . . that they had not used the equipment." "This happens over and over," May protested; "we call, or write the authorities and we get no relief."

Calling on the federal government to intervene to protect citizens like her from the pollution, May pleaded, "Do they have the right to take away the life savings and chance of independent livelihood from people who are so helpless in defending their helplessness?"[37] Exemplifying the uncertainty surrounding the federal responsibility he was helping to define, Muskie replied: "Control measures are under the jurisdiction of the state health department, however, I am hopeful that the hearings held in Tampa will have the effect of stimulating accelerated activities in air pollution control measures."[38] While that vague answer may have given little comfort to May, the attention of the subcommittee amplified the idea that the federal government was responsible for addressing the air pollution problem. Jacksonville activist Ann Belcher had been unable to attend the Tampa hearings, but she had written to Senator Muskie to share her utter lack of faith in Florida's state government. While Belcher and her fellow activists would use existing channels to press for state-level intervention, their appeals had already begun to lay the foundation for the vast expansion of the federal government's authority over the nation's environmental health at the end of the decade.[39]

The immediate response from federal policymakers was more research. Following the Tampa hearings, the PHS launched a study of the monetary damage that phosphate mining and manufacturing was doing to cattle ranchers and citrus growers. It was this study that brought Tom Crocker to Florida in 1964. From an office in Winter Haven, a small town forty miles east of Tampa with angry agriculturalists and a local office of the State Board of

Public Health, Crocker studied shifts in real estate values around phosphate mines and manufacturing plants, corroborating complaints that mining and manufacturing reduced the value of neighboring land.[40]

Tom Crocker's interest in the phosphate manufacturing problem soon expanded beyond the falling prices of grazing acreage and orange groves. As Crocker would later write, far from avoiding phosphate manufacturing, some citrus growers and cattle ranchers appeared to be moving toward the pollution. The PHS contract had said nothing about such behavior, and it ran contrary to the narratives collected by Muskie in his hearings the year before. But Crocker recounts that in conversations around town, he heard rumors of citrus growers choosing to plant trees and ranchers deliberately grazing cattle right next to the settling ponds where processing companies extracted phosphorous from phosphate ore.[41] If such actions seem unlikely today, they came to seem perfectly logical as Crocker puzzled upon them and he would later turn his account of that perverse location strategy into an influential early argument for a market-based approach to pollution control.

Digressing, for a moment, into Crocker's biography sheds light on the mental model in which such arguments took hold. A Maine native, Crocker spent his teenage years working as a surveyor for lumber companies in his home state as well as the Canadian Maritimes and Washington State. This work allowed Crocker to observe firsthand how different compensation models affected the way in which timbering crews treated the forest. As Crocker found, crews paid by the hour cut only the trees they were supposed to harvest, while crews paid by the yard foot tended to cut everything, marginal trees included. Crocker followed his interest in the environment to a PhD in economics at the University of Missouri, where the land economics field founded by Richard Ely in the 1920s had broadened its focus from soil conservation and other strictly agricultural topics to the economics of air and water pollution.[42] Crocker trained with Mason Gaffney, a well-known economist who studied the inefficiency of the existing system of water rights in the American West—where the doctrine of prior appropriation granted usage rights on a first come, first served basis, regardless of the economic gain that different future uses of the water might have attained under a model that granted rights to users according to their maximization of the water's productive capacity. Crocker also spent time at the Wisconsin Water Resources Institute, where he met Jacob Bucher, a legal scholar who encouraged Crocker to think broadly about what constituted a property right in practice.

From these various experiences, Crocker gathered the components of the emerging neoclassical revolution in economics. Popularized by Milton Friedman and other economists at the University of Chicago, neoclassicism imagined a world of self-interested individual actors, rationally seeking the greatest personal gain based on the specific incentives of whatever system of social organization they happened to find themselves. Such actors would maximize public welfare by putting everything from air to labor to its most efficient usage. In markets free from state intervention, the prices of various inputs would perfectly signal their value. Neoclassicists urged elected officials to limit government action to enforcing property rights, allowing individuals to transact for and use resources however they wished.[43] Prior to traveling to Florida, Crocker had begun to wonder about the possibility of extending property rights to the atmosphere, allowing profit-minded individuals to make the most efficient use of a resource that was currently free and thus poorly managed.

Crocker believed that citrus growers and ranchers near Winter Haven were moving in closer proximity to the phosphate pollution because courts in torts cases had directed phosphate manufacturers to pay damages to the agriculturalists that often exceeded what they could earn from oranges or beef. Conceiving of individuals as profit minded and incentive driven, Crocker could readily understand such behavior. The courts' damage assessments had created a perverse incentive to plant trees and raise cattle in unsuitable locations. By deliberately locating near phosphate mines and manufacturing plants, agriculturalists were hurting overall public welfare since the damages that phosphate manufacturers were being forced to pay raised the price of fertilizer for consumers without yielding any higher quality or quantity of beef or oranges. In Tampa, Crocker saw a perfect opportunity to apply his system of atmospheric property rights. If agriculturalists could own property rights to the air, they would create areas of citrus growing and cattle ranching where the air they owned was kept free of pollutants. Phosphate manufacturers, meanwhile, could buy up the air rights over their manufacturing areas to ensure that they could emit fluorine and other pollutants without any threat of lawsuits.

Receiving what Crocker described as enthusiastic response to this scheme from the Resources for the Future (RFF) economist Allen Kneese when they met at a conference, Crocker wrote up his ideas for a 1966 paper. Bucking contemporary enthusiasm for Pigouvian taxes, Crocker argued that taxes required an omniscient central authority that could continuously adjust the tax rate to capture the changing social cost of various pollutants. A market, on the other hand, would generate the same, or better, information on social costs from the expressed preferences of its participants.[44] In later writings, Crocker acknowledged the problem of transaction costs that Coase had identified as the most serious constraint on the use of private property rights to protect large resources like the air. But Crocker maintained that a careful assignment of property rights could help minimize these costs and make a property rights system the best route for maximizing public welfare.[45]

In 1968, a Canadian economist named J. H. Dales introduced the idea of markets as tools of environmental governance in his *Pollution, Property, & Prices: An Essay in Policy-Making and Economics*. Building on the idea of an inevitably exploited commons that Garrett Hardin and others were then popularizing, Dales argued that the indivisibility of air and water meant they were always overused relative to private property and public property for which users could be charged a fee. A new administrative state was being formed to address this unrestrained pollution, Dales continued, but uniform standards and regulations did not address the specific benefits and costs experienced by each user and thus were inefficient and potentially unfair. Pollution charges tailored to mitigate the costs of each resource usage were fairer and more efficient but required constant, time-consuming, and politically difficult tinkering. In place of these suboptimal alternatives, Dales suggested that pollution "rights" be created for each region that businesses would be required to buy to continue to emit various pollutants. A central authority would retain a reserve of unsold rights to limit sharp price increases and would possess the ability to buy back rights at a fixed discount to limit any sharp deflation. Thus, predetermined levels of different pollutants could be fairly and efficiently maintained with very little government involvement."[46]

It would take a full decade, an energy crisis, and an ailing economy before the idea of tradable atmospheric rights gained traction with policymakers. In the meantime, Crocker published his original research showing that pollution from phosphate manufacturers had driven down the property values of nearby citrus orchards and cattle-grazing land by as much as 40 percent— an alarming decrease for a citrus industry that produced over $30 million in annual sales and a cattle industry with over 100,000 head.[47] To local agriculturalists as well as concerned officials like Senator Muskie, those falling property values marked yet another cost of pollution—a problem that the American population increasingly believed only the federal government could address.

Meanwhile, RFF was steadily expanding its own research into the economics of pollution, led by Allen Kneese, who joined RFF in 1961 to study water pollution. Kneese echoed Gordon and other economists in maintaining that unregulated shared resources were often very inefficient, since upstream polluters had no incentive to control pollution that incurred costs for downstream users, even if the cost of potential controls was much less than the existing damages of the unchecked pollution. For many problems, Kneese argued, market solutions were simply impossible, because some of the benefits of clean water would remain forever "unsalable," as he put it. Instead, Kneese wrote, "Communities that want the unsalable benefits have to get them through political action." The task for lawmakers was to devise "a system that takes into account the nonsalable benefits of pollution control and at the same time is economically efficient for those values that are measurable by market standards."[48]

Under Kneese, RFF quickly became one of the most important centers of research and thinking on the economics of pollution.[49] In the early 1960s, RFF funded research on water pollution on the Ohio and the Potomac rivers and studied the Ruhr River in Germany for its successful coordination of industrial production and pollution control through a regional authority.[50] In 1965, the Ford Foundation granted RFF an additional $1 million to form a research program in environmental quality, which Kneese was chosen to direct. In addition to funding research on water quality—including a grant to Harvard to improve techniques of cost-benefit measurement—Kneese's program began funding research on air pollution, including studies into how the damage of urban pollutants might be calculated in the monetary costs to public health.[51] In 1966, RFF held its first Forum on Environmental Quality, a two-day conference in Washington, DC, at which the presenters made the collective point that environmental degradation forced policymakers into new realms that demanded new ways of thinking. In a talk titled "Economics of the Coming Spaceship Earth," economist Kenneth Boulding laid out what soon became a popular metaphor. The proliferation of waste, Boulding told his audience, posed an acute threat to humanity, which was stuck on a global spaceship with all the pollution it would ever generate. To ensure future prosperity, society would need to figure out how to satisfy its needs with a minimum amount of material inputs.[52]

The notion of a natural limit to growth aligned economists like Boulding with the ascendant ideas of ecologists, who in turn echoed a much older fear that humanity was outstripping its natural resource base. The most enduring expression of that old fear came from English economist Thomas Malthus, who warned at the beginning of the nineteenth century that growing populations would eventually be checked in brutal fashion by the fixed carrying capacity of the land to support agriculture, provided humans did not regulate their own reproduction.[53] The rise of ecology in the 1960s, with its explanation of the intricate webs that connected every organism, also gave rise to new expressions of those fears about population growth and carrying capacity. In 1968, ecologist Garrett Hardin published "The Tragedy of the Commons" in the prestigious journal *Science*, in which he argued that heedless expansion in a world of limited resources would soon lead to environmental collapse. Calling attention to the tendency of private actors to overuse resources that are collectively available to all, Hardin suggested both population control and new rules to stop private actors from freely dumping their waste into the air and water.[54] That same year, fellow ecologist Paul Ehrlich published *The Population Bomb*, in which he and his wife Anne Ehrlich warned that the Malthusian crisis brought on by overpopulation had not been escaped but only delayed by the great boosts in agricultural productivity that had occurred since Malthus's writing. In the coming years, Ehrlich would become a national celebrity, appearing numerous times on Johnny Carson's *Tonight Show* and helping to popularize the idea that humanity would have to reckon with its environmental degradation.[55]

Making Air Pollution a Federal Responsibility

In the late 1960s, environmental activists across the country pushed up against the capacity of state-level responses to air pollution. In California, environmental activists grew impatient with state authorities that had done much to advance the science of air pollution without managing to resolve the long-standing smog issue in Los Angeles.[56] Meanwhile, their counterparts on the East Coast confronted a growing interstate pollution problem as New York's fledging efforts to clean up its air proved impossible as long as industry in New Jersey continued to freely pollute. In 1965, New York governor Nelson Rockefeller appealed to the federal government to organize a regional pollution control strategy, which New Jersey's leaders agreed to in 1967, partly in a gambit to stave off greater federal intervention.[57] But as state-level authorities continued to struggle to act against powerful local industrial interests, activists increasingly turned to the federal government.

Congress responded by passing the Air Quality Act of 1967, which increased federal funding to state and local governments, empowered the federal government to set up interstate air quality control regions, and gave the secretary of Health, Eduction, and Welfare (HEW) responsibility for developing scientific definitions for the six most prevalent pollutants. These "criteria" documents were to serve as the official record of the atmospheric characteristics and medical risks of each pollutant. But the legislation left it up to the states to create their own standards for the permissible ambient concentrations of each "criteria" pollutant and to develop their own plans for enforcing those limits.[58] Senator Muskie, one of the Air Quality Act's principal authors, defended this approach as allowing each state to focus on the particular pollutants that posed the biggest problems in their areas. Though Muskie championed an expanded federal role, he resisted taking over completely from the states, explaining to one inquiring constituent that developing a national bureaucracy to administer a set of national standards would simply be too expensive.[59] Over the next few years, Muskie emerged not just as a national environmental champion but a leader in the Democratic Party—including representing the party as the vice presidential candidate on the 1968 ticket. Despite the failures of the Air Quality Act to address the recalcitrance of the states to act on their own laws, the senator and his increasingly influential Subcommittee on Air and Water Pollution continued to insist that the states, and not the federal government, should set air quality standards, including going so far as to critique the criteria documents issued by HEW in 1969 as being so prescriptive in their recommendations as to establish de facto national standards.[60]

But the momentum for a federal assumption of authority continued to mount. In 1969, proponents of federal pollution control gained support when consumer advocate Ralph Nader decided to take up their campaign. Fresh off a stunning victory over General Motors regarding unsafe vehicle design, Nader was enjoying a meteoric rise as the head of a new group dedicated to protecting the public interest from profit-minded businesses. Drawing on the energy of law and medical school students and other volunteers who flocked to his Center for Responsive Law, Nader and John Esposito founded the Summer Task Force in 1969 to investigate Congress and the National Air Pollution Control Administration's effectiveness in reducing air pollution. Nader's Raiders, as the Task Force became known, soon levied a harsh critique of the existing system for protecting corporations rather than the general public by confining federal activity to research that primarily benefited polluters while avoiding any responsibility on the part of the government. In a widely publicized report (published in 1970 as *Vanishing Air* but earlier reported on by the press), the Task Force pointed out that, as of 1969, not a single state had submitted air quality standards as required under the Air Quality Act of 1967. The reasons for delay varied, but the result was the abject failure of the state-led pollution control program to actually address the problem.[61]

Along with this challenge from public interest advocates, the state-centered approach to air pollution control faced growing opposition from many business executives, who complained about the difficulty of complying with an unwieldy array of different laws and regulations in different states. In 1968, for instance, the vice president of the Continental Can Company (operating 143 plants across the country) wrote to the United States Conference of Mayors advocating federal standards for air and water pollution to replace local and state "standards that vary all over the map."[62] Continental's aluminum can factories, like almost every industrial manufacturing process, emitted fine particulate material, which tended to lodge inside human lungs and damage tissue. The Air Quality Act of 1967 had designated particulate matter as one of the six "criteria" pollutants deemed especially dangerous to public health but left it to the states to determine how much pollution a plant emitted as well as how that limit would be calculated. Thus, Continental's plant in Mankato, Minnesota, might be allowed to emit up to 100 tons of particulates per year, while its plant in Stockton, California, could emit no more than one ton per calendar month—a variation that made it difficult and expensive for companies to standardize pollution control equipment and operations.[63] For business executives like Continental's vice president, a single set of federal standards would come as a welcome consolidation of regulations that they were resigning themselves to.[64]

The environmental movement that had been building throughout the 1960s erupted onto the national scene in 1970. As historian Adam Rome explains, a diverse set of actors focused on a variety of environmental problems coalesced around the teach-ins that were held across the country on April 22. After Senator Gaylord Nelson, a Democrat from Wisconsin, had suggested teach-ins across the country, thousands of organizers from a wide variety of backgrounds turned that first "Earth Day" into a truly national event. Great Society liberals, ecology-minded scientists, middle-class suburban women, countercultural youth, old-school conservationists, and other groups joined together to express their concern for environmental degradation and their demands for an adequate government response. An estimated 20 million people participated in that first Earth Day, nearly 10 percent of the total population. It brought Republican and Democratic elected officials and the leaders of the nation's largest corporations together with activists on Earth Day stages across the country. While the day itself captured the headlines, the surging public concern and the organizing behind Earth Day established modern environmentalism as a potent political force.[65] Historian Chris Sellers points out that in 1970, fully 82 percent of Americans identified air and water pollution as their top priorities for government spending, a level not equaled before or since.[66]

Congress and President Richard Nixon responded to this wave of public concern with a flurry of legislation. Even before Earth Day, the Nixon administration had identified environmentalism as one of its most important political issues. Nixon had little personal interest in environmental protection, but environmental advisor John Whitaker and others convinced him that environmental quality had become a popular concern of such magnitude that he could not afford to ignore it if he hoped to be reelected.[67] Whitaker was a conservationist of an older ilk with a background in oil and mining, and he pushed Nixon to embrace new environmental responsibilities for the federal government when he joined the administration in 1968 as the domestic policy advisor responsible for natural resources and the environment.[68] Like other advisors, Whitaker saw environmental policy as a potential concern for Nixon heading into the 1972 election, where he seemed likely to face Senator Muskie.[69] At the encouragement of those advisors, Nixon supported the National Environmental Policy Act, which mandated environmental assessments throughout the federal government's activities and established a new federal council to advise the president on environmental matters. Signing the act into law on New Year's Day in 1970, Nixon declared that the country was "determined that the decade of the seventies will be known as the time when this country regained a productive harmony between man and nature."[70] With the clamor of Earth Day, his advisors pushed Nixon to continue supporting strong new action to blunt the possibility that environmentalism would become a major liability in the 1972 election.

Responding to their own pressure from the environmental movement, Muskie's subcommittee moved toward new legislation to strengthen the federal government's oversight. In a May 1970 press conference that Muskie held in response to the charges of inaction leveled in Nader's highly critical *Vanishing Air*, the senator defended the subcommittee's continued preference

Figure 1.2 Senator Edmund Muskie addressing a crowd of approximately 50,000 in Philadelphia on April 22, 1970, part of the 20 million Americans who participated in that first Earth Day. https://commons.wikimedia.org/wiki/File:Ed-Muskie-at-Earth-Day-1970-web.jpg.

for state-level standards while admitting that implementation had been slower than expected and that better laws would need to be written.[71] By summer 1970, the environmentalist campaign for expanded federal responsibility had eroded Muskie's defense of state-administered standards. The subcommittee had already endorsed the federal government's duty to protect the public's interest in clean air, especially the minority of the population whose age or infirmity led them to suffer most acutely from air pollution. Rejecting the suggestion of one lobbyist who testified before the subcommittee in 1968 that air conditioned indoor retreats could be created for the most acute victims of air pollution, Leon Billings, a Muskie staffer who had become the subcommittee's staff director, wrote that the proposal raised serious ethical and legal questions in suggesting that people ought to adapt to pollution rather than confront it. Besides, Billings noted, the primary pressure for pollution control came not from the sick but "from the urban, upward-striving, middle class who are offended by the aesthetic insults of smog, smut, and filth."[72] In the face of the failure of the state-led program, the subcommittee gradually accepted national standards for ambient air.

By June, the subcommittee staff had moved from debating whether there should be national standards to how they should be designed. How many pollutants would be covered? How long would states have to comply? And how would the standards balance feasibility with the health risks posed by pollutants?[73] Over the subsequent month, the subcommittee settled on using the preexisting criteria documents to select and define the pollutants to be controlled through national standards. The Air Quality Act of 1967 had identified six air pollutants deemed the most pressing threats to human health because of their prevalence and risk—carbon monoxide, sulfur dioxide, ground level ozone, particulate matter, nitrogen dioxide, and hydrocarbons—and tasked the National Air Pollution Control Administration with issuing a criteria document describing the health effects for each pollutant. When the legislation that became the Clean Air Act Amendments of 1970 reached the Senate floor, it included the new concept of National Ambient Air Quality Standards (colloquially referred to by the acronym NAAQS and pronounced "knacks"). The NAAQS would draw on the criteria documents to create national standards for each of the "criteria" pollutants. The federal government was to set a primary and a secondary standard for each criteria pollutant. The primary standard would spell out a permissible concentration of the pollutant below the threshold that the criteria document had established as a threat to public health. The secondary standard would be set at a stricter level to protect the public welfare from things like damaged plant foliage. While the states retained responsibility for devising plans for emissions sources to comply with the NAAQS, the setting of the standards would take place at the federal level. The Clean Air Act bill gave the federal government six months to set the NAAQS and the states five years to comply with the primary standards.[74]

In addition to the NAAQS, the proposed Clean Air Act included mandatory pollution controls on any major new source of emissions (defined according to the tons of pollutants emitted annually). These New Source Performance Standards (NSPS) would identify a numerical emissions limit that a new source could not exceed, with the limit based on what the best available pollution control equipment could achieve. For example, the NSPS for a new coal-fired boiler in an electric power plant would specify the pounds of particulate matter that could be released per BTUs (British thermal units) of coal burned based on what the best available "baghouse" fabric filtration system could achieve. By forcing businesses to install the best available control technology (variously referred to as "control devices," "control equipment," or, simply, "controls"), NSPS ensured that future growth would not cause air quality to backslide.[75]

While NSPS would consider technical feasibility in determining the best controls available to industry at the time, the NAAQS deliberately omitted any such weighing of feasibility in their deliberate disregard of whether local areas could meet the new standards by the specified deadlines. Nader had recommended this course to Muskie in late June 1970 by instructing the senator to delete any mention of "economic or technical feasibility" from the bill. Responding to news that Muskie intended to so, the Nixon administration noted that they too supported NAAQS free of economic considerations.[76] As a result of this political jockeying, the Senate version of the Clean Air Act ended up being a much tougher piece of legislation than the House's version.[77]

Defending his claim as the nation's environmental champion, Muskie supported a prohibition on considering economic costs in the NAAQS when the Clean Air Act came up for debate in the Senate in September 1970. The duty of Congress, Muskie declared, was not to make technological or economic considerations but rather to "establish what the public interest requires to protect the health of persons."[78] So that there would be no mistaking the intention of Congress regarding the NAAQS, Muskie took the floor again the next day, declaring, "I would like to reemphasize that the concept of this bill as it relates to national ambient air quality standards and the deadlines for the automobile industry is not keyed to any condition that the Secretary [of Health and Human Welfare] finds technically and economically feasible. The concept is of public health, and the standards are uncompromisable in that connection." Acknowledging the ambition of that concept, Muskie appealed to American ingenuity and perseverance in the face of great challenges, citing the country's recent moon landing and its building enough airplanes to defeat the Axis powers in World War II.[79] Calling for a similar heroism in defending the public health, Congress deliberately left off the table the relative difficulty or cost for private enterprise in complying with the national standards.

In debating the Clean Air Act, Congress clearly recognized that enforcement of strong standards would prompt businesses to pass on its resulting costs by raising the price of consumer goods and services. The Air Quality Act of 1967 required the secretary of Health, Education, and Welfare to make an annual accounting to Congress of the costs to both industry and government of complying with the legislation.[80] By the time Congress was debating the Clean Air Act amendments of 1970, the legislators had received the first report and could see that expanding the nation's environmental regulations would increase already significant compliance costs. Senator Jennings Randolph, a powerful Democrat from West Virginia, declared on the Senate floor that "this legislation will test the willingness of the citizens of this Nation to control and abate environmental pollution. Ultimately every individual citizen would be called on to pay the increased costs associated with the achievement of an environment that protects and improves the public health within this country."[81] Proponents of the act were equally forthright about the anticipated expense of the Clean Air Act in speeches and other communication with the public. Senator Muskie's letters to constituents on the subject noted that the public would eventually pay for pollution controls—whether in the form of higher taxes or higher consumer prices.[82] When a radio broadcaster wrote Muskie in 1969 to convey a series of editorials in support of pollution control, Muskie thanked him for educating the public about the problem, since that awareness would be crucial in creating a "willingness to pay for abatement." "If we are going to succeed in building a wholesome environment," Muskie informed the broadcaster, "everyone will have to pay a share of the cost."[83]

Many of Muskie's colleagues in the Senate and House echoed his handling of the costs of pollution control in their speeches on behalf of the Clean Air Act. While higher prices would be painful and easily attributable to the new regulation, the act's supporters argued, the public would bear the increased cost of living in exchange for the benefits of cleaner air. Bolstering the confidence of the act's supporters on the Senate floor, Senator Gaylord Nelson warned potential detractors that the public supported strong environmental protection. "Would-be polluters are forewarned," Nelson declared. "A livable environment is more important to man and his survival than all the market-able gadgets produced by our economy to make our life easier."[84] Nelson's claim shared the language and philosophy of Boulding's spaceship earth: the postwar generation, raised in comfort in the suburbs, was nonetheless willing to see that prosperity as a threat to the underlying environmental quality on which a fuller conception of the good life rested.

For all the speech making about the inevitable costs of protecting the public interest in clean air, Congress spent very little time on the specific economic implications of the NAAQS. Not one senator or representative, for example, asked what would happen if a state could not meet the standards within the five years allotted under the act. That neglect can likely be explained by Congress's preoccupation with the fate of the automobile industry under the new mobile source standards included in the act. While all industrial producers were subject to the New Source Standard and state implementation of the NAAQS, the act singled out the automobile industry for additional controls.

Automobiles had been a primary subject of air pollution debates since the 1940s, when local environmental advocates in places like Los Angeles determined that the sickly white smog that increasingly shrouded their cities could be blamed on the internal combustion engine. Air pollution experts discovered that refining oil into gasoline and burning that fuel in cars released large amounts of nitrogen dioxide and hydrocarbons, which reacted with volatile organic compounds (occurring naturally but also expelled by industry) to produce photochemical oxidants. Oxidants react with and disintegrate living tissue, from the leaves on a plant to the lining of a human lung.[85] In high concentrations and the right environmental conditions, oxidants can also produce visible smog. For most people, smoggy days were merely an aesthetic nuisance, or, at worst, a cause of watery eyes and itchy throats. But for asthmatics, the elderly, and others with compromised lungs or for people who lived in cities where the smog increasingly lasted for weeks, oxidants were dangerous—even deadly. Since the 1950s, when air pollution experts recognized that automobiles produced two-thirds of the hydrocarbons and an even greater percentage of nitrogen dioxides, regulators had focused their efforts to combat smog on automobile manufacturers.[86]

In addition, automobiles were increasingly identified as a chief culprit behind a host of growing health concerns. Automobiles produced nitrogen dioxide, which can damage the immune system and increase respiratory illnesses. Cars also generated carbon monoxide, which reduces the amount of oxygen the blood can carry and can also damage the cardiovascular, nervous, and pulmonary systems. And mid-century automobiles also emitted lead, which can lead to severe brain damage, with special risks to the developing brains of young children.[87]

Deflecting demands from state and local regulators to reduce the pollutants coming out of their cars, automobile manufacturers claimed that control technology did not exist or that control devices were infeasible because of their costs. Absent strong laws, automobile manufacturers delayed investing in devices such as catalytic converters that could reduce emissions from vehicles. The Department of Justice eventually sued the four largest automobile manufacturers in 1967 for anti-trust violations in preventing catalytic converters from coming to market.[88]

This long experience with resisting pollution controls prepared automobile manufacturers for the Clean Air Act of 1970. Their organized protests dominated the attention of legislators. As a result, both supporters and critics of the Clean Air Act focused on cars when it came to the feasibility of the act's requirements and its likely economic effects.[89] Underscoring the preoccupation of the Clean Air Act's critics with the implications for the automobile industry, Senator Robert Griffin, a Republican from Michigan, emerged as the most vociferous opponent of the act in the Senate. Deeply concerned about his home state's most important industry, Griffin assailed the act as risking catastrophic shutdowns and the loss of up to 15 million jobs in the event that manufacturers could not develop the requisite emissions controls before the deadline. "This bill holds a gun at the head of the American automobile industry in a very dangerous game of economic roulette," Griffin declared. Questioning the wisdom of attaching such severe repercussions to pollution control, Griffin continued, "President Kennedy announced a goal when he said we would go to the moon by a certain date but no one suggested a law that would have put space industries out of business if we had fallen short in developing the needed technology." To mitigate catastrophic dislocations that might result from the fixed deadlines mandated by the act, Griffin called for an ongoing review of the feasibility of emissions standards in light of manufacturers' progress toward a technological solution.[90]

Despite Muskie's continued insistence that Congress's responsibility lay in protecting public health rather than considering the economic situation of any particular industry, Griffin's critique did force the act's defenders to engage in a debate about whether the proposed automobile controls were in fact feasible. Muskie's subcommittee had previously held hearings on the subject,

collecting extensive testimony from representatives of all the major automobile manufacturers as well as other engineering experts. Griffin, Muskie, and
others reviewed that testimony, debating the product development process
and entering copious technical evidence into the *Congressional Record*.[91]
Debate over the automobile standards consumed the vast majority of the
time allotted to the act. Though Griffin at one point noted that little consideration had been given to stationary sources, the act's proponents declined to
expand their inquiry into the feasibility of the NAAQS.[92] So while Congress
intentionally left economic considerations out the national standards,
supporters of the Clean Air Act paid less attention to the full implications of
that decision than they might have had automobile emissions not dominated
the debate. In September, the Senate voted 73 to 0 to pass the Clean Air Act
legislation and send it into conference with the House, which had passed its
own bill in June on a vote of 374 to 1.[93]

Within the Nixon White House, new regulations on automobiles also pre-
occupied administration officials and advisors who evaluated the Clean Air
Act. In November, a Nixon advisor outlined the administration's priorities
in shaping the final bill that Senate and House members would hash out.
Various issues related to the new automobile standards compromised five of
the fourteen priorities. The remaining concerns focused on new provisions
for citizen suits, national security exemptions, and compulsory sharing of
patented pollution control technology. The advisor did include a provision
for the extension of implementation deadlines where feasible technology
could not be found. But the standards set by the NAAQS themselves did not
make it onto Nixon's list of priorities. Discussing the likely outcome of the
conference, the Nixon advisor stated that while the tougher provisions from
the Senate bill would probably prevail over the House bill, the administration should not try to intervene on behalf of the weaker House bill because
of the remarkable degree of support for the stronger legislation in Congress
and among the general public. Despite hundreds of millions of dollars in
expected federal expenditures under the strongest Clean Air Act, the same
advisor cautioned against intervening on spending provisions as well, since
doing so would "too easily lend itself to characterization of being 'soft on air
pollution.'"[94]

Some voices within the Nixon administration warned against such blanket
support for the proposed legislation. Secretary of Commerce Maurice Stans
sent a list of particularly worrisome provisions in the Senate bill to Nixon
advisor John Ehrlichman, including citizen suits, automobile emission

controls, mandatory patent sharing, and "unrealistically short statutory deadlines," for achieving the NAAQS.[95] Rejecting a full-scale attempt to revise the legislation, the Nixon administration opted for a narrow appeal to ease the automobile standards in a letter to the Senate and House conferees. Even that limited request managed to provoke an outcry from several senators, who critiqued the president for improper interference.[96]

Meeting in conference in early December, the Senate and House conferees produced a final bill in which the stronger Senate provisions prevailed in nearly every important account.[97] By the middle of December, both houses agreed to the conference legislation and sent the Clean Air Act to Nixon. Eager to seize the mantle of environmental champion from Senator Muskie, Nixon's advisors organized a grand signing ceremony for the Clean Air Act.[98] On the last day of 1970, reporters gathered in the Roosevelt Room to watch Nixon sign the Clean Air Act into law. Pointing to the room's namesake as a precedent for making environmental protection a national goal, Nixon claimed responsibility for the passage of the legislation. If 1970 had been the year in which the nation finally began to address the problems of clean air and water, Nixon declared, "1971 will be known as the year of action," above all else in controlling automobile emissions, a "plague" to not only Nixon's "native area of southern California but all the great cities of this nation."[99] Though Nixon did not to mention it, the new Clean Air Act had also created a binding set of national air quality standards for the first time in United States history, promising to clean up the air across the country, from Chicago to Central Florida.

* * *

Over a few short years, the environmental movement had transformed popular understandings of the environmental responsibilities of the federal government, spurring Democrats and Republicans alike to significantly expand federal authority over air pollution and other environmental problems. As with the other legislation passed at the height of the environmental environment, the Clean Air Act Amendments of 1970 grounded these new federal responsibilities and authorities in the notion of a natural right to enjoy an environment free of degradation.[100] Economists too had grown concerned about the social costs of environmental degradation. But rather than natural rights, these economists tended to think in the monetary terms of externalities—a niche perspective in the heyday of the environmental movement.

However, as the country would soon find out, keeping the Clean Air Act's promise to meet national air quality standards that had been set without regard to the costs of compliance would be an expensive proposition. The cost of pollution control would prompt elected officials from both parties to join regulators at the EPA, representatives of regulated industries, environmentalists, and many others in questioning what price society ought to pay for clean air. Having spent the previous decade answering that question, environmental economists would soon make themselves indispensable in the policy debates.

2

The Doer

The EPA and the Power in Implementation

In November 1970, on the eve of creation of the Environmental Protection Agency (EPA), Richard Nixon summoned William Ruckelshaus, soon to be appointed the agency's first head, to give him his marching orders. As Nixon put it to the thirty-eight-year-old Ruckelshaus, the EPA was to be a "doer," not a "thinker." Policy strategy would come from elsewhere, Nixon explained, and the EPA and Ruckelshaus's job was to implement those ideas by writing and enforcing regulations that would reduce pollution. Though the new agency had a staff of nearly 6,000 and a budget of $1.4 billion, Nixon and others involved in the creation of the EPA could be forgiven for envisioning a quiescent agency, dutifully executing plans formed elsewhere. From the White House and Congress's perspective, the EPA was first and foremost a reorganizational measure intended to make the Executive Branch more efficient by consolidating environmental staff from a dozen preexisting agencies and departments into one new institution. Business representatives shared that viewpoint, imagining that the EPA might be easier to influence than the multitude of different agencies it replaced, since all those regulators would be collected together in one place. Environmental organizations also saw new opportunities to influence policy, but these groups were still small or largely disinterested in national politics in 1970. For the time being, most observers assumed that the EPA would do what the Nixon administration asked.

It did not take long for Nixon and everyone else to realize how wrong that assumption had been. New legislation, especially the Clean Air Act Amendments of 1970, gave the EPA vast new authorities and responsibilities. Eager to establish the new agency's credibility, Ruckelshaus and the EPA's early leadership embraced those mandates, writing and enforcing strong standards that quickly disabused the business community of any notion that the EPA would be easy to wrangle. Moreover, the consolidation of environmentally focused civil servants in one agency had sown the seeds of a strong institutional culture that quickly grew up around the EPA's mission

Valuing Clean Air. Charles Halvorson, Oxford University Press (2021). © Oxford University Press.
DOI: 10.1093/oso/9780197538845.003.0003

to protect human health and the environment. As the EPA's implementation of the Clean Air Act would soon demonstrate, the regulations and enforcement mechanisms that career staff and political appointees created were at least as important as the underlying legislation in determining what pollution control looked like on the ground. By the end of the agency's first year in operation, it was clear that contests over environmental protection would be waged in the corridors of the EPA as much as in the halls of Congress.

This chapter focuses on the Clean Air Act's National Ambient Air Quality Standards (NAAQS) and the plans that the states developed to implement those standards as key parts of the EPA's development as a critical site of policymaking. To explain the contingency and significance of the implementation process, the chapter begins with the formation of the EPA and the growth of an institutional culture that supported strong oversight. For the first time, a majority of the federal employees whose professional duties lay in environmental protection worked for the same agency. Environmental advocates appealed to the EPA's environmental sympathies as they learned to navigate the new levers of power in the Clean Air Act and other legislation—especially the provisions for citizen suits that environmental advocates quickly proved adept at using before a friendly judiciary. But widespread support for enforcing strong NAAQS did not mean that the EPA was ever of one mind, as the legal fights over attempts to moderate the mandates of the standards made clear. Among other things, these contests revealed the utility of economic analysis in political debate.

The NAAQS and corresponding implementation plans also marked a key juncture in the evolving relationship among local, state, and federal authorities concerning environmental governance. Finding wide discrepancies in aptitude and appetite for strong regulations among local and state bodies, the EPA worked to raise competencies through training and the funding of external, expert consultants. While these efforts and the EPA's regional structure ensured that much of the work of pollution monitoring and control would continue to be done at the state level, the EPA's influence over how the states did so contributed to the consolidation of power over environmental protection in the federal government.

The Origins of the EPA

An archaeology of federal administration reveals layers of offices, bureaus, departments, services, commissions, councils, agencies—built on top of one another and borrowing construction material. This building got started in earnest at the end of the nineteenth century, when an increasingly complex industrial economy outgrew the governing capacity of legislatures, which created commissions to oversee the railroads, regulate commerce, police the financial markets, and so on. The densest layers date to the middle of the twentieth century, when swelling faith in the federal government's capacity and liberalism's rapidly expanding sense of the government's responsibilities combined to drive a frenzy of institution building. Though unknown at the time, the EPA would be among the last of these layers, created as much to make the federal government more efficient as to expand federal responsibilities and authority.

One of the insights of the field of American political development has been to show how the layering of regulatory agencies on top of each other often involves granting new authorities to the state that do not neatly supersede those they are built on, leading to contradictory imperatives in different parts of the federal apparatus that have spurred ongoing controversies over priorities and authority.[1] In the EPA's case, much of this layering involved a rebalancing of state and federal power, a task made more confusing by the fact that the EPA lacked an organic congressional act—the enabling legislation that typically delineates the power and responsibilities of agencies such as the National Park Service. As a result, the decisions made by the EPA's first officials, and the groups that were able to influence those decisions, would have an outsized role in determining the EPA's shape.

The EPA emerged as part of a flourish of institutional building around the environment. In one year, Congress and the White House created the Council on Environmental Quality, the EPA, the National Oceanic and Atmospheric Administration, and the Occupational Safety and Health Administration. All of this happened in spite of Richard Nixon's efforts to limit the size of the federal government and his skepticism about the lasting political salience of environmentalism. Pushed along by his advisors to keep pace with a Congress rushing to respond to public demands, Nixon oversaw arguably the most important period of environmental policymaking in the country's history.

The Council on Environmental Quality (CEQ) was the first in this administrative burst, created by Congress as part of the National Environmental Policy Act of 1969 and signed into law on January 1, 1970. Having bucked calls to create a new environmental Cabinet position, Nixon accepted the CEQ as an advisory body to replace his own half-hearted attempts at ensuring environmental counsel in the executive branch.[2] Congress also tasked the CEQ with administering the new Environmental Impact Statement program, which required an environmental accounting for all major projects that involved the federal government, as well as issuing a yearly report on the state of the environment. To accomplish these objectives, the act granted the council twelve employees and a $300,000 budget for year one, set to expand to thirty and the budget to $1 million by 1972.[3] As some of Nixon's own advisors celebrated, the CEQ promised an environmental voice in the White House, checking what had been an unquestioned faith in development among offices like the Army Corps of Engineers.[4]

Nixon was responsible for appointing the three council members who would oversee the CEQ, and the selection process reveals something of the dance that presidential administrations face in appointing officials who share their political vision and are yet acceptable to a variety of interested parties. Consulted on possible members, Russell Train, the under secretary of the Interior, argued that Nixon should choose "environmental generalists" of "real stature" such as Dr. Luna Leopold, a senior scientist at the Geological Survey in the Department of the Interior and the son of the famous naturalist Aldo Leopold—a selection sure to appease any "conservation or ecology group."[5] The only problem, Train wrote, was that Leopold was probably a Democrat, though fortunately not "in any way a political activist." Passing on Leopold, Nixon's advisors instead chose Robert Cahn, a Pulitzer Prize–winning reporter who could "spot the strong controversial issues," together with Dr. Gordon MacDonald, a geophysicist and administrator at the University of California at Santa Barbara who could "cut through the scientific data in each agency," and Train himself, who as chairman could be expected to "fight the bureaucrats, cut through red tape, sell the Congress and get things done."[6] Train fit the criteria of a respected conservative conservationist. Born to a politically well-connected family in Rhode Island, Train attended Princeton University and then served as an artillery officer in the US Army during World War II. Following the war, Train graduated from Columbia University's Law School before going to work on Capitol Hill—eventually becoming an advisor to the powerful House Committee on Ways and Means. In the 1960s, Train helped found a series of conservation organizations, including the African Wildlife Leadership Foundation and the World Wildlife Fund. After a stint as the head attorney in the Treasury Department, Train left government to become the president of the Conservation Foundation. By 1969, Train had been appointed the undersecretary of the Interior, the position he held when Nixon tapped him to be the first chairman of the Council on Environmental Quality.[7] A statesman of conservation, Train lent stature and authority to the council while at the same time affirming Nixon's conservative outlook on environmental policy.

One of the first things Train had to do was to convince important allies in the business community that the Nixon administration was still receptive to their concerns. In January 1970, the Republican National Committee sent word to Nixon advisor John Whitaker that representatives from Dow Chemical and other industrial titans, including Republic Steel and Monsanto, were upset that appointees to the new council seemed to consist entirely of conservationists. Deflecting a request to meet with these disgruntled business representatives, Whitaker told his aide to "just ignore [the request]—don't say no—yet."[8] Such important supporters could not be completely neglected, however, and by February, Whitaker was coordinating the appearance of Train and other council representatives at a conference on environmental regulation organized by paper manufacturers in order to demonstrate the administration's commitment to industry-led solutions to environmental degradation.[9] To placate the business community, Nixon created a National Industrial Pollution Control Council composed of representatives of industry, though this supposed counterweight to the CEQ was in reality largely ignored by his administration.[10]

Having centralized environmental strategy in the new Council on Environmental Quality, Nixon and his advisors also sought to bring together the various offices and groups that implemented and enforced environmental policies, which were then split between the Department of the Interior, the Public Health Service, the Department of Agriculture, and several other offices. A task force set up by Whitaker recommended the creation of a new Department of Environment and Natural Resources to replace Interior and consolidate environmental protection and environmental development in one body, allowing disputes between those two impulses to be worked out internally with the involvement of the White House. Nixon liked the idea and asked a committee led by industrialist Roy Ash to develop the plan. Congress had recently granted short-term authority to the White House to propose executive branch reorganizations for an up or down vote, and Ash hoped to increase the efficiency of the executive branch through the creation of four super-departments. But environmental advocates on the Ash committee opposed the idea of forcing environmental protection and environmental development to report to one cabinet official, fearing that development would always have the upper hand. The president and his cabinet also rejected the idea, partially because of Nixon's distrust of the current secretary of the Interior, whose powers would have been dramatically increased.[11]

In place of the new department, Ash recommended that Nixon create a new Environmental Protection Agency (EPA) dedicated solely to environmental protection. Nixon saw the EPA as a means of satisfying all of the parties involved while gaining a political boost among environmentalists with a demonstrated commitment to moving forward on environmental protection, and he set his advisors to planning how the EPA would function.[12] One option was to abolish the CEQ and replace it with the EPA. Another was to retain the EPA and have the agency report to Nixon through the council— an idea that Train endorsed.[13] Ultimately, Nixon decided to keep the CEQ as the chief environmental advisor and create the EPA as a separate executive branch agency to implement the policy that the council created. As Nixon himself described the arrangement, the EPA was to be the "doer," while the CEQ would continue to be the "thinker."[14]

In June 1970, Nixon circulated his plan to create the Environmental Protection Agency. The proposal quickly gained the support of influential congressional representatives, several of whom (including Senator Ed Muskie) had recently proposed bills to consolidate implementation and enforcement.[15] The proposal also won the support of environmental groups including the Conservation Foundation, and public health advocates, including the American Medical Association.[16] Though traditionally wary of new regulatory bodies, the business community embraced the consolidation of authority that the EPA's creation promised. As political scientist David Vogel explained, most businesses understood the EPA's creation as a shuffling of bureaucratic functions within the executive branch rather than as an expansion of the federal government.[17] Nixon's advisors worked hard to assuage any concerns, including holding meetings with chemical manufacturers and others to assure them that the EPA would not threaten their business.[18] Some business leaders seem not to have anticipated much of a change, among them executives in the electric power industry, whose monthly trade journal ran frequent articles on the dangers of overly stringent environmental regulation throughout the 1960s and into the early 1970s without a single note of caution about the new EPA.[19]

In July 1970, Nixon formally proposed the creation of the EPA under Reorganization Plan Number 3, the same plan under which he proposed the National Oceanic and Atmospheric Administration.[20] Though some

members of Congress continued to grumble about the lack of an environmental Cabinet position, the House and Senate gave the EPA their approval,
and in early October 1970, the new agency was given sixty days to get organized before it began operation on December 2.

Like other regulatory agencies, the EPA was designed to operate according
to a set of principles that would give it the capability to fulfill its mission
while also remaining accountable to the general public. In 1946, Congress
had passed the Administrative Procedure Act in 1946, codifying a standard
process across the agencies charged with administering federal statutes.
Under the act, an agency would develop a proposed regulation (or "rule")
to fulfill statutory obligations created by an act of Congress, announce the
proposed "rulemaking" in the daily federal journal, the *Federal Register*, and
then invite public participation through a formal public comment process. In
practice, while individual citizens shared their opinions through the public
comment process, carefully formulated arguments from special interest representatives (spanning public interest groups to individual businesses and
trade associations) carried the most weight. Responding to those comments
(which might mean adjusting or abandoning the proposed rule) the agency
would then issue a final rulemaking, which would function as law and be
published in the *Federal Register* and the annual *Code of Federal Regulations*.
Like laws passed by a legislative body, such rulemakings were subject to ju-
dicial review in federal court, giving the public and special interest groups
another opportunity to appeal administration decisions.

Getting the EPA up and running was an organizational feat. As Chuck
Elkins, who worked on the Ash Council that designed the EPA, later
explained, it was not clear in 1970 what responsibilities the EPA should take
on. Many different federal offices had environmental components and, while
it was obvious that air and water pollution authorities would go to the EPA,
programs such as rat control or microwave oven regulation or workplace
environmental hazards were trickier. In the end, Elkins and his boss Doug
Costle chose some and left others, emphasizing a focus on pollution as the
criterion for inclusion.[21] In the end, the EPA brought together fifteen preexisting offices along with their staffs and budgets into a new agency with
5,743 employees and a collective budget of $1.4 billion. At the head of the
agency was the presidentially appointed administrator, assisted by a deputy
administrator who ran the day-to-day operations. The EPA's formation came
in the midst of the new federalism movement, which, among other things,
advocated the physical dispersal of federal power across the country.[22] The

Ash Council's plan followed that idea in splitting the country into ten regions, each with its own regional office and presidentially appointed regional administrator and deputy regional administrator to serve as the first point of contact with state pollution control authorities and the businesses they regulated.

As the EPA took shape, the institution's creators debated whether to organize the agency by environmental medium (e.g., air), which is how the programs that the EPA was inheriting were laid out, or by function (e.g., enforcement), which might yield a more comprehensive approach to complex problems. Doug Costle recommended a staged transition from medium to function, retaining the divisions along program lines for the time being to minimize disruption and then slowly phase them out into functional offices. Under the EPA's first administrator, the agency adopted a middle approach, creating divisions organized by function (Planning and Management, Enforcement and General Counsel, and Research and Monitoring) while leaving the program offices intact. Presidentially appointed assistant administrators or commissioners were to run each of these divisions and programs.[23] The EPA would reorganize several times over the ensuing decades, but the basic architecture dividing the EPA's programs by environmental medium endures.

By budget and personnel, the water program was the largest, inheriting the Federal Water Quality Administration from the Department of the Interior with its $1 billion budget (mostly earmarked for sewage treatment plant construction) and its staff of 2,650. The EPA's new water program also took the Bureau of Water Hygiene from the Department of Health, Education, and Welfare (HEW), with its $2.3 million budget and 160 employees. From HEW also came the Bureau of Solid Waste Management, with a staff of 180 employees and a budget of $15 million as the new core of the EPA's solid waste program. Meanwhile, the EPA's pesticides program collected 425 employees and a budget of $5.1 million from the Department of Agriculture's Pesticide Regulation Division, pairing them with 275 employees from the Federal Drug Administration's Office of Pesticide Research and nine employees from Interior who studied the effects of pesticides on fish and wildlife. The EPA also received responsibility for the rapidly evolving field of radiation, with 350 staff from HEW's Bureau of Radiological Health joining the four person Federal Radiation Council and three staff from the Atomic Energy Commission to make up the agency's radiation program. To create the EPA's air program, HEW transferred the National Air Pollution Control

Administration from the Public Health Service, with its 1,100 employees and $110 million budget.[24] Finally, to support its program offices, the EPA took responsibility for ten national research laboratories scattered throughout the country.

Together with budgets, staff, and responsibilities, the EPA also inherited the institutional dynamics, quirks, and politics of those various bureaucracies. As Doug Costle explained, this inheritance included a water pollution office that was "independent even of its own top staff," an air pollution office that was "traditionally weak on enforcement" and "very independent," a solid waste program that had "great public expectations" but "little money," and a pesticides office that faced "tricky politics" as a result of "wide scientific dispute," "heavy public pressure," and "great resentment" in the Food and Drug Administration.[25] The decision to organize the EPA by environmental medium contributed to the retention of these administrative cultures. Staff from the various program offices remained organizationally and even physically distinct. Meanwhile, the political appointees that ran the various programs worked with their staffs out of the agency's headquarters in Washington, DC, fueling a sense of autonomy along program lines. This arrangement was most pronounced in the Air Office, which maintained most of the staff it inherited from the National Air Pollution Control Authority in their former offices in North Carolina's Research Triangle Park.

Compounding the difficulty of organizing all those different offices, the EPA's responsibilities seemed to expand by the day, as Congress passed one bill after another. In the realm of solid waste, for instance, the 1970 Resource Recovery Act authorized $460 million to be used by the EPA to upgrade local disposal sites and fund recycling research.[26] An even larger expansion of responsibility loomed under the Clean Air Act, which was making its way through conference committee as the EPA came together in November 1970.

Like other administrative institutions, the EPA's career staff were part of the federal civil service, the nation's public sector workforce, with set pay schedules and hiring authorities determined by the White House and Congress. With popular interest in the environment at a fever pitch, especially among young people, the EPA had no trouble attracting talented employees. For many, this was the beginning of a long career with the agency. Kerry Clough, who joined the EPA as a management intern in 1971, has what must be the most colorful story of coming aboard. Competing for the position against fellow applicants with PhDs from prestigious universities, the twenty-three-year-old Clough figured that his master's degree in physical geography gave him little chance of obtaining one of the coveted spots at the EPA. But Clough's interview took a fortuitous turn when Howard Messner, the director of the White House task force assembled to do the initial hiring, saw something that caught his eye. Clough had had a summer job building sewage treatment plants in Virginia and had recently been painting black creosote on the insides of trickling filters under the hot Virginia sun. Slowly rotating his body along the contours of the pipe as he painted, Clough acquired a spectacular sunburn down the entire right side of his face, arm, and body. At the beginning of the interview, Messner leaned far over his dais, inspecting Clough in silence before finally asking what was wrong with him. Having heard Clough's explanation of the task that had created his striking appearance, Messner dismissed him without another question. Figuring his prospects were sunk, Clough was shocked to receive an offer letter. When Clough finally gathered the courage to ask about it later, a colleague told him that Messner had been so taken by Clough's apparent familiarity with the work the EPA would soon be doing that he decided to hire him on the spot. Clough would go on to become a trusted aide of two administrators and eventually a deputy regional administrator as part of a thirty-seven-year career at the EPA.[27]

In addition to the career staff they inherited from the program offices and the idealistic young employees they hired, the EPA's planners had the support of the White House to tap top talent for the new agency. Chuck Elkins remembers targeting a high-level attorney in the civil service whom he knew to be working on environmental protection, someone who ordinarily would not be asked to leave his post, and convincing him to come over to the EPA.[28] There were many such stories around the EPA's founding. One expert who did not get the call was the Ash Council's Doug Costle, who despite "know[ing] more about the EPA . . . than anyone else in Washington," in the words of an advisor, was passed over for a top appointed position because he was a Democrat.[29]

To run the new agency, Nixon's advisors settled on William Ruckelshaus, who had quickly risen through the ranks of state politics in Indiana to an assistant attorney general post. Holding a BA from Princeton and a law degree from Harvard, Ruckelshaus had started his career in the Indiana State Board of Health, representing the state in pollution control litigation and helping to draft the Indiana Air Pollution Control Act in 1963. In the mid-1960s, Ruckelshaus entered Indiana state politics, rising to Republican majority leader of Indiana's House of Representatives and running and losing a close

race for the US Senate in 1968, before being appointed assistant attorney general of the Civil Division in the Department of Justice by Nixon in 1969.
When Nixon tapped Ruckelshaus to be the first EPA administrator, he was
thirty-eight years old, a decade younger than his nearest competitor.[30]

On November 6, 1970, Nixon, his chief environmental advisor John
Whitaker, and CEQ chairman Russell Train gathered to announce Ruckelshaus's
nomination to the press. In a private meeting before the press announcement,
Nixon emphasized that Train's CEQ would continue to be the chief source of
policy advice on environmental matters.[31] Nixon and his advisors also stressed
that in implementing the administration's environmental policy, Ruckelshaus
was expected to tread lightly on the administration's allies in the business community. As Whitaker put it, Ruckelshaus's job was "to get industry cooperation
in cleaning up the environment without outright harassment of industry."[32] In
December 4, with the president looking on, Ruckelshaus was sworn in as the
first administrator of the EPA.[33]

A Pirate's Ransom

Ruckelshaus's first speech as administrator painted a bleak portrait of the
nation's environment. From the proliferation of dangerous pesticides to effluent fouled rivers, environmental conditions were deteriorating, dragging
down human health along with them. But it was air pollution that represented
the nation's most urgent problem, Ruckelshaus explained, because unlike
water or soil, specific parcels or streams of air could not be cleansed before
their consumption. Centuries of treating the air like a "gigantic sewer" had
created an array of problems. For the urban resident, the degradation took
the form of "the sickening yellow smog that lands over his city, irritating his
eyes and nose, filtering out the sunshine, and preventing his children from
seeing what he used to see." For "the housewife it is the dirt that collects on
her wash when she hangs it out to dry. And to her husband, it is what causes
the paint on their house to discolor and peel more quickly than it used to."
As air pollution increased across the nation, the toll of the economic damage
had become staggering. "The 200 million tons of pollutants with which we in
the United States infect our air every year extorts a pirate's ransom in dollar
costs," Ruckelshaus declared. "The yearly total amounts to many billions, including $500 million in damage to crops and livestock and $800 million in
added laundry bills."[34]

Ruckelshaus recognized that the EPA had a popular mandate to act decisively to reduce these mounting costs. "For a century," Ruckelshaus stated, "industrial smokestacks belching their poisons into the air were symbols of progress . . . celebrated by poets." But in recent years, the American public had come to see the trade-offs that such progress entailed. Out of this recognition had come an "environmental ethic—the discovery of a new reverence for all forms of life and their systems of support." The present challenge, Ruckelshaus declared, was to enact "reasonable standards" of air quality and to hold industry and the general public to those standards.[35] It is a testament to the sea change in values occasioned by the environmental movement that the "reasonable standards" that Ruckelshaus and the EPA developed nevertheless represented a radical expansion of federal authority. As Ruckelshaus would later recount, "the public was insistent on absolute purity" and had little patience for a gradual approach to cleaning up the environment.[36] In the EPA's first few years, Ruckelshaus and other EPA officials would find themselves propelled by this swell of popular support for strong new protections.

The Air Office's first major task underscored the EPA's importance in determining what the sweeping ambitions of landmark legislation would look like in practice. The Clean Air Act of 1970 had instructed the EPA to promulgate National Ambient Air Quality Standards (NAAQS) for the nation's most pressing pollutants, building on previous research conducted by one of the EPA's predecessor agencies, the National Air Pollution Control Administration (NAPCA). In 1969, NAPCA received the findings of a commissioned study that identified thirty airborne pollutants as threats to human and environmental health. NAPCA initially picked six pollutants— carbon monoxide, nitrogen dioxide, total photochemical oxidants, sulfur dioxide, particulate matter, and hydrocarbons—on the basis of their threat to public health, though the administration had indicated that additional pollutants might be considered. For each of the six, NAPCA convened a Science Advisor Board that canvassed existing research to produce a "criteria document" that spelled out the pollutant's particular properties and dangers at different concentrations in the air.[37] The Clean Air Act of 1970 instructed the EPA to set a national standard for each of the "criteria" pollutants based on this collected research. The permissible ambient concentration of each criteria pollutant would be different, depending on the particular risks of that pollutant. But across the board, the statute specified that the NAAQS were to be set at levels that, "allowing for an adequate margin of safety, are requisite to protect the public health."[38]

Figure 2.1 President Richard Nixon signs the Clean Air Act of 1970 into law with EPA administrator William Ruckelshaus and Council on Environmental Quality chair Russell Train looking on, December 31, 1970. Nixon White House Photographs, 1/20/1969–8/9/1974. White House Photo Office Collection (Nixon administration), 1/20/1969–8/9/1974. Richard Nixon Presidential Library, National Archives and Record Administration.

Having inherited responsibility for the criteria documents alongside the NAAQS, the EPA chose not to expand its list of the "criteria" pollutants beyond the initial six.[39] Even with this focus, the EPA faced a monumental task in devising standards for pollutants whose unifying risk factor was their pervasiveness. The automobile, the basic unit of transportation for the bulk of the country, was the primary producer of carbon monoxide, nitrogen dioxide, and hydrocarbons. In the atmosphere, nitrogen dioxide combined with hydrocarbons and other volatile organic compounds emitted by industry or naturally by vegetation to form a fourth pollutant, total photochemical oxidants. Electric utilities and other industries that burned coal produced sulfur dioxide, the fifth pollutant. The sixth and final pollutant, particulate matter, may have been the most endemic, consisting of microscopic particles suspended in the air as a result of the combustion of fossil fuels by industry and automobiles, and, to a lesser extent, generated by other industrial activities such as powder coating. These anthropogenic particles tended to be smaller, more toxic, and thus more hazardous than naturally occurring particles such as dust or pollen and wreaked havoc on the body when they entered the lungs. Mindful of earlier failures of the National Air Pollution Control Administration to issue its own standards, Congress wrote a tight deadline into the new Clean Air Act legislation. Proposed NAAQS were due in January 1971 and the EPA had until the end of April 1971 to issue the final standards.[40]

Those first proposed standards upended the Nixon administration's assumption that the EPA would play a moderating role in the nation's expanding pollution control programs. Drawing on the public health research of the criteria documents, the EPA's Air Office set the permissible concentrations well below existing ambient emission levels in most of the country.[41] Violations of the carbon monoxide standard in its first year in operation in 1971 give an idea of the toughness of the new standards. In Los Angeles, pollution monitors in Long Beach County recorded 1,015 exceedances of the carbon monoxide standard, exactly 1,014 more exceedances than were permitted under the NAAQS. No city faced a harder road to controlling automobile emissions than Los Angeles, but even places like St. Louis (with barely a fifth of Los Angeles's population and none of the topographic constraints) exceeded the carbon monoxide standard four times in 1971, each time by more than 10 percent.[42] The story was the same for the other five criteria pollutants. Cities and regions differed substantially in air quality, but every city was well out of compliance with one or more of the NAAQS.

Back in January 1971, Nixon's advisors declared that the proposed standards portended doom—Ruckelshaus remembers John Ehrlichman telling him that the standards threatened to "shut the country down." Having received assurances from the Air Office that economists in Congress and the White House had vetted the proposed standards, Ruckelshaus was as surprised as the White House by the strictness of the NAAQS.[43] So, with Ehrlichman's assistance, Ruckelshaus set out to bolster the EPA's economic expertise to avoid similar surprises in the future.

By congressional directive and bureaucratic design, the EPA already had the ability to assess the costs for enforcing clean air standards. The Ash Council saw economic expertise as a tool for the EPA's leaders to evaluate different regulatory alternatives presented by the program offices.[44] In keeping with the Nixon administration's wariness about overly zealous environmental regulators, economic expertise would help to "balance economics, health, aesthetics," alongside other "competing, often conflicting considerations."[45] In addition, the Clean Air Act tasked the EPA with publishing an annual report for Congress on the economic costs of controlling air pollution for industry and government. In March 1971, the EPA issued its first report, estimating that it would cost $15 billion to clean the nation's air over the following five years—$1.2 billion of it in government spending for the development, monitoring, and enforcement of regulations, $6.5 billion by the owners of stationary sources of pollution to implement those rules, and the remaining $7.1 billion in investment on automobile emission controls.[46]

To augment the EPA's economics after the rude surprise of the proposed NAAQS, Ehrlichman transferred to the EPA an economist named Robert L. Sansom, who had previously worked for Henry Kissinger in the White House.[47] Under Sansom's direction, the EPA created several economic analysis programs within the agency to serve different purposes. First, Sansom created an Economic Analysis Division in the Office of Policy Planning and Management to provide quick feedback on the costs of particular EPA policies for EPA officials to use in discussions with the White House and regulated industries. The eight staff researchers in the Economic Analysis Division also set standards for how economic analysis would be conducted elsewhere in the agency.[48] Cost/benefit analysis was particularly useful for these quick reports, and the Economic Analysis Division made developing those techniques a funding priority.[49] Meanwhile, Sansom created a separate group in the Office of Research and Development, with a $3 million annual budget to fund longer-term research on the broad macroeconomics of pollution control.[50] EPA officials also decided early that program offices needed their own analytical capabilities. In the Air Office, a Policy Analysis Staff consisting of three economists, two analysts, secretaries, and a consultant provided that capability.[51] Across the rest of the agency, a dozen additional staff studied the various economic implications of the EPA's activities.[52]

Congressional mandates and popular support for environmental protection put the NAAQS themselves out of reach for Sansom's economic advisors. Congress had instructed the EPA to issue NAAQS with the sole goal of protecting public health, insisting that the EPA ignore economic costs and technological feasibility in setting the standards. Nixon knew that wide popular support for strong regulatory protections meant that he would suffer politically if he tried to interfere with this mandate. During debate on the act, Muskie and other senators and congressional representatives had frequently appealed to Nixon's own public claims regarding the importance of environmental quality to demonstrate the depth and the bipartisan nature of support for the act and to tie Nixon's public record on the environment to the EPA's implementation of the Clean Air Act.[53] Given the political salience of environmentalism in the early 1970s, any perception that Nixon did not support regulatory protections would have damaged his chances at a second term in office.[54] The act's supporters made it clear that Nixon would face great political peril if he stood in the way of the mission Congress had given the EPA. In case such admonishments fell short, Muskie had warned that the Senate would be reviewing the EPA's implementation of the Clean Air Act to ensure that the Nixon administration had not "watered down" the legislation.[55] In such a climate, the EPA retained the strict NAAQS when the agency promulgated the final rule in April, setting an ambitious course for the country even as the agency's own head publicly lamented the near impossibility of achieving the standards by the deadline Congress had specified.[56] But the battle over the cost of pollution control was just beginning.

While the expanding of the EPA's economic expertise sprang from White House efforts to restrain the agency, Ruckelshaus and other officials quickly recognized that this economic expertise could also help protect regulations that they deemed wise. Beginning with the proposed NAAQS in January 1971, the EPA found itself buffeted by business representatives insistent that the agency's standards would be ruinous to their industries. On the other side, environmental advocates demanded that the EPA strengthen this or that regulation, often arguing that the attendant costs were not nearly as high as the agency claimed. For the EPA's leaders, it quickly became clear that defending the agency's programs and navigating through fusillades of competing claims required a strong economic game.

Within the Nixon administration, the Department of Commerce emerged as a vocal critic of the compliance costs of the EPA's regulations. Citing industry reports that the high costs of introducing new equipment could not be recouped or would come at the expense of other capital investments, Secretary of Commerce Maurice Stans called for the business-friendly National Industrial Pollution Control Council in the White House to form a new environmental quality control cost council.[57] Stans also urged the EPA and the Nixon administration to evaluate each regulatory proposal through cost/benefit analysis.[58] The Nixon administration, while recognizing the frequent hyperbole of business complaints (including those funneled through Commerce), nevertheless pressured the EPA to reduce the costs of its programs to business or at the very least to justify those costs through economic research.

All of this meant that economics as logic or justification became an integral part of the EPA's policymaking. By April 1971, the EPA had begun work on a study titled the Economic Effects of Pollution Control on Industry, contracting with Chase Manhattan bank to plan the research and drawing on the expertise of economists on the Council of Environmental Quality and elsewhere in the executive branch.[59] The EPA officials saw such expertise as a shield for the EPA's rulemaking (as the administrative formulation of regulations is known) against both environmentalists and regulated businesses. Laying out a calendar for the study, an EPA staff member noted that while the final report would not be ready until June, an interim draft would be available when Senator Muskie's review of the EPA's implementation of the Clean Air Act began in May.[60]

Implementation

The EPA's implementation of the stringent NAAQS quickly became a key battleground in the contest over the cost of pollution control. The Clean Air Act required each state to submit a State Implementation Plan (SIP) detailing how it planned to reduce emissions from existing sources of air pollution such that the six NAAQS would be attained by May 31, 1975, for each of the Air Quality Control Regions—geographic entities laid out by the EPA's predecessor agency according to atmospheric circulation patterns and land use patterns that drove pollution such as concentrations of population or industry—within the state.[61] The Clean Air Act required the EPA to evaluate those plans and to reject any SIP that did not appear sufficiently vigorous to meet the NAAQS by the 1975 deadline. If a state failed to submit an acceptable SIP by January 1972, the Clean Air Act required the EPA to create its own plan for that state. Once a SIP was approved, it would have the force of law and the states, and the EPA could take enforcement actions to force businesses to comply with the plans.

In the early 1970s, the states differed widely in their competence and enthusiasm for controlling air pollution. As an informed observer told the Nixon administration's John Whitaker, few states had a comprehensive environmental agency. Many had pollution control authorities scattered around by medium (air, water, etc.); others had only a council or commission, often

working in a strictly advisory capacity. States with longer histories of industrialization had much more developed control authorities than states
without: Massachusetts was in the midst of organizing its various administrative bodies into an Office of Environmental Affairs; Arizona had only the
Governor's Commission on Beauty.[62] In order to assist states like Arizona in
preparing their SIPs, the EPA identified environmental consultants and set
aside $2 million to help pay for expert guidance.[63]

Of course, the same endemic pollution problems that built up control expertise in a state like California tended to create many more difficulties for
officials in coming up with a viable plan to meet the NAAQS by the 1975
deadline. Los Angeles had more than 1,000 violations of the carbon monoxide standard in 1973—a predicament of geography and economic growth
that no amount of experience or sophisticated control authority could resolve before the 1975 deadline. What's more, a long history of environmental
action in states like California brought much more public scrutiny to their
State Implementation Plans.

Though the SIPs were prepared by the states, the process turned on the
EPA's evaluation of the plans. For states that exceeded one or more of the
NAAQS, the EPA required that the implementation plan specify the annual
emission reductions that would enable reasonable further progress toward
attaining the standard by the deadline. But with no precedent for a nationwide reduction in pollution, what constituted an acceptable plan for attainment was an open question. Business representatives and environmental
advocates both recognized that the SIP process represented a critical juncture in translating the goals of the Clean Air Act into the actual pollution
controls that firms would be forced to install, and they jockeyed for influence
within the EPA's rulemaking. Business representatives used the Department
of Commerce and the White House's Office of Management and Budget
(OMB) to get at the EPA's policymaking. But environmentalists fought back
with allies of their own in Congress and within the EPA.

The contest over the state plans coalesced around a set of guidelines
that the EPA proposed in April 1971. The guidelines were technically nonbinding, but state authorities, environmentalists, and businesses recognized
that the EPA's suggestions effectively amounted to the criteria by which the
agency would evaluate the SIPs. Sure enough, when the EPA opened the proposed guidelines for public comment, the agency received more than 400
responses, making clear that all parties involved understood the guidelines
as more requirement than suggestion.[64] Within the Nixon administration,

the Department of Commerce lobbied hard against the EPA's strong hand. In July 1971, Commerce's General Counsel William Letson wrote Whitaker as well as the assistant director of the Office of Management and Budget to complain that the EPA's proposed SIP guidelines had effectively shifted responsibility for air pollution control from the states to the federal government. In Letson's opinion, by creating a detailed set of criteria by which the SIPs would be judged, the EPA had usurped authority that Congress had intended to reside in the states. In addition, by insisting on such stringent NAAQS, the EPA had effectively instituted "air rationing for large parts of the nation, with all of the coupon books spoken for." Letson argued that the EPA should accept any "reasonable" plans the states put forward so long as each governor certified that he would act in good faith to implement the plan.[65]

State officials served as another conduit for complaints about the EPA's handling of the SIPs. In May 1971, an aide to California governor Ronald Reagan wrote a Nixon advisor to warn that Ruckelshaus's anticipated critique of the deficiencies of California's SIP at a news conference the next day would likely embolden the proponents of a far more disruptive plan then up for consideration in statewide referendum. Among other things, the 1972 ballot referendum authorized shutting down factories and other businesses that violated air quality standards.[66] Reagan's aide took pains to avoid suggesting that Ruckelshaus ought to be pressured into silence regarding California's plan. Besides, the aide noted, "my impression is that Mr. Ruckelshaus does not respond readily to pressure anyway." Reagan's aide simply hoped that Nixon might impress upon Ruckelshaus that the ordinary citizen would not understand the "potential for economic dislocations . . . lurking" in the referendum proposal and thus he should take a positive tone in describing California's present efforts and accomplishments. Perhaps, Reagan's aide suggested, Ruckelshaus could avoid bringing up California entirely until the press asked him about the state.[67]

Despite sympathies that leaned more toward the business than the environmental community, Nixon was willing to shoulder some criticism for pollution controls that Whitaker and other advisors told him were politically popular. A November 1971 memo recounted Nixon laughing with Ruckelshaus about "all the flack" Nixon took from industry due to Ruckelshaus "being too zealous in getting industry to stop pollution." The president jokingly inquired whether Ruckelshaus might consider holding a "be kind to industry week," but congratulated him for being "a fine strong man in an impossible job," suggesting that Nixon anticipated some business criticism as both inevitable and tolerable.[68]

Within the EPA itself, staff and officials held different opinions about how hard to push the states, with the Air Office leading the charge for stronger SIPs. The Air Office's George Walsh exemplified this position when he appeared in December 1971 on behalf of the EPA at a public hearing in Montana on that state's proposed SIP. Copper smelting produced the bulk of Montana's sulfur dioxide emissions, and the State Board hearings had been organized to consider a proposal by the smelters to avoid stringent caps on their facilities in exchange for an operational plan whereby firms would curtail production on days with poor air quality.[69] Walsh discouraged the operational method and testified that a simple limit on all smelters would be more effective and easier to enforce than trying to regulate when smelters operated. Furthermore, Walsh told Montana's State Board of Health that the National Ambient Air Quality Standards (NAAQS) represented only "minimum goals" and that the board could be far more aggressive in reducing sulfur oxides if it wished.[70]

Walsh's testimony outraged copper producers, including Kennecott Copper Corporation and Anaconda Copper Mining Company, whose representatives wrote to the EPA and the Nixon administration to protest what they declared to be Walsh's urging of Montana's Board of Health to follow the EPA's preferences rather than the letter of the Clean Air Act. Those copper producers objected especially to Walsh's remark that the market would capably absorb the 3 percent to 5 percent increase in copper prices that a uniform standard on smelters might bring, noting (in White House paraphrasing) that "Walsh was nowhere qualified as an economic expert," and that this particular assumption was in fact incorrect. The copper smelter industry had also proposed an operational method of control in Arizona and Nevada—states, which together with Montana, contained nearly all the smelting activity in the country. Kennecott and Anaconda asked that the EPA not testify at future hearings in any of those states and issue a formal letter withdrawing Walsh's remarks from Montana's public record.[71]

Called in for a meeting with Nixon's advisors about the issue, Ruckelshaus refused to withdraw Walsh's letter but issued a clarifying statement that the NAAQS were an acceptable target for state SIPs, that operational changes could be used in place of uniform limits to meet the NAAQS, and that Walsh's statement reflected only information he had personally collected and did not represent the agency's economic analysis.[72] Walking back Walsh's claims about the industry's financial situation, Ruckelshaus and the EPA nonetheless refused to retract Walsh's encouragement of Montana to go above and beyond the national requirements or Walsh's cautionary note about the difficulty of meeting the NAAQS through operational adjustments. Still, the correction amounted to EPA headquarters tempering the Air Office's push for more stringent controls.

In the eyes of many environmentalists, Ruckelshaus's addendum to Walsh's testimony represented yet another weakening of the Clean Air Act under the Nixon administration. With help from the courts, environmental advocates pushed back. Environmentalists' access to the courts as a site for contesting the EPA's decisions was a recent but vital development, as the courts became a critical space for shaping the agency's policies. In 1965, a federal court decision had given environmentalists the ability to file lawsuits against public and private development projects where the public interest was threatened.[73] The National Environmental Policy Act of 1969 established a statutory basis for that standing by creating the environmental impact review process, which to this day requires that all major developments with federal involvement (defined broadly as anything from issuing permits to securing loans) include a publicly reviewed study. Believing outside review to be a bulwark against industry capture of the EPA, the authors of the Clean Air Act included provisions that allowed private citizens to bring civil suits against any person or firm alleged to be in violation of the NAAQS and to sue the agency for failing to uphold any part of the act.[74] While environmental advocates certainly did not win every case they brought, and regulated businesses also found juridical ways to advance their agendas, on balance, the courts served as a powerful ally for environmentalists in their push for strong regulatory protections.

With recourse to the courts, environmental organizations patrolled the EPA's development of the State Implementation Plan approval process. One of the most effective organizations was the newly created Natural Resources Defense Council. Formed in New York in 1970 with an initial staff of nine lawyers, NRDC was built on a substantial grant from the Ford Foundation to further the development of public interest law.[75] NRDC's strategy targeted areas in which grave threats to the environment had not received adequate attention from other environmentalist organizations and where legal statutes or jurisprudence presented an opportunity to establish important legal precedents for environmental protection.[76] A long-term goal of NRDC was to secure a thorough and universal environmental impact review process such that businesses would come to consider the potential environmental effects of every major decision they made.[77] To help finance expensive litigation, NRDC quickly developed a robust fundraising operation.[78]

Despite this strong base of support and legal toolkit, NRDC could hardly afford to take the EPA to court over every single dispute. Nor did NRDC have the political clout to intervene in the agency's rulemaking through a senator's office, as well-connected business lobbyists often did. So, in addition to bringing lawsuits, NRDC lawyers built personal relationships with sympathetic EPA staff who shared NRDC's goal of creating a robust set of regulatory protections. Dave Hawkins, a NRDC lawyer who was instrumental in shaping the organization's air pollution control program, describes the strategy thus: "We tried to develop persuasive analyses to inject into the Agency's thought process at the lowest level possible and at the earliest point in the process possible. You're always advantaged if you can convince people that are writing the first draft of these things to embrace your ideas."[79] Surveying published literature, NRDC created technical and legal analyses that they distributed to EPA staff in the Policy Office and in the Air Office.[80] NRDC lawyers also lobbied attorneys in the EPA's Office of General Counsel, offering legal opinions that the EPA's attorneys could use in response to questions from EPA staff.[81] The Natural Resource Defense Council's reputation for high-quality analysis extended to EPA officials, including Ruckelshaus himself, who recounted that NRDC's analysis convinced him to reverse course on at least one regulatory decision.[82] When that collegial approach failed, NRDC could and did sue the administrator under the agency-forcing provisions in the Clean Air Act.

That the EPA's rules often incorporated NRDC's recommendations reflected the trust that the NRDC cultivated as well as the fact that much or maybe even most of the EPA's staff shared its desire for robust regulatory interventions. In a process similar to what historian Daniel Carpenter found in his study of the Food and Drug Administration, career staff at the EPA soon developed a personal stake in the reputation of the EPA as a strong regulatory agency.[83] Insulated from the pressure that politically appointed officials and higher-level managers faced, the EPA's technical and legal staff were a receptive audience for NRDC lobbying, especially as they learned to trust its analysis. Where EPA staff disagreed with the decisions made by higher-level managers, the NRDC proved a discreet and supportive ally.[84]

The Natural Resource Defense Council's cultivation of close relationships with EPA staff quickly proved critical in the fight over the state implementation guidelines. Back in April 1971, the NRDC had assumed that the EPA would review the public comments on the proposed SIP guidelines and then quickly issue final recommendations for the states. Instead, the NRDC found itself waiting alongside state officials for months without a final set of guidelines. When Ruckelshaus eventually announced the final guidelines in August, NRDC attorneys were dismayed to see substantial revisions that they believed drastically weakened the potential of the act to clean up the nation's air. Two internal EPA memos provided to the NRDC by a source in the EPA's Air Office indicated that the revisions had come in response to suggestions made by the Office of Management and Budget in the White House. In June 1971, the EPA had sent a revised set of SIP preparation guidelines to the Office of Management and Budget, where economic advisors joined officials from a number of other federal offices (including the Department of Commerce) in offering additional feedback. With the official comment period closed, the EPA did not include this review in the official record. It was not until environmentalists cried foul later that fall that the agency even acknowledged that the Office of Management and Budget had reviewed the guidelines at all. The revisions to the guidelines and the process by which they had been made set off a firestorm of criticism from environmental groups—including venerable organizations like the Izaak Walton League—which charged the Nixon administration with improperly meddling in the EPA's affairs and weakening the Clean Air Act.[85] Whitaker and Ruckelshaus's denial of the charges did little to mollify concern that soon spread to Congress.

Declaring the presidential intervention contrary to the intent of Congress in assigning the EPA responsibility for implementing the Clean Air Act, environmentalists turned to the sympathetic Senate Subcommittee on Air and Water Pollution to force the EPA to insist on more robust state controls. In February 1972, the subcommittee finally opened its long-promised hearings on the Clean Air Act, eventually taking thirteen days of testimony on all aspects of the EPA's implementation of the legislation. Underscoring the importance of the subcommittee as a platform for environmentalist voices, the hearings began with the testimony of NRDC chairman Richard Ayres. Prior to the hearings, Ayres's Project on Clean Air had studied the viability of twenty-four of the fifty-odd SIPs submitted to the EPA.[86] Ayres began his Senate testimony by lamenting that the plans, "which were to have been comprehensive blueprints for new action, have mostly become little more than weak-kneed apologies for each State's present program." Two-thirds of the surveyed plans would not achieve the NAAQS by the 1975 deadline, Ayres reported, and "most of the rest are so hobbled by other infirmities that their promises to meet standards cannot be taken seriously." "The major blame for this situation," declared Ayres, "must be placed squarely on the Nixon administration," which had reviewed the SIPs in secret and forced the EPA to issue the "drastically weakened final guidelines."[87]

As evidence for the White House's nefarious intervention, Ayres held up the two leaked memos sent by the deputy administer of the Air Office to Ruckelshaus in August 1971. Transmitting the final guidelines to Ruckelshaus, the memos described the revisions that had been made in response to the review led by the Office of Management and Budget. That review, complained Ayres, had not been publicly announced and occurred after the public comment period, preventing NRDC and others from responding to the claims made by the White House. Ayres argued that the Office of Management and Budget review had allowed opponents of strong regulation in the business community to effectively veto offending aspects of the SIP guidelines, using the Department of Commerce as their voice within the administration. Noting that Ruckelshaus had "vehemently denied" NRDC's complaints about this unwarranted interference, Ayres asked why the final guidelines departed so dramatically from earlier drafts, and seemingly without any basis in the publicly available information filed during the public comment period. While Ayres neglected to say how exactly he had obtained the memos, his source was almost certainly inside the EPA, since the White House (as the only other party with access to the memos) had no incentive to make them public.[88]

Led by encouraging questions from Senator Thomas Eagleton, Ayres detailed the many specific ways that the Office of Management and Budget review had weakened the SIP guidelines and thus the plans put forward by the states. The final guidelines left out land use and transportation controls, and so most states had neglected to do anything about the automobile emissions that were a principal source of air pollution. The few that had were hardly encouraging in their scale: a stricter review process for parking garages in Portland, a proposal to use propane in New York's taxis, and a carpooling incentive for the Bay Bridge between Oakland and San Francisco. The new guidelines also omitted suggestions that states with good air quality create rules to prevent that quality from degrading. Perhaps most troubling, the final guidelines encouraged states to consider economic costs and feasibility in deciding between alternative plans, effectively creating an avenue for industry across the country to successfully block pollution control requirements they deemed too expensive. Questioning Ayres at length about this new economic language, Senator Eagleton repeatedly declared this final revision to be the most pernicious, since Congress had expressly omitted such considerations of economic costs from the Clean Air Act itself.[89] Following Ayres, the subcommittee heard from several other environmental and public health advocates, who added to the damning account of White House intrusion into the implementation of the Clean Air Act.[90]

When Ruckelshaus appeared before the subcommittee, Senator Eagleton and other members used the testimony of Ayres and other environmentalist critiques to grill the EPA administrator about the OMB's interference. Welcoming Ruckelshaus, Senator Eagleton noted that the subcommittee had heard testimony, "with rather strong supporting evidence, that serious compromises have occurred in the implementation of the Clean Air Act of 1970." Reiterating the many specific accusations made by Ayres, Senator Eagleton asked for Ruckelshaus's response. Rejecting all assertions that the White House had rewritten the guidelines or taken over the SIP implementation, Ruckelshaus laid out a narrowly defined interpretation of the EPA's duties under the Clean Air Act. The agency had only been given responsibility for ensuring that the NAAQS were met, Ruckelshaus asserted. How the states got there was their business. The EPA could no more insist on a fundamental rethinking of a state's transportation system than it could insist that a state that already met the NAAQS prevent its air quality from degrading. Confronted with a flow chart that the Air Office had produced, which suggested that the OMB had the final say on SIP approval, Ruckelshaus rather unconvincingly declared the chart a mistaken response to misinformation in the press. With the exception of a brief reprieve from Senator Bob Dole, who stopped by the hearings to offer his support for Ruckelshaus and take a swipe at Senator Muskie for being away from the hearings on the presidential campaign trail, Ruckelshaus bore a steady stream of criticism over the SIP guidelines.[91]

Repeatedly questioned about the newly added recommendation that states consider costs to businesses in deciding between different ways to reach the NAAQS, Ruckelshaus maintained that the Clean Air Act only prohibited cost considerations in setting the NAAQS—a requirement he said that the EPA had followed. Telling states to avoid unnecessary economic dislocations in reaching the NAAQS was common sense, Ruckelshaus averred. Eventually growing exasperated with Eagleton's repeated questions on the subject, Ruckelshaus declared, "I can't believe that we are unable to communicate ... The law does not say, 'Let's do it the most expensive way we can figure out.'" Instead, Ruckelshaus explained, "We said to the States, 'If you can come up with others that are enforceable and will meet the standard, let us see them.' What we are telling them is do it in a way that has the least negative impact on your State."[92]

Ruckelshaus's testimony and the subcommittee hearings took place within a growing conversation about the economics of environmental protection. In a May 1971 speech to the Audubon Society in Milwaukee, Ruckelshaus had asked the environmental community for patience in restoring the nation's environmental quality. Treating every act of moderation as a betrayal, Ruckelshaus warned, risked alienating the average American, who was worried about the high costs of pollution control and would be unlikely to "pay for ecological frills," or to listen to "anyone who cries 'wolf!' too often."[93] In his 1971 environmental message to Congress, President Nixon warned against overly stringent regulations that would bankrupt the very firms whose profits the nation depended on to fund improvements in environmental quality, citing a CEQ report that estimated the annual compliance costs of pollution control at $4.7 billion.[94] CEQ's chairman, meanwhile, acknowledged those costs but noted that an economic accounting found regulation to be a financial windfall for the nation. As Train told the National Soft Drink Association in November 1971, environmentalists should be asked about the costs of their proposed programs. But a clear-eyed assessment would find that most regulations were justified. After all, Train reminded his audience, a polluted environment also cost money in damages to human health, industrial materials, and agriculture.[95] Meanwhile, Ruckelshaus told an audience of reporters that economic feasibility needed to be a consideration in evaluating regulations.[96] And the EPA's first report to Congress on the economics of air pollution control warned of the substantial costs to businesses of complying with the EPA's regulations.[97] To get a better handle on those costs, the EPA began the first of many comprehensive studies of the economic effects of implementing the Clean Air Act. Contracting with the CONSAD Research Corporation, the EPA produced reports on the seventeen industries most affected by the act as well as two new macroeconomic models to use in assessing the broader effects of the SIPs across cities and regions.[98] As the EPA's Robert Fri told Whitaker, the EPA would use those models to assess the cost effectiveness of the state plans as well as to provide a comprehensive report on the costs of meeting the NAAQS to the Office of Management and Budget before the agency approved the final state plans.[99]

Meanwhile, NRDC and other environmental groups turned to the courts to spur the EPA to strengthen the Clean Air Act at the state level. In 1972, NRDC filed suit against the EPA for approving Georgia's implementation plan, which included a provision allowing electric utilities to construct taller smokestacks to more thoroughly disperse emissions into the atmosphere instead of installing pollution control devices on those stacks. The case was eventually settled against NRDC in 1976, but not before the EPA issued a rule in 1973 disallowing the use of tall stacks, demonstrating that the scrutiny and political pressure brought in a lawsuit could compel the EPA to strengthen regulations regardless of what happened in court.[100] In another important early case, the Center for Law in the Public Interest, a California public interest advocate, successfully sued the EPA in 1972 to compel the agency to include transportation controls in California's SIP.[101] The following year, NRDC defeated the EPA's attempt to allow California and other states to delay their required transportation controls.[102]

With environmentalists watching over their shoulders, EPA officials took a hard look at the first set of implementation plans submitted by the states in January 1972. The EPA broke down SIPs by criteria pollutant, reviewing and approving plans in parts—for example, a state could have its SIP for carbon monoxide approved but not its SIP for sulfur dioxide. As the EPA sent one plan after another back to the states for revision, it became clear the agency would approve only those plans that contained sufficiently stringent measures to meet the 1975 deadline. Reporting on the review process to Whitaker in May 1972, the EPA's Robert Samson noted that twenty states had not yet established satisfactory SIPs for lowering the emissions of one or more criteria pollutants emitted by stationary sources. For many of these, Samson stated that the EPA would move forward by prescribing its own plans for the states. In addition, roughly half the nation's states did not have an adequate plan for blocking future construction of major emission sources in the event that the standards were not met by the 1975 deadline required by the Clean Air Act. The same proportion also lacked sufficient plans for emergency pollution episodes. And thirty states had not made sufficient provisions for the public availability of emissions data, a necessity if organizations such as the NRDC were going to be able to monitor their progress (and sue as necessary). However, Samson concluded that the situation was changing rapidly as the states strengthened their SIPs in response to the EPA's complaints.[103]

Figure 2.2 Under the Clean Air Act of 1970, state and local regulators, such as this representative of the Air Pollution Control Board in San Joaquin, California, worked with local sources including this asphalt batching plant to reduce their emissions in order to meet the terms of the EPA-approved State Implementation Plans. EPA Documerica, National Archives and Record Administration 542546.

On May 31, 1972, Ruckelshaus announced that the SIPs for eleven states and territories had been approved in their entirety. Unsurprisingly, the eleven states with fully approved SIPs largely lacked major industrial or automotive concentrations of pollutants. Endemic air pollution issues trumped pollution control expertise in states like California and New York, which did not have their SIPs approved. Nevertheless, Ruckelshaus stated that large portions of the SIPs for the remaining forty-one states and territories had been approved and the EPA would soon promulgate its own regulations to fill in the remaining missing or deficient areas.[104]

In addition to highlighting the enforcement costs of pollution control, the SIP process raised the question of the EPA's autonomy. Modifying the EPA's guidelines after the public comment period, the Nixon administration asserted the right to direct the EPA's policies. But the blowback and subsequent retreat left that prerogative unclear. In many instances, the White House elected merely to try to shape the optics of the EPA's policies, as when Whitaker asked Ruckelshaus to rewrite a letter the administrator had drafted to reject Arizona senator Barry Goldwater's request that the EPA defer the enactment of a permit program. Implicitly acknowledging that Ruckelshaus was not going to grant Goldwater this deferral, Whitaker merely noted that the draft had been "too cool and unresponsive," and that Ruckelshaus ought to see Goldwater personally to deliver the bad news.[105]

* * *

The fight over the EPA's review of the state implementation plans solidified the agency's place at the center of environmental governance. By the beginning of 1972, industry, environmentalists, and the Nixon administration had all realized just how much was at stake in the seemingly mundane decisions the EPA made in implementing the Clean Air Act. Would the nation's cities be forced to move away from the polluting automobile as the primary means of transportation? Would firms be required to install the latest pollution control technology regardless of the compliance costs involved? And that was just in regard to the air. Scores of other rulemakings determined how businesses, cities, and individuals treated their wastewater, disposed of their garbage, and tended their crops. Furthermore, the EPA's responsibilities appeared likely to expand in 1972, with new legislation in the works targeting air, water, radioactive substances, and even noise. Spending several million dollars to install a state-of-the-art video conferencing system in the EPA's headquarters, regional offices, and laboratories, Ruckelshaus began 1972 with an agency-wide meeting of the EPA's nearly 6,000 employees. First and foremost, Ruckelshaus declared that the EPA would continue to insist on strong regulations. That remark drew laughter from some watching the broadcast in the Denver Regional Office who believed that the agency had capitulated on automobile standards.[106]

But the business community was not laughing, not with the EPA's budget soon to expand to nearly $2.5 billion dollars. Reporting on a February 1972 meeting with a group of business representatives, Nixon advisor Ken Cole noted that the EPA's implementation of the Clean Air Act represented one of the top four concerns of industry and business allies in the Department of Commerce.[107] Thus far, businesses had been largely ineffective in limiting the expansion of the new environmental regulatory regime over which the EPA presided. As it became increasingly clear that the EPA determined billions of dollars in annual compliance expenses, industry scrambled to find a more reliable way into the EPA's policymaking. In the early 1970s, with the surging popularity of environmentalism among the general public, groups such as the Natural Resources Defense Council enjoyed far more influence with the EPA than business representatives. As the subcommittee hearings suggested, Nixon faced political peril when he directly intervened in the EPA's decision making. So business and their allies turned to an alternate means of shaping environmental policy: creating a regulatory review process to "balance" national priorities.

3

A Balancing Act

Regulatory Review

From the beginning of the environmental decade, almost everyone who worried about the expansion of regulation did so by calling for "balance." In 1970, the council that created the EPA promised plenty of checks to ensure that the new agency would "balance economics, health, aesthetics," and other concerns.[1] The following year, Nixon advisor John Whitaker instructed the president to conclude a meeting with his environmental advisors by stressing within earshot of the departing press the "need for a balanced approach to the whole environmental question so that the economy doesn't suffer." In 1972, Carl Bagge of the National Coal Association followed up on a meeting with Whitaker by reiterating his "sincere hope that we have initiated a dialogue that may lead to a more balanced implementation program which will not result in economic dislocation and unemployment."[2] And in 1975, the Office of Management and Budget revised Gerald Ford's State of the Union Address to better demonstrate the administration's commitment to "balance development and conservation."[3] Balancing was still the metaphor of choice in 1979 when Carter advisor William Nordhaus circulated "economic and legal background to assuring better balancing in the regulatory process" in a memo to other members of the economic team with the subject line: "A Balancing Act."[4]

All this talk of balancing can be explained by the enduring popularity of environmental protection, which made questioning the merits of regulatory programs politically risky for elected officials. The language of balancing, by contrast, framed constraint as a reasonable and necessary moderation, especially as the prosperity of the postwar period ran up on the shoals of the energy crisis and rising inflation. Under such conditions, only the wild-eyed could protest against balanced policy. Supporters of strong regulations soon found that they too had to adopt the sobering rhetoric of balancing to make their case for maintaining or expanding environmental protection.

Valuing Clean Air. Charles Halvorson, Oxford University Press (2021). © Oxford University Press.
DOI: 10.1093/oso/9780197538845.003.0004

In the hands of business interests, balancing conjured a zero-sum world of trade-offs in which environmental quality and economic prosperity were inversely correlated. New regulations inevitably meant higher prices, lost productivity, and, above all, rising unemployment. Increasingly concerned about such economic woes, first Nixon and then Ford expanded the White House's authority over the EPA. Defining a new prerogative to evaluate the costs and benefits of proposed regulations before the EPA and other agencies issued them, Nixon and Ford tried to assert control over an environmental protection regime that seemed insufficiently concerned about the economic consequences of its multiplying interventions.

Environmental advocates protested, but the notion of inevitable trade-offs gained traction with EPA officials who were themselves wary of the ambitious mandates created by Congress. The EPA's first administrator, William Ruckelshaus, was deeply concerned that complying with overly stringent restrictions on pollution might cripple key industries such as steel and automobile manufacturing and that intrusive limits on private behavior might cause mainstream voters to turn against environmental protection. As a result, he and other EPA officials adopted the rhetoric of balancing to moderate the agency's rules. Throughout the 1970s, environmental organizations used a sympathetic judiciary to prevent the EPA from considering compliance costs in setting the national air quality standards. But by elevating compliance costs as a key variable in the application and enforcement of those standards, proponents of balancing brought economic considerations to the forefront of the EPA's policymaking.

Increased attention to the economics of regulation privileged a monetary valuation of the environment and human health. It also threatened the dichotomy between environmental protection and economic development that business interests appealed to through the rhetoric of balancing and the idea of a trade-off. Pressed to defend its interventions on economic terms, the EPA closely analyzed the economic effects of its policies, funding and helping to spur the new field of environmental economics. This attention revealed that environmental protection was not necessarily detrimental to the economy and in fact might even have a positive effect, though the certainty of short-term compliance costs were typically more politically salient than the long-term benefits of intervention. Nevertheless, a new relationship arose: as new research threw the economics of regulation into sharper relief, the calls for balancing grew more fuzzy and abstract.

Regulatory Review

The EPA's power expanded in leaps and bounds during the agency's first year, upending the assumptions of many Nixon advisors that the EPA would merely apply policies devised elsewhere. This disconnect was the result of a lack of comprehension about the EPA's purview in the implementation of vast new legislative mandates as well as the fervor with which the EPA's first leaders pursued those responsibilities. Though the states were technically responsible for devising their own plans to meet the goals of the Clean Air Act, the EPA oversaw those plans and determined the criteria by which they were judged. The EPA set standards for what constituted acceptable pollution control technology. And the EPA was charged with ensuring that the states actually enforced the plans they established. Where the EPA found states unwilling or unable to enforce their state plans or federal standards, the agency's administrative law judges were to issue binding legal orders and fines, effectively taking control over particular companies from the states. For serious violations, the EPA was supposed to refer enforcement cases to the Department of Justice, which would initiate civil suits or criminal proceedings based on evidence that EPA agents collected.[5] The EPA enjoyed wide discretion over enforcement, deciding where and how hard to push industry to clean up pollution. The Clean Air Act allowed private citizens to sue the EPA if they thought the agency was ignoring its mandates, and Congress and the White House both weighed in on the agency's enforcement decisions.

Recognizing that the EPA's legitimacy and his own credibility in the environmental community depended on the agency's ability to actually reduce pollution, Ruckelshaus made enforcement one of his top priorities. In his first two months, he initiated five times more enforcement actions against polluting firms than the agencies from which the EPA had been assembled had ever undertaken over a similar time period. To maximize the publicity of this effort, Ruckelshaus targeted major corporations including Armco Steel (for polluting the Houston Ship Channel) and Union Carbide (for particulate emissions in West Virginia and Ohio). Ruckelshaus knew that such a brash beginning would upset the White House administration, but he gambled that the president would not interfere in his development of a strong enforcement program with environmental champion Senator Ed Muskie waiting in the wings as his likely Democratic challenger in 1972.[6]

Nixon's advisors started instead on the EPA's proliferating regulations. In May 1971, the White House's OMB instructed the EPA to start clearing the economic impact of major regulations with the president. Established as part of the same 1970 executive branch reorganization that created the EPA, the OMB quickly became one of the most powerful bodies in the Nixon administration. Under the pretext of coordinating the executive branch budget, the OMB was given the final word on the reports and even the public pronouncements of other White House offices.[7] In that May directive, OMB's director explained to Ruckelshaus that the White House was concerned that the EPA was failing to properly consider the full costs of its programs to the general economy as well as failing to provide an adequate defense of the benefits of its many programs. Henceforth, the EPA would be required to notify the OMB of any proposed regulation that appeared likely to have a significant impact on the economy and to send the OMB an economic assessment of the costs and benefits of the regulation for businesses and the federal government.[8]

Over the next several months, Nixon's advisors moved to strengthen their powers to evaluate the policies devised by administrative agencies. In June 1971, Nixon's Domestic Council undertook a study of different ways that the administration might ensure that regulations achieved a "balance of many interrelated Quality of Life variables—particularly consumer and environmental interests, industrial requirements, and safety aspects."[9] The study group recommended the creation of a new White House office. Nixon approved the recommendation and a month later, the Quality of Life Review Committee was quietly formed.[10] The Quality of Life Review allowed White House advisors to increase the weight of compliance costs in the rulemaking under the pretext of safeguarding the public interest. The heads of each executive branch agency were required to inform the OMB about any proposed rulemaking of "important consequences" and to provide the OMB with a preliminary analysis of the effect the rule was likely to have on economic factors like employment and inflation.[11] As Whitaker explained the process, the review "allows all other competing constituencies . . . to take a crack at proposed regulations prior to their being publicly announced."[12] Furthermore, regular reports from the EPA and other agencies would allow the White House to stay abreast of the hundreds of proposed administrative actions across the executive branch. Finally, by compelling the regulatory agencies to produce the initial economic analyses of their proposed rules themselves, regulatory review pushed those agencies to consider "alternative courses of action with a comparison of their relative benefits and costs," as one advisor put it.[13]

Though Nixon's advisors publicly denied any anti-environmental bias in the review, the private records tell a different story. In 1972, Whitaker told fellow Nixon advisor Ken Cole that "largely because of concern that the EPA was setting standards and making administrative decisions without a balanced view of costs of compliance as compared with benefits, we instituted last Summer the 'quality of life' review process."[14] In a 1974 memo, Jim Tozzi, an OMB economist who built a career reviewing EPA regulations, bragged that "practically all" of the EPA's proposed regulations had been reviewed since the process began.[15] Looking back on the first five years of White House review of administrative policies, a 1976 news article concluded that it had "been applied primarily, and some would say almost exclusively to EPA." OMB officials interviewed for the 1976 article did not deny the EPA's centrality, citing the EPA's unparalleled impact on the economy and other regulatory agencies.[16]

From the perspective of the environmental community, this concentrated attention on the EPA deliberately limited the agency's speed and effectiveness in responding to new problems. From the beginning, environmentalists recognized regulatory review as a critical threat to their hard-won access to the rulemaking process, and they fought back accordingly. Environmental advocates repeatedly challenged the legality of regulatory review in the courts and, when the courts upheld the process, served notice through public complaints and congressional hearings that the reviewers would be closely watched. In 1972, the Natural Resource Defense Council's Richard Ayres complained to the Senate Subcommittee on Air and Water Pollution that public interest organizations like the NRDC were being shut out of the OMB's secret proceedings, while "antienvironmental Federal agencies" like the Department of Commerce used the reviews as an "effective power to veto EPA's actions."[17] This perception has endured. Dave Hawkins, an NRDC attorney who was intimately involved in the formation of the EPA's air pollution programs, suggests that H. R. Haldeman and John Ehrlichman, Nixon's top domestic advisors, created the review "as a way to fix regs that economically powerful interests didn't like. It was a way for them to be able to call up EPA and say, 'slow down, or change this.'"[18]

In the end, determining how influential OMB review was on the EPA's policymaking depends on the specific regulation and the perspective of the observer. Ruckelshaus maintains that the process could only delay the EPA's development of new policies, resulting in missed congressional deadlines from time to time, but it never prevented the agency from eventually promulgating its rules.[19] Roy Gamse, who joined the EPA's Economic Analysis Division in 1972 and was its head by the following year, likewise dismisses the supposed potency of White House meddling, arguing that the EPA's biggest threat came instead from direct complaints from regulated industries.[20] On the other hand, Bud Ward, a journalist whose weekly newsletter *Environment Reporter* was the authoritative insider account of the EPA from its founding in 1970, remembers the Nixon administration's pressure as intense and influential. In Ward's telling, EPA employees were acutely attuned to White House scrutiny. "EPA regulators shook in their boots at a phone call from Jim Tozzi," Ward said later, referring to the notorious OMB staff member.[21] Kerry Clough, a key advisor to two EPA administrators (Russell Train and Doug Costle), argues that while direct White House intervention was very rare, the interventions that did occur were influential and discrete, targeting top political appointees at the agency and bypassing even senior-level career employees.[22]

Informal White House pressure was often more effective in tamping down the EPA's regulations than the formal Quality of Life Review process. Though such pressure left little evidence in the written record, anecdotal accounts shed light on these interventions. Clough recounts that EPA officials discussed major policies with Nixon's advisors before the formal proposal and regulatory review process even began.[23] Such confidential discussions were well within the letter of the law under the Administrative Procedures Act and sometimes found their way into writing, as when Nixon advisor Peter Flanigan noted in an October 1972 memo to Ehrlichman that the EPA, at the administration's request, had delayed proposing regulations for the removal of lead from gasoline until after the presidential election.[24] Supporters of strong regulations were not without recourse. Aware that a behind the scenes request for delay could only be accommodated if the public remained ignorant of the proposed initiative, EPA's career staff sometimes leaked potential EPA policies to the press before White House advisors had had a chance to review them. Publicly revealing the EPA's position forced the White House to either accept the proposal or incur the political risks of publicly overriding the agency.[25]

Beyond its immediate effect on any particular rule, regulatory review privileged economic analysis as the most important measure of the EPA's program within the Nixon administration. The OMB parsed the compliance costs and benefits of every major regulation, which forced the EPA to do the same. While the EPA technically had the authority to ignore whatever critique the OMB might offer and issue the final rules without making any of the changes, no political appointee wanted to flagrantly disregard the suggestions of advisors who clearly had the president's ear. The preferred option was to minimize the chances that the OMB would object to a new policy or, failing that, to have an excellent economic defense prepared. Thus, even where the Clean Air Act prohibited economic considerations in setting the national air quality standards, regulatory review pushed costs to the forefront, which naturally had a moderating effect on what the EPA chose to propose. As Whitaker put it a year into the Quality of Life Review's operation, the "system is working well to keep EPA from getting 'too far out.'"[26]

Seeking Numbers

For the EPA, the practice of governance quickly came to orbit around the aggregate costs of regulation—especially the question of whether regulation threatened jobs. Businesses wasted little time in blaming the burden of complying with the EPA's standards for all manner of plant closings and job losses. In January 1971, when the EPA was barely a month old, the chemical manufacturing giant Union Carbide Corporation publicly accused the agency of imperiling over 600 jobs at its Marietta, Ohio, plant by denying the company's request for a three-year extension on a compliance deadline for fly ash controls on its coal-fired generator.[27] Environmentalists were equally quick to reject these complaints, sharing consumer advocate Ralph Nader's opinion that such accusations amounted to nothing more than "environmental blackmail," as Nader put it in a letter to Senator Ed Muskie. The EPA's requirements for the Marietta plant would not force the factory to close, Nader told the chairman of the Senate Subcommittee on Air and Water Pollution. Instead, the threat of job loss was just another ploy by the company in a long-running program of "duplicity and intimidation evidently designed to discredit the Environmental Protection Agency and frighten the people of the Marietta region into quiet submission." Agreeing with Nader's assessment, Muskie demanded a response from Union Carbide's vice president and appealed successfully to the EPA's leaders to reject such threats.[28] In this case, Union Carbide's own workers refused to support the company in blaming regulations for the threatened shutdown, echoing other refusals from organized labor in these early years to endorse business attempts to fight pollution control with threats of layoffs.[29] But the risk remained that this narrative might shift, and the EPA's leaders increasingly looked to economics to prevent this from happening. The White House too was hungry for reliable information about plant closings. As Whitaker put it in a request to the heads of the EPA, the CEQ, and the Department of Commerce in July 1971, Nixon's advisors wanted to know "precisely what jobs have been lost by a plant closing down due to pollution enforcement. Not the *threat* to close a plant," Whitaker underscored, "but *actually being closed* and the number of jobs lost."[30]

Moving to provide that reliable accounting and preempt business complaints, the EPA and the Department of Labor joined together in November 1971 to form the Economic Dislocation Early Warning System.[31] With special attention given to economically depressed areas, the EPA would flag imminent plant closures that might be the result of environmental regulations. The Department of Labor would then supply retraining and financial assistance programs to the displaced workers.[32] In this way, the Early Warning System would both alert the EPA and the White House to potential political controversies and preempt criticism of the agency with a ready-made response for job losses.

The Early Warning System began operation in spring 1972, with the EPA issuing quarterly reports analyzing each instance in which a plant had reportedly closed, significantly curtailed operations, or seemed likely to do so because of environmental regulations. The reports were broken down by EPA Regional Office as well as the type of pollution, industry, enforcing agency (local, state, or federal), and a variety of other variables. Appendices included a description of the economic context of each local community. For example, the July 1972 report described the closure of the Big Bear Board Products Company in Redlands, California, noting that the plant was "already uneconomial [*sic*] and likely to close" due to "poor quality timber supply and thus a poor quality product." Big Bear might have "struggled by" using its marginal wood, but the $60,000 that the firm needed to spend for a new particulate emissions incinerator had eliminated the firm's meager profit margins. Though the plant only employed forty workers, the report warned that the "local economy will not absorb unemployment labor," since the "company is within a designated Economicly [*sic*] Deorssed [*sic*] Area."[33] As Roy Gamse, the director of the EPA's Economic Analysis Division, later recounted, such detailed reporting on the fate of firms like the Big Bear Board Products Company helped EPA officials to anticipate and respond to businesses that would blame the EPA for closures that would likely have happened anyway, while preempting workers' from souring on environmental regulations by making sure they received the assistance they needed.[34] According to Gamse, the EPA erred on the side of caution in attributing shutdowns to regulation, seeking above all else to avoid surprise accusations. While EPA staff knew that shutdowns occurred primarily in marginal industries, agency officials still fought to avoid blame for any loss of employment. [35]

For his part, Ruckelshaus saw economics as the means of crafting a moderate and enduring system of environmental governance. In 1972, he delivered a speech to the Los Angeles Chamber of Commerce in which he assessed his entire regulatory program on its economic merits. "Just as in physics there can be no action without a reaction," Ruckelshaus told his audience, "in economics there can be no benefit without a cost." And the costs of environmental regulation were quite significant, so much so that "at first glance, pollution control looks like a prohibitively expensive proposition." Anyone who would claim otherwise, Ruckelshaus said, or who would try to "remove every ounce of pollution from the environment is simply practicing the same old demagogy of overpromising, which guarantees underperforming and disappointment." Putting himself at least partly at odds with the Clean Air Act's cost-blind national air quality standards, Ruckelshaus declared that "we should undertake no action whose costs and benefits have not been carefully weighed and we should make every effort to predict the effects of a given policy on society as a whole."[36] In order to do so, Ruckelshaus reported that the EPA, together with the Council on Environmental Quality and the Department of Commerce, had "commissioned a task force of impartial consultants to get the answers." The results, Ruckelshaus happily continued, suggested that the nation could "actually afford the costs of a major environmental renovation. . . . [W]e are going to get back much more than we pay out."[37] There was the rub: an EPA administrator charged with implementing legislation that declared clean air to be a national right regardless of the cost, evaluating his success in dollars and cents.

In debating the economics of environmental regulation, the EPA, businesses, and the Nixon administration all confronted the basic problem of determining how much pollution control really cost. The first step lay in figuring out what information could be trusted. Businesses blamed environmental regulation for those woes. The EPA and environmentalists disagreed. And the Nixon administration was stuck trying to figure out the truth—in part so it could decide where and how strongly to intervene in the

EPA's activities.[38] Although the Council on Environmental Quality and the EPA both produced annual reports tallying the costs of regulations, Nixon's advisors would not rely solely on estimates from sources they considered overly sympathetic to the environmentalist cause. Aware that economic analyses figured centrally in the Nixon administration's evaluation of the EPA's policies, business interests invested in such research and enthusiastically offered it to the White House and the EPA.[39] Despite a cozy relationship with industry, the president's advisors knew that businesses inflated the compliance costs they reported. They also viewed with skepticism the reports produced by administrative bodies with a "developmental" bias, as Whitaker put it in declaring that the Department of Commerce, the Department of Interior, and the Department of Transportation had "done a much better job of producing rhetoric than facts."[40] So while Nixon's advisors did not lack for economic reports to sift through, none of their many sources could be fully trusted.

Furthermore, many of Nixon's advisors shared the EPA's opinion that environmental regulations brought economic benefits that, while difficult to quantify, nevertheless needed to figure into an honest accounting. The challenge lay in how to quantify those uncertain benefits, both at the macroeconomic level and in evaluating proposed rulemakings. As environmental economists had long known, regulation was a difficult subject for cost/benefit evaluations because many of the costs and benefits of pollution control would only be experienced in the long term—over decades, or generations. But if those real long-term effects were to figure into the calculation, they had to be quantified in the present. For example, in 1971, Nixon's advisors considered a number of options for measuring the inflationary effect of automobile manufacturers' spending to control carbon monoxide and other harmful pollutants, ultimately deciding that the associated health benefits would increase the value of the cars to consumers and thus the expenditures should not be tallied as contributing to rising inflation.[41] Some advisors disagreed, however, and commissioned their own studies to show that pollution controls might lower the value of the cars by decreasing consumer satisfaction, since the modified cars would likely be less powerful and less fuel efficient.[42] Who was to say on the basis of such information whether Nixon should press the EPA to suspend its recently announced requirement that manufacturers introduce catalytic converters by 1975?

To gain a better perspective on the macroeconomic costs of pollution control, Nixon's advisors solicited two reports—one from the Council on Environmental Quality (CEQ) and another from the Department of Commerce—thinking that the environmental and business biases might cancel each other out. But on receiving the reports in September 1971, the advisors were dismayed to find themselves no closer to an answer.[43] Critiquing the reports, Whitaker lamented that "the premise of the Commerce analysis was to take particularly egregious examples relayed to them through the NIPCC [National Industrial Pollution Control Council] and extrapolate those to show effects on the economy as a whole." Not much better, the CEQ approach focused on boosts in employment from the emergent pollution control industry and then relied on "guestimates" regarding the additional costs of pollution in terms of health care, cleaning bills, and so on.[44] Making "responsible policy decisions" from the two reports, another aide complained, was "extremely difficult in light of the wide divergence between the factual assumptions."[45] Rather than pointing the Nixon administration toward a moderate compromise, the two reports simply illustrated how little was settled about the economics of pollution control.

Dissatisfied with both reports, chief domestic advisor John Ehrlichman commissioned another study later in 1971 with the dual objectives of providing a more accurate assessment of the long-term costs of enforcing environment protections and identifying the most effective analytical tools to generate such assessments. Overseen by Paul McCracken, chairman of Nixon's Council of Economic Advisors, the study contracted with consultancies to produce a dozen microeconomic surveys of various industries and one study of valuation methods. Assessing the findings from all that research, the McCracken report eventually concluded that pollution control "would not cause a recession or seriously threaten the long-run economic viability of the industrial activities examined." The report indicated that prices would rise about 2 percent annually from 1972 to 1976 as a result of expenditures on pollution control and that between 50,000 and 250,000 jobs would be lost over the same period, though these would be nearly offset by new jobs created in the pollution control industry. Pollution control would also cause some upsets in manufacturing, where smaller firms might find it harder to make necessary capital investments and where the added costs of domestic manufacturing could not be passed along to consumers because foreign competitors would undercut those prices.[46] Reviewing the findings, Nixon's Department of Commerce conceded that the overall economic effects would not be devastating but underscored the report's warning that "serious dislocations" would be experienced in marginal industries.[47]

Less remarked on within the Nixon administration was the McCracken report's finding that microeconomic industry studies perpetuated a common error in undercounting or ignoring the likely benefits from increasing environmental protection—such as new jobs generated by the pollution control industry or added efficiency through the closure and absorption of inefficient firms. None of the studies, the report lamented, had even attempted to quantify the benefits of a cleaner environment, such as additional output from a healthier working population or increased crop yields. For that same reason, the McCracken report concluded, measures like gross national product (GNP) were a poor gauge of the overall costs and benefits of pollution control.[48] Not surprisingly, representatives of the Department of Commerce and other opponents of regulatory expansion disregarded those last sets of observations.

So, despite quieting fears about imminent economic catastrophe, the McCracken report did little to reverse a situation in which proponents of stronger regulation often found themselves playing defense when it came to the economics of environmental protection. In March 1972, the same month the report was released, Nixon's Office of Science and Technology reported that new research conducted under its auspices suggested that the benefits of the EPA's automobile emission standards did not outweigh the costs. Ford Motor Company president Lee A. Iacocca was elated, declaring the report "the best news the public has had in years." Ralph Nader took the opposite stance, calling the report a "mockery of scientific integrity and competence."[49]

Reflecting the importance of economics in evaluating policy, the Nixon administration pushed the EPA to improve its analytical capacity. When the top job at the EPA's Office of Policy, Planning, and Evaluation opened up, Whitaker recommended CEQ's Al Alm for the post. Alm had managed all the economic analysis produced by the CEQ, Whitaker informed Ehrlichman, analysis that had contributed to the administration's lobbying for less restrictive water pollution controls. The White House could expect sober, accurate analysis from the EPA under Alm's watch. Best of all, Whitaker continued, Alm's "key role at EPA will be to manage the Quality of Life Review so that the product that arrives at OMB will really have inputs from the other agencies."[50] Alm got the job, providing high-level support for the development of economic expertise already under way at the agency.

Though many environmental advocates looked askance at this emphasis on costs and benefits, they too recognized that the fight for expanding environmental protection would be contested in dollars and cents. As early as 1971, Senator Muskie was giving speeches in which he made the case for pollution control on its economic merits, telling the Florida Senate that year that they ought to protect Florida's environment as a key, revenue-generating asset for the state.[51] During the hearings by the Senate Subcommittee on Air and Water Pollution on the Clean Air Act's implementation the next year, subcommittee members affirmed the testimony of environmentalists that the OMB was improperly inserting economic considerations into statutes that had been explicitly written to disallow such consideration of costs. But the subcommittee also acknowledged that affected industries would make their case against pollution control on the costs that compliance entailed and that environmental agencies needed to be capable of responding in kind. As Senator Hale Boggs (D-Louisiana) described it, "EPA and the State environmental agencies have their own capability for economic analyses. . . . Whether it is presented by testimony before a hearing board or whether it is just news articles, economics is going to be involved."[52] In 1972, the subcommittee solicited a report on the "costs and benefits of air pollution control" from the Congressional Research Service, underscoring the subcommittee's recognition that industry complaints and White House pressure on the costs of regulation would have to be engaged on those terms.[53]

For his part, Senator Muskie's interest in establishing the pecuniary benefits of environmental protection was also prompted by his emergence in the fall of 1971 as the Democratic presidential frontrunner. As one of the key proponents of the Clean Air Act and other landmark environmental legislation, Muskie had an obvious constituency among environmentalists, but the Muskie camp also recognized that the cost of environmental regulations would be a major issue in the campaign, as Nixon cast about for a scapegoat for the ailing national economy. As subcommittee staffer and chief aide Leon Billings described Nixon's likely argument, "their facts and their figures would show that you cannot have a clean and healthful environment and a productive economy at the same time." To counter those claims, Muskie would have to engage Nixon on "the facts." Taking the Nixon administration's estimates of $100 billion in spending for pollution control, Billings sketched out a retort by calculating the benefits of that spending. Money spent on pollution control did not vanish, Billings argued, but instead "will buy cars, will buy clothes, will buy food and it will buy homes."[54] On the campaign trail, Muskie drew on such reasoning to challenge what he called Nixon's meddling in the economically beneficial work of regulatory agencies like the EPA.[55]

The Politics of Economics

In the 1972 presidential campaign and in American politics more generally, the economics of environmental regulation came to serve as ammunition in a wider contest over federal priorities. As in other areas, economics provided sums that could be easily compared and carried an imprimatur of neutrality that all sides in the contest gravitated toward. Demand and funding for economic analysis swelled accordingly. But as the debate over environmental regulations would show, the political utility of all those numbers lay less in their ability to adjudicate between competing claims and more in the authority they conveyed in answering what were, at their root, political questions about the responsibility, capacity, and legitimacy of the state when it came to governing the environment.

When Nixon and Muskie looked out on American voters in 1972, they saw a majority that favored government interventions to promote environmental quality but revolted from programs that imposed significant costs in their everyday lives. As he had in debating the Clean Air Act of 1970, Muskie chose to embrace the notion of trade-offs between economic prosperity and environmental protection, likely to the detriment of his campaign. On one issue after another—from strip mining in Kentucky to billboards in Florida—Muskie publicly ruminated on the benefits and costs of regulatory intervention. Instead of coming across as thoughtful consideration of complex issues, these deliberations looked like "waffling," as his advisor Leon Billings put it in a memo to his files. "It was extremely difficult to portray the gray areas of the environment issues," Billings lamented, "especially in light of the fact that the majority of the environmental constituency sees only blacks and whites."[56] Though Billings counseled his boss to run as an uncompromising defender of the environment, Muskie chose instead to run as a moderate, disappointing environmentalists and allowing Nixon to neutralize the environment as an issue in the race. [57]

Despite having little personal interest in environmental protection, Nixon nevertheless followed the advice of his advisors and evinced just enough concern to stake a claim as a moderate on the environment. Though he signed many of the nation's signature environmental programs into law, Nixon questioned the merits of strong federal policies and the endurance of popular support for such measures. To convince a skeptical president, environmental advisor John Whitaker drew on the findings of electoral and public opinion pollster Robert Teeter and his Opinion Research Corporation (ORC). Teeter had been one of the EPA's first advisors, brought on by Ruckelshaus to help the agency stay abreast of public opinion.[58] Whitaker used Teeter's findings of strong support for environmental protection among key voting demographics to convince a skeptical president to tolerate the EPA's strong regulatory interventions.[59] On the national level, Teeter had found that more than three-quarters of Americans supported forcing businesses to invest large amounts of capital in pollution control so long as that spending translated into no more than a "small increase" in prices for consumer goods. But that ratio of support flipped to 60 percent against if the price increases were "large."[60] To appeal to this wide and moderate base, Whitaker advised, Nixon should propose "a balance between environmental and economic concerns."[61]

Teeter's polling over the course of the campaign affirmed Whitaker's counsel. While 74 percent of respondents in a January 1972 survey considered environmental issues "extremely" or "very" important, those same respondents were evenly divided as to whether promoting economic growth should be emphasized at the expense of the environment. Furthermore, despite Muskie's strong environmental record, respondents considered Nixon only slightly less competent to handle environmental issues. While less than 1 percent of subjects polled considered environmental improvements to be an important accomplishment of the Nixon administration, only 1 percent considered pollution to be a major failure.[62] In that context, Whitaker's moderate approach toward environmental regulation effectively eliminated the environment as a variable in the campaign. By September, the environment had fallen off Teeter's list of major issues, with roughly 6 percent of interview subjects reporting environmental issues among the top three most important problems facing the nation. By that time, Teeter's pollsters were tracking another issue—public awareness of a break-in at the Democratic National Committee's offices in the Watergate complex.[63] On Election Day, facing only flickers of the Watergate firestorm that would soon consume his administration, Nixon won in a landslide, capturing over 60 percent of the popular vote and carrying every state except Massachusetts.[64]

Among many other things, the Watergate scandal claimed Ruckelshaus as collateral damage. Eager to capitalize on the EPA administrator's reputation for integrity, Nixon pulled Ruckelshaus from the EPA to serve as acting director of the Federal Bureau of Investigation and then deputy attorney general as part of his desperate efforts to contain the spreading scandal. In October 1973, Nixon made Ruckelshaus the second victim of the Saturday

Night Massacre, firing him after he refused to dismiss the special prose-cutor appointed to investigate Nixon. By August 1974 Nixon had exhausted every option to contain the crisis and became the first president to resign the office.[65]

As the new president, Gerald Ford, set about governing after Nixon's resignation, the domestic policy advisors who survived Watergate pressed forward with plans to elevate economic considerations in the EPA's deci-sion making. Within Ford's first month in office, Glenn Schleede, Nixon's former science advisor, proposed a new group to collect and assess infor-mation from regulatory agencies, industry, academics, consultants, special interest groups, nonprofits, and others. Schleede called for the new analyt-ical group to report directly to the science advisor and to be funded in large part by the National Science Foundation. Rather than interfere directly in agency rulemaking, the new analytical group would inform White House in-tervention.[66] Persistent mistrust of the EPA's own economic analysis drove Schleede's proposal. Endorsing Schleede's idea, economic advisor Alan Pulsipher complained that the current assessments available from the EPA were of such poor quality that they contributed little to policy discussions. Pulsipher absolved the EPA and the CEQ from any need to improve their analyses, noting that they could hardly be expected to do so, given their "cli-entele," echoing old suspicions regarding the loyalties of the EPA and the CEQ to the environmentalist community.[67] Ford's chief domestic advisor Ken Cole (also inherited from Nixon) liked the proposal and presented the idea to the president in September 1974.

Though Ford ultimately shelved the proposal in order to honor his pledge to forgo further executive branch spending, its promulgation exemplified the president's thinking about environmental policy.[68] Three characteristics stand out. First, the proposal emphasized the inevitability of conflict between improving environmental quality and fulfilling other national objectives such as increasing energy self-sufficiency.[69] Unlike Nixon, Ford insisted on the impossibility of meeting all the nation's goals—at least immediately. In speech after speech, Ford reminded audiences that the environmental problems facing the nation had been created over more than a century and thus would require more than a decade to correct. Second, the memo pro-posed technically sophisticated analysis as a means of balancing these com-peting objectives. The group would consist of approximately five members from a variety of backgrounds and an ample budget to contract additional research. Third, and perhaps most important, the memo reflected the Ford administration's conviction that public support for such balancing could be achieved by laying out the scientific and economic implications of specific policies. The reports of the new group were to be distributed to Congress and other agencies, as well as to the general public by request. Together, these three elements held out economic analysis as a neutral authority, which, tellingly, could be expected to moderate environmental regulation.

Business representatives continued to suggest that the EPA needed outside help to balance costs to industry with environmental benefits to society. Dismissing the EPA's analysis of proposed rules, trade associations often commissioned their own economic studies and offered them to sympathetic White House advisors. Such was the case with a 1975 report produced by the American Paper Institute that argued that the EPA's proposed water pollution controls would be more inflationary than the agency had acknowledged.[70] In a testament to the soft touch that well-connected lobbyists were able to employ, a memo describing the American Paper Institute's complaint noted that "an acquaintance dropped off" the report in a visit to one advisor's office, and it was promptly sent around to the White House for review and comment.[71]

Russell Train, who replaced Ruckelshaus as EPA administrator, presented himself as acutely sensitive to these complaints. In his first meeting with the new president, Train emphasized his commitment to balancing environmental goals with the economic costs of enforcing environmental standards. Distinguishing his tenure from that of his predecessor, Train told the president that he had devoted a great deal of his time to meeting with business representatives.[72] In short letters sent throughout the Ford administration, Train made a point of reminding Ford of his sensitivity to business concerns.[73] In addition to defending his agency, he used the EPA's economics to go on the offensive, as when his assistant administrator for the Air Program called the White House to warn that new vinyl chloride regulations proposed by the Occupational Health and Safety Administration to protect workers would set a strict standard on the basis of bad science, forcing the EPA to issue unnecessarily stringent and expensive vinyl chloride regulations of its own.[74]

But appealing to the compliance costs of regulations remained a politically powerful tool for businesses. In the fall of 1974, for instance, American Electric Power (AEP), an electric utility holding company operating in the Northeast and Midwest, spent over $3 million on an advertising blitz attacking the EPA's requirement that coal-fired electric power plants install flue gas desulfurization systems (known colloquially as "scrubbers").[75] One such advertisement in *Newsweek* typified AEP's campaign to bury the scrubber requirement. In copy written across a tombstone as an epitaph, AEP declared that the supposed benefits of the scrubbing technology had been reached through faulty cost/benefit analysis. Appealing to growing public concerns over energy supplies and prices, the *Newsweek* advertisement also warned that the scrubber requirement had created tremendous uncertainty in whether the nation's coal reserves could be utilized. In conclusion, AEP asked, "Isn't it about time someone redirected E.P.A.'s energies into more constructive channels?"

American Electric Power's question caught the attention of President Ford, who asked EPA officials for their response. Scrambling to answer the president, the EPA drew on its own economic and technical studies to insist on the feasibility and necessity of scrubbers.[76] Responding to Ford's letter, the EPA's Mike Duval refuted American Electric Power's claims point by point, apparently settling the matter since Ford declined to intervene further on American Electric Power's behalf.[77] As the EPA's response to the scrubber controversy demonstrated, quality economic analysis could sometimes protect the agency's proposals. But this was a war waged continuously and on multiple fronts. In September 1975, the Third Circuit Court of Appeals sent the EPA's economists back to the drawing board when it rejected the EPA's analysis that scrubbers were economically feasible, citing the electric power industry's own studies as more convincing than the agency's and ordering the EPA to revise the scrubber requirement.[78]

Contests over the economics of pollution control funneled millions of dollars into research on the subject, spurring the growth of environmental consultancies and the discipline of environmental economics. A 1974 survey revealed that twelve federal agencies and departments had more than 300 ongoing studies on the costs and benefits of pollution control. The Department of the Interior led the way with ninety-eight studies under way. The EPA was sponsoring sixty studies; the CEQ another forty-one; NASA had fifteen, as did the Department of Defense. The Department of Urban Development had contracted twenty-one studies and several other agencies were each sponsoring a handful more. Most were concerned with the costs of new regulations, though a handful focused their attention on monetary benefits of expanded protections.[79] The tens of millions of dollars funding this research went primarily to consulting firms and new environmental economics departments in universities across the country.[80] This money fueled the growing prowess of outfits like Stephen Sobotka & Co. (paid $30,000 to study the viability of the coal industry under the implementation of state pollution controls), and academic research, such as that at Oregon State University (where a $115,000 grant explored the economic impact of fluoride production on orchards).[81] Economics departments across the country drew on this federal and industry funding to build and expand programs in environmental and natural resource economics. Tom Crocker, whose research on air pollution in central Florida had helped chart important ideas in the young field, drew on funding from the EPA to grow an environmental economics program at UC Riverside. By 1971, the EPA was sponsoring several millions of dollars of environmental economics research each year, including Crocker's study on the correlation between air pollution and property values in Chicago.[82]

By the early 1970s, environmental economists had begun drawing borders around their discipline. Early participants had included scholars who questioned the dynamics and even the desirability of continued economic growth.[83] Popular books by economist E. F. Schumacher and biologist Paul Ehrlich demonstrated the continued public appetite for such radical stances in the early 1970s.[84] But most environmental economists gathered around the consensus that the social costs of environmental degradation could be addressed through taxes on pollution that would encourage companies to reduce their damaging activities and generate revenue that could be used to resolve any lingering problems. Whatever the particular tax arrangement, this model promised to reconcile industrial capitalism with environmental protection.[85] In 1973, Allen Kneese, together with A. Myrick Freeman and Robert Haveman, published the field's first widely used textbook.[86] Students taking the new environmental economics courses learned to make room in existing models to account for environmental externalities but encountered no radical rethinking of the desirability of continued economic growth.

At UC Riverside, Crocker and a close colleague, Ralph D'Arge, found themselves embroiled in what Crocker describes as increasingly contentious disputes with other economists in the department and made it known that they were ready to leave. The enterprising president of the University of Wyoming convinced Crocker and D'Arge to bring a dozen graduate students to Wyoming and take charge of its small economics department. The investment paid off, with Crocker and D'Arge building one of the premier environmental economics departments in the country in Laramie. Crocker established himself as an important distributor of EPA funding, serving as project director for grants worth hundreds of thousands of dollars, which he dispensed to economists at Wyoming as well as the University of New

Mexico, the University of Colorado-Boulder, Cornell University, and the University of California, Los Angeles.[87]

During the same period, environmental consultancies sprang up to assist agencies and businesses in compliance matters, positioning themselves as experts on the microeconomics of pollution control in particular industries. A 1974 national directory of environmental consultancies listed hundreds of experts on air and water pollution. States with long histories of pollution control efforts had dozens of consultants working within their borders (California had more than ninety). States where pollution control had begun only recently had far fewer (Arkansas listed two consultancies and Arizona had only one).[88] Consultancies became such an important part of policymaking, according to a former EPA manager, that experienced staff at the EPA's headquarters would have had little need for such a directory, since they knew offhand which firms to contact on any given issue.[89] Consultants looking to drum up business "roamed the halls" of the EPA during the 1970s, in the words of another former EPA manager, asking EPA staff whether they needed any help.[90]

Economics gained another boost from a new White House directive, Executive Order 11821, which instructed federal agencies to include a statement on the inflationary impact of any major regulation they proposed. [91] In close consultation with the Office of Management and Budget, the EPA and other agencies began writing Inflation Impact Statements.[92] When EO 11821 expired in December 1976, Ford issued EP 11949, extending and rebranding the review as the Economic Impact Statement Program to reflect its evolution from inflation toward broader economic concerns.[93]

In the absence of a White House group dedicated to analyzing the economic and social impacts of new environmental regulations, the task of reviewing those incoming statements fell to the Council on Wage and Price Stability (COWPS). The council had been formed in August 1974 as part of President Ford's campaign to reduce inflation and engaged in what policymakers called "jawboning"—the use of a public platform to critique businesses and public agencies in the hope of browbeating the targeted firm or agency into changing its decisions about prices, wages, and regulations. COWPS was also given the authority to review the Inflation Impact Statements produced by the EPA and other agencies. The cost/benefit framework employed in such review could be quite reductive, as exemplified by one memo that simply stated: "OMB/COWPS should see to it that E.P.A. prove benefit/cost = more than 1.0."[94] Against such a rubric, short-term compliance costs inevitably loomed larger than the more difficult to estimate and quantify long-term benefits. And, as Ford's advisors intended, the evaluation of potential regulations through that prism made the EPA more "inflation-conscious" in its own deliberations, as a transition memo praising the program later put it.[95]

Appealing to Balance in Complaining about Costs

No matter how "inflation-consciousness" regulatory review might have made the EPA in issuing new rules, regulated businesses could hope for little relief from appealing directly to the EPA to ease regulations that had already been enacted. Instead, many firms followed American Electric Power's example and fought regulations by appealing to sympathetic elected officials and the general public. Those appeals frequently used the rhetoric of balancing, particularly in areas where much of the population was dependent on a particular industry or firm. In such places, looming compliance deadlines under the Clean Air Act standards provoked consternation and fear that business leaders could whip into a frenzy by claiming that enforcement of the deadlines might force them to shut down vital industries.

Such was the case with the Kennecott Copper Corporation's smelting operation in McGill, Nevada. Despite being located in a rural area, the McGill plant generated enough sulfur dioxide that the surrounding area violated the National Ambient Air Quality Standard for the pollutant. Under the original State Implementation Plan submitted by Nevada in 1972, Kennecott was to increase the height of an emissions stack and install an acid plant, at a combined cost of approximately $23 million, in order to allow the area to meet the 1975 deadline for attaining the sulfur dioxide standard. In contrast to Kennecott's smelting operations in Arizona and Utah, the company declined to install more comprehensive measures in McGill, explaining to the EPA that the mostly exhausted copper reserves in Nevada could not justify such a large expenditure. Unconvinced, the EPA rejected Nevada's state plan because of Kennecott's failure to install the most advanced controls. Though Kennecott revised its plan and received the EPA's approval for more substantial controls, the firm soon lagged behind its approved compliance schedule and took to the courts and the public sphere to oppose the EPA's requirements.[96]

In 1974, struggling to meet the deadlines of the modified State Implementation Plan, Kennecott indicated to the residents of McGill and nearby Ely that it might have to close the McGill plant if an extension could not be secured. The threat of the region's largest employer shutting down prompted widespread panic among local residents and officials. Underscoring the importance of the firm to the area's livelihood, Nevada governor Mike O'Callaghan successfully petitioned the EPA to open hearings about whether the company should be granted an extension.

W. Howard Winn, Kennecott's general manager for Nevada, set the tone for the hearings when he took on the public welfare premise at the heart of the national standards, arguing that, despite the pollution it generated, the McGill plant was essential to the health of a county without viable economic alternatives. The hearings brought out nearly every elected official in the town and region, including the mayor, the city councilmen, the county assessor, the county recorder and auditor, and the board of county commissioners. One by one, those officials painted a dire picture of school closures and other wrenching dislocations that would result if the McGill plant shut down. As one official put it, "I've looked down this valley when there was no smoke coming from those stacks and it wasn't a good picture." Kennecott's peril also drew the support of the local labor council, which was concerned about

Figure 3.1 Emissions from the processing operations of extractive industries pushed areas of the southwest out of compliance with the Clean Air Act. Pictured here is Kennecott's copper mines and smelter in Salt Lake City, Utah, 1972. EPA Documerica, National Archives and Record Administration 544788.

workers' livelihoods as well as a previously planned strike, and even the local branch of the Jaycees civic organization. Other business leaders, including the general manager of the local electric utility, testified that Kennecott's closure would likely bankrupt their enterprises, dependent as the area was on its largest employer. [97]

Although such complaints drew the attention from top EPA officials, the agency ultimately refused to grant Kennecott an extension. And so, in the summer of 1976, with the McGill plant still not in compliance, the EPA shut down operations. Kennecott and elected representatives of Ely and Nevada appealed to the Ford administration to reverse the EPA's decision. Kennecott's supporters likely took heart in the Ford administration's intervention in national copper smelter regulations proposed by the EPA two years earlier. In that case, the OMB negotiated exemptions with the EPA that allowed copper smelters to avoid the New Source Review process, with its strict technology standards, that was required for major modifications.[98] Hoping for a similar intervention, Nevada's attorney general joined a US congressman, Nevada's governor, and the president of the local Chamber of Commerce in petitioning President Ford to appeal the EPA's 1976 shutdown order.[99]

While the appeals sent several of Ford's advisors scrambling to assess the situation, the Ford administration ultimately declined to intervene, citing court rulings that prevented exemptions that violated the national standards.[100] Over the next six years, Kennecott waged a protracted legal battle with the EPA over its Ely operations, whipsawing the fortunes of the local community as the smelter opened and closed and opened and closed.[101] Legal battles and the intermittent operations of the smelter continued until 1983, when Kennecott shuttered the McGill plant for good.[102]

The efforts of the Ford administration to scale back proposed EPA smelter regulations while simultaneously refusing to get dragged into the fight between Kennecott and the EPA exemplified a larger pattern of White House involvement in environmental policy. When EPA regulations were in the drafting stage, White House advisors often campaigned with gusto to make the rules less burdensome on business. But once the regulations had been promulgated, presidential advisors tended to sympathize with disgruntled individual firms while declining to intervene in the EPA's decisions.

The McGill story also underscores the challenge that the EPA faced in negotiating plant closures in a globalizing economy. Kennecott's general manager stated the obvious when he spoke of the binding connections between Ely's livelihood and the plant's pollution control requirements. But in keeping with a larger asymmetry in industry's relationship to local places, Kennecott Copper Corporation faced no such existential crisis in Ely. Kennecott owned and operated mines and smelters across the American Southwest as well as in the Ozarks, Canada, Alaska, Chile, and South Africa. Pollution control requirements made McGill and other US smelting operations increasingly expensive to operate. In 1976, the $1.4 billion company reported less than $10 million in profits despite collecting nearly $1.8 billion in revenue—a poor performance that Kennecott's president and CEO explained to the shareholders by citing $100 million in pollution control expenditures, amounting to three-quarters of Kennecott's total capital investments that year.[103] Given that Kennecott's reserves in Nevada were already running out, it can hardly be surprising that the company found it more profitable to run the McGill smelter for a decade without the full pollution controls demanded by the EPA than to make an expensive investment to sustain its operations.[104] Appealing to local livelihoods in court and the public sphere bought Kennecott that additional decade at McGill, while Kennecott's geographically diversified holdings permitted the firm to detach its own fortunes from Nevada (and the United States more broadly) when that extra time ran out. Thus, the balancing to which Kennecott appealed amounted to compromises made by the local populace. When McGill ceased to generate sufficient profit margins, Kennecott simply left. Furthermore, while Kennecott shut the McGill plant because of a range of factors, the EPA's pollution control mandates gave the company an easy villain for the closure, directing the blame at the federal government and away from the firm's own profit-seeking decisions.

Occasionally, the EPA recognized that howls from businesses and the public could be directed toward its own ends. EPA administrator William Ruckelshaus had long expressed reservations to Congress and the general public about the states' ability to achieve the National Air Quality Standards by the act's 1975 deadline but had found his calls for moderation repeatedly rebuffed. In the case of the state of California, reducing automobile emissions of criteria pollutants like carbon monoxide and total photochemical oxidants by the 1975 deadline could have been achieved only by devising a plan to drastically reduce the number of cars on the road—a responsibility the EPA had no interest in assuming.[105] But as historian Tom McCarthy has described, a series of court victories for environmental organizations in the early 1970s forced the EPA to propose a transportation control plan for California.[106]

Figure 3.2 In the 1970s, as cities across the country choked in air pollution created by the automobile, Los Angeles suffered worst. This photo shows the city in 1973, enveloped in smog. EPA Documerica, National Archives and Record Administration 552379.

Having been forced by the courts to address transportation controls, Ruckelshaus turned to public protest to seek relief for California and his agency. In 1973, the EPA introduced a traffic reduction plan under which California could meet the 1975 deadline. The plan called for severe limits on vehicle use, especially in southern California. In addition to some features that eventually survived (such as carpool lanes on highways), the plan called for gasoline rationing as well as surcharges on all new parking lot construction and the removal of parking lots from several downtown areas. These parking lot proposals aimed to make it so expensive to park that residents would be forced to use public transportation or carpools, thereby lowering emissions.

If the plan sounds politically impossible in the context of automobile dependent Los Angeles, that was Ruckelshaus's intent. A memo written by Nixon advisor Ken Cole to the president in January 1973 suggests that the EPA's proposed transportation controls were a careful strategy to raise public protest against the current Clean Air Act requirements and spur Congress to allow the EPA more leeway around the transportation controls until a technological solution obviated the problem. As Cole laid out in the memo:

The EPA plan is unworkable. We know it and Ruckelshaus will say it. It would require an 80% traffic reduction in the Los Angeles area. Our intention is, of course, never to put such a plan into effect, but to ultimately amend the Clean Air Act to permit administrative discretion in achieving the legislative requirements so that we can permit the technology of the automobile industry to in effect solve the problem itself over time. To do so, we need to call the problem to the public's attention. Public hearings will take place shortly after the plan is published. Ultimately we will move legislation to the Congress to amend the Act.

To prevent the outcry from getting out of hand, Cole noted that Governor Reagan had been briefed on the real purpose of the announced transportation controls and that he supported the plan.[107]

Together with Ruckelshaus's earlier complaints about the severity of the NAAQS, the transportation controls appear to have been one part of a wider strategy on Ruckelshaus's part to create public support for a moderation of the EPA's responsibilities under the Clean Air Act.[108] Ruckelshaus recalls that he met with John Ehrlichman and convinced him to let the EPA follow the letter of the law in order to "make it very clear what is unadministrable" to the public and "see if we can convince Congress to give us some adjustment." With the much larger threat of the emerging Watergate scandal dominating his time, Ehrlichman assented.[109] Describing for Nixon the intent behind several of Ruckelshaus's contemporaneous pronouncements, Ehrlichman noted that they were a "deliberate and calculated preconditioning" on Ruckelshaus's part, "designed to shock the consumers into a realization that the cost of the environment will be very high and that the air quality laws are very impractical."[110] As Ruckelshaus later described, he used the court mandate to help "both the people in California and the broader public to understand the implications of this law." The EPA could "vigorously [go] after compliance but it had to be done on a more reasonable basis."[111]

As expected, Ruckelshaus's proposed transportation controls succeeded in generating a swift and angry response. Business representatives predominated among the complainants, writing to the White House to denounce the proposed parking lot surcharge and gasoline rationing as a threat to the survival of their enterprises. An owner of a packaging plant grossing $2 million in annual revenue summoned bleak imagery akin to the Great Depression, writing, "I believe that industry in California will be brought right down to its knees. I can see nothing but plants closing, chaos, unemployment, and a relief roll and an unemployment compensation roll . . . the like of which would stagger the imagination."[112] Also opting for a stark portrait of catastrophe, the Los Angeles Chamber of Commerce declared that the proposed gasoline rationing "would simply destroy this area and the way of life of our residents in an effort to meet an arbitrary date."[113] A report commissioned by California estimated that the controls would cost the state some $1.5 billion per year in development and result in the loss of over 150,000 jobs as 80 percent of the workforce found it impossible to commute to work using public transportation.[114] Elected officials also denounced the proposed controls as an overreach of the federal government. The mayor of Santa Ana wrote Nixon to warn that "the powers delegated to the Environmental Protection Agency far exceed anything ever developed in our history," and that parking lot surcharges would "disastrously affect this City's economy."[115] Despite their frustration, the majority of these various petitioners allowed that air pollution needed to be controlled—just not so drastically or quickly. Succinctly articulating that sentiment, the residents of Sunnyvale, California, wrote in their petition that the parking lot controls would have disruptive economic effects so acute as to "have a greater deterrent upon the health and public welfare than the dirty air itself."[116]

Across the country, the EPA announced similar transportation requirements in places like New Jersey that were also poised to miss the 1975 deadline. Ruckelshaus and the EPA did not want to inflame public opinion so far that Congress might gut the Clean Air Act, however, and so subsequent transportation control proposals emphasized aspects like parking surcharges rather than the more contentious gasoline rationing.[117] Upon his appointment, Russell Train found himself immediately besieged by real estate developers and construction unions over the possibility that parking lot controls would halt the building of suburban shopping malls and other car-dependent landscapes. Under Train, the EPA backpedaled from parking restrictions in California and from a similar plan to compel private employers in Boston to remove a quarter of their parking spaces.[118] With outrage still simmering, Congress included an explicit prohibition against such controls in 1974 legislation designed, somewhat paradoxically, to safeguard fuel supplies during the OPEC oil embargo.[119] The EPA finally had its reprieve from the statutory mandate to yank people out of their cars.[120] Prevented by the Clean Air Act from proposing standards that explicitly weighed economic costs, the EPA's transportation control plans show the agency's capacity to manipulate public opinion as an alternate route to more reasonable standards. Facing unworkable mandates, the EPA could sometimes generate a pragmatic solution by proposing regulations like parking lot controls that so obviously upset popular notions of balance.

However, the unintended ricochet of outrage is worth dwelling on. Ruckelshaus believed in the merits of a substantive shift away from polluting cars, just at a more gradual pace than the Clean Air Act required. But many of the people inflamed by his parking lot controls and gasoline rationing plainly did not believe that they should have to change their behavior in the name of clean air. By amplifying those voices in response to such a disruptive plan, Ruckelshaus helped to politicize environmental regulation.[121] Telling ordinary Americans that they could not drive their own cars created the perfect image of unaccountable bureaucracy—calling forth the specter of the overreaching state that Reagan and other Republican political candidates would soon run against.

* * *

Regardless of whether the speaker was the administrator of the EPA or the executive of a multi-national firm, the rhetoric of balancing increasingly depended on quantified costs and benefits—but especially costs. While economists did tend to emphasize short-term costs of regulations over the long-term benefits of protection, the growing influence of the field was not a straightforward coup for regulated industries. Most of the first practitioners of environmental economics had been drawn to the work out of a conviction that environmental protection was undervalued and institutions like Resources for the Future supported studies that found wide benefits in the sort of regulatory protections that businesses angrily opposed. From the first months of the EPA's existence, senior agency officials funded economics research that further established the pecuniary benefits of protection.

As a result, opponents of environmental protection appealed to the pecuniary costs of regulation at their own risk. By the mid-1970s, environmental advocates had built their own expertise with economic calculations and could cite a wide range of research suggesting that regulatory protection was, on balance, an economic boon for the nation.[122] Getting too specific in lamenting the costs of regulation was particularly risky, as President Ford found out the hard way when he claimed in an April 1975 speech that federal regulations cost the average American family $2,000 each year. As the *Washington Post* described the aftermath of that claim, Ford's figure "sent a number of people to their pocket calculators," where they determined that

Ford's numbers added up to $125 billion in annual spending, or a clearly inaccurate one-tenth of the country's GDP. Critics such as California's congressman John Moss were quick to pounce, citing studies by the US Government Accountability Office and other sources that estimated far lower per family totals. The White House eventually had to admit that its analysis might have been inaccurate, an embarrassment the OMB addressed by directing the National Science Foundation to fund further research on the subject.[123] Taking heed of such risks, most critics of regulation found it safer to claim that the rule in question upset a balance between economic and environmental objectives—a quotidian weighing of emphasis and priorities that had more to do with a gut reaction to fewer parking spaces or the closure of a local plant than a cost/benefit accounting.

4

Put the Profit Motive to Work

Regulatory Reform

In May 1976, a new think tank called the Center for Policy Process sponsored a National Conference on Regulatory Reform in Washington, DC. Executives from many of the nation's largest companies gathered at the L'Enfant Plaza Hotel with the heads of administrative agencies, prominent academics, leading consumer advocates, and elected officials at the highest levels of government to consider the future of government regulation. Attendees were treated to an opening debate between Ralph Nader and Milton Friedman, kicking off a program that aspired to a lively exchange of wide-ranging perspectives. Senator Edward Kennedy, who was leading the push for opening up the airline industry to greater competition, addressed the conference. So did Senator Charles Percy, co-sponsor of a bill that would require Congress and the president to evaluate, amend, and potentially abolish regulatory agencies on an annual basis. If the three-day affair ultimately failed to "define an appropriate role for government regulation in our changing society," as a conference objective envisioned, participants and observers certainly came away convinced that something about the federal regulatory state demanded reform.[1]

The 1976 conference was one piece of a much larger conversation about reducing the administrative state's oversight of business practices in the mid-1970s. As with the conference, what exactly needed reducing or reforming was up for debate. Public interest advocates such as Ralph Nader sought to reduce or remove regulations that governed competition in specific industries, arguing that restrictions on the routes that airlines could fly, for example, tended to benefit incumbent firms at the expense of consumers. Business representatives, for their part, complained that environmental and safety regulations that cut across industries (such as the national air quality standards) were eating up precious capital, damaging the productivity of American companies, and forcing them to raise prices and lay off workers. A swelling cohort of free market proponents led by economists at

Valuing Clean Air. Charles Halvorson, Oxford University Press (2021). © Oxford University Press.
DOI: 10.1093/oso/9780197538845.003.0005

the University of Chicago blamed regulation and government interference more broadly for the nation's growing economic woes. Think tanks like the Center for Policy Process incubated and amplified those various critiques, cultivating a growing conviction among voters and elected officials that future prosperity depended on scaling back rather than building up the federal government's oversight of firms. The 1976 election underscored the appeal of this reform message among Republicans and Democrats, and the victor, Jimmy Carter, made reducing state management one of the primary objectives of his presidency.

Environmental protection, the locus of so much of the federal government's recent growth, occupied a central position in debates about regulatory reform. Cleaning up the environment was expensive, even if the Environmental Protection Agency (EPA) could usually prove that the long-term monetary benefits of intervention exceeded the short-term costs of compliance. Economists had long encouraged the EPA and other agencies to ditch proscriptive rules that told every firm exactly how to achieve a fixed set of standards in favor of alternative policies that used markets or economic incentives to reach those same goals.

And yet, for all this talk of reforming environmental regulation to reduce the active role of the government, the reforms passed in the Clean Air Act Amendments of 1977 actually expanded the EPA's purview. By mandating that the EPA protect clean air as well as dirty air, Congress broadened the agency's focus from polluted cities and industrial sites to the whole country. And by strengthening the EPA's responsibilities for a wider range of hazardous air pollutants and compelling the agency to revisit the underlying National Ambient Air Quality Standards, Congress pushed to make the EPA responsive to rapid advancements in scientific knowledge about the full risks of air pollution. These new mandates revived debates about environmental economics, as proponents and opponents of expanded protections squared off on the costs and benefits of pollution control, as well as the very legitimacy of monetary approaches to environmental value.

The amendments did create new opportunities for market-based compliance strategies. With the encouragement of the Carter administration, the EPA experimented with policies that "put the profit motive to work for pollution control," as a guide to one policy put it.[2] Under the new administrator Doug Costle, the EPA played a leading role in the Carter administration's efforts to articulate a new liberalism that turned away the direct mandate model in favor of steering private actors toward desired outcomes with nudges and incentives. But as proponents of such reforms tried to shift how the EPA approached pollution control, they ran up against concerted opposition from career staff and environmental organizations to changes that seemed to weaken the EPA's authority. The result was a set of policies that proved more important in rhetoric than they did in practice. Nonetheless, these new policies and, just as important, all this talk of reform contributed to an intellectual climate in Washington in which expansions of government authority were increasingly treated as something to lament rather than celebrate. In this way, environmental policymaking took part in a bipartisan framing of government as a necessary evil, even as the expansion and strengthening of environmental regulations continued to improve the public welfare.

Economic Malaise and the Case for Reform

The growing salience of regulatory reform as a political issue was primarily the result of the economic woes that descended on the United States in the early 1970s. The price shock and recession that followed the 1973 oil embargo marked the end of the remarkable period of postwar prosperity. From 1974 to 1981, the real growth of the Gross National Product and the per capita share of that wealth both fell significantly, and inflation rose from 4.8 percent to an annual average of 9.3 percent. Real hourly wages peaked in 1972 and then declined over the next decade. Productivity fell from an average growth rate of 3 percent in the postwar period to just 1 percent after 1973. While structural economic forces were mostly responsible for the economic downturn, pollution control represented a significant and increasingly visible cost: American industry claimed that it spent almost $7.5 billion in 1974 to comply with regulatory mandates, amounting to nearly 8 percent of total capital expenditures in 1974. This was double the share that businesses had spent on pollution control in 1969, before the EPA's creation and the dramatic expansion of environmental protection under the Clean Air Act and other programs.[3]

The EPA's struggles to clean up the steel industry illustrate how environmental regulation came to be tied up in these economic struggles. In the early 1970s, American steel companies ran into a perfect storm of foreign competition, labor strife, aging technology, and expensive new pollution control mandates from the EPA. Like many other American businesses, steel producers had enjoyed a halcyon period following World War II, which devastated the capital stock of European and Japanese competitors and created vast reconstruction projects that undamaged American plants happily supplied. By the 1970s, however, foreign producers had largely rebuilt, incorporating modern technology that many American firms had not yet adopted. Modernization, coupled with the comparatively low cost of labor in Japan, made Japanese steel 15 to 20 percent cheaper to produce than American steel, allowing Japanese firms to significantly undercut American firms on price.[4] At the same time, as one of the nation's worst polluters, the steel industry faced new regulatory pressures from the EPA's enforcement of the Clean Air Act Amendments of 1970.

From its inception, the EPA had focused special attention on the steel industry as one of the country's largest sources of pollution. But, to the chagrin of agency staff and officials, the steel industry quickly developed a miserable record of compliance with the EPA's standards. In the agency's first year, Bill Ruckelshaus brought well-publicized and hotly contested enforcement actions against U.S. Steel and other major steel firms to prove the mettle of the new agency.[5] The relationship between the EPA and the industry did not improve much from there. Significant differences in pollution control among firms suggested to regulators that compliance was possible if every firm pursued pollution control in good faith.[6] But industry leaders like U.S. Steel routinely threatened to close plants and lay off thousands of workers rather than comply with regulatory mandates.[7] In response, the EPA would often intervene and work out an administrative order with a particular firm that laid out a path to compliance tailored to that firm's specific challenges.

The challenges confronting the steel industry made it difficult for the EPA to move either specific firms or the industry as a whole toward compliance. Industry representatives argued that American steel could not afford both the modernization expenditures necessary to keep pace with foreign competitors and the pollution controls mandated by the EPA. In 1975, the American Steel and Iron Institute commissioned a study from the consultancy Arthur D. Little Inc. that predicted the industry would spend $12 to 14 billion complying with federal standards through 1983—a sum that would comprise more than 20 percent of total capital investment over the eight-year period and would drive up the price of domestically produced steel. Firms with prices that were already on the high end of the market would likely have to close, the study reported, threatening the loss of 90,000 jobs. U.S. Steel chairman and CEO Edgar Speer cited those dire forecasts in

Figure 4.1 U.S. Steel's massive Birmingham, Alabama, operations were a major employer for local residents, while also making the city one of the most polluted in the country, threatening the health of this local resident and the paint on his car, 1972. EPA Documerica, National Archives and Record Administration 545391.

publicly questioning whether Congress would have passed the Clean Air Act if legislators had known the economic effects would be so severe.[8] As it had many times in the past, the EPA quickly summoned its own economic expertise to critique the study. In this case, however, chief EPA economist Al Alm noted that the predicted dislocations and tens of billions of dollars in compliance costs appeared worrisomely accurate.[9] As EPA administrator Russell Train noted in 1975, not a single firm was in compliance with the Clean Air Act, and he refused to hazard a guess as to when one might be.[10] Part of the problem was the EPA's own tendency to negotiate administrative orders that were less demanding than the state implementation plans that they replaced.[11]

In addition to the EPA's particular struggles with the steel industry, the agency faced an increasingly organized push by the wider business community to roll back the expansion of the regulatory state that had occurred earlier in the decade. In addition to lodging their own complaints or lobbying through trade associations, many of the nation's largest firms formed a new organization called the Business Roundtable in 1972 to advance shared goals that included lower corporate tax rates and a reduction in government oversight. In 1974, the Business Roundtable formed a special task force on regulation to collect and amplify its members' grievances.[12] The Ford administration's strengthening of cost/benefit tests for new regulations marked one victory for the business community. But emboldened business leaders pressed on in an effort to roll back regulations that already existed. In 1974, the coal and energy industries tried to amend the Clean Air Act to permit utilities to burn coal, even if that meant their states would not meet the National Ambient Air Quality Standards (NAAQS). Despite the souring economy, public support for environmental protection remained high enough to beat back that particular effort.[13] But business interests eagerly pushed forward against federal programs that appeared increasingly vulnerable.

Simultaneous to this business campaign, two sets of reformers challenged the capacity and authority of the state to act in the public interest. One complaint came from economists such as Milton Friedman, who argued that government intervention prevented markets from allocating resources according to their actual utility. The resulting inefficiencies lowered economic output and thus overall public welfare, according to these free-market thinkers, who called for reforms to untether or introduce markets. Meanwhile, a second complaint came from social liberals including Ralph Nader and Senator Ted Kennedy, who argued that the regulation of specific industries favored not consumers but incumbent firms, which used their superior resources to capture regulatory bodies and thwart competition. Paring back or removing regulations in such cases, these reformers argued, would increase competition and thus drive down prices and improve products and services for consumers.[14] In the environmental realm, this push for public accountability often took the form of lawsuits that challenged the administrative discretion of agencies such as the EPA. Ironically, while this litigation was aimed at strengthening environmental protections, it also opened up the authority of the EPA and other agencies to attack from regulated industry.[15] While consumer interest advocates like Nader insisted that environmental and safety regulations were necessary because no market existed for clean air, the push to find market alternatives swept into the EPA and its programs.

Ideas for regulatory reform proliferated in the 1970s. *The Public Interest*, the popular conservative policy journal, published frequently on the subject, including a 1972 article by economists Myrick Freeman and Robert Haveman lamenting that the EPA had adopted a standards-based approach to water pollution control that was very difficult to enforce when it should have chosen a far more efficient system of user charges.[16] Think tanks also supported the development and dissemination of market alternatives, including a collaborative study by RFF economist Allen Kneese and Brookings Institution economist Charles Schultze that found that economic incentives could replace direct enforcement of standards, lowering the cost of environmental protections while making them more effective.[17]

Emission taxes were the first alternatives to proscriptive regulations to gain traction among policymakers. Nixon's advisors had bandied about ideas for a tax as early as January 1970, eventually settling on sulfur emissions from coal-burning electric utilities as their first target.[18] As the Council on Environmental Quality explained, a sulfur tax would not only reduce overall control costs but would actually lead to a quicker reduction in pollutants by incentivizing firms to invest research and development capital in new control technologies. Since every pound of emissions reduced was money saved under a tax system, profit-minded firms would naturally seek out the most efficient means of making reductions. Furthermore, a sulfur tax would expose electricity consumers to the full environmental costs of power generation.[19] Economists loved Nixon's proposed tax. Many environmentalists liked the idea as well; several prominent organizations, including the Sierra Club and Friends of the Earth, even formed the Coalition to Tax Pollution in 1972.[20]

But the EPA resisted Nixon's sulfur tax proposal (and emission charges in general) as too difficult to graft onto the existing pollution control regime, which was built around the idea that the EPA, and not firms, would determine how pollution was controlled. Ruckelshaus himself was intrigued with taxes and other incentive-based programs. But he recognized that the EPA had little room to experiment with such alternatives under the mandates in the Clean Air Act and other statutes. Perhaps more important, Ruckelshaus believed that public opinion strongly favored firm, proscriptive rules that enforced minimum standards.[21] But the EPA was not entirely closed off to the possibility of developing taxes or other alternatives. Informal conversations that included RFF's monthly brown bag lunch talks served as channels for reform ideas to seep into the EPA. Within the agency, the EPA's economic analysis division provided an institutional basis for such ideas.[22] In September 1973, EPA administrator Russell Train reversed his predecessor's position and endorsed the idea of a sulfur tax, albeit as a complement to the existing approach of enforcing uniform standards.[23]

Despite their promise to reduce compliance costs, taxes and other alternatives to proscriptive rules faced a tough road with businesses that were determined to resist any new pollution controls, whatever their form. Arguing against a 1971 proposal to tax the lead content of gasoline, the American Petroleum Institute (API) unconvincingly claimed that paying such a tax would siphon off funds that the industry would otherwise have devoted to researching and developing pollution controls. API claimed that instead of spurring cost-conscious firms to develop new control technology as a means of lowering their taxes, a charge would dry up funding for new technology and thus halt progress toward pollution control. That logic was evidently as shaky in the early 1970s as it is today, because the API spokesperson soon admitted the real reason for the industry's opposition: the lead tax would create a precedent, the spokesperson said, from which the taxing of a wide range of other pollutants might follow.[24]

By the mid-1970s, the EPA's reliance on proscriptive regulations was a major source of concern for the Ford administration. In April 1975, for instance, economic advisor Alan Pulsipher wrote to fellow advisor Alan Greenspan to recommend a tax-based system to encourage technological innovation and to account for regional differences in compliance costs. Pulsipher noted in his letter that he had been prompted to write in part because of the EPA's intransigence in maintaining its existing system of uniform standards. The EPA had a large economics division, Pulsipher complained, but it only used that division to evaluate the effects of its programs rather than to make new policy.[25]

In response to such complaints, Russell Train generally noted that the EPA was also concerned about regulatory compliance costs and was already reforming its policies. Writing to Ford in October 1975, Train described an extensive study the agency had recently conducted of its regulations and rulemaking process. He included in his letter a long list of rules that the EPA had singled out for potential revision: from aircraft emission standards, which had been deferred for reexamination "in light of low environmental payoff," to the registration of fuel additives, which was to be reexamined to see whether consumers could be provided the information through less expensive means. He also sent along a pile of memos detailing internal EPA review and reform meetings.[26]

But where Train portrayed a nimble and reasonable agency, business representatives continued to paint a picture of the EPA as a rule-bound bureaucracy that stubbornly refused to make even minor adjustments to help American firms and workers. Ford advisors' folders are full of letters from executives and sympathetic legislators, including a January 1975 letter from Indiana Senator Vance Hartke, who asked for Ford's help in keeping open a U.S. Steel Plant in Gary, Indiana. Finding itself in violation of the EPA's standards for open-hearth production, U.S. Steel agreed to a consent decree to install new pollution control equipment. But when U.S. Steel fell behind the timeline it had agreed to with the EPA, the agency refused to offer further relief and rejected the company's offer to post a $200,000 performance bond in order to continue operations. With 2,400 jobs hanging in the balance, Senator Hartke hoped that Ford might be able to find some means of "rectifying this miscarriage of equity."[27] As such complaints piled up, Train's request to let the EPA handle itself ran up against a growing conviction among Ford's advisors that the agency required outside direction.

The EPA's ascendance as a source of concern for Ford's advisors came as the agency expanded its regulatory purview. Although the Clean Air Act Amendments of 1970 called for the quality of the nation's air to be protected or enhanced, the EPA had initially resisted taking responsibility for maintaining pristine air. But this decision left much of the West and Southwest facing the reality that the growth of cities such as Phoenix, Denver, and Los Angeles would come at the expense of the regions' clear air, as electric utilities built new generating facilities and tapped the region's extensive coal reserves to keep up with growing demand for electric power.[28] Environmental advocates thus strongly objected to the EPA's refusal to prevent degradation, especially since the regions most threatened by declining air quality contained the majority of the nation's national forests, national parks, and other federal lands that environmentalists held dear.[29] In 1972, the Sierra Club won a lawsuit in the Second Circuit that forced the EPA to throw out all state implementation plans that did not include provisions to prevent significant deterioration, a decision that the Second Circuit Court of Appeals and the Supreme Court upheld on appeal.[30] And so, in 1974, the EPA announced a prevention of significant deterioration program (PSD) to begin in January 1975. The PSD program grouped areas across the country into three classes according to their air quality and prohibited additional industrial development that would worsen air quality in Class I pristine areas.[31]

Over the next two years, environmental organizations including the Natural Resources Defense Council and congressional advocates such as Senator Muskie repeatedly pressed the EPA to strengthen the PSD program, while the courts continued to hear a series of challenges to the EPA's authority to enforce such regulations.[32] Congress, meanwhile, proposed to clarify the EPA's PSD mandate in 1975 legislation. Though businesses welcomed clarification on what was becoming a major source of uncertainty, the strong PSD program outlined by the Democratic Congress was met with condemnation. The Phoenix Chamber of Commerce, for instance, published a report entitled "The Air Pollution Maze" that described the chaos and devastation that the proposed amendments would bring. As the chamber explained, the PSD provision would create whole swaths of the West and Southwest where industrial development would be prohibited. In August 1975, the National Association of Manufacturers began to distribute maps that depicted whole zones of the country blocked off from any further development.[33] The Phoenix Chamber of Commerce included such a map in its own report, describing the resulting geography as a "plague of idiocy in the land."[34]

The electric power industry chose to make its case using more specific economic analysis. Beginning in 1975, the National Association of Electric Companies contracted with National Economic Research Associates to research the specific rate increases that could be expected from the PSD legislation under consideration in Congress. Since the Clean Air Act was subject to a flurry of proposed amendments in this period, National Economic Research Associates issued a monthly report detailing the implications of PSD on the electricity rates of their utility clients. A representative of the National Association of Electric Companies dutifully sent each report to Ford advisor William Gorog, whose detailed handwritten summaries of each demonstrated the political utility of investing in such careful economic analysis.[35]

Environmental advocates engaged in this debate about the economics of the prevention of significant deterioration expansion, while at the same time continuing to argue that the environment could never be fully valued through a monetary lens. Writing the Ford administration in opposition to a bill the president had proposed that eliminated the EPA's PSD program, Richard Ayres of the Natural Resources Defense Council argued that economic analysis of the bill had hitherto focused only on the costs faced by industry when "a systematic economic study would reveal a great many hard economic costs of allowing significant deterioration." Ayres went on to

enumerate a few examples of these costs, including a shift of industry west-
ward that would deeply hurt many northeastern communities.[36] But then he
changed tack, concluding his letter by asking, "Who is really willing to decide
how many dollars an unpolluted Grand Canyon is worth to those alive now,
let alone those to come?"[37]

In 1975, Ford advisor Judith Hope was assigned to write a special report
on the EPA to help the Ford administration get a handle on the agency. Hope
noted that the EPA had not been intended by Nixon to make policy but that
subsequent legislation and executive orders had dramatically expanded the
agency's responsibilities until it had become effectively the center of national
environmental policy. The EPA's areas of responsibility had grown so vast,
Hope noted, that the federal government published a "*one inch thick index*"
of all the statutes and orders granting authority to the EPA.[38] She then went
on summarize the many critiques of the agency—from environmentalists
complaining about missed compliance deadlines to the National Association
of Manufacturers, which directly blamed the EPA for undermining industrial
growth. By way of conclusion, she summarized the advice of a "number of
experts," who recommended that the EPA substitute economic incentives for
uniform standards to allow firms to clean up the environment according to
their own economic circumstances. As Hope wrote, "The present EPA complex of statutes and Executive Orders is full of 'sticks' with very few 'carrots.'"
Unfortunately, substituting carrots for sticks required legislative changes, the
prospect of which appeared doubtful to her given the current Congress.[39]

While White House economists struggled to introduce taxes and incentives
into regulatory policy, substituting such market approaches for directly enforced standards grew ever more popular among economists. In 1975, RFF
and the Brookings Institution published Kneese and Schultze's study on
replacing proscriptive regulations with economic incentives. Trotting out
the usual troupes of well-intentioned but misguided bureaucrats, Kneese
and Schultze's *Pollution, Prices, and Public Policy* described how the air and
water pollution control programs introduced in the early 1970s would soon
grow so expensive as to forestall continued improvements in environmental
quality. The problem, Kneese and Schultze argued, lay in the impossibility of
regulators trying to devise a detailed set of rules for every industry in the face
of constant technological and economic change. Furthermore, an increase in
marginal costs made each additional unit of pollution more expensive than
the last to control. The nation was poised to spend half a trillion dollars on
pollution control over the next decade, Kneese and Schultze warned. Under

the present approach, much of this spending would be wasted as regulators attempted to force smaller and smaller reductions out of recalcitrant industries.[40]

The solution, Kneese and Schultze declared, was to harness rather than fight the profit-maximizing impulses of industry. Pollution was not the inevitable product of capitalist production but rather the unintended byproduct of a misaligned pricing system. If the price of consumer goods and industrial inputs incorporated their real environmental costs, businesses and consumers would soon figure out ways to reduce pollution. In the same way that rising labor costs had spurred the development of new technology to reduce labor inputs, rising environmental costs, if properly conveyed in new prices, would drive innovations in pollution control. The tool that Kneese and Schultze suggested for that realignment was a new system of effluent and emission charges to replace uniform standards. The federal government would institute a series of stiff taxes on every unit of pollution emitted into the air and water. These taxes would be set at levels that were slightly higher than the cost of installing control technology so firms would find it less costly to reduce their emissions than to pay the charge. Over time, the charges could be adjusted upward to make polluting more expensive and thereby drive technological innovation. Since it relied on incentives rather than directly applied and enforced mandates, the system would also be less costly to administer. By constantly promoting new innovation, Kneese and Schultze promised that their system would be more effective, resisting the tendency of well-intentioned regulatory interventions to be taken over (or captured) by incumbent firms, and used a shield against competition.[41]

While public welfare advocates such as Ralph Nader also worried about captured regulators, they tended to resist such calls to replace proscriptive programs that had successfully reduced environmental and safety risks. Writing in the Yale *Law Journal* in 1973, Nader and his fellow consumer rights advocate Mark Green drew what they said was a vital line between rules that limited competition in specific industries and health and safety protections that extended across industries. Regulatory reform ought to use a "scalpel, not a scythe," Nader and Green argued, to protect environmental and safety regulations that could not be met by "a market system incompetent or uninterested in fulfilling certain social needs."[42] In June 1975, Nader expounded on the distinction before the Senate Committee on Commerce, which had convened a special symposium on "Regulatory Myths." In front of that friendly audience, Nader warned that business voices such as the

American Enterprise Institute were deliberately conflating "wasteful cartel regulation with life-saving consumer regulation" and provoking the Ford administration into a misguided attempt to scale back both types. Consumers could decide between air fares in a deregulated airline industry, Nader exclaimed, but they could not "taste the cancerous pesticides that went into the production of their food" or avoid purchasing "the air pollution given off by local steel mills."[43] On the same day as the hearing, Nader and Green published an editorial in the New York Times that challenged the supposed benefits of regulatory reform to consumers. Deregulating airlines, Nader and Green noted in one example, would benefit consumers by lowering prices, thus helping to reduce inflation nationwide. But removing controls on air pollutants promised no analogous benefits for consumers, because the general public could not go out into a marketplace to buy the health and safety protections they required.[44]

Russell Train made a similar distinction as a voice within the Ford administration. In a meeting with James Cannon and other White House advisors in September 1975, Train argued that President Ford had missed a major difference between regulatory reform in agencies like the Interstate Commerce Commission "that were established to make the market mechanisms work right, and agencies, such as the EPA, FDA, and OSHA, which were established because the free market system didn't work, for example in reducing pollution. It is not the natural function of the marketplace to protect the public health and safety," Train insisted.[45]

In trying to separate environmental and safety standards from rules governing prices or competition, environmental advocates confronted a political conversation that preferred to consider "regulation" as a problem that could be approached holistically. The 1976 National Conference on Regulatory Reform held by the Center for Policy Process illustrates this tendency. John Naisbitt, the business consultant who founded the Center for Policy Process, would soon establish himself as a popular futurist, predicting "megatrends" for business leaders and policymakers, and the 1976 conference shared a similarly reductive approach to regulation.[46] While offering a stage for many different ideas, the conference framed regulation as something that could be approach in the singular. An introduction for the opening debate between Milton Friedman and Ralph Nader described regulatory reform as "a highly complex and controversial issue," with a multitude of perspectives, while also holding that "to achieve improvement, a greater convergence of thought, objectives and agreement must occur." By bringing the EPA's top leadership together with their counterparts from a dozen administrative agencies, representatives of industry, consumer advocates, economists, and political pundits, the conference framed regulatory reform as a universally necessary pursuit. Though environmental advocates would continue to protest against policies that conflated environmental protection with regulations on pricing and competition, the notion that regulation writ large needed reforming increasingly became a basic assumption of political conversation.

While national actors were busy debating the legal and economic basis of reform, pollution control authorities at the state and regional levels experimented with policies that transferred authority to businesses to ease the challenge of meeting pollution control targets. One such experiment occurred in Connecticut, where the Department of Environmental Protection (DEP) struggled to implement pollution standards with clumsy enforcement mechanisms. Under the law, if the DEP found that a business was in violation of a standard, the only recourse available to the regulators was to ask a court to issue an injunction against the continued operation of the business. The likely economic and political repercussions of that option meant that the DEP hardly ever used it, which taught recalcitrant firms that they could defer pollution control requirements without penalty. In 1972, the DEP commissioner formed a task force to consider alternate enforcement mechanisms, appointing as its director a young consultant from McKinsey & Company named William Drayton. Working with funding that the EPA had supplied in the hope of generating new enforcement techniques, Bill Drayton and his staff decided to figure out how much a particular firm was saving by not complying with a given standard and then charge the firm that amount as a noncompliance penalty. The task force called this approach "Economic Law Enforcement." Conducting complex financial analysis for every violator across the state was infeasible, so engineers on the task force developed a set of cost curves for different types of industry and control equipment that regulators could use to easily calculate the appropriate penalty.[47] In 1973, the task force introduced a bill into the Connecticut legislature granting the DEP the authority to assess those penalties. With support from prominent economists including William Baumol, the act passed and was signed into law.[48] Doug Costle, the Ash Council member who had helped design the EPA before becoming commissioner of Connecticut's DEP, made implementing the Economic Law Enforcement program a priority during his tenure.[49]

In California, by contrast, regulators at the nation's largest air pollution control agency had plenty of enforcement resources and political muscle, but they faced seemingly insurmountable air pollution in Los Angeles. Under the terms of the Clean Air Act Amendments of 1970, if one of the roughly 150 air quality control regions around the country failed to attain one or more of the ambient air quality standards by May 1975, the control authority for that region was prohibited from issuing construction permits for any major new source of that pollutant. California's South Coast Air Quality Management District, which encompassed the area in and around Los Angeles, exceeded the national standard for photochemical oxidants over a hundred times in 1975.[50] In response, the California Air Resources Board began denying building permits to major new sources of photochemical oxidants, including a new petroleum pipeline in Long Beach, which Standard Oil of Ohio wanted to build to offload Alaskan crude. The Clean Air Act had effectively shut down economic development by denying the ability of new firms to move into the area and by preventing existing firms from investing in new productive capital. In response, the EPA's Region IX office (which covered California, Arizona, New Mexico, and Hawaii) devised a solution: firms that wanted to build new factories or other new sources of emissions could pay existing emission sources to reduce their emissions by a commensurate amount, thus "offsetting" the new emissions. The program included a discounting requirement whereby the new emissions source had to buy a few more offsets than it required, slightly improving the overall air quality with every transaction. The "trade-off" or "offset" policy had, in effect, created the nation's first cap-and-trade system for pollution control, with a market rather than a central regulator determining where and how pollution was controlled.[51] The first application of the offset policy came in January 1976, when the Region IV office denied PAKTANK Pacific Company's application to build new oil storage facilities near Los Angeles—the first time the EPA had ever denied a permit because the new source was in a nonattainment area. Region IX offered PAKTANK the opportunity to resubmit the project with the provision that it would have no net increase in photochemical oxidant emissions, introducing the trade-off policy into practice for the first time, although PANTANK eventually elected to pursue a different strategy.[52]

EPA officials in Washington embraced Region IX's "trade-off" or "offset" plan as a solution to the thorny problem of permitting new sources in polluted areas, adopting the policy in 1976 as the Offset Interpretive Ruling for California. The agency extended the policy to the entire country later that year, tweaking the exact rules in a series of subsequent interpretive rulings and announcements. While describing the program as a much-needed solution to a critical problem, EPA officials avoided pitching it as a major regulatory reform. Roger Strelow, assistant administrator for the EPA's Air Office, noted that the trade-off policy might inspire firms in the steel and chemical industries to search out and make additional emission reductions they would otherwise have had little incentive to pursue.[53] But Strelow's comments were about as far as the agency would go, despite the fact that later observers credit the program as one of the first significant departures from the direct enforcement model and an early precedent for the market trading of pollutant rights.[54] The EPA's reticence owed to the widespread opposition that the plan aroused. Environmentalists such as the Natural Resource Defense Council's Dave Hawkins complained that the policy violated the Clean Air Act by enshrining the status quo of bad air quality in the most polluted areas, stifling further improvements.[55] A state-level regulator from Texas charged that the policy amounted to selling a "repugnant" right to pollute.[56] At the national level, the board of directors of the Air Pollution Control Association overwhelmingly voted to condemn the trade-off policy as unworkable and illegal, with the only dissenting vote coming from the EPA official on the board.[57]

Business interests likewise warned that the policy stood on shaky legal grounds or complained of perverse capital investment incentives and new geographical constraints on industrial production. A representative of the American Petroleum Institute worried that the policy could not be legally justified under the Clean Air Act and indicated that the refining industry would not support regulations that were likely to be soon overturned.[58] At a public hearing on the plan in Dallas in which 300 people testified, representatives of Sun Company and Dow Chemical Company warned that businesses would delay investments in control projects so that they could be sure to receive the rights to existing emissions. A member of Houston's Chamber of Commerce complained that those businesses that had obediently reduced their emissions years ago were being punished by losing out on the emission rights they would have gained if they were still belching that pollution. A representative from the chemical manufacturer ICI United States, Inc., testified that his firm had recently been denied a building permit for a new site near Bayport, Texas, because the existing industries in Bayport had already installed the best available pollution controls and so could not make any further reductions to generate the necessary offset rights for ICI. A member of the Greater San Antonio Chamber of Commerce worried that a similar fate would befall his community, where industries had few offsets to sell.[59]

Against such a negative reaction, it is no surprise that EPA officials avoided touting the program as a significant departure from existing practice.

Despite these halting starts on the ground, proposals for sweeping regulatory reform featured prominently in the 1976 presidential election. In the Republican primary, Ford battled a strong challenge from former California governor Ronald Reagan, who made reducing the size of the federal government a central component of his promise to restore American prosperity. In response, Ford redoubled his own commitment to scaling back regulations. Throughout the spring, Reagan traded victories with Ford in Republican primaries across the country, taking his campaign all the way to the floor of the Republican National Convention in August before Ford finally managed to secure the nomination.[60]

The specter of a bloated federal government persisted into the general election, where Ford faced a Democratic challenger who, like Reagan, positioned himself as a reformer who would cut through stifling bureaucracy and regulation. Jimmy Carter boasted of his success in streamlining the state government as governor of Georgia and promised to make the federal government more transparent and accountable to ordinary citizens. Ford's campaign paid close attention to Carter's pronouncements on regulatory reform, underscoring the importance of the issue to the 1976 election.[61] Carter also ran as a conservationist, attacking Ford as weak on environmental protection.[62] Tying together those two positions, Carter often mentioned his work in stopping the Army Corps of Engineers' Sprewell Bluff Dam, which he described as not only imperiling a scenic landscape and critical habitat but also as an example of wasteful and unnecessary government spending.[63] In November, Carter's campaign as an outsider willing to take on Washington carried him into office.

Carter's election galvanized proponents of regulatory reform. In December 1976, the Department of Economics at the Massachusetts Institute of Technology convened a two-day conference on Air Pollution and Administrative Control. Aiming to move past a theoretical discussion of the desirability of different types of regulation in the abstract, the conference organizers solicited papers on the costs and benefits of the implementation of the Clean Air Act and how alternative approaches might be realistically substituted.[64] Karl Braithwaite, who handled the daily operations of Senator Ed Muskie's Subcommittee on Air and Water Pollution, was among the many policymakers to attend. Although he returned home annoyed with the prevailing assumption that economics was inherently objective, Braithwaite was nonetheless intrigued by the ideas he had heard, including a talk by Connecticut's Bill Drayton on using a penalty fee approach to encourage the maintenance of pollution control equipment.[65]

Braithwaite also carried back with him a draft copy of a lecture that economist Charles Schulze had given earlier in the week at Harvard University.[66] In the "Public Use of Private Incentives," Schultze argued that by modifying price signals, institutional structures, and incentives of these alternative systems, policymakers could encourage private firms to reach a desirable level of pollution control on their own terms. Obviating the need for continuously writing new regulations to close loopholes opened by enterprising firms, such market-oriented approaches would reduce the costly burden of red tape on businesses and thus consumers.[67] Schultze delivered his third and final lecture on December 9, 1976, and began combining his lectures into a book, *The Public Use of Private Interest*, which became one of the most important treatises on the use of incentives in public policy when the Brookings Institution published it the next year. Already by the final lecture in December, Carter's transition team had tapped Schultze to join the new administration as chairman of the Council of Economic Advisors. As the Carter administration prepared to take office, regulatory reform was on everyone's minds, not least in the area of environmental protection.

As president-elect, Carter asked the EPA to prepare a transition memo on possible alternatives to the uniform standard model. In "Non-Regulatory (Economic) Approaches to Environmental Problems," economic analysis office director Roy Gamse offered a thoughtful consideration of the theoretical advantages and practical obstacles to alternative approaches to the existing model, principally a system of emission charges.[68] Echoing the conclusions of economists like Schultze and Kneese, Gamse's memo described how emission charges promised to be more equitable in rewarding firms that pursued pollution control in good faith, more effective in removing the incentive to delay controls, less expensive since firms with low abatement costs would reduce their pollution well below the level they would have under uniform standards, and easier to administer because regulatory agencies would have only to calculate the charge.[69]

Yet, as Gamse noted, Congress had never seriously considered such a system. Indeed, despite considerable scholarship on the subject, very few incentive alternatives had ever been implemented around the world. As Gamse explained, the reason for this mismatch between academic praise and real-world application lay in the failure of economists to demonstrate that an emission charge system could actually yield more effective and less costly controls. Seasoned in the practical challenges of administering a regulatory regime, environmental advocates in Congress and the EPA worried that emission charges would be undone by technical issues, which included building and maintaining a national monitoring system as well as significant uncertainty regarding the social costs of environmental resources and the actual control costs firms would encounter. Furthermore, even if these practical barriers could be overcome, grafting a charge system onto existing controls risked halting or reversing the progress that had already been made by creating potentially contradictory incentives for firms.[70]

Despite those obstacles, Gamse and his staff believed that the oft-touted benefits of alternative approaches might be finally realized if the EPA were to develop test cases for environmental advocates. Sidestepping the many practical issues of transforming existing policies, these test cases should be conducted in new control areas, of which there were many, thanks to the EPA's expanding responsibilities. For instance, under the Resource Conservation and Recovery Act of 1976, the EPA might try leveling a sales tax on consumer products and packaging to cover the environmental cost of producing and disposing of toxic materials. Or, to address the newly discovered problem of chlorofluorocarbons eating a hole in the ozone layer, the EPA might create a system of tradable chlorofluorocarbon production rights, which would be bought and sold by manufacturers to ease the transition away from the dangerous compound. With congressional permission and funding, the EPA could develop a test case that might finally convince environmental advocates that charges or markets presented a viable alternative to enforcement of uniform standards.[71]

Reform in the Carter Administration

Carter's presidency saw a tug of war between an older liberal consensus that the government needed to direct private industry in realms such as pollution and the reformers' insistence that government direction was inherently inefficient compared to what private industry would devise with the proper incentives. Within the administration itself, this contest was embodied in Carter's appointees. Carter repaid strong support for his candidacy from the environmental community by appointing environmental officials who endorsed a robust role for the federal government. At the EPA, Carter installed Doug Costle, who had initially helped design the agency. To direct the EPA's Air Office, Carter selected Dave Hawkins, the Natural Resources Defense Council attorney who had helped shape the EPA's implementation of the Clean Air Act. But even as Carter's appointees pointed the EPA toward a strong regulatory program, the reform-minded president also hoped to foster the fledgling attempts to shift some of the decision making to the business community. To help Costle spur regulatory reforms at the federal level, Carter appointed Bill Drayton to run the EPA's Office of Planning and Management. Over the next four years, Hawkins and Drayton repeatedly found themselves on opposite sides of reform proposals, with Costle mediating between them and between his own commitments to strong regulations and reform.

The first task for Carter's EPA officials was to implement the Clean Air Act Amendments of 1977, which had their own balance of traditional mandates and new market-based compliance innovations. After several years of contest between environmental groups and industry representatives, Congress finally managed to agree on legislation to update the Clean Air Act, passing legislation in August 1977 that Carter quickly signed. Much of the news about the legislation focused on the loosening of automobile standards, uncertainty over which had convulsed the automobile industry.[72] But the real changes were in the stationary sources. As the historian Samuel Hays described it, the Clean Air Act Amendments of 1977 reflected three underlying shifts in thinking about air pollution that had filtered up from researchers to advocates to policymakers. The first was a shift in concern from acute air pollution episodes to the longer-term effects of chronic exposure, including cancer. The second was rising awareness of the synergistic effects of pollutants, with adverse effects multiplying rather than simply adding up as more and more pollutants were pumped into the air. Tied to this second point was a rising awareness of long-distance transmission of pollutants, during which they often transformed into new threats. Finally, the amendments reflected the recognition that air pollution could not be eliminated and instead would need to be managed on an ongoing basis to limit its risks.[73]

Those shifts in thinking manifested in several policy changes in the Clean Air Act Amendments of 1977. Recognizing that the EPA's standards had failed to keep pace with rapid advances in air pollution science since 1970, the amendments provided for the ongoing review of the National Air Quality Standards based on a periodic updating of the underlying criteria documents to reflect the latest science. The amendments also pushed the EPA to expand the pollutants it regulated, including giving more attention to potential carcinogens. To account for the synergistic effects and long-distance transmission, the amendments strengthened the EPA's ability to dictate control technology at the point of emissions. Perhaps most important, the amendments confirmed the EPA's responsibility for preventing clean air from deteriorating. In nonattainment areas, the amendments required the EPA to oversee the revision of the State Implementation Plans to require that existing sources of emissions retrofit their operations to install reasonably available control technology (RACT), a somewhat ambiguous definition determined by the EPA in conjunction with the states on the basis of the prevailing industry standard for different industrial processes and pollutants. Firms that wished to add or modify emission sources would be required to undergo a New Source Review and install control technology that met a new, especially stringent standard for the lowest achievable emissions rate (LAER). In areas that did meet the national standards, the Prevention of Significant Deterioration (PSD) program required that new sources install the best available control technology (BACT) to make sure that air quality did not backslide and to protect clean areas from an influx of polluting industry from nonattainment areas. In both cases, the legislation left considerable discretion with the EPA in determining those standards and making sure that states followed the review process. One further point of emphasis on control technology came not from a shifting perspective but from horse trading in Congress to get the legislation passed. Worried that electric utilities would shift to lower sulfur coal to meet limits of sulfur dioxide emissions, representatives from eastern coal states succeeded in inserting a requirement that coal-burning utilities had to use some form of mechanical controls, keeping eastern coal competitive by obviating any cost savings that switching to western coal might have provided.[74]

The Prevention of Significant Deterioration (PSD) program thrust the EPA even further into thorny debates about economic development and environmental preservation. Prior to construction of a power plant or other source of emissions, businesses would be required to use air dispersion computer modeling to prove that the additional emissions would not deteriorate air quality in surrounding pristine (Class I) areas. As Allen Kneese and Resources for the Future argued in their survey of growth and environmental quality in the Southwest, the EPA was required to force states like

New Mexico to insist on expensive air pollution control devices or even ban new industry if sufficient control technology did not exist.[75]

At the same time, the amendments also reflected the realization that air pollution posed an endemic problem that could not be resolved within the time frame envisioned by the Clean Air Act Amendments of 1970, even with the best possible efforts. The 1977 amendments extended the deadlines for when specific industries would need to meet technology standards, including copper smelting and coal-burning electric utilities. The amendments also provided a break for the states on the widely unmet national air quality standards, extending the attainment deadline until the late 1980s for the most severe cases. To allow for economic growth in those nonattainment areas, Congress adopted the EPA's trade-off policy, with a provision for states to develop their own means of coordinating growth and emissions reductions if they could convince the EPA they had a viable plan.[76] The new law also included an experimental technology program that delayed compliance deadlines for firms that installed innovative control technology and instructions for the EPA to conduct two studies for Congress on how economic incentives might be used in environmental policy.[77]

As the Carter administration set about implementing the new legislation, the economic implications of the strengthened rules were a central concern, especially as reports came in that the industry was trying to turn its workers against environmental regulations as a threat to their jobs.[78] In September 1977, Carter met with members of the newly formed "Steel Caucus" in the House of Representatives, hearing from fellow Democrats and Republicans alike that the industry could not afford to match Japanese modernization and at the same time comply with pollution control requirements. Asked for his response, Costle argued that the industry might have been able to comply with the EPA's rules and still modernize but had instead chosen to drag its feet, "stretching out all proceedings by maximum litigation and delay."[79] An updated report on pollution control within the steel industry suggested that producers did have the capacity to clean up their operations. What's more, the report found that improvement over the previous four years was strongly correlated with enforcement pressure.[80] Under Costle, the EPA was already taking action to shut down the most egregious plants. [81] Nonetheless, Costle told Carter, the EPA was willing to make adjustments to its policies to help the industry come into compliance.[82]

One idea, articulated by Council of Economic Advisors chairman Charles Schultze, was to let firms reduce emissions from a given factory however they wanted so long as overall emissions did not increase. In this way, the EPA could take advantage of the superior knowledge of corporate engineers about the possibilities for emission reductions in their plants and still meet air quality objectives.[83] The EPA had already introduced an analogous program in 1975 whereby heavy metal smelters could avoid stringent control requirements on new equipment if they reduced emissions elsewhere in their plants such that the overall increase in emissions remained below the tons per year threshold of the New Source Performance Standards. Environmental advocates fiercely resisted this attempt to introduce a workaround into the applicability of the EPA's technology standards, and the Sierra Club had sued the agency over the 1975 proposal. In January 1978, the DC Circuit Court of Appeals ruled that the EPA did not have authority under the Clean Air Act for this plant-wide definition of an emissions source in nonattainment areas.[84]

Undeterred, Carter's EPA continued to experiment with a "bubble concept" that would draw a legal dome over industrial facilities that were subject to emission reduction requirements under a state implementation plan. Within that dome, corporate engineers and their managers could choose where and how to reduce emissions among the various sources of a given pollutant so long as the total emissions of that pollutant across the plant was less than the aggregate reductions required under the EPA's standards for all those different sources. While the smelter case was being litigated, the steel manufacturer Armco, Inc., the cleanest firm in the industry, had approached the EPA with a novel proposal to bring one of its mills into compliance.[85] Armco had controlled the particulates from its smokestacks but still faced requirements for additional controls on the fugitive emissions that escaped out of roof vents, doors, and other openings. Instead of installing expensive control devices on these various openings, Armco proposed to invest a much smaller sum in water sprayers for the mill's unpaved roads and in tarps to cover raw material piles—investments that Armco claimed would substantially reduce the particulates blown up into the air by the wind. The substitution would save the firm millions of dollars in capital and maintenance costs, Armco estimated, while achieving greater overall particulate reductions.[86] Substituting tarps and sprinklers for advanced control technologies was, at that point, too far afield, and the EPA rejected Armco's proposal. But Costle formed a Bubble Concept Task Force to pursue the idea and put Bill Drayton in charge.[87] Chemical manufacturers joined steel producers in encouraging this shift, noting as they did that the new policies should be as permissive as possible and that an overly restrictive bubble would be of no use in the dirtiest areas, where a new, flexible approach was most needed.[88]

The bubble policy was part of a set of new policies with which Costle's EPA was assuming a central role in Carter's regulatory reform program. In 1978, Carter appointed Costle as the first chair of his new Regulatory Council, which collected the heads of agencies across the executive branch to disseminate ideas like the bubble policy.[89] Stumping for Carter's proposed Regulatory Reform Act, Costle described the president's care in distinguishing necessary health and safety standards from regulations that benefited few people and yet cost an enormous amount, quoting the president's declaration that "if we are to continue our progress, we must ensure that regulation gives Americans their money's worth."[90]

For Carter, a key means of doing so was by strengthening the White House's purview over the EPA's rulemaking to give more weight to the economic costs of new regulations. Previous administrations had carved out regulatory review authorities to review (and typically scale back) the decisions made by the EPA and other executive branch agencies, and Carter built on

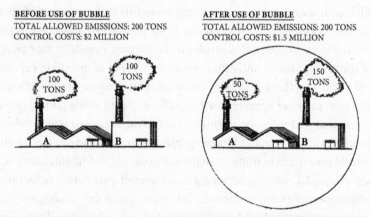

USE OF THE BUBBLE CAN REDUCE COMPLIANCE COSTS

EMISSION CONTROL COSTS:
PLANT A: $ 5,000 PER TON
PLANT B: $ 15,000 PER TON

BEFORE USE OF BUBBLE
TOTAL ALLOWED EMISSIONS: 200 TONS
CONTROL COSTS: $2 MILLION

AFTER USE OF BUBBLE
TOTAL ALLOWED EMISSIONS: 200 TONS
CONTROL COSTS: $1.5 MILLION

Figure 4.2 An illustration in an EPA guide to the bubble policy explains its promised savings over the older, proscriptive model of uniform standards.
US Environmental Protection Agency, *The Bubble and Its Use with Emission Reduction Banking* (Washington, DC, 1982).

this foundation. In 1978, he issued Executive Order 12044, which instructed the EPA and other agencies to forward to the White House for further review any proposed rules with compliance costs totaling more than $100 million annually. The process would be overseen by a newly created White House body, the Regulatory Analysis Review Group (RARG).[91]

In fall 1978, the Carter administration decided that the EPA's proposal of a new National Ambient Air Quality Standard (NAAQS) for photochemical oxidants would be the RARG's first test. The 1977 amendments had directed the EPA to update the NAAQS to account for new scientific knowledge. Since much of the regulatory system was built atop the NAAQS, even a slight adjustment in the standard could have major economic implications, which is what the Carter administration was counting on in the case of the photochemical oxidants NAAQS. As with many pollutants, pinning down a threshold at which photochemical oxidants did not threaten the public health, as the Clean Air Act required, was nearly impossible, since the oxidants were technically reactive at very low concentrations and underlying health conditions such as asthma produced widely ranging thresholds for adverse effects among the general population. Attaining the tight NAAQS set back in 1970 had proven difficult and costly to attain, given the prevalence of photochemical oxidants in every major metropolitan area.[92] Arguing that some adverse effects were inevitable, the RARG pushed the EPA to take a cost/benefit approach to the new standard, arguing that some adverse effects were inevitable and that the EPA should ease up on photochemical oxidants and tighten its standards elsewhere, where the payoff of monetized health benefits relative to the compliance costs faced by private industry was higher.[93]

The RARG's logic found support from Bill Drayton and others in the EPA's policy offices but was fiercely rejected by the Air Office's Dave Hawkins and environmental advocates, who pointed out that the Clean Air Act forbade such economic considerations. Over the next few months, the White House and the EPA's various offices went back and forth on the proposed standard. Drayton and other reform advocates at the agency eventually helped the White House ease the standard, with Costle and the EPA dancing around the prohibition on considering costs by not formally making economic analysis the determinant of the new NAAQS, even though the costs and benefits of the new NAAQS drove the internal conversation.[94] Environmental advocates protested loudly, but while Senator Muskie held hearings on the RARG's involvement in the national standards, Congress chose to not get further involved.[95]

As with the RARG review, the bubble policy faced its most concerted opposition from Dave Hawkins and the Air Office. Like many of the Air Office staff, Hawkins believed that the bubble let firms claim a right to existing emission levels from outmoded production facilities, foregoing the slow but steady improvements in air quality obtained by forcing businesses to meet technological standards. If businesses could reduce pollution more than the EPA was asking for in a particular area, Hawkins thought that the EPA should expand the technological standard to require that reduction for all firms.[96] As the Bubble Policy Task Force worked at implementing the policy, Hawkins repeatedly introduced constraints. In September 1977, he cordoned off the bubble from revisions to state implementation plans, telling the EPA's regional administrators that the states should revise their plans according to the Clean Air Act Amendments of 1977, which had no bubble component.[97] The next month, Hawkins critiqued Armco's proposed bubble for "fugitive dust" emissions, telling Costle that the switch from sophisticated fugitive dust controls to the management of open dust presented a monitoring headache and might prove more dangerous to human health.[98] As Costle prepared to formally propose the bubble in November, Hawkins went so far as to object to the wording of the announcement, advocating language that conveyed the EPA's "neutral position" toward the policy rather than Costle's "more positive statement of encouragement."[99]

As Hawkins would later recount, his repeated introduction of qualifications and constraints on the bubble policy was a strategy born of the recognition that the steel industry had too much clout for the air office to simply kill the policy. Instead, Hawkins set out "to restrain, and condition, and limit [the bubble's] use as much as possible by negotiating all of these criteria conditions." By weighing down the bubble with onerous requirements, Hawkins calculated that state agencies would spurn the policy as a drain on their limited budgets and staffs. At the same time that the EPA's policy office was encouraging state regulators to embrace the bubble, Hawkins was making sure that they would have "to jump through seven hoops to do it."[100]

Costle's announcement in December 1978 that he would soon propose a bubble policy immediately aroused concerns at the state level about the bubble's potential disruption to existing programs—exactly the sort of objections that Hawkins was counting on to limit the policy's adoption. George Ferreri, administrator of Maryland's Air Quality Program, wrote Hawkins in December 1978 that the bubble contained enough hidden problems that "to call it a can of worms would be a gross understatement."

Passing Ferreri's note along to Drayton, Hawkins urged delay, noting that Ferreri was upset about being pressured into adopting the policy "before he has figured out where and how to apply it."[101] The EPA's regional offices, which dealt most closely with the states, likewise reported in December 1978 that state regulators strongly supported a delay in the EPA's announcement of the bubble policy to avoid interfering with the state implementation plan revisions and to allow time to consider the policy in more depth.[102] In public letters and complaints to the agency, environmental advocates also voiced concerns about the imposition of the bubble on the limited resources of state and local regulators.[103]

Beyond worries about the taxing or disruptive effects of the bubble, state and local regulators shared the opinion of many in the air office that the bubble threatened continued improvements in air quality by surrendering the EPA's ability to dictate specific control technologies and to push states to continue to clean up their air. John Wise, who helped states formulate their implementation plans in the EPA's Region IV office, recalls that state regulators were especially leery of the bubble's use in poor neighborhoods and communities of color, which had historically been exposed to higher levels of dangerous pollution.[104] Proponents of the bubble wrestled with these problems, eventually devising trade-off requirements such that any bubble would result in a net air quality improvement and establishing that regulators could always go back to sources that had bubbled and demand further reductions. But many regulators remained convinced that the best way to clean up the air was to stick with strict, uniform standards that every company had to meet.

Regulators also worried about a range of side effects ignored by the bubble's proponents. Bill Becker, who became president of the national association of state air regulators in 1980, described one such issue in how businesses hedged against the risk of pollution control–equipment failure. In designing pollution control technology, corporate engineers typically reduced emissions below what the EPA's standards required. This margin of error was not required by law, but firms preferred to spend the extra money to hedge the risk that control equipment would fail to deliver the promised reductions, a failure that could bring fines and expensive retrofitting. If a given stack had to meet an emissions standard of no more than 100 tons per year, Becker estimated that the typical firm would design controls that limited emissions to 80 or 90 tons. Since that hedge more often than not went unused, it yielded a 10 to 20 percent bonus in reduced emissions from that emissions source. Under the bubble policy, the risk of control equipment not performing up to expectations would be spread over the plant as a whole. Engineers would still build overly stringent controls to guard against control-equipment failure, but the hedge could be much smaller, since the chance of all the control equipment simultaneously failing to meet expectations was vanishingly slim. Under the bubble, that substantial air quality bonus would largely disappear.[105]

Tracing a related line of critique, an environmental analyst named Richard Liroff found that many state-level regulators objected to the EPA's policy because they were already striking similar bargains with industry. In a comprehensive history of the bubble policy produced for the Conservation Foundation, Liroff reported that local and state regulators had always enjoyed some leeway in deciding what technical standards would apply to emission sources under their jurisdiction. These local and state regulators periodically allowed companies to exceed one of these technological standards in exchange for tightening controls in another part of their operations—informal deals that gave local regulators valuable flexibility in negotiating with politically powerful firms.[106] EPA staff in the regional offices and at headquarters could in theory identify and reject such accommodations through a careful review of the applications that state agencies were required to submit for any proposed modification of their implementation plans. But the practical difficulty of such painstaking review and the political consequences of rejecting all but impeccable state plans obviated against such intervention. As with the unrecorded air quality bonus from risk hedging, informal bubbling was an instance in which the dynamics of pollution control in the real world created entrenched interests against change.

Predicting legal difficulties and counseling an abundance of caution, Hawkins and his fellow skeptics at the EPA convinced Costle to propose a conservative bubble in January 1979. Announced with great fanfare and the enthusiastic endorsement of prominent economists and advocates of regulatory reform, the initial bubble policy in reality changed very little about how most firms actually complied with the Clean Air Act.[107] Bubbles were only allowed by firms that were in compliance or on an approved compliance plan for meeting statutory deadlines for standards, no open dust swaps were allowed, trading between pollutants was not allowed, trading between plants in the same area was not allowed, and each bubble proposal had to be reviewed by EPA officials as an official revision to the state implementation plan.[108] Nevertheless, representatives from the steel and other industries pressed on, hoping that Drayton and other regulatory reform advocates would prevail over Hawkins and other skeptics to create a more liberal bubble before the final policy was implemented.[109] Indeed, Drayton was busy trying to resolve each issue raised by Hawkins and other critics.[110]

In addition to pushing for the continued liberalization of reforms like the bubble, Drayton and his staff imagined a transformed regulatory landscape in which such reforms would function, discussing, for instance, how financial firms might be enticed into creating insurance policies for bubbles.[111] Recognizing the need to sell the bubble outside of the EPA, Drayton extolled the policy's merits in speeches and publications.[112] In 1979, Drayton created a regulatory reform staff in the policy office, hiring attorney Michael Levin as its first director. Drayton's efforts came in the midst of sweeping bipartisan reforms that opened the airline and trucking industries to far greater competition, a climate that no doubt encouraged him and others who hoped to achieve equivalent transformations at the EPA.[113]

In December 1979, Costle issued a final bubble policy that removed many of the constraints that the air office had fought to include. Fulfilling Armco's request, firms could control particulates across their operations, provided they could establish through monitoring that the promised reductions were in fact occurring. Firms could use bubbles to come into compliance and also draw bubbles across multiple plants in the same geographic vicinity.[114] Nevertheless, significant constraints limited the new policy's effect on how the majority of businesses controlled pollution. As Hawkins and the air office had long insisted, bubbles were available only in areas that were on an EPA-approved plan to achieving the air quality standards by the 1982 deadline. And firms that wanted to use the bubble still had to complete an implementation plan revision, allowing regulators who were wary of the policy to closely interrogate each proposed usage. The review process could take a year or more—an unappealing prospect for firms that needed to build new facilities in response to market signals and did not want to hear eighteen months later that their application under the novel policy had been rejected.[115] Though the potential savings of the bubble were substantial, most firms chose to avoid the uncertainty of a policy that many regulators plainly mistrusted.

Within industry, enthusiasm about the new direction the EPA seemed to be taking under Carter and Costle was soon replaced with disappointment. As National Steel executive Fred Tucker complained to a reporter, "What we asked EPA to do was to legalize the bubble, not to qualify it so badly that nobody uses it."[116] Anticipating the challenges that would arise from the permitting requirements, New Jersey asked for permission in 1979 to approve bubbles without revising its implementation plan for each application—an arrangement that became known as a "generic bubble." Wary of surrendering control to state authorities who might not insist on the same high standards for each and every bubble, the EPA rejected New Jersey's request in March 1980, prompting an immediate legal challenge from the Manufacturing Chemists' Association.[117]

In the summer of 1980, the bubble's proponents fanned out to promote the policy. Levin toured the country explaining the mechanics and merits of the bubble and other market alternatives to skeptical business representatives and state and local regulators. As Levin explained in a slide deck he used on his tour, the bubble would significantly reduce compliance costs for businesses as corporate managers "put the profit motive to work for pollution control."[118] To convince regulators of the benefits of adopting such reforms, Levin's staff collected data from industry adopters such as DuPont that showed significant improvements in air quality to go along with the economic savings.[119] Drayton's policy office formed a Bubble Clearinghouse to collect and disseminate reports about every proposed bubble in the country along with other literature about the policy.[120] Costle met with industry representatives, including the Council of Industrial Boiler Owners, to try to nudge them into proposing bubbles for new and expanded plants.[121] Writing to the president in August 1980, deputy EPA administrator Barbara Blum touted several imminent success stories, including DuPont's projected savings of $12 million on its Chambers Works facility in New Jersey.[122]

As EPA staff promoted the bubble, proponents within the agency fought for further liberalization of the policy. In 1980, the policy office's Roy Gamse put together a list of remaining constraints. In addition to the problem of delays in revisions of state implementation plans (for which Gamse singled out the air office's Dave Hawkins as the principal obstacle), Gamse flagged restrictions on using bubbles in the areas without a plan to attain the national air quality standards.[123] Drayton took Gamse's analysis to Costle, emphasizing that this nonattainment prohibition, despite appearing legitimate at the time the bubble policy had been formulated, revealed itself to bar bubbles where they were most appealing. Acknowledging that environmental groups would object, Drayton advised Costle to lift the restriction to prove to industry that the bubble had not been a "hollow gesture."[124] Meanwhile, Drayton's staff pushed Hawkins and the air office to accept other liberalizations of the bubble policy, including bubbling across different volatile organic compounds, precursors to smog that are also one of the most

commonly emitted pollutants among the small—and medium-sized—
industrial sources of pollution that Levin and others hoped to reach with
the new policies.[125] Though Hawkins did eventually give in on a number
of fronts, he managed to protect key restrictions, including the provision
against bubbling in areas that did not meet national standards and could
not agree with the EPA on a plan to do so, withstanding even White House
pressure.[126]

The hobbling effect of these remaining constraints on the bubble policy
was made clear during a September 1980 conference organized by the EPA
that brought regulators, business executives, local elected officials, academic
economists, union leaders, congressional leaders, and EPA staff together
to consider the implementation of regulatory reform initiatives to date.[127]
According to Liroff, the results were not pretty. Conference participants
expressed deep disappointment with the EPA's reforms, particularly the
bubble policy. For all the hype, the EPA had yet to approve a single bubble.
Of the many hindrances to the policy's success, participants singled out the
state implementation plan's review requirement as the most pernicious.
Liroff argued that the conference represented something of a turning point
for Costle, with the avalanche of criticism convincing him that the promised
benefits of the bubble would never be realized unless the EPA removed the
bulk of the remaining constraints.[128] Two weeks later, Costle announced that
the EPA would allow states to submit plans for generic bubbles that did not
require EPA review. Writing Carter's economic advisor Stuart Eizenstat to
inform him of the impending change, Costle noted that DuPont would be
among the first companies to take advantage of the change, finally realizing
that $12 million in savings that the EPA had bragged about in August.[129]

On October 22, 1980, the EPA announced its provisional approval of the
nation's first bubble. The EPA's press release explained that the bubble would
allow Narragansett Electric Company of Rhode Island to burn high-sulfur
oil at one plant in exchange for shutting down another plant or converting
it to natural gas. Behind the scenes, Drayton and others had tried and failed
to speed through approval of a 3M bubble to make it the nation's first, in
place of Narragansett's less politically appealing fuel swap.[130] Nevertheless,
the EPA celebrated the "landmark regulatory reform action," which promised to reduce sulfur dioxide emissions by nearly 1,400 tons and imported
oil by 600,000 barrels each year while saving the utility and its customers almost $3 million annually in projected costs.[131] Another press release touted
Armco's soon-to-be-approved bubble for open dust control at its Ohio plant,

with anticipated savings of $14 million to $16 million and exciting prospects of reproducibility across Armco's other facilities.[132] In a private letter to two of his former McKinsey colleagues, Drayton pointed to the Narragansett and Armco bubbles, together with the generic bubble program, as the long-awaited "clear commitment to making regulatory reform work."[133] Critics and supporters alike made the imminent bubble an important topic in policy circles.[134] Change finally seemed to be coming to the EPA.

The bubble policy's tentative ascent exemplified the Carter administration's complicated record on regulatory reform leading up to the 1980 election. The administration led the charge to deregulate the trucking and the airline industries, convinced by reform advocates that removing restrictions on pricing and routes would benefit consumers.[135] But the sweep and pace of such changes contrasted markedly with the halting embrace of market-oriented strategies at the EPA. In the lame duck session following the 1980 election, Carter would add to the ambiguity of his regulatory record, signing two new pieces of legislation that simultaneously expanded the EPA's mandate while circumscribing the agency's authority vis-à-vis the White House.[136]

Carter's mixed record reflected the complexity of the regulation he set out to reform. While many in the think tank world liked to speak of regulation as a single subject, the reality of governance was far more complicated. With environmental advocates at the EPA and elsewhere watching closely, Carter tended to adhere to the distinction that Ralph Nader and other public interest advocates insisted on between regulations governing competition that could be abolished to the benefit of consumers shopping in a more competitive market and regulations that protected things like clean air for which there could never be a market. But a complex record proved to be a political liability against a Republican candidate who could paint a compelling image of a federal state run amok in large, uncomplicated brushstrokes. Supporters of tentative reforms such as the bubble would have to wait and see whether their careful work would flourish under the new administration.

* * *

In 1980, the EPA and the environmental governance regime over which the agency presided stood at a crossroads. At 14,500 employees, it was one of the country's largest and arguably most successful regulatory bodies. In the decade since its formation, the EPA's proscriptive rules and energetic enforcement had produced remarkable improvements in air quality and public health. Particulate levels had been cut in half, sulfur dioxide was down

44 percent, and carbon monoxide levels were 36 percent of what they had been in 1970—despite a 35 percent increase in vehicle miles traveled. Ozone and nitrogen dioxide levels remained high, but the EPA had managed to reduce the threat from all the major air pollutants.[137] In perhaps the most compelling testament to the agency's success, the EPA's air program had extended the average life expectancy of an American by an entire year.[138] Recognizing the EPA's capability, Congress continued to give the agency new responsibilities, including the 1980 legislation that created the Superfund program. Despite skyrocketing inflation, stagnating wages, energy crises, and industrial woes, public support for environmental protection remained high.

At the same time, the ambitious objectives of the Clean Air Act remained largely unmet. Indeed, cleaning up the nation's air had proven so hard and costly that Congress had granted long extensions to the statutory deadlines with the 1977 amendments. Faced with the task of meeting increasingly difficult mandates in a challenging economy, the EPA had tentatively embraced new policies that used market incentives to ease compliance, cheered on by a swelling chorus of regulatory reformers, who heralded the bubble and other innovations as the harbingers of a fundamental shift in governance. Meanwhile, opponents of the EPA were gathering. Unmoved by the agency's hesitant reforms, these opponents would soon challenge the EPA's basic legitimacy with a deregulatory assault on the agency's legitimacy and capacity to govern.

5

Are You Tough Enough?

Deregulation

Three years after her ouster from the Reagan administration, Anne Gorsuch published a tell-all about her two years as administrator of the EPA. From the beginning of her tenure in 1981, Gorsuch had been a deeply divisive figure. Environmental advocates accused her of sabotaging the EPA by neglecting statutory responsibilities and overseeing deep budget cuts that hobbled the agency's work. Thousands of career staff had been fired or quit. Among those who remained, Gorsuch's imperious management style had earned her a nickname: "the Ice Queen." In the months before her resignation, Gorsuch's refusal to provide investigators with documents related to a scandal in the Superfund program had led Gorsuch to become the first Cabinet-level official in history to be cited for contempt of Congress. By popular account, Gorsuch had been an embarrassing failure. Her memoir punched back, portraying her as a well-meaning newcomer to Washington who had fallen victim to an environmental governance regime that would not yield to new ideas.[1] Gorsuch may not have been well meaning, but she was correct in claiming that she had faced fierce resistance from within the EPA as she faithfully tried to implement Reagan's vision. "Are You Tough Enough?" asked the title of Gorsuch's later memoir, ironically echoing the question countless EPA employees asked themselves during Reagan's presidency.

Ronald Reagan was elected in 1980 on the premise that the country's economic woes had been caused by an overlarge and overzealous government, which had stifled free enterprise in a mess of rules and regulations and misguided interventions. The EPA had become one of the most prominent parts of the regulatory state by the time Reagan took office, and the agency's programs were a key target of Reagan's campaign to reduce the scale and scope of the federal government. A former state representative in Colorado, Gorsuch won the top job at the EPA after making a name for herself as one of the "the crazies," a group of lawmakers who aggressively pushed to cut regulations and taxes. In appointing Gorsuch and other westerners

Valuing Clean Air. Charles Halvorson, Oxford University Press (2021). © Oxford University Press.
DOI: 10.1093/oso/9780197538845.003.0006

to run his environmental agencies, Reagan was endorsing a powerful anti-government protest that took its rhetoric from the Mountain West but appealed to Americans across the country to see themselves as cowboys in a grassroots uprising against the federal government. Reagan was unapologetic in looking to industry for direction—a confidence borne of the ascent of free enterprise as an article of faith in the Republican Party. But like their counterparts in what became known as the Sagebrush Rebellion, Reagan's environmental officials were the public faces of a campaign that was driven by conservative business interests who were far more embedded in the politics of Washington than the image of the outsider cowboy would suggest. Reagan himself perfectly embodied these politics: a national celebrity courtesy of General Electric who would don a cowboy hat and take reporters riding on his ranch.

While officials in the Reagan administration openly solicited deregulatory ideas from the business community and enthusiastically launched initiatives to block new regulations, they moved with more circumspection in challenging the EPA's capacity to govern. As they worked to relieve the agency of its statutory mandates through amendments to the Clean Air Act, Reagan's advisors also proceeded with budget and staffing cuts and careful reorganization plans designed to maximize disruption to the agency while minimizing public and congressional awareness of their actions. Initially, Gorsuch implemented those cuts with gusto. Later, she would come to chafe under White House direction, clashing more frequently with Reagan's advisors just as she was becoming a political liability for the administration.

Confronted by political appointees and an administration that they believed to be undermining the agency's mandates, the EPA's career staff fought back. A network of former environmental officials called Save EPA organized to spread the word about what was happening to the agency, channeling that internal resistance into congressional and media scrutiny. At the same time, many of the business interests that Reagan had courted began complaining that Gorsuch and Reagan's indiscriminate cuts and hostility to new regulations were hobbling the nascent market-based reforms left by the Carter administration. As this negative attention intensified, Reagan's advisors came to see that they had underestimated the political liability of undercutting the EPA's work. Gorsuch's forced resignation was an implicit admission that the Reagan administration had miscalculated in its attack on the EPA. After Gorsuch's departure, Reagan made a show of backing away from his deregulatory environmental agenda, though it would take nearly a decade for the EPA to fully recover. Beginning with the election of 1980, this chapter discusses Gorsuch's brief tenure to consider the politics of deregulation, showing how the EPA's opponents worked to limit the agency's legitimacy and capacity to govern and investigating the resistance that resulted.

Government Is the Problem

The 1980 presidential election was in many ways a contest over the idea of an interventionist federal government. Against a backdrop of crises at home and abroad, the Democratic incumbent Jimmy Carter and the Republican challenger Ronald Reagan debated whether the government could and should act to improve public welfare. The fight was not black and white—Reagan chastised Carter for not deploying the military to safeguard American oil interests in the Middle East, and Carter infamously asked voters to look not to government but rather inside themselves for the spiritual strength to revive a sputtering economy. But, on the whole, Carter argued that the government could and should manage matters such as the country's energy supply through proscriptive regulations, while Reagan tended to argue that more rules would simply make the fuel shortages and most other problems worse.[2] When it came to environmental policy, Carter had promoted new policies such as the bubble that shifted some authority over compliance from the EPA back to industry and he held these out as evidence that the economic costs of regulation could be reduced through careful reforms.[3] But Carter remained committed to the idea that the federal government should preside over a strong regulatory regime, setting and enforcing the standards that had produced remarkable improvements in environmental quality.

Reagan challenged the capacity and the legitimacy of federal interventions to improve the environment. A former actor and one-time Democrat who had found national celebrity as a spokesperson for General Electric, Reagan emerged as a popular voice for free enterprise in the Republican Party in the 1960s, warning of the threats to prosperity and freedom posed by the federal government, then nearing the peak of its Great Society expansion. Though he supported some conservation measures as governor of California, Reagan generally held that the federal government had overstepped its constitutional authority in telling the states how to handle environmental problems. He echoed a growing skepticism among many Republican voters that environmental issues were as serious as the EPA and the environmental community contended. Air pollution had been "substantially controlled" and was caused mostly by trees anyway, Reagan declared as a candidate, and if the EPA continued unchecked, "you and I would live like rabbits."[4]

The myriad and serious problems facing the country in 1980 posed a major challenge for Jimmy Carter as the incumbent candidate. Sluggish growth coupled with a rapid rise in the price of consumer goods had produced a painful new malaise called stagflation. A second oil shortage following the Iranian revolution underscored the country's debilitating dependence on energy supplies that it did not control. The humiliating Iranian hostage crisis exposed the weakness of American power abroad. From the beginning of his presidency, Carter had told the country that it must accept the reality of natural limits on resources and growth, famously donning a cardigan and turning down the thermostats in the White House. Reagan rejected the very notion of limits, appealing to a faith in American exceptionalism and a growing belief in the salvation of free enterprise. The United States did not need more rules to prosper, Reagan argued, but simply to get government off the backs of hardworking Americans. In November 1980, that vision of prosperity through deregulation helped to sweep Reagan into office as the nation's fortieth president in an election that saw Reagan carry forty-four states and Republican candidates pick up seats in the House and win a majority in the Senate—the first time since 1954 that the Republican Party had controlled a congressional chamber. Reagan and his allies saw the commanding victory as a mandate for their vision. As Reagan famously put it in his inaugural address, "In this present crisis, government is not the solution to the problem; government is the problem."[5]

As with much of his agenda, when it came to environmental policy, Reagan was deeply influenced by conservative business interests, who had regrouped after the surge of new regulation in the early 1970s to help build an intellectual and legal case against the expanding mandates of the EPA and other agencies. In addition to supporting pro-business organizations like the Business Roundtable and the Chamber of Commerce, major companies built powerful lobbying operations and funded new political action committees.[6] Business interests also funded a series of new think tanks that incubated and disseminated policy ideas and legal arguments for scaling back the federal government. These included the Heritage Foundation, founded in 1973 by the Colorado brewer and energy and minerals investor Joseph Coors, and the Cato Institute, founded the next year by the industrialist Charles Koch and others. Several of these new organizations developed a specific focus on rolling back federal interventions in the environment. James Watt, a former official in the Department of the Interior and the Federal Power Commission, built the Coors-financed Mountain States Legal Foundation into a sophisticated opponent of federal conservation programs.[7] The emergence of these think tanks intersected with the growth of free market environmental economics programs at western universities. Scholars at these schools often challenged the efficacy of centralized government control, and by the late 1970s, some of the programs were receiving substantial funding from foundations that were closely aligned with business groups.[8]

The western locus of much of this business organizing owed to the perceived alignment between corporate priorities and long-standing grievances among small western producers. The federal government owned significant portions of the land in many western states (nearly 50 percent in Wyoming in 1979, for example, compared to 12 percent in Florida or 3 percent in Pennsylvania). Dating back to Theodore Roosevelt, Republican leaders had played a prominent role in conservation efforts that set aside subsets of this territory as national parks and developed policies to protect the remainder from overuse. Nevertheless, ranchers, timber operations, mining companies, and other agriculturalists and natural resource extractors leased large swaths of this land from the Bureau of Land Management and the Forest Service on what tended to be generous terms. New land use policies in the 1960s and 1970s intended to tighten those terms to better protect the underlying environments ignited protests against federal control among resource users. This grassroots critique was quickly taken up by conservative legal activists, who built a case against regulatory interventions as takings of private property for which compensation was required. Holding up the cowboy as a totem of the hardworking American imperiled by overzealous and unconstitutional federal regulation, what came to be called the Sagebrush Rebellion swept into office a set of libertarian politicians who demanded less regulation and the release of millions of acres of federal land. As a presidential candidate, Reagan had aligned himself with this anti-federal politics, at one point telling a crowd in Utah to "count me in as a rebel."[9]

With his cowboy persona and pro-business politics, Reagan fit neatly with the hostility that these different parties expressed toward environmental regulation, and his election in 1980 opened up the possibility of major policy changes. On the advice of Coors, who was a key member of his kitchen cabinet, Reagan installed prominent western critics of the regulatory state atop the agencies they had formerly opposed. To head the Bureau of Land Management, Reagan chose Robert Burford, a former rancher turned conservative Speaker of the Colorado House of Representatives. At the Department of the Interior, Reagan appointed the Mountain State Legal Foundation's James Watt as Secretary. For EPA administrator, Reagan chose Anne Gorsuch, the young Colorado state representative whose intelligence and pugnaciousness had made her a rising star in Sagebrush politics. At thirty-eight-years-old, she was the same age as William Ruckelshaus when he became the EPA's first administrator, though she did not have the same familiarity with the federal government. What Gorsuch lacked in experience, she made up in commitment to the Reagan revolution, impressing Reagan's advisors with her professed willingness to make major cuts to the agency she was being appointed to run.[10] For Coors and the other business interests who had supported the anti-government turn in Republican politics, Reagan's appointments promised a direct channel into the regulatory state. For conservative voters, the appointments were a delightful rebuke to a federal bureaucracy they were learning to distrust and fear. Nodding to this outsider's disdain, Gorsuch replaced her predecessor's midsize Mercury Zephyr with a luxurious Oldsmobile Ninety-Eight Regency Brougham, which cost the EPA nearly four times as much to lease and emitted more pollutants than the majority of new cars for sale.[11]

Relief

Despite Reagan's anti-government rhetoric, an older set of Republican environmental leaders had looked to the incoming administration as a chance to build on a long history of Republican leadership in environmental protection. To assuage fears about his intentions, Reagan formed an environmental transition team staffed by members of this old guard. Chaired by Dan Lufkin, a prominent conservationist and former state official, the team consisted of the sort of Republicans who had played critical roles in environmental protection over the past thirty years, including the EPA's first two heads, William Ruckelshaus and Russell Train. Harkening back to the politics of Reagan's Republican predecessors, the team declared that the new administration would promote economic growth alongside environmental quality, returning "the good name of balance" to environmental policy, as a statement of philosophy put it. The transition plan called for Reagan to build on Carter's fledging market-oriented reforms to achieve environmental objectives in a less costly and less intrusive fashion. More authority would be returned to the states for administering national standards. The new administration would avoid pursuing minute pollution reductions at very high prices. Though they sought to elevate considerations of efficiency in environmental policy, the transition team articulated a commitment to environmental protection as a "major concern" of Reagan's presidency.[12]

But the new administration was not interested in balance or careful reform but rather in reining in the federal government as quickly and as thoroughly as possible. To do so, Reagan's advisors set about expanding White House control over the EPA and other administrative agencies. The first step was to centralize power within the Office of Management and Budget (OMB), whose principal responsibility had been to assist the White House in evaluating the budget requests of federal agencies.[13] Reagan's OMB director, David Stockman, was a former congressman from Michigan who had won the job with his fiery critiques of intrusive government and his recommendations for sweeping cuts to health and safety regulations. In the months between the election and the inauguration, Stockman created a list of deregulatory priorities with the help of the OMB's longtime Environment Branch director Jim Tozzi, whose sharp criticism of the costs of regulations to businesses had made him a familiar and feared antagonist at the EPA. Tozzi and Stockman's deliberations soon expanded to include James Miller, an economist who Reagan appointed to a key OMB post, and C. Boyden Gray, chief counsel to Vice President George H. W. Bush.[14] Recognizing a deregulatory ally in the president-elect, representatives of the coal companies and other businesses that had long resisted the EPA's direction eagerly sent in recommendations for rules they wanted changed.[15]

Reagan's initial steps as president made clear that he viewed regulation as something to be resisted as an article of faith. On his first day in office, Reagan chastised Jimmy Carter for issuing a rash of "midnight" regulations at the end of his presidency, many of which Reagan promised to reverse. Reagan also declared a sixty-day freeze on the enactment and proposal of any new rules and announced the formation of a Task Force on Regulatory Relief that would make changes to existing regulations as well as the underlying rulemaking process. The EPA and other agencies were told to bring forward recommendations for reducing their own programs but otherwise sit on their hands, with one exception: any new rules that diminished the "regulatory burden," as the Reagan administration put it, were exempt from the freeze.[16]

With the freeze in place, Reagan's Task Force on Regulatory Relief launched into its work. Chaired by Vice President Bush and managed by Boyden Gray and Jim Miller, the task force was staffed with OMB members who were familiar with the agencies they scoured for deregulatory opportunities. Cuts were to come from across the federal government, but environmental protections drew special scrutiny as candidates for the axe.[17] Much of this direction came from the business community. The Department of Commerce reported to the task force that large and small businesses both identified the costs of meeting the EPA's standards as their top regulatory concern.[18] In March, Vice President Bush mailed a formal request for deregulatory proposals to hundreds of executives and other business representatives. Nearly 300 replied, from major chemical manufacturers to fast food chains.[19] The EPA dominated among the concerns of large businesses and was matched only by the Department of Labor among small businesses.[20]

To continue blocking the expansion of environmental regulations after the sixty-day freeze ended, the Reagan administration turned to the longstanding process of regulatory review. Regulatory review had begun under Richard Nixon, who deployed White House economists to recommend changes to the rules issued by the EPA and other agencies, and who faced sharp criticism from environmental advocates and congressional representatives for this intervention. But Nixon and each president since had nevertheless taken steps to strengthen and formalize the review process. Recognizing that proposed standards would be evaluated on their economic merits, the EPA had learned to support its proposed rules with a thorough accounting of their costs and benefits.

Reagan decided to build on this regulatory review foundation. Moving his regulatory review staff into a new office in the OMB, Reagan transformed one of Carter's last initiatives as president into a potent deregulatory cudgel. In December 1980, Carter had signed the Paperwork Reduction Act with the intention of making the regulatory process more efficient, granting the newly created Office of Information and Regulatory Analysis (OIRA) the power to limit the amount of physical paperwork that agencies like the EPA could require companies to complete. Adopting the most literal reading of that prerogative, the Reagan administration used the Paperwork Reduction Act to assert White House authority over even the most minute proposals made by the EPA and other agencies so long as they happened to require a single form.[21] Economists who had reviewed a small subset of the rules issued during the Carter administration were transferred to a new office in OIRA with the purview to look at virtually any regulation they wanted.[22]

The consolidation and strengthening of regulatory review came as part of Reagan's push to insert economic considerations into the heart of the EPA's governing. In February 1981, Reagan issued Executive Order 12291, which required the EPA and other agencies to submit a Regulatory Impact Analysis detailing the estimated economic costs and benefits to businesses and the federal government of all major proposals to the OMB for review. Carter's own Executive Order 12204 had enabled similar scrutiny. But Reagan's EO 12291 added a significant new requirement: agencies could only issue regulations for which the monetary benefits exceeded the monetary costs.[23]

Regulatory review had been challenged by environmental advocates from its inception, but Reagan's use of OIRA and EO 12291 marked a new threat. Critics had complained under previous administrations that regulatory review opened a back door into rulemaking through which business interests could lobby White House advisors and EPA officials outside of public view. But the privileges that Carter had claimed paled in comparison to Reagan's consolidation of authority in the White House. When Congressman John Dingell asked that the Reagan administration keep a public log of all contacts involved in regulatory rulemakings (something Carter had been forced to do), Reagan's advisors declined, noting among themselves that such a log "could have a chilling effect on their ability to meet with the outside world."[24] Procedures introduced by the Reagan administration did nothing to allay environmentalists' concerns. When the OMB released conduct guidelines for regulatory review in June 1981, the Environmental Defense Fund's Chuck Ludlam was among those who complained that the OMB's rules did not require material given to OMB staff to be placed in the public record, did not require disclosure of any conversations with private parties, and did nothing to limit the OMB's consultation of EPA officials. "It is hard to imagine," Ludlam wrote, "OMB adopting guidelines imposing less meaningful protections against back-door manipulation of the regulatory process."[25] In a meeting later that year with the public interest group the National Consumer League, Reagan advisor Chris DeMuth declared that he would refuse to even acknowledge whether a particular regulation was under review without a subpoena or a Freedom of Information Act request.[26]

Environmental advocates also protested against the strengthening of cost/benefit analysis, which they argued systemically undervalued the benefits of environmental protection. As those advocates explained, the benefits of environmental protections (such as the reduced risk of lung cancer from tighter emission standards) were more difficult to quantity than the costs. Even after settling thorny questions about what not getting lung cancer should be worth, the underlying risks of pollution tended to manifest over a longer term, with more uncertainty than the short term, easily established costs associated with compliance, with a result that the cost/benefit scale tended to be weighted against environmental protection. Nevertheless, organizations such as EDF hired economists and invested in economic expertise in an implicit admission that the cost/benefit rubric was there to stay.[27] In a testament to both that growing acceptance and the enduring controversy, the New York Times editorialized in 1982 for the virtues of using monetary calculations to weigh new regulatory proposals.[28]

In his haste to gain control over the rulemaking process, Reagan often ignored or dismissed the advice of environmental policymakers who might have helped moderate his vision into workable policies. Shortly after taking office, Reagan relegated the Council on Environmental Quality (CEQ), which had functioned as an important source of policy advice for the White House since the Nixon administration, to a merely symbolic role. In his first year in office, Reagan cut the CEQ's staff from sixty to just six and made the council vacate the Jackson Place townhouse that had been its home since its inception.[29] Caroline Isber, who had been CEQ's legislative and public affairs director, was one of the many dismissed employees forced to look on from the outside as nearly everything she had been working on ground to a halt.[30] While cutting the CEQ may have made some sense given Reagan's disinterest in expanding environmental protections, it also eliminated an important source of advice on environmental policy and removed what had been a historical counterweight to the OMB's persistent push for easier standards.[31] Without the CEQ, Reagan's advice on environmental policy came primarily from economic advisors and business voices. At the time, Reagan likely saw nothing wrong with that arrangement. But the absence of counsel from knowledgeable insiders eventually revealed itself as a strategic weakness as Reagan's deregulatory ambitions collided with a governance regime that he often did not understand.

The Ice Queen's Reign

Perhaps the clearest case where hostility and indifference to the regulatory system he inherited ultimately hurt Reagan was at the EPA, where administrator Anne Gorsuch was quickly at war with the agency she had been appointed to run. The antagonism began before she had even set foot through the door. Following her nomination in February 1981, Gorsuch moved into a suite of offices in Jim Watt's Department of the Interior while she prepared for her confirmation hearings. Declining invitations to meet with former EPA administrators William Ruckelshaus and Doug Costle and turning down nearly all briefings with EPA staff, Gorsuch instead hunkered down with a cadre of Reagan advisors and planned how she would implement budget and personnel cuts that the OMB's David Stockman and other Reagan advisors were planning. Recounting the strategy behind these first few months, Gorsuch's deputy chief of staff recounted Watt's advice: "It's a lot easier to fire people you don't know."[32] That might have been true, but Gorsuch's detachment was also a liability, especially as her confirmation dragged into May.

With input from industry, Stockman and Tozzi had prepared a detailed analysis of the EPA's regulations and plans for how to go about scaling them back.[33] Such cuts required careful management. As Stockman had put it in an earlier memo urging Reagan to prioritize the EPA appointments, the agency was "filled with career staff who are hostile to the President's philosophy." Without a strong set of Reagan appointees on the ground, the EPA's staff would start to work against the White House.[34] Instead, Reagan lagged in his appointments and did not invest his political capital in speedy confirmations; top positions at the EPA remained open for over a year and one job went unfilled until 1983. The people Reagan did appoint were selected for their political loyalties or their ties to industry rather than their experience with the offices they were supposed to manage.[35]

Meanwhile, the EPA's acting administrator Walt Barber followed Stockman's direction and asked for a significant reduction in funding in the EPA's first budget request. The EPA's responsibilities had dramatically increased with the creation of the Superfund program at the end of the Carter administration and the continuing work of implementing standards for toxic substances. But instead of seeking a bump in funding to cover these new duties, the EPA asked for a 12 percent reduction in the agency's budget with an attendant reduction in force (layoffs) among the career staff.[36]

Facing what was already an acute leadership challenge in implementing a major budget and staffing cut, Gorsuch and her top deputies ensured their unpopularity with an imperious management style. Ensconced on the top floor of the EPA's headquarters, Gorsuch's team largely ignored the expertise of

Figure 5.1 Reagan with Anne Gorsuch in March 1971, as her nomination as EPA administrator made its way through the Senate. Ronald Reagan Presidential Library and Museum.

the EPA's staff as they set about enacting Reagan's policies. Career employees were rarely invited to advise the administrator on her agenda, which was just as well since at least one staffer ended his briefing only to be told that he was fired and that his office had been locked while he was upstairs.[37] Rumors circulated of a color-coded hit list of everyone Gorsuch wanted to get rid of, and people told horror stories of longtime employees who had been transferred across the country or made to work in a broom closet because of their ties to the Carter administration.[38] The EPA's regional administrators reported being told that every enforcement case referred to headquarters would be a "black mark" against them. A sweeping reorganization of the enforcement team carried out in the name of efficiency seemed instead to leave the agency less able to fulfill its duties. And abrupt reversals of decisions throughout the agency left managers increasingly unwilling to provide guidance on policy they did not understand.[39] Demoralized by their inability to do what they understood to be their jobs and the shocks happening round them, a growing number of the EPA's career staff began to quit.

In those early months, the EPA's former policy head Bill Drayton increasingly found himself serving as a sounding board for current and recently departed employees who were alarmed by what was happening to the agency. As he heard their stories, Drayton grew more and more frustrated by the vindictive treatment of career staff and the steep cuts to the EPA's capacity at a time when the agency's responsibilities were multiplying. Reporters covering the EPA soon realized that they could turn to Drayton for insight into what was happening. As Drayton himself learned more, he began to realize that the EPA was in real danger.[40]

Meanwhile, the Reagan administration proposed to overhaul the Clean Air Act. Funding for implementation and enforcement was due to expire in September 1981, requiring Congress to pass legislation to reauthorize the law. With widespread concerns among Republican as well as some Democratic legislators about the economic effects of many of the mandates in the existing act, Reagan's advisors saw an opportunity to weaken the statute on which the nation's entire air pollution control regime was based. In March, the National Commission on Air Quality, which had been created by the Clean Air Act Amendments of 1977, issued a long-awaited report that supported changes to the law. The report concluded that while the health-based national air quality standards were sound, compliance deadlines as well as automobile pollution controls should be relaxed and the Prevention of Significant Deterioration program (PSD), which mandated that areas with clean air protect that quality, should be eliminated.[41] For the steel and automobile industries in particular, loosening the compliance schedule of the Clean Air Act was an urgent priority.[42] Representatives of the larger business community, including the Business Roundtable and the National Association of Manufacturers, indicated their hope for even more sweeping reforms—including the creation of an independent scientific body to evaluate the air quality standards that the EPA had developed, a simplification of the permitting process, and looser guidelines on pollution control technologies.[43] Nonetheless, with Democrats in control of the House and important Senate committees chaired by longtime Republican supporters of the Clean Air Act, the road ahead was steep.

Over the course of the spring, the Reagan administration formulated an ambitious set of goals for the amendments. The PSD would be eliminated, authority over inspection and maintenance programs and implementation plans would devolve to the states, the permitting of new sources of air pollution would be eased, and air and water pollution control would be coordinated. Perhaps most important, the air quality standards and other critical components would be reevaluated from the "realization and recognition that economic and energy development must enter the calculus of environ-mental improvement," a reframing that would be in large part accomplished by injecting cost/benefit analysis, risk assessment, and cost-effectiveness considerations into "all regulatory actions."[44] OMB staff and other economic advisors had long bemoaned the Clean Air Act's prohibition against consid-ering economic consequences in setting the national air quality standards. Acknowledging the inevitable backlash to introducing economic consider-ations into an area from which they had been expressly prohibited, the OMB nevertheless urged Reagan to try.[45] As OMB economist Art Fraas argued, without a legislated cost/benefit mandate, Reagan would be stuck like his predecessors trying to work in economic considerations during regula-tory review.[46] In June 1981, the Supreme Court found that administrative agencies could issue rules even if the costs outweighed the benefits, invali-dating EO 12291's cost/benefit test and thus amplifying the importance of Reagan's efforts to create a statutory basis.[47] During the spring of 1981 and into the summer, the Clean Air Act Working Group—a new outfit of Reagan advisors and business representatives led by Administrator Gorsuch and Secretary of the Interior James Watt—laid out a plan for the amendments.[48] Leaked in June, the amendments were met with immediate and widespread public disapproval. A public opinion survey in July found that 86 percent of respondents opposed easing the requirements of the Clean Air Act.[49] In late July, Reagan announced that he would send a set of objectives to Congress in lieu of a full bill, thus insulating the president from the potential polit-ical consequences of sponsoring what increasingly looked to be unpopular legislation.[50]

By this point, Drayton was convinced that the Reagan administration was trying to destroy the agency. Over the course of the spring, he had grown increasingly alarmed as he learned that the budget cuts that Reagan had pro-posed were only the first step in a wider plan to severely disrupt the agency's operations. Today, Drayton still is not sure exactly where or when this plan was formulated, but he identifies OMB director David Stockman as one of its principal architects. Drayton had worked closely with the OMB and some of his contacts there confided in him that Gorsuch intended to ask for not just one cut in the agency's budget, but five. Carried out over a period of eighteen months, these cuts would amount to a full 50 percent reduction in the agency's budget but spread out in smaller increments so as to minimize awareness and outcry. In addition, Stockman and other Reagan advisors had carefully planned the related staffing reductions to maximize turnover at the agency. As part of the federal service, the EPA's career staff were governed by a fixed set of rules concerning promotions and other personnel changes. By letting employees go in just the right places, Stockman could trigger a vast reshuffling of the EPA's bureaucracy. According to Drayton, of the 4,500 employees in the Headquarters office, only 200–300 would be in their original positions when Stockman's Reduction in Force was complete. Combined with the skyrocketing attrition rates, the personnel changes and the budget cuts would effectively sap the life from the EPA while leaving a husk in place to deflect any questions.[51]

Working with a group of equally alarmed volunteers over the summer of 1981, Drayton built an organization titled Save EPA. The strategy was simple: cultivate relationships with sympathetic EPA employees, collect internal documents detailing Reagan's plans, verify and collate the information they shared, package it in an easy to understand form, and share it with allies in the press, Congress, and environmental organizations who could get the word out about what was happening at the EPA. With a series of small grants from friends in the environmental community, Save EPA operated out of a donated suite of offices, drawing on the subject matter expertise and professional networks of a core group of nine volunteers, who included Doug Costle. The organization's small budget went to secretarial services, printing reports, and photocopying—that last budget item growing larger and larger as more and more EPA employees and other policymakers heard about the group and reached out to leak memos and other documents that detailed the plans of Gorsuch and Reagan.[52] Caroline Isber, who had been dismissed from the Council on Environmental Quality as part of Reagan's dismantling of that advisory group, was one of Save EPA's first members, where she quickly put her knowledge of public affairs and extensive contacts on the Hill to work. As Isber would later recount, one of her biggest tasks was simply coordinating her meetings with Save EPA's burgeoning ranks of sources to protect the confidentiality of her many informants.[53]

Attracting interest in the EPA's plight was more difficult. As Drayton described it, few environmental organizations were focused on the EPA's internal capacity, and political reporters also tended not to latch onto the relatively intricate budget and staffing changes he was describing. Members of Congress, meanwhile, were initially reluctant to publicly challenge Reagan in the wake of his landslide victory, though a young representative from Tennessee named Al Gore did make a symbolic move to restore $10 million to the EPA's enforcement budget.[54]

But by the fall of 1981, Save EPA's critique was gaining traction. Save EPA's first reports were little more than sheets of figures and facts, cut and pasted from leaked budgets. Still, they revealed a startling image of the dangers that the EPA faced. Drayton and other volunteers used the data to help journalists understand the threat, slowly convincing Philip Shabecoff of the *New York Times* and other members of the press to start paying attention. In September and October, newspapers across the country began reporting on the EPA budget cuts, with the help of leaked documents and colorful quotes from Drayton and Costle. Leaked EPA database printouts revealed that the EPA had effectively stopped asking the Department of Justice to prosecute violators.[55] Leaked budget documents showed that Gorsuch had asked for a 28 percent cut in funding and a reduction in force of 30 percent and suggested that Stockman was pushing even further—a situation that Save EPA's Costle characterized as "a wrecking crew at work" and Drayton described as a "radical bomb-in-the-basement budget."[56] Picking up on a moniker that was by then well-known at the EPA, *Newsweek* ran a story in October on "The 'Ice Queen' at EPA."[57] Worry over disruptive budgetary cuts and drastic policy changes penetrated the boardroom, with the chemical industry weighing in with an October 1981 editorial in a trade publication on the necessity of predictable regulations for business planning.[58] Meanwhile, Gorsuch was growing frustrated with serving as the scapegoat for the OMB's budget cuts, warning Stockman and then the president in a November letter of severe political repercussions if they continued. After a contentious back and forth, the OMB and Gorsuch settled on a compromise. The final budget, while not quite as severe as Stockman had sought, nonetheless reduced the EPA's funding and staff by nearly 30 percent while leaving Stockman increasingly at odds with Gorsuch, who he believed had betrayed her promise to implement his vision.[59]

Save EPA was also drawing a growing audience among Democratic and Republican lawmakers, increasing scrutiny of Gorsuch's management and frustrating her attempts to dismiss Save EPA as merely a partisan ploy. Senator Robert Stafford, Republican from Vermont, was one of the first members of Congress to turn his attention to the agency.[60] Another Republican, Dan Lufkin, who had chaired Reagan's environmental transition team, wrote a stinging open letter to the president in October denouncing Reagan's "extreme" and "bizarre" appointments of environmental officials like Watt and Gorsuch, whose conduct in office had upended the environmental ethic that Reagan had expressed as a candidate. Lufkin also questioned Reagan's proposed amendments to the Clean Air Act, which he described as throwing the baby out with the bathwater rather than trying to fix a fundamentally sound and popular statute.[61] John Dingell, chairman of the Subcommittee on Oversight and Investigations of the House Committee on Energy and Commerce, held hearings on the EPA's enforcement program in fall 1981. In October, Drayton also appeared before the House Subcommittee on Environment, Energy, and Natural Resources to convey concerns that were a growing national issue.[62]

Growing controversy at the EPA served as the backdrop for the continued fight over Reagan's proposal to amend the Clean Air Act. Environmental organizations, whose membership had surged as they increasingly positioned themselves as national advocates for strong environmental protection in Washington, joined together in the Clean Air Coalition against Reagan's proposed amendments.[63] In the fall of 1981, these opponents doubled down on the unpopularity of the legislation. Louis Harris, the pollster who had found a whopping 86 percent of Americans were opposed to weakening the act, condemned the proposed amendments before Henry Waxman's environment subcommittee in the House of Representatives. "You mess around with the clean air and clean water acts and you're in the deepest trouble in the 1982 elections," Harris declared."[64] Save EPA's Doug Costle sent Harris's poll and testimony around to legislators and pundits as evidence that Reagan's proposals should be rejected.[65] Businesses did not cede the question of public support without a fight. In December 1981, the Chamber of Commerce announced that its own poll found most Americans did in fact support amendments to the act.[66] Along with the poll, representatives of the Chamber of Commerce also sent Reagan's advisors a survey they had conducted of key players—including the National Governors Association, the National League of Cities, and the professional association that represented local and state environmental regulators across the country—that again reported that the Reagan administration would have wide support for its proposed amendments.[67] Meanwhile, a bill approximating Reagan's ambitions was eventually introduced in the House in December 1981 by North Carolina Republican James Broyhill and Michigan Democrat John Dingell, who, despite his concerns about cuts to the EPA, had long served as a key champion of the beleaguered automobile industry, which, he argued, needed relief from impossible mandates.

Meanwhile, worse and worse news was coming out of the EPA. EPA employees increasingly found they were being blocked from doing what

they understood to be their jobs. This was especially acute in the enforcement realm. In 1981, the number of civil enforcement actions forwarded
to the EPA's headquarters from the regional offices declined by 79 percent
compared to Carter's final year, while the EPA's civil referrals to the Justice
Department fell 69 percent.[68] As career enforcement employees and others
at the EPA recognized, by not going after the most egregious offenders,
Gorsuch was encouraging other businesses that might have followed the
law in the past to also cheat, since they would be at a competitive disadvantage if they continued complying while their competitors did not. A decline
of as little as 2 percent in compliance rates would double the enforcement
workload and could have spiraling effects, as the EPA's resource-strapped
enforcement attorneys failed to keep up with a steadily growing chunk of
noncompliant businesses. No wonder that by the end of Reagan's first year in
office, the EPA's monthly attrition was at nearly 3 percent—three times what
it had been under Carter.[69]

As Congress recessed for the winter holidays, Save EPA prepared a media
campaign to catapult the EPA to the center of the political conversation in
the new year. In a letter to Al Gore and other Democrats, Drayton wrote
that Reagan's "extraordinary combination of ideological blindness, special
ineptness, special interest greed, and ignorance" offered a political gift to
Democrats if they could take advantage of the president's folly.[70] Timed to co-
incide with the January period in which congressional committees set their
hearing schedules for the following session, Save EPA's blitz included newspaper articles, editorials, nightly news stories, and the macabre *Doonesbury*
narrative of the demoralized EPA attorney contemplating suicide. The following week, the *Washington Post* ran an op-ed from Russell Train. Entitled
"The Destruction of EPA," Train's piece was sharply critical of Gorsuch and
Reagan's attacks on the EPA. "It is hard to imagine any business manager un-
dertaking such a personnel policy unless its purpose was to destroy the enterprise," Train declared.[71] The op-ed came at considerable personal cost for
Train, who was reportedly under consideration for a future post as secretary of the interior, but it opened up new space for Republicans to speak out
against the cuts. Feeling the pressure, the Republican National Committee
was circulating defensive talking points on Gorsuch's and Reagan's environmental policies by February.[72]

But Save EPA had seized control of the narrative, and, together with critics
in Congress, the press, and the environmental community, it continued to
pummel Gorsuch and the Reagan administration. In February, Save EPA

and the National Wildlife Foundation published an alternative EPA budget, which juxtaposed the funds requested by Gorsuch against "EPA's real program needs." With clean graphs and reams of data, the report was a powerful tool for reporters and lawmakers, who could use it to question Gorsuch and the Reagan administration on every line of their proposed cuts.[73] In March, the ten most powerful environmental advocacy organizations published a sweeping critique entitled *Indictment: The Case against the Reagan Environmental Record.*[74] Staff at Gorsuch's EPA scrambled to rebut the many accusations, but the charges kept coming.[75] That same month, Dingell's committee opened widely publicized hearings in the House that were sharply critical of Gorsuch's management of the enforcement program.[76] If Stockman had hoped to hobble the EPA before anyone realized what was happening, Save EPA had ensured that Reagan would have to own up to his attempts to dismantle the EPA.

Convinced that the Clean Air Act might still be amended, industry mobilized on behalf of HR 5252. The National Environmental Development Association, which represented many of the nation's largest industrial conglomerates and was chaired by former EPA official John Quarles, lobbied hard to convince Washington's policymakers of the bill's merits.[77] General Motors and other business representatives from Reagan's Clean Air Act Working Group launched an educational campaign in an attempt to spur grassroots support for the bill among organized labor.[78] But union representatives largely rebuked that effort, rejecting the amendments as a threat to vital protections in exchange for false promise of jobs.[79]

Before HR 5252 could make it to the House floor, the bill first had to clear Representative Henry Waxman's Subcommittee on Environment, Energy, and Natural Resources. Opening the first hearing in February 1982, Waxman made it clear that HR 5252 would face a tough challenge. Waxman derided the bill for foregoing intelligent tweaks in favor of "a radical crusade to rewrite and weaken this law that has the broad support of the American people." Lamenting the proposed relaxation of automobile standards, Waxman noted that the adjustment would make it impossible for many cities to meet the national air quality standards while netting only the meager "savings of $40 to $100 per car." Questioning the larger value of that small reduction in price, Waxman continued, "I cannot believe that this pittance would reopen the closed assembly lines or put American workers back to work."[80] With the help of a variety of environmental advocates, Waxman and his allies on the House subcommittee on the environment maneuvered to keep HR 5252 in

committee hearings until they had transformed the bill into un-passable legislation. Over the course of the spring and summer of 1982, Waxman took a
bill that eased regulations for nearly every industry and turned it into a bill
that granted relief to only some industries while imposing tougher standards
on others and the industry coalition fractured.[81]

To the consternation of business interests, environmental advocates
largely controlled the public narrative around the Clean Air Act, portraying
almost any effort to amend the act as countenancing a return to dirty, dangerous air.[82] Despite the protests of supporters of HR 5252, that narrative
prevailed.[83] By August, Waxman was able to pass a motion to suspend consideration of HR 5252, effectively killing Reagan's best chances of securing
his desired amendments.[84] In a last ditch effort, Gorsuch proposed enforcing drastic sanctions provided for in the existing Clean Air Act to force
legislators back to the drawing board. Under the 1977 amendments, areas
that had not met the air quality standards by the end of 1982 could face bans
on the construction of new sources of emissions as well as a suspension of
federal highway and sewer funding. William Ruckelshaus had once pulled
off a similar trick to avoid implementing transportation controls. But by the
fall of 1982, Reagan advisors were no longer certain that Congress would respond to the threat of sanctions by weakening the Clean Air Act. Congress
might instead call the administration's bluff, a November memo warned, and
so Gorsuch's proposal was rejected.[85]

Deregulation, Not Reform

As he faced mounting opposition to his cuts at the EPA, Reagan was also
confronted by growing disappointment among regulatory reformer
proponents who had hoped the president would lead a shift toward market-
oriented policies. For these reformers, Reagan's election back in 1980 seemed
to offer an opportunity to expand on the work of the Carter administration.
Bill Drayton and other key champions of market-oriented policies would
be replaced by new political appointees, but Reagan, as a candidate, had repeatedly stressed the need for a regulatory overhaul to put pollution control
back in the hands of corporate managers and his environmental policy transition team had identified the bubble and other fledging Carter policies as
the logical starting point for that transfer of power.[86] Despite Carter's loss
in the election, Drayton and other Carter officials continued to promote the

bubble and other reforms. In November 1980, the EPA held a conference on regulatory innovation to improve what was called the Controlled Trading Program, which encompassed both internal shuffling of emissions under a bubble and the trading of emission rights to other firms.[87] In December 1980, Administrator Costle had convened a roundtable of key agency officials with the goal of "easing restrictions in the bubble policy."[88] On his way out of office in January 1981, Costle expanded one form of bubbling to nonattainment areas (where the policy was most appealing) and promised that a consolidated controlled trading policy would be released within weeks.[89]

Even more promising for reformers, several prominent firms had created bubbles by the time Reagan took office. An article in *Chemical Week* in January 1981 described DuPont's newly approved bubble to control volatile organic compounds (VOCs) at its Chambers Works plant in New Jersey. Prior to the bubble, DuPont had been required to install control equipment on every one of the 205 sources of VOCs at Chambers Works—a system that yielded an 85 percent reduction in smog-causing VOCs but at considerable cost. Using the bubble policy, DuPont installed advanced control technology far surpassing the EPA's standards on the five largest emission sources, leaving the other 200 uncontrolled, managing in the process to reduce overall VOCs emissions by 99.9 percent while saving $1 million a month in compliance costs. As *Chemical Week* reported, those savings quickly attracted the attention of other chemical manufacturers.[90] Cheering on such successes as he left the EPA, Drayton published an article in the *Harvard Business Review* urging business managers to come forward with other proposals, which he insisted would have "the new administration's strong support."[91]

Yet the bubble and other reforms faced concerted resistance from many within the agency, who were skeptical that such policies would continue the environmental progress achieved by the proscriptive mandates and uniform standards that they proposed to replace. Before he departed with the other Carter officials, Air Office head Dave Hawkins had expressed his skepticism of the bubble with a long set of qualifying conditions on its use.[92] Outside the agency, the Natural Resource Defense Council's David Doniger spoke for other environmental advocates when he registered his protest against the continued liberalization.[93] Overcoming this continued resistance would require strong support from the White House for the careful work that Drayton and other reformers had laid out.

When Reagan arrived at the White House, Mike Levin and his Regulatory Reform Staff in the EPA's Policy Office were in the midst of an ambitious campaign to expand the agency's fledgling emissions trading program into a new regulatory paradigm in which firms across the country could buy and sell the right to emit pollutants like any other aspect of their business. If an electric utility wanted to upgrade its transmission infrastructure but was being forced instead to invest its capital to meet an impending pollution control deadline, the utility could turn to an offsets market to buy the temporary right to emit excess pollutants while it invested in transmission.

The key was an active market with many offsets offered for sale. Without a market, buyers faced the formidable task of cold calling neighboring firms to propose a novel and risky transaction. Would-be sellers would have to attract buyers for an untested, uncertain product. Under Carter, the EPA managed to create a legal basis for the trades, and a handful of intrepid firms had experimented with such policies. But the transactions typically required the active participation of local pollution control officials, who knew which firms could generate excess reductions and paired them with firms seeking to buy those emission rights. As an article in *Industry Week* in March 1980 noted, authorities often simply made the reductions themselves, as when the State of Pennsylvania switched to a new road paving material to reduce hydrocarbon emissions and create room under the state's emissions cap for a new Volkswagen assembly plant.[94] Individually, such arrangements were heralded as great successes. But Levin and other reform proponents recognized that a meaningful shift away from directly enforcing uniform standards would require much greater participation from industry and other private actors. If trading was to become commonplace, a market needed to be created.

Levin and the Regulatory Reform Staff saw banks and brokers as key components of a viable market, and they were busy coaxing both into existence when Reagan came into office. Less than a week after the new president had arrived, the EPA held its first Conference for Potential Brokers of Emission Reduction Credits in Washington. Intended to attract and educate entrepreneurs, the one-day conference covered the finer points of financing offsets, analyzing markets, and paying taxes on the handsome profits that brokers could be expected to reap.[95] Levin welcomed the participants by pointing to the auspicious timing of holding the conference on the "first Monday of a new administration committed to free enterprise, the market system, [and] getting government off the backs of the people." The EPA, Levin continued, was rolling out policies to make pollution control "quicker, simpler, cheaper," while simultaneously "making large profits for brokers too." Though Levin cautioned later in his remarks that an active market did not yet exist, he urged the audience to create one by getting out there and negotiating some trades.[96] If participants failed to take adequate notes at the conference, they could refer to *Brokering Emission Reduction Credits: A Handbook*, which Levin's Regulatory Reform Staff published that same month.[97] Cheering on those efforts, think tanks including the Heritage Foundation encouraged Reagan to lend his support.[98]

To the dismay of these advocates of market-oriented reform, Reagan and his OMB showed little interest in the bubble and other innovative ideas, much less in the substantive regulatory work required to turn those ideas into viable policies. This neglect began with Reagan's regulatory freeze, which failed to distinguish between the proscriptive directives that the EPA had long issued and the innovative, market-oriented policies that reformers at the agency had worked so hard to offer as alternatives. Levin and his regulatory reform staff at the EPA found this out the hard way in January 1981, when they began mailing *Smarter Regulation*, a primer on the bubble and other incentive alternatives developed by Drayton, to tens of thousands of business representatives and policymakers across the country. Before even 5 percent of the mailings had been sent, an abrupt hold came down from the White House. *Smarter Regulation* had run afoul of the blanket prohibition on new activities. Though the White House later released the mailing, the episode revealed a disturbing inability or unwillingness on the part of key Reagan advisors to distinguish reforms like the bubble from the EPA's older, proscriptive model.[99] Three months later, Levin was once again appealing to his superiors to make an exception to a printing freeze so that he could publish promotional reports on marketable emission rights.[100] In that first year, the Reagan administration tended to view regulation simply, as a menace to be fought wherever found. Roy Gamse, serving as the acting head of the EPA's Policy Office, briefed the OMB on a set of possible reforms that the EPA might pursue in lieu of the regulatory freeze, but was told that the administration was interested only in cuts.[101]

Gorsuch also showed little interest in the nascent reforms she had inherited. In her first month in office, staff from the American Enterprise Institute (AEI) met with her to present several opportunities where economic incentive alternatives could be implemented. To their surprise, AEI's representatives found Gorsuch to be ignorant of and totally disinterested in such reforms. As one participant recounted, Gorsuch made it clear that she was not interested in better regulation, but simply less regulation.[102] Ultimately, it took Gorsuch nearly fifteen months to issue the Interim Emissions Trading Policy Statement, and the EPA did not release the final version until 1986.[103]

Neglect at the top repeatedly hamstrung the work of reform proponents within the agency. Recognizing that state authorities might create markets if they could assemble large amounts of offsets, Levin and the Regulatory Reform Staff set out to build local banks where firms could deposit credits for their excess emission reductions, which other businesses could purchase to expand their own emissions. In 1981, only Louisville, San Francisco, and the Puget Sound had established banks, though Levin noted that twenty other areas were in the process of adopting banking regulations. Toward that end, the Regulatory Reform Staff distributed model banking rules and other technical guides to control authorities across the country.[104] In at least one case, Levin's office offered to provide financial assistance to a local authority to set up a banking system in New Brunswick, New Jersey.[105] Here as elsewhere, Gorsuch's disregard for the work needed to create such a banking system undercut Levin and his staff. The EPA proposed a unified set of banking regulations in 1981 but did not finalize them until 1986. Local regulators who had started down the road of creating a bank were left hanging as to whether their particular banking systems would meet the long-delayed federal rules. Witnessing this, regulators in other areas shied away from developing banks. And the businesses that banks needed to function steered clear of an uncertain and risky enterprise.[106]

Nonetheless, under Levin's direction, the EPA's regulatory reform staff slowly expanded the use of the bubble and other market-oriented policies. The EPA's Policy Office produced guides marketing the bubble to business representatives and regulators, including one whose cover drawing depicted smokestacks emitting dollar signs directly into a corporate bank vault.[107] In winter 1981 and spring 1982, Levin organized a series of regulatory reform conferences across the country, each co-sponsored by the EPA and a corporate leader in pollution control such as 3M or Armco.[108] Along with summaries of the great savings to be had, Levin sent business representatives home with personal letters of praise from the EPA in the hope of raising the stature of environmental compliance managers within their companies.[109] But without support from the EPA's senior officials, innovations like the bubble languished in uncertainty.

Reagan's failure to support the substantive work required of regulatory reform was met with growing frustration among the Beltway policymakers who had aligned behind market-oriented reforms during the Carter administration. At a dinner hosted by the American Enterprise Institute in December 1981, Brookings Institution economist Robert Crandall criticized the administration for not supporting marketable emission permits and for its failure to amend the Clean Air Act, giving voice to a growing bipartisan complaint when he lamented that Reagan had managed "almost no accomplishments" in regulatory reform.[110] Throughout the following spring, criticism of Reagan's disinterest in new policies like the bubble continued to mount.[111] The EPA did finally issue its interim Emissions Trading Policy Statement in the *Federal Register* in April 1982—nearly a year and a half after the previous administration had promised.[112] That did little to quiet the critics who believed that Reagan and his appointees had little interest in substantive reform.

For bipartisan supporters of the bubble and the alternative model it represented, Reagan's blunt deregulatory ambitions posed a threat not just to specific initiatives but to market-oriented reform as a new approach to government oversight and enforcement. Proponents of reform had long faced charges from environmental and public health advocates that innovations like the bubble were merely a cloak for deregulation, and Reagan threatened to validate those accusations. In June 1982, the Council for a Competitive Economy organized a dinner with the Brookings Institution, the Heritage Foundation, and other think tanks, along with representatives of major regulated industries including the American Petroleum Institute, in an attempt to demonstrate to Reagan's administration the merits of market approaches to enforcing environmental standards. The dinner invitation left no doubt about the perceived danger of Reagan's current approach, warning that "the free market perspective has been discredited even though it has not been tried."[113]

By the fall of 1982, this chorus of criticism finally prompted the Reagan administration to change course. In October, Reagan's top advisors gathered for the first meeting of the Working Group on Regulatory Reform. As a memo for a later meeting explained the group's rationale, Reagan's regulatory relief program had lost momentum, taking on a "stop-gap character" because "the Administration had failed to develop and articulate a unified approach to regulation."[114] Developing that unified approach evidently required educating many of Reagan's advisors on the basics of economic incentive alternatives, as an earlier memo circulated a reading list to bring members of the working group up to speed.[115] Having at last expressed an interest in substantive regulatory reforms, Reagan could fall back on the foundation laid by

Carter as well as the ongoing work of the EPA's regulatory reform staff. In the fall of 1982, Levin took advantage of the Reagan administration's changing attitudes to create the Emissions Trading Standing Committee to coordinate the development of economic incentive approaches, dispense advice to the EPA's regional offices, and push the EPA's air office to incorporate trading schemes into the "main stream" air pollution control program.[116] After a long period of disinterest, the free-market president was finally supporting the legwork needed to create viable alternatives to proscriptive regulations.

Yet Reagan's earlier neglect continued to present obstacles. Though Gorsuch was convinced by Levin and others to support reforms like emissions trading, her earlier restrictions on the agency's work delayed the EPA from developing the theoretical and empirical support needed to protect such rule changes from environmentalists' legal challenges. In August 1982, following a suit brought by the NRDC, the DC Circuit Court of Appeals rejected the EPA's expansion of the bubble policy to the many industrialized and polluted areas of the country that did not have approved plans toward compliance. The court explained in its ruling that Gorsuch's EPA had changed critical definitions in the rule without producing a single study or other piece of supporting evidence.[117] Policy advisor DeMuth angrily denounced the DC Circuit's "liberal Democratic judges" in a letter to Vice President Bush and Stockman.[118] But in reality, Reagan had only himself to blame for appointing EPA officials focused on deregulation at all costs. Over the following year, environmental advocates including the NRDC, the Environmental Defense Fund, and Citizens for a Better Environment continued to take advantage of the EPA's poor planning, limiting the bubble's expansion through administrative hearings and public complaints that challenged the bubble's expansion across the country.[119]

Proponents of regulatory reform also lamented the missed opportunities in Reagan's regulatory review program, built as it was around the singular goal of reducing regulation. These complaints had begun early. In 1981, Antonin Scalia, editor of the American Enterprise Institute's *Regulation* magazine, described Reagan's EO 12291 and the resulting review process as "basically meaningless," given that the EPA already used cost/benefit analysis to develop its rules and Reagan lacked the legal authority to force the EPA to evaluate and redirect its underlying regulatory mandates on a cost/benefit basis.[120] Two years later, at a conference on EO 12291 at the University of North Carolina, the assessments were even worse. The uncertainty of environmental risks and the difficulty of translating those risks into monetary assessments left the OMB to evaluate rules on the basis of shaky and often controversial information. Moreover, the EPA still lacked the authority to reprioritize its underlying programs on a cost/benefit basis and so could not refocus its attention on the pollution problems that promised more bang for its buck. Finally, while more and more environmental advocates had come to accept economic analysis as a key criterion in rulemaking, EO 12291 risked discrediting the legitimacy of cost/benefit analysis by exempting new deregulatory initiatives from the cost/benefit test. If the ultimate goal was to devise regulatory policy that maximized benefits and minimized costs, deregulatory proposals should be subject to the same cost/benefit test as new regulations. Simply giving deregulation a pass threatened to undercut the supposed neutrality and thus the political utility of the cost/benefit approach.[121]

Taking Down the Lightning Rods

In the fall of 1982, the growing controversies over Gorsuch's management came to a head in the Superfund program. The Comprehensive Environmental Response, Compensation, and Liability Act had been signed into law at the very end of the Carter presidency, creating a new set of enforcement tools and a pool of money to clean up illegally dumped waste. Trying to avoid confrontation with industry as well as the creation of a new major federal spending program, Gorsuch tried to avoid both prosecutions and major expenditures under the law. In her first year, the number of toxic substances enforcement cases referred to the Department of Justice for prosecution decreased by over 90 percent from the level during the Carter administration.[122] In addition, Gorsuch made it difficult for states to tap into the $1.6 billion fund created by Congress to assist with cleanup by implementing new policies that required states to front a portion of the funds and restricting Superfund designation to only those sites in which a public health emergency could be proven to be occurring at that very moment.

The attention that Save EPA had brought to the EPA made Superfund an increasing liability for Gorsuch. In June 1982, Representative John Dingell's Subcommittee on Investigations and Oversight sent the EPA a formal request for agency records related to the enforcement of the Superfund program. In a related investigation, members of the House Subcommittee on Investigations and Oversight traveled to an EPA regional office in September 1982 to view enforcement records in person. To their surprise, EPA staff rebuffed their demands, claiming that Reagan enjoyed executive privilege over the records, even though they had been created at the EPA without any input from the White House. Reagan's advisors had decided to use the Superfund records as a chance to test an expansive interpretation of executive power and told Gorsuch to withhold the records, spurning her repeated requests to allow her to comply with the congressional request. Furious, Dingell subpoenaed Gorsuch and ordered her to appear before Congress in early December with the documents. Gorsuch showed up but refused to release the records, citing Reagan's instructions to withhold them. In December, Dingell's committee and then the full House of Representatives voted to hold Gorsuch in contempt of Congress, the first time a Cabinet-level official had been so charged. This was followed by the even more remarkable development of the Department of Justice filing suit to prevent the enforcement of the congressional subpoena.[123]

As congressional and media attention intensified, so too did controversy at the EPA. Accusations swirled that Gorsuch and her deputies had used Superfund monies to interfere in the political campaigns of state officials.[124] Those charges were soon joined by claims that Rita Lavelle, the EPA's top toxic waste official, had failed to recuse herself from a series of Superfund negotiations in California that involved her former employer.[125] Gorsuch's often dismissive approach to the EPA's mandates also created problems. In December 1982, news leaked that Gorsuch had told representatives of the Thriftway gasoline company that they did not need to worry about complying with existing regulations under the Clean Air Act's lead standard because the Reagan administration would soon be easing those requirements.[126] By the beginning of 1983, the EPA seemed to be overrun with scandals.

Worried about a dip in polling, with the president's approval rating sinking as low as 35 percent in early 1983, the Reagan administration moved to anesthetize the environmental issue.[127] After Rita Lavelle refused to resign, Reagan fired her in February.[128] The scandal only worsened with new revelations that Lavelle's office had frantically shredded documents before her firing, followed by Lavelle's accusations in front of Congress that senior officials within the Reagan administration also had ties to the firms involved in the California Superfund site, offering an explanation for Reagan's unusual claim of executive privilege.[129] February also brought new embarrassing information detailing punitive transfers and firings of career staff in the EPA's General Counsel's Office, the head of which was soon forced to resign.[130] Making matters worse, the Second Circuit Court of Appeals rejected the Department of Justice's attempt to block congressional access to the Superfund records.[131] Still charged with contempt of Congress, Gorsuch pleaded with Reagan officials to release the records. Reagan's advisors responded by telling Gorsuch that because she was under investigation by the Department of Justice, they could no longer defend her in court. On March 9, 1983, Gorsuch resigned.[132] Later that day, the White House and Congress reached an agreement to release the Superfund documents.[133]

Eager to put the EPA's controversies behind him, Reagan convinced the agency's first head, William Ruckelshaus, to leave a senior position at the Weyerhaeuser Corporation and return as administrator. Reagan promised Ruckelshaus a free hand in directing the agency, as well as the ability to choose his own deputies. From the beginning, Ruckelshaus worked to reverse all the complaints about management from the Gorsuch years, including the welcoming of congressional and media probes. As the EPA's enforcement, budget, and staffing slowly began to increase, Save EPA ceased its public attacks of the agency's management, but it continued to watch over the Reagan administration.[134] "We're going back to work," Ruckelshaus told the EPA's staff on his return, and Save EPA was there to make sure they did so.[135]

By the end of 1983, the most visible signs of Reagan's deregulatory environmental agenda were gone. Vice President Bush's Task Force on Regulatory Relief disbanded.[136] Jim Tozzi, the EPA's longtime antagonist at the OMB, retired.[137] In October, beset by his own controversies, James Watt resigned as secretary of the interior.[138] Making the case for change, a Republican pollster told a reporter, "I used to think that Watt was a lightning rod who deflected animus away from the President. But now I think if the lightning rod goes away, the environmentalists won't be able to make as much of an issue out of it."[139] After a highly publicized trial, Rita Lavelle was sentenced to six months in prison in December for lying to Congress about her conflicts of interest in the Superfund site. Though Lavelle was the only Reagan official to be held criminally responsible for her conduct, nineteen other EPA officials followed Gorsuch in resigning amid congressional investigations.[140]

* * *

At the beginning of the Reagan administration, acting administrator Walt Barber met with the Task Force on Regulatory Relief to give his recommendations for reducing the costs associated with the EPA's regulations. With the help of the EPA's Policy Office, Barber had put together an extensive list of suggestions, many of which built on the market-oriented reforms begun during the Carter administration. Following up on the meeting, Barber told the OMB's Jim Miller that he agreed that Reagan's EPA should "move promptly" to "mark the clear change in direction which the public expects after the election." But it was essential, Barber told the White House, that any changes be seen as part of a "well-planned, long-term environmental policy."[141] Instead, Reagan allowed Stockman and business executives such as Joseph Coors to lead a thinly disguised attack on the regulatory state, including through the installation of top environmental officials who showed little interest in careful reform and instead seemed intent on demolishing the agencies they had been appointed to run. While appealing to Sagebrush politics may have been good campaign strategy, putting contemptuous cowboys in charge of environmental protection proved to be a miscalculation. Confronted with political appointees who seemed indifferent or hostile to the EPA's responsibilities, the EPA's career staff revolted.

The campaign to Save EPA revealed the power of the agency's career staff to define and defend what they understood to be the EPA's responsibilities. Barber and other EPA employees were prepared to make changes to reflect the new administration's priorities, but only up to a point. Pressed to say what that point was, most would probably point to the law: statutory requirements could not be ignored simply because Gorsuch and Reagan did not want to follow them. But Gorsuch and Reagan also challenged a deeper understanding of the agency's mission. Career staff leaked EPA documents and environmental advocates, lawmakers, and much of the public rallied around the EPA because they supported a strong agency, one that had made great strides in improving the nation's environmental quality and needed to retain its capacity as it took on a new set of problems. In this respect, Gorsuch's contemptuous attitude toward the EPA turned out to be a something of a gift since it yielded damaging scandals and an easy narrative for the press and public to follow. Even Gorsuch herself seemed to yield to appeals to the EPA's mission, opening a fissure with the White House as she bucked Stockman's most radical cuts.

But the EPA's resilience too had its limits. The EPA's budget declined substantially during the early Reagan years. By the time Gorsuch left, the EPA's funding had been cut to what it had been in 1973, even though the agency's responsibilities had more than doubled since that time. Under Ruckelshaus and his successor, the budget was slowly restored, though it was not until 1990 that the EPA had as much spending power as it had had in 1980.[142] The drop-off in enforcement led to a sharp reduction in voluntary compliance, making the process of restoring the EPA's credibility costly and prolonged and raising new political liabilities as the agency was forced to come down hard on offenders as it had during its first years of operation.[143] A shift toward market-oriented compliance strategies was put on hold as Reagan missed an opportunity to take advantage of growing bipartisan support for regulatory reforms. Finally, the layoffs and mass waves of resignations took a severe toll on the agency's institutional capacity and memory. Almost 40 percent of the EPA's staff left in Reagan's first year alone.[144] The staff who left tended to be the ones with the strongest belief in the EPA's mission as well as those of the highest caliber—who could most easily find opportunities in the private sector, often for consulting firms where they soon represented business clients in their dealings with the agency. In the 1970s, the EPA had attracted remarkable talent. After Gorsuch, the agency never regained its full luster. Drayton, who arguably did more than anyone to save the EPA, does not believe the agency ever fully recovered.[145] Within the next five years, the EPA would be called on to dramatically expand its responsibilities again to address the problems of acid rain and then global warming. Whether the agency had the capacity to do so was an open question.

6

Markets for Bads

Cap-and-Trade and the New Environmentalism

In 1987, the American Enterprise Institute published an article on the state of emissions trading at the Environmental Protection Agency (EPA) in its quarterly journal *Regulation*. "The Market for Bads" acknowledged the seeming perversity of buying and selling the right to emit pollution but urged the EPA on in creating such markets. Existing programs such as the bubble policy, though inadequate in scope and underutilized in application, offered a tantalizing glimpse of the market-based governance system that might be.[1] The authors did not have to wait long. By the end of the decade, the EPA had developed cap-and-trade systems to solve two of the most high-profile environmental problems of the era: ozone depletion and acid rain. In the early 1990s, it seemed likely that a cap-and-trade approach would soon be deployed to address the greenhouse gases that were accumulating in the atmosphere. Markets for bads had moved from the margins to the mainstream of environmental policymaking. Each program worked differently, but they all shared a single assumption: by allowing polluters to decide how they controlled emissions and incentivizing them to make those cuts as deep as possible, market-based approaches could harness capitalism's profit-seeking to drive innovation and meet environmental goals at a lower cost than if policymakers told every firm how to cut emissions.

Several factors underlay the ascent of market-based approaches. Within the EPA, regulatory reformers led by Mike Levin had overcome the neglect of the early Reagan years to expand the bubble policy as part of a growing emissions trading program. These efforts gained a significant boost in 1984, when the Supreme Court affirmed a key idea underpinning the bubble and other reforms in the landmark *Chevron v. NRDC* decision, which granted the EPA and other regulatory agencies considerable autonomy to make policy where the underlying statute was unclear. Market-based approaches permeated other parts of the agency, including a new push to remove lead from

Valuing Clean Air. Charles Halvorson, Oxford University Press (2021). © Oxford University Press.
DOI: 10.1093/oso/9780197538845.003.0007

gasoline—one of the instances where regulations were strengthened during Anne Gorsuch's tenure.

William Ruckelshaus' return as administrator coincided with and helped to spur the rise of risk management. This new framework for governance held that environmental dangers could never be fully eliminated and that policymakers should instead focus on the biggest threats and the areas where their limited resources would go furthest. Continued under Ruckelshaus's successor, this risk management framing directed the EPA toward a new suite of problems, including acid rain. As with the phasing out of leaded gasoline, the application of market-based approaches to new problems tended to encounter less resistance than when regulators attempted to graft them onto issues that the EPA was already addressing through enforcement of uniform standards. Staff at the EPA helped to formulate a cap-and-trade model to finally address the problem of acid rain, which had worsened throughout the Reagan administration. Electric utilities would be required to reduce sulfur dioxide emissions below a certain threshold (the "cap"); but how they got there was their choice, with tradable emission allowances enabling utilities to direct pollution reduction to where it was most efficient and least expensive.

Cap-and-trade's promise to minimize compliance costs helped convince George H. W. Bush to throw his new administration's support behind acid rain intervention in the Clean Air Act Amendments of 1990. These promised savings also made cap-and-trade attractive to Congress, whose members were eager to avoid business complaints about the supposed economic damage of expanded regulation. In addition to reducing compliance costs in the aggregate, the cap-and-trade approach promised to minimize political struggles with the most difficult firms, since a business that did not have the capital on hand to invest in the necessary expenditures to reduce its own pollution could buy the continued right to pollute while it accumulated funds. As industry leaders recognized the cost savings of cap-and-trade over proscriptive standards, concerted opposition would disappear, and any laggards would have only themselves to blame.

Environmental advocates had long resisted the EPA's relinquishing any control over how businesses reduced their pollution, but here too market approaches began to catch on as a way out of stalemates over regulatory standards that had characterized much of the past two decades. The first organization to change course was the Environmental Defense Fund (EDF), whose new president Fred Krupp encouraged other advocates to join him in launching a third stage of environmentalism predicated on finding economic solutions for job losses or any dislocation that resulted from complying with federally mandated standards. In addition to helping to design the trading system that lay at the heart of the 1990 Amendments, Krupp and EDF helped to make cap-and-trade acceptable for environmental advocates in Congress, building a constituency among both Democratic and Republican lawmakers that was key to the passage of the legislation. Gradually, other environmental organizations came to endorse market-based approaches, including the Natural Resources Defense Council (NRDC), whose longtime strategist Dave Hawkins threw his critical support behind the 1990 amendments.

But as trading programs spread, they helped to spur the formation of a new wave of environmental activism that looked rather different from what Krupp had envisioned. What became known as the environmental justice movement fought back against the shift toward market-based policies, arguing that surrendering authority to industry over where and how to control pollution would hurt poor communities and communities of color, whose residents were already exposed to a disproportionate share of the risks and degradation of industrial society. In drawing attention to distributional inequities, the environmental justice movement pushed policymakers to refine and adjust cap-and-trade programs to eliminate loopholes and unintended consequences.

In raising the issue of power, environmental justice advocates pointed to a subtle but important shift in the flourish of market-based policies. For all the talk of revolutionary shifts, market-based programs in the 1990 amendments and elsewhere changed very little about environmental protection in practice. Lawmakers set goals in response to popular demand and charged the EPA with implementing and enforcing them. Companies had much more flexibility in how they met those goals, but policymakers still held the power and responsibility of determining the ultimate objectives. The old Coasian vision of assigning property rights to the underlying environmental resources and letting markets actually determine the allocation of value was reenergized in the 1990s as "free market environmentalism," but remained little more than a fantasy. What was changing was the underlying faith in the capacity of the EPA and the federal government. Market-based programs like the cap-and-trade approach to acid rain reflected a new consensus that private firms were inherently more efficient than public regulators in determining how pollution should be controlled. As time passed, the corresponding notion that the government was inherently inefficient in tackling problems would erode support for new expansions. Thus, new ideas about the capacity of the federal government would drive new questions about its responsibility and authority.

Unfinished Business

Economists tended to praise market-based models for their efficiency and cost savings. For regulators, as much of the appeal came from the prospect that a trading option might smooth the disruptions and industry complaints associated with the introduction of any capital-intensive program to meet standards for air quality. The EPA's first foray into markets for bads was an offset trading program in the 1970s that allowed businesses to effectively pay other businesses to reduce their emissions and thus make space for major industrial expansion in areas where the air quality was worse than the national standards.

In the early 1980s, a similar desire to minimize the economic disruption associated with ending production of leaded gasoline inspired the EPA to develop another market-based program. Leaded gasoline dated to the 1920s, when refiners and automobile manufacturers realized they could add lead to reduce the engine knock associated with low octane gasoline. From the beginning, researchers warned of the dangers of depositing a known poison into the air, but corporate obfuscation blocked public awareness of the risks until the 1960s. Around the same time, the introduction of new refining techniques allowed for the production of high-octane gasoline, which did not cause engine knocking. In 1974, the EPA mandated catalytic converters on all new cars, which removed harmful pollutants from exhaust, but which could not function with leaded gasoline, jump-starting the market for unleaded gasoline and raising the prospect of ending production of leaded gasoline.[2]

Under a court order resulting from a lawsuit by the NRDC, the EPA issued a National Ambient Air Quality Standard (NAAQS) for lead in 1978 and began a program to phase out the production of leaded gasoline. Recognizing that small refineries would have a harder time than larger companies with raising capital for the necessary upgrades to produce high-octane gasoline, the EPA designed the phasedown to be easier for smaller firms, which tended to be privately owned and politically powerful. Despite these efforts, many of these companies warned that they still could not meet EPA deadlines and would go out of business. When environmental and public health advocates blocked an attempt to ease the deadlines, the EPA faced the possibility that many small refineries would indeed close.[3] Meanwhile, an EPA study using cost/benefit analysis reported in 1983 that the cost of lead to society as measured in public health spending dwarfed the cost to manufacturers of removing it. The study concluded that the EPA should insist on an even steeper and faster phasedown. In a rare instance of regulatory fortitude, Administrator Gorsuch decided to accelerate the phasedown.[4]

Casting about for a means of quickly phasing out lead from gasoline without radically disrupting the refining industry, the EPA and White House staff decided to allow refineries to buy and sell emission credits that could be used to meet the reduction deadlines. Under this approach, a large refinery with capital on hand could reduce the lead content in its gasoline below what was required by the EPA and then sell those excess reductions as credits to a smaller refinery to use to continue producing gasoline that exceeded the EPA's standard while building up the capital to upgrade its own refining process.[5] Firms could also bank excess reductions for use or sale in the near future.

The phasedown proved to be a major success, reducing lead emissions by over half a million tons from 1979 to 1988, while the trading provisions saved over $200 million in compliance costs that would have resulted had every company been required to meet the uniform standards.[6] Different from other early emission trading programs, a robust market for lead credits quickly developed. Over half of the leaded gasoline produced in 1987 was manufactured by refineries that had bought lead credits to do so. An active market made lead credits easy to buy and sell, driving down transaction costs. The program did encounter the unexpected enforcement problem of the roughly 600 "alcohol blenders," who sprang up to buy and dilute supplies of leaded gasoline with alcohol and then sell the resulting credits to refineries.[7] Here and elsewhere throughout the phasedown, monitoring was made difficult by small operations that popped up and disappeared before the EPA could audit their operations.[8] But through trial and error, EPA staff figured out how to administer the trading process in such a way as to end the production of leaded gasoline while keeping compliance costs to a minimum and thus making the policy politically acceptable to the Reagan administration.[9]

The expansion of market-based approaches at the EPA was slow going. In the early 1980s, environmental advocates remained deeply skeptical about any shift away from enforcing uniform standards. One area that especially animated environmentalist opposition concerned "shutdown credits." If a firm closed a factory or production line, did it have a right to use or sell the attendant reduction in emissions? Business interests and reform proponents believed that firms should receive shutdown credits, while environmentalists and many regulators argued instead that any improvement in air quality that resulted from a shutdown should be preserved as a boon to public health. The two sides went back and forth, including a long fight in San Diego over the Merck Corporation's efforts to upgrade the power generators on a massive kelp processing operation that employed about 500 workers. At question was whether Merck could count the nitrogen oxide emissions from the old generators against the emissions of the new generators, a claim opposed by local California regulators but which Merck insisted was vital in keeping the kelp refining plant economically viable.[10] In a testament to the stakes involved, Merck's case was taken up by the Chemical Manufacturers Association, which eventually reached a settlement with the EPA after two years of litigation whereby firms could claim shutdown credits under certain stipulations.[11]

Allowing business to claim and sell emission rights for major pollutants like sulfur dioxide also raised the worrisome prospect of shifting emissions of less prevalent but no less dangerous toxic pollutants. A new set of environmental advocates coalescing around the framework of environmental justice complained that by encouraging such shifts, emissions trading could further concentrate environmental hazards in poor neighborhoods and communities of color.[12] Environmental justice advocates tapped into a longstanding revulsion to emissions trading among an important contingent of environmentalists, who ethically opposed what they derided as selling the right to pollute.[13]

By the time William Ruckelshaus returned to the EPA in 1983, the agency was growing more familiar and more comfortable with market-based approaches, even if the majority of its activities continued to focus on writing and enforcing proscriptive, uniform standards. A report on market approaches prepared for Ruckelshaus on his return counted 179 approved bubbles, with compliance cost savings of over $600 million.[14] After a long legal battle with environmental advocates over what counted as an emissions source (a key part of the bubble policy and other reforms), the agency finally prevailed in the *Chevron v. NRDC* decision in 1984. In accepting the EPA's plant-wide definition of an emissions source, the Supreme Court affirmed the principle of judicial deference to administrative interpretation. Where the underlying statute was unclear and where the court deemed the resulting policy to be reasonable and rational, the EPA and other agencies were given great latitude to make policy.[15]

Though *Chevron* gave the EPA more leeway in developing new compliance strategies, proponents of market-based approaches struggled to get congressional support for a larger program. According to Ruckelshaus, Gorsuch's combative tenure left environmental advocates in Congress suspicious of any attempts to change how the EPA operated for the remainder of Reagan's presidency.[16] Reform proponents also had to contend with continued resistance from the Air Office, the EPA's regional offices, and at the local and state levels.[17] When bubble advocates finally won permission in 1985 for bubbling in areas that had not attained national air quality standards, the Air Office quickly moved to restrict this expansion to only those areas with approved attainment plans—a stipulation that prohibited the use of the bubble in the heavily polluted areas where the bubble was the most appealing to industry.[18]

The EPA's regulatory reform chief Mike Levin devoted much of his time during this period to assuaging concerns within and outside of the agency about the efficacy of the bubble and other market-oriented policies. Levin's staff kept a running list of issues raised by critics, and his Standing Committee on Emissions Trading met frequently to address questions and concerns from the air office and regional offices.[19] In an effort to build support for the bubble and other reforms, Levin continued to promote the policies in academic and policymaking circles.[20] Levin also collected endorsements from outside parties, including environmental consultancies, who Levin contracted to produce credible assessments of the bubble's success.[21]

Though he supported the development of market-oriented approaches, Ruckelshaus prioritized restoring the agency's integrity in the eyes of the public during his short second tenure as administrator.[22] The EPA consolidated its various economic incentive programs in the long-awaited final Emissions Trading Policy Statement. But Ruckelshaus announced his retirement from the agency shortly after Reagan's reelection in November 1984 and left the agency in February 1985. The emissions trading policy was not released until 1986.[23] Among other things, the policy finally extended bubbling to the most intransigent compliance problems—the nonattainment areas without approved attainment plans—where the policy was most attractive. The policy also aimed to create predictability around the bubble and other market-based forms. Among other provisions, the final policy prevented regulators from simply tightening standards to capture any excess reductions that firms proposed to use in a bubble. Regulators could still go back to firms that had bubbled and ask for further reductions, but it would have to be done across the entire source category in the given air quality area.[24]

Though Ruckelshaus supported market-based innovations such as the bubble as an attractive means of achieving the agency's objectives at lower cost, his real interest lay in introducing risk management into the EPA's governance model.[25] Popular in policymaking circles in the early 1980s, risk management called for policymakers to prioritize interventions according to the magnitude of the threat and the likelihood of successful mitigation given existing resources.[26] In the 1980s, new scientific understanding of carcinogens revealed that such substances could cause cancer even in minute concentrations. A steadily expanding roster of suspected carcinogens affirmed a long-standing belief among policymakers, including Ruckelshaus, that environmental health threats could never be entirely eliminated. Instead, policymakers needed to figure out how to best manage the various risks. To make policy amid uncertainty, risk management called for experts to provide their best estimates of the magnitude of a given threat along with the actions and economic investment that would be required to reduce that risk by varying degrees. Policymakers would then manage all known risks, intervening on the basis of relative danger and cost effectiveness.[27]

As he worked to restore the EPA's credibility, Ruckelshaus also began a long process of convincing the EPA's many stakeholders that the agency's mission and priorities ought to be recalibrated from the perspective of risk management. In his first public speech in his second stint as administrator, Ruckelshaus told an audience at the National Academy of Science that the public should be educated on the inevitability of environmental risks and then asked to help the EPA decide on where and how to intervene. Though he subsequently backed away from the public participation component, Ruckelshaus made increasing the agency's capacity for risk assessment and its reliance on risk management one of his top priorities.[28] In an editorial in *Science*, Ruckelshaus argued that the EPA needed to become more comfortable weighing the costs and benefits of various interventions as well as with the reality that absolute certainty on many matters would remain elusive. The best approach would be to continue to invest in the EPA's risk assessment capacity while improving the agency's ability to communicate complicated threats to the general public. Here, as elsewhere, Ruckelshaus argued that while risk assessment should be a neutral survey of issues, risk management was fundamentally a political question, one that would require the public and its representatives to decide where to intervene according to how they valued the threats.[29] In this, risk assessment broke from an older model in which Congress had mandated complete protection from air pollution and other threats—though Ruckelshaus and others at the agency would likely say that the EPA had always revised that mandate according to the agency's actual capacity. Though Congress remained skeptical about major changes to the EPA's mission, Ruckelshaus generated enough support for risk management to launch the Comparative Assessment of Environmental Problems project.

Lee Thomas, the former head of the EPA's Solid Waste and Emergency Response program who succeeded Ruckelshaus as administrator in 1985, also viewed risk management as a valuable means of directing the agency's focus. Continuing the project that Ruckelshaus had launched, Thomas assembled a task force to evaluate the entire purview of the EPA's responsibilities from a risk management perspective while also conducting surveys to find where the greatest areas of public concern lay. The work culminated in the 1987 report *Unfinished Business: A Comparative Assessment of Environmental Problems*, which was intended to orient the EPA toward the most pressing problems and the best use of its resources as the agency entered its third decade. One key area flagged by the report was the rise of international environmental issues, especially acid rain.[30] But as with *Unfinished Business*'s other recommendations, the EPA would need a new mandate from Congress to take on the problem.

The Silent Plague

Like lead, acid rain was an old problem that had bedeviled the EPA throughout its existence. The term acid rain and the basic mechanics of the phenomenon it described had been known since 1852, when a Scottish chemist noticed that coal-fired industrialization was turning rainwater acidic near British cities. For the next hundred years, acid rain remained a local curiosity, overshadowed as an environmental concern by more immediate problems such as smog. In the 1960s, environmental advocates in Norway began complaining that the burning of coal in factories in Germany and England was generating vast sulfur emissions that blew up away from industrial areas into the atmosphere, only to descend hundreds of miles away in Norway in rain that killed forests and sterilized lakes. Subsequent research identified sulfur dioxide (emitted primarily by industry) and nitrogen oxides (emitted by automobiles and industry) as the two primary contributors to acid deposition, which studies showed could come down to earth in the form of rain, snow, and dust.[31]

In the late 1960s, environmental advocates in North America had recognized that sulfuric emissions from the Midwest were traveling on prevailing westerly winds to settle in lakes and forests in New York, New England, and Canada. In 1972, the United States and Canada joined European nations in signing the Stockholm Declaration, which committed its signatories to using their domestic natural resources in such a way as to prevent harm to neighboring nations.[32] But the hopeful accord did little to check soaring consumption of coal and other fossil fuels and, by the second half of the environmental decade, acid rain had become a serious threat to ecosystems, the object of growing public alarm, and a significant diplomatic issue with Canada.[33]

Beginning in the mid-1970s, EPA officials tried in vain to come up with a solution to eliminate acid rain. Congress had created a National Ambient Air Quality Standard for sulfur dioxide (SO_2) in the original Clean Air Act of 1970. But SO_2 was monitored at ground level, making the standard largely ineffective against acid rain, since SO_2 could concentrate higher in the atmosphere even when the standard was being met on the ground. Officials considered developing a new national standard for total sulfates in 1975 but ultimately abandoned that route. Several states instituted sulfate standards on their own accord, but sulfates blew across state borders, out of reach of frustrated state authorities.[34] In the Carter administration, EPA officials returned to the position that acid rain could be addressed only if Congress granted new statutory authority to the EPA—an unlikely outcome given that Congress had amended the Clean Air Act in 1977 and had little appetite for further reforms.[35] What's more, representatives of eastern coal-producing states, where the sulfur content was generally higher than in western coal, opposed any intervention that would encourage utilities to switch to western coal. Prospects for a successful intervention dimmed further during the energy crisis, which Carter addressed in part by allowing electric utilities to switch back to burning coal to reduce the nation's dependence on imported oil. Anguished over the worsening problem, EPA administrator Doug Costle had gone so far as to draft a resignation letter to Carter in 1980 to protest the coal conversion. Carter's commitment to new safeguards on worsening air quality saved Costle from having to make good on that threat.[36] But the problem and public frustration only worsened.[37]

Acid rain also became an increasingly contentious issue in relations between the United States and Canada. Pollutants, of course, did not recognize international borders. Prevailing wind patterns and the geography of
American industry combined to deposit American sulfates in Canadian
lakes and forests. While the 1972 Stockholm Declaration committed both
the United States and Canada in principle to avoid damaging each other's
environments, it did not deal with specific issues like acid rain, nor did it
provide any means of addressing damage when it did occur. After a series
of negotiations, the two countries joined many European nations in signing
the 1979 Convention on Long-range Transboundary Air Pollution, which
directly addressed the problem of acid rain and committed the United States
to a good faith effort to prevent its sulfates from blowing over the border.[38]
Within a year, however, the Canadian Embassy filed an official complaint
with the United States, charging its neighbor to the south with neglecting the
1979 commitment in its scramble to convert electric power plants to coal.
With no legal avenue for recourse, the Canadian communiqué prevailed
upon the Americans to at the very least undertake a study of what such
conversion might mean for worsening acidification problems north of the
border.[39]

Reagan's election cast even these fragile agreements into doubt. In a testament to Canadian frustration over the persistent failure of the United States
to address the problem, Reagan was met with protests in Ottawa's streets and
chants of "acid rain, go home!" during his first official state visit.[40] The suspicion was mutual, with an internal Reagan memo reporting later that year that
Canadian prime minister Pierre Trudeau was using acid rain as a "smoke-
screen" for his own efforts to centralize power over the provinces and pos-
sibly nationalize American energy investments.[41]

Back in the United States, growing worry over acid rain focused unwel-
come attention on the electric power industry.[42] By the early 1980s, electric
utilities were generating 60 percent of national sulfur dioxide (SO_2) emissions
and over a third of national nitrogen oxide emissions, making them the chief
culprits for what environmental advocates warned was a dangerous growth
in acid deposition.[43] To fend off new controls that the EPA might implement,
the electric power industry turned to the reliable shield of scientific uncertainty. In 1980, American Electric Power (one of the nation's largest utilities and a ferocious opponent of environmental regulation) contracted with
the nonprofit research institution Battelle Columbus Laboratories to conduct a survey of all known acid rain research. Allowing that SO_2 emissions

had increased rapidly, the report nonetheless downplayed the problem.[44] Demonstrating the political utility of funding such research, Ohio governor James Rhodes sent American Electric Power's report to the recently elected President Reagan.[45] Reagan likewise made a shield of scientific uncertainty, insisting to Congress time and again that more research was needed before the country could take action.[46]

However, rising public alarm about acid rain forced the Reagan administration to do something, lest the issue become another political liability. Despite the efforts of American Electric Power and others to cast doubt on the severity of the problem, solidifying scientific consensus held acid rain to be a major threat. Popular accounts of that threat proliferated in television specials and magazine articles like *Time*'s November 1982 cover story— "Acid Rain: The Silent Plague."[47] A worried internal report by the electric utility trade organization, the Edison Electric Institute, claimed in 1983 that the Democratic Party had taken up acid rain as a potentially powerful campaign issue, forcing the Reagan administration and the Republican Party to respond.[48] With the acquiescence of the Reagan administration, William Ruckelshaus prioritized acid rain as a major issue, assigning a special staff to the issue and holding dozens of fact-finding meetings.[49]

While Ruckelshaus and the EPA followed the scientific community and environmental advocates in calling for electric utilities to reduce their SO_2 emissions, the Reagan administration cast about for an alternative response that would avoid new controls. By December 1983, Ruckelshaus's fact-finding mission had settled on an SO_2 cap for utilities in eastern states, with limits to be considered for midwestern utilities as well.[50] Allowing for the possibility that Congress would develop a new mandate for the EPA as part of the Clean Air Act amendments under consideration, Reagan advisors surveyed a wide variety of control options including sulfur taxes or emissions fees, capital subsidies for scrubbers, and tax credits for compliance to help offset SO_2 compliance costs that utilities might otherwise pass along to their ratepayers.[51] In an effort to forestall such measures, Reagan advisors simultaneously considered a $10–$15 million program in concert with the Canadian government to "lime" lakes that had acidified to toxic pH levels by adding alkaline substances like calcium carbonate. Preliminary studies suggested that "liming" could restore pH levels to a normal range without any reduction in SO_2 emissions, although Reagan advisors acknowledged that the proposal would be met with complaints from environmentalists and the Canadian government that the United States was ducking the central problem.[52]

The Reagan administration's toying with miracle cures like lake liming and its repeated calls for more research did little to reduce international tensions. In 1983, for instance, the United States Department of Justice went so far as to require a Canadian documentary on acid rain to be labeled propaganda from an agent of a foreign country.[53] But Reagan's appointment of special envoys and other largely symbolic gestures allowed his administration to avoid any further controls on SO_2 during his presidency, despite acid rain becoming, as a report among his advisors described, the major political issue in the relations between the United States and Canada.[54]

Even as Reagan continued to oppose action on acid rain, the political landscape was changing. In the 1980s, redistricting reduced the number of congressional representatives from Detroit and other Midwestern and Northeastern industrial areas, who had long opposed additional pollution control as a threat to automobile manufacturing and other imperiled industries in their districts. The elevation of Michigan representative John Dingell to chair of the Energy and Commerce Committee provided some check on that loss of influence for Midwestern industry. But California's Henry Waxman proved an adept legislative steward and defender of environmental laws as chair of the Environmental Subcommittee. In the Senate, West Virginia's Robert Byrd, who had long opposed any legislation that would damage his state's high sulfur coal industry, was replaced as the Democratic Party's leader in 1989 by Senator George Mitchell of Maine. In addition to representing a state that was suffering the ravages of acid rain, Mitchell was a protégée of former senator Edmund Muskie.[55]

Meanwhile, a growing number of economists saw the problem of acid rain as an opportunity to develop an emissions trading program in the foundation of a pollution control program rather than as an add-on compliance option. To push a trading program into the forefront, economists and other proponents produced detailed thought pieces on how SO_2 trading could work. Economists Robert Hahn and Roger Noll began work on the technical aspects of such a market in the early 1980s, including possible pitfalls a market might encounter.[56] Another early sketch came in the *Canadian Journal of Economics*, underscoring the desire north of the border to kickstart a control program.[57] By 1986, the idea of using tradable permits to address acid rain had circulated to the extent that Massachusetts's Division of Air Quality Control conducted an entire report on the experience, capabilities, and attitudes of their region toward developing a trading program.[58] Later in the decade, Hahn and another economist published a retrospective on the EPA's past experience with such policies, which positioned a potential "market for bads" in line with EPA programs going back to the first 1976 emissions offset policy.[59] In 1987, another pair of economists laid out a detailed plan for instituting a market approach.[60]

Critically, the trading approach to acid rain also gained the support of a prominent environmental advocate when the Environmental Defense Fund (EDF) departed from two decades of environmentalist resistance to market approaches to take a leading role in devising a viable trading scheme for SO_2. EDF had previously sought out environmental economists to help them convince policymakers that federal regulations were sound investments. Along with the ability to assemble a case for intervention, environmental economists brought to EDF their long-standing enthusiasm for using tradable permits and other market-based schemes to lower the cost of regulatory compliance. With the acid rain problem worsening in the mid-1980s and no solution in sight, EDF's president Fred Krupp turned to those economists to craft an alternative approach.

As an undergraduate at Yale University and a law student at the University of Michigan, Krupp had encountered the promise that markets could help reduce the compliance costs of environmental protection. After a short time in private practice in New Haven, the thirty-year-old Krupp became EDF's president in 1984 on a platform to work with, rather than litigate against, industry.[61] In 1986, Krupp hired Dan Dudek, an environmental economist at the University of Massachusetts, to translate the myriad trading schemes then circulating among academic economists into a politically viable proposal.[62] That same year, Krupp published an op-ed in the *Wall Street Journal* heralding the launching of a new stage in environmental advocacy that would focus on resolving any economic problems associated with strong environmental protections.[63] Krupp and Dudek's work attracted the attention of Democratic senator Timothy Wirth of Colorado and Republican senator John Heinz III of Pennsylvania, close friends who were married to EDF board members. Wirth and Heinz decided to sponsor a report on the possibilities of using markets and economic incentives in place of enforcing uniform standards, hiring the Harvard University economist Robert Stavins to put together a set of case studies on how market approaches might be adopted.

The eventual report, *Project 88: Harnessing Market Forces to Protect Our Environment*, drew on over fifty experts from academic institutions, environmental organizations, industry, and government to lay out a blueprint for using marketable permits to address acid rain, water quality, and a host of other issues. For acid rain, *Project 88* proposed a cap-and-trade program that promised to dramatically reduce SO_2 emissions while limiting costs. By letting electric utilities determine where and how the reductions were made, *Project 88* predicted that the program would save up to $3 billion in annual compliance costs over a uniform standard model.[64]

Like Krupp himself, *Project 88* won support from policy observers who believed that environmental protection was at a crossroads. As a *New York Times* reporter described it, the report marked a long overdue embrace of efficacy rather than fairness on the part of environmentalists, who for too long had focused on punishing corporations rather than on delivering the greatest pollution reductions at the lowest price. This sea change in attitudes, the reporter argued, made it possible for Democratic and Republican legislators to forge a new consensus on pollution control programs that promised both environmental quality and substantial savings.[65]

The prospects for action on acid rain shot up during the 1988 presidential election, during which the Republican nominee, Vice President George H. W. Bush, used environmental protection as a chance to distinguish himself from the Reagan administration. Like Richard Nixon, Bush was counseled by advisors that a strong environmental platform would prevent his Democratic opponent, Michael Dukakis, from making the environment a partisan issue in the campaign.[66] Declaring that he would be the "environmental president," Bush promised to address the problem of acid rain if he was elected, which he was that November.[67]

Although most environmentalists voted for Dukakis, the president-elect came as a welcome change from the Reagan administration, and environmental advocates worked to ensure that he kept his campaign promises. The early signs were good. In a meeting with environmental leaders a few weeks after his election, Bush impressed with his openness to their concerns.[68] As his EPA administrator, Bush chose William Reilly, a well-respected member of the environmental community who had worked in Nixon's Council on Environmental Quality before becoming the president of the Conservation Foundation and then the World Wildlife Fund.[69] While Bush assured Reilly that he was committed to keeping his campaign promises, he also told him that these objectives would have to be accomplished with minimal additional funding and limited disruption to industry.[70] To run the Air Office, Bush appointed William Rosenberg, who worked in the Energy Department and Michigan politics and whose close relationship with Bush confidant Robert Teeter gave the EPA another channel to the White House.[71] The prospects for movement toward an acid rain solution also gained a boost from Bush's interest in international issues and diplomacy and his personal friendship with Canadian prime minister Brian Mulroney. North of the border, Canadians greeted Bush's election as an indication that the United States would finally control the sulfur emissions raining down on Canadian lakes and forests, with crowds cheering on the president when he arrived for his first state visit.[72] Back home, Reilly decided to prioritize acid rain intervention as a program that would be popular with the new White House and would fulfill his own convictions that the EPA should be focusing more on ecological issues and international problems. Alongside Reilly and Rosenberg, Bush's emerging acid rain team included his longtime legal counsel, Boyden Gray, whose work with Bush in the Reagan administration had given him ample experience with market-based approaches.[73]

To satisfy Bush's request for an acid rain solution that would minimize EPA spending and compliance outlays from private industry, Gray, Reilly, and Rosenberg turned to EDF's well-regarded *Project 88* proposal. At Gray's request, EDF economist Dudek worked with the EPA and the White House to develop legislation around that model.[74] The resulting bill proposed a cap-and-trade system to reduce annual SO_2 emissions by 50 percent. Electric utilities would be allocated a portion of the remaining emissions allowances under that cap according to their existing levels. Each utility would choose how it would reduce emissions—whether by retiring coal-fired plants, switching to lower sulfur coal, improving efficiency, or investing in devices that scrubbed sulfur from smokestack emissions. Each utility would also decide how deep to make its cuts. If a firm went below its allocated total, then it could sell the rights to its extra allowances in one-ton increments to other emitters. If a firm's emissions remained above its share, it could buy allowances to cover the difference. At the end of the year, any utility that had not made or purchased sufficient emission reductions would be fined $2,000 per excess ton, which could quickly add up to a significant fine.[75]

Perhaps even more important than EDF's contributions to the design of the Bush's acid rain proposal was the support it offered the proposal and the notion of emissions trading. From the beginning, Dudek and EDF president Fred Krupp enthusiastically promoted the president's plan to Congress, industry, environmentalists, and the general public.[76] Krupp even advised Gray on public relations matters, including the best language to use in describing the trading provision during television interviews.[77] In exchange for EDF's support, Krupp received Bush's promise to maintain the 50 percent cut in

SO_2 emissions—an ambitious target that Bush might have otherwise shied away from.[78]

Improving its chances for success, Bush's acid rain bill encountered a Congress that was eager to update the Clean Air Act but divided on how aggressively to do so. Democrats controlled both chambers, but they were internally divided about what the new clean air legislation should accomplish. This debate played out primarily in the House. A camp centered around John Dingell of Michigan accepted the need for new legislation to respond to acid rain, urban smog, the ozone hole, and other issues that had emerged or grown worse in the thirteen years since the Clean Air Act had been amended in 1977. But Dingell, who was a key champion of the Detroit automobile companies, and those around him worried that expansive new mandates would weigh too heavily on the industries in their home states. On the other side was Henry Waxman of California and a group of representatives who believed that the federal government needed to be much more aggressive in addressing acid rain and other issues. In pairing a strong new acid rain program with a moderate approach to urban smog and other issues, Bush's bill was one that both sides could conceivably agree to.[79]

The legislation came at a time when the EPA was increasingly comfortable with market-based approaches. In addition to its flourishing emissions trading program and the remarkable success of the lead phase-down, the EPA had helped to design a trading program to eliminate the chlorofluorocarbons (CFCs) that had been dramatically revealed to be depleting the earth's ozone layer. Since the early 1970s, environmental advocates, many scientists, and a few members of Congress had warned that CFCs—in wide use as refrigerants and propellants—degraded the protective stratospheric ozone layer that shields earth's surface from harmful ultraviolet rays.[80] Environmental and public health advocates warned of a coming epidemic of skin cancer and other maladies but struggled to convince Congress or the EPA to prohibit the manufacture or use of CFCs.[81] Subsequent EPA studies revealed that the current rate of growth of CFCs would lead to a 200–300 percent increase in skin cancer and in 1978, the EPA banned the use of CFCs as propellants.[82] But the physical properties of CFCs and their place in global commerce stopped the Carter administration from supporting a full ban. CFCs accumulate in the stratosphere, far away from their point of origin. Banning their production and usage in the United States would do little to reduce the risk of skin cancer for Americans if CFC producers elsewhere around the world continued to manufacture and use them. An American ban without international counterparts would disadvantage domestic producers of CFCs and domestic manufacturers of appliances like air conditioners and refrigerators that relied on CFCs. Substitute chemicals could no doubt be found, but in an era of increasing global trade, business interests repeatedly claimed that the added expense of those substitutes would hurt the competitiveness of American companies.[83]

But as ozone depletion worsened, pressure on the United States to act intensified.[84] In 1985, the problem became a major public concern, after researchers found that ozone depletion was particularly acute in the Antarctic, yielding the terrifying (if not entirely accurate) notion of an ozone hole.[85] Finally, in 1987, the United States helped to negotiate the Montreal Protocol, which created an international schedule to phase out CFCs. EPA economists had considered using tradable permits to phase out CFCs as early as 1977, and they continued to sketch out ideas throughout the 1980s.[86] After Reagan signed the Protocol in 1988, the EPA set to work devising a system that would parcel out tradable CFC production rights to manufacturers and then slowly phase those rights out of existence.[87] Manufacturers that needed to save up capital to finance a switch to a substitute could buy CFC rights from other manufacturers and continue producing CFCs a little while longer.[88] With the CFC implementation under way as the EPA took up the Clean Air Act amendments, market-based approaches enjoyed a new level of legitimacy at the agency.

In July 1989, Bush sent his bill to Congress with EDF's enthusiastic endorsement and support from Reilly's EPA.[89] Reflecting the multitude of air pollution issues facing the nation, various provisions addressed attainment areas, toxics, mobile emissions, enforcement, and urban smog, generally taking a moderate approach toward addressing these long-standing concerns, and charted an aggressive approach on acid rain whose impact on the utility industry was tempered by the promised cost savings of the allowance trading program.[90] To help establish a market price for the emission allowances and prevent existing firms from hoarding allowances to block possible competitors from entering their markets, the EPA would hold back about 2 percent of the allowances each year to sell in an annual auction.[91] As the historian Samuel Hays points out, in addition to the novel trading program, the bill also departed from past legislation in establishing its target of a 50 percent reduction in SO_2 emissions politically rather than allowing the EPA to come up with a reduction target through the agency's own science-based criteria document process. The 50 percent figure represented a long-standing scientific consensus, but it also let Bush come up with a politically acceptable target himself, rather than leaving it in the hands of the EPA. The bill further dictated a list of 190 toxic air pollutants that were subject to strict control technology mandates, bypassing the EPA's identification process, which had long been delayed by uncertainties in the standard setting.[92]

The legislation faced a challenging road, with the biggest opposition coming from the electric utilities, which organized a variety of challenges to the legislation. One tack challenged the bill's supposed shortsightedness in restricting usage of the country's "most abundant energy resource" in coal.[93] Another challenged the viability of the tradable allowances that lay at the heart of the bill, arguing that individual firms would hoard any allowances they acquired in anticipation of future growth, killing a market for excess allowances and Bush's purported compliance cost savings along with it.[94] By pivoting away from proscriptive standards in favor of letting utilities decide how to reduce SO_2 emissions on their own, the legislation also attracted fierce opposition from eastern coal companies, many of whom depended on the EPA's uniform technology mandates to remain competitive with western coal, which was naturally lower in sulfur content.[95] Labor organizations lobbied Bush to require all electric utilities to use scrubbers as part of an effort to avoid a shift to non-unionized western mines.[96] Western coal companies, on the other hand, cheered the legislation alongside railroad companies, which stood to make a handsome profit hauling lower sulfur coal east.[97] For Gray, these contrasting business perspectives were a major reason to favor emissions trading, which would "cut through these political struggles by asking the *marketplace* to make the ultimate allocation decisions," as he told another member of the Bush administration.[98] The market, not policymakers, would decide who won and who lost, insulating Bush and other elected officials from bearing responsibility for the distributional effects of their policies.

Alongside coal and electric power, a constellation of business representatives and conservative think tanks challenged the bill. The National Association of Manufacturers warned that the legislation failed to "consider the delicate balance of protecting our environment and destroying the growth potential for our nation's small businesses."[99] Meanwhile, the Heritage Foundation tried to disrupt the scientific consensus around the problem—continuing to advocate lake liming even though scientists had long concluded that confronting acid rain required reducing SO_2.[100]

But the majority of the business community accepted Bush's intention to support the bill through Congress and worked to shape rather than defeat the amendments. In 1988, 200 of the nation's largest companies formed the Clean Air Working Group, hiring policy insiders like former EPA Regulatory Reform Chief Mike Levin.[101] The Working Group agreed to support Bush's amendments on the condition that they would be allowed to provide input into the bill to insure that it would not be overly "disruptive."[102] Bush's advisors accepted that arrangement and the president himself met with representatives to discuss their suggestions for the legislation.[103]

Bush's proposal also faced opposition from environmental advocates, many of whom had long opposed emissions trading not just because they believed it was less effective than a proscriptive approach but because they believed that it was unethical for the federal government to grant businesses the right to pollute. Clear air, this objection held, should never be transacted. An expression of this line of thinking came in a *New York Times* editorial in July 1989 that sarcastically asked if emission rights would be followed by "pesticide residue rights" or "fouling rights" in professional basketball. Continuing in a darker vein, the editorial imagined a world in which "felony rights" were created for "murder, rape, armed robbery and so forth." The United Nations might even create "torture rights," the editorial concluded, to be stored in Swiss bank accounts.[104] In such morbid questions, the editorial was pushing back against a growing tendency to view public welfare through a market lens, making a case instead for the legitimacy of government interventions that drew inviolable lines, regardless of their supposed inefficiency. Such critiques carried weight, underscoring the importance of EDF's endorsement of the market turn.

As Bush's Clean Air Act bill wound its way through Congress, EDF provided critical support in convincing skeptical legislators and environmental advocates that trading would produce real emission reductions. Krupp, Dudek, and other EDF representatives testified before congressional committees and worked behind the scenes to convince legislators that the trading approach was viable and necessary.[105] Preparing a list of rebuttals to environmentalist criticisms that the Bush bill did not go far enough in reducing SO_2 emissions, the EPA's Air Office quoted EDF's pronouncement that Bush's bill was "forging an iron linkage between robust market incentives and environmental integrity."[106] As well, EDF's support pushed other leading environmental organizations to support (or at least consider) the legislation.[107]

One matter on which these various environmentalists were adamant was that the trading provisions avoid any indication that SO_2 allowances amounted to property rights in air. Environmentalists feared that framing allowances as property rights would stymie future pollution reductions, since authorities would have to either abrogate those rights and risk legal battles or spend large amounts to compensate owners. Fulfilling that demand, even though doing so risked generating uncertainty that firms might shy away from, Bush's bill explicitly stated that SO_2 allowances were not property rights and that the EPA could withdraw allowances at a later date without being forced to pay compensation.[108]

As the legislation moved through Congress, the Bush administration rolled out support to keep the trading program intact. A dozen winners of the Nobel Prize in economics wrote an open letter to Congress in 1989 endorsing the tradable allowances approach.[109] The chairwoman of the Federal Energy Regulatory Council wrote Representative John Dingell in September 1989 to assuage fears that SO_2 allowances would lead to anti-competitive behavior by incumbent emission sources.[110] And the chairman of Bush's Council of Economic Advisors as well as EDF's Dudek worked closely with Democratic congressman Philip Sharp, who introduced legislation on emissions trading provisions in the House, to ensure that Sharp's legislation protected the mechanics of EDF's original proposal.[111] In May 1990, both the House and Senate passed legislation modeled on Bush's proposal. Though the conference process proved grueling, a result of continued contests among Democrats over how aggressive the various provisions should be, the House and Senate worked out a conference bill in October. On November 15, 1990, Bush signed the amendments into law.[112]

Worried that business interests would lean on Bush's EPA to weaken the amendments in the implementation, Congress had been much more proscriptive in its instructions than it had been in past legislation.[113] Nevertheless, the EPA still had a great deal of work to do in determining how the amendments would function.[114] Air Office head Bill Rosenberg assigned the implementation of the Acid Rain Program to the Office of Atmospheric Programs, bypassing the Office of Air Quality Planning and Standards, which typically handled implementation, in what was likely an attempt to minimize the internal resistance that had delayed past reforms such as the bubble, according to Eileen Claussen, who directed the Office of Atmospheric Programs. Claussen assembled an advisory committee that included environmental advocates alongside representatives of the utility industry, and she conducted her implementation process in public meetings. The result was an Acid Rain Program that had wide buy-in from both the business and environmental communities.[115] As the *Wall Street*

Journal reported in April 1991, many electric utilities had come around to support the program as the compliance savings of the trading approach became clear.[116] On the environmental side, the Natural Resource Defense Council's Dave Hawkins also gave his organization's critical endorsement. As Rosenberg explained, Hawkins deftly exchanged this endorsement for a new continuous emission monitoring provision. Regulators had previously been forced to estimate emissions based on equipment type, fuel intake, and so forth. With the installation of continuous monitoring equipment, regulators could see in real time exactly what was coming out of the smokestacks. This requirement helped win the support of career staff in the Air Office. And it set the EPA up to take on an even more fearsome problem than acid rain, as the new monitors reported not just on SO_2 and nitrogen oxides, but also carbon dioxide.[117]

Since the 1960s, researchers had warned that carbon dioxide and other byproducts of the fossil fuel age were accumulating in the earth's atmosphere, where they functioned like a greenhouse, trapping solar radiation that would otherwise have reflected back into space, and as a result raising global temperatures. In the 1980s, growing scientific understanding and alarm about sea level rise and other potential consequences of global warming led the United Nations to call for a global treaty to address the problem. By the late 1980s, the United States was drawing more and more attention as the world's largest emitter of greenhouse gases. Though the Bush administration disputed this primacy, international pressure mounted for the United States to address the issue.

As they drafted the Clean Air Act Amendments, Gray and other Bush advisors tried to position the legislation as a demonstration of the United States' leadership on climate change. In doing so, they had to rely considerably on the ancillary effects of controlling SO_2. The biggest benefit came from a switch away from coal, which, when burned, releases great quantities of carbon dioxide in addition to the SO_2 targeted by the amendments. The Environmental Defense Fund had celebrated this ancillary benefit in its lobbying of Congress to support the legislation.[118] Bush's advisors did the same on the international stage.[119]

Beyond serendipitous carbon reductions, the Bush administration saw the Clean Air Act Amendments' SO_2 trading provisions as a model for addressing climate change through a cap-and-trade approach. Explaining the need for Bush to put his weight behind the passage of the amendments, several of his advisors noted in a December 1989 memo that SO_2 trading could serve "as a tool ... [for] a new generation of environmental issues, such as global warming."[120] Addressing a diverse crowd of environmentalists, business representatives, and other policy makers following the amendments' passage, Council of Economic Advisors chairman Michael Boskin remarked that the "whole world is watching the acid rain program, the first large-scale attempt to use market incentives to promote environmental protection ... to see if the theoretical promise of this approach as a means of reconciling environmental protection and economic growth can be realized in practice."[121]

In addition to minimizing the costs of intervention, the Bush administration saw a cap-and-trade approach to climate change as a way to ensure that the United States was not forced to do more than its share in addressing the problem. As Gray described it, creating a market required a clear-eyed assessment of total greenhouse gas emissions, which would reveal global warming to be the entire world's fault. A proscriptive, standards-based approach would likely focus on countries like England and Germany that relied heavily on coal, as well as the United States and its many automobiles; however, an international market for greenhouse gases would capture a wider range of activities, including "rice cultivation in the Far East," which Gray noted was "the largest single contributor to methane." Moreover, controlling greenhouse gas emissions through exchangeable rights would allow countries like the United States to claim credits for pulling carbon dioxide out of the atmosphere through reforestation efforts.[122] In the minds of many Bush advisors, a market approach would allow the United States to claim leadership on climate change without assuming more than its share of the responsibility.

Adam Smith's Green Thumb

The acid rain emissions trading program was part and parcel of a flourishing number of market approaches to environmental protection in the early 1990s. Moving beyond air pollution, the proponents of the SO_2 market identified scores of environmental problems that could be better addressed through market approaches. EDF proposed that the Bush administration create a wetland mitigation credit system through which a company wishing to build in an ecologically sensitive and protected area could pay for the conservation of adjacent wetlands to replace those being destroyed.[123] An internal Bush memo entitled "Environmental Peristroika" reported on a range of areas in which markets might be applied, including water treatment and tropical deforestation.[124] The EPA laid out its own set of options ranging from municipal waste to climate change.[125]

Another set of suggestions came from a new movement that took its name from the 1991 book *Free Market Environmentalism*. Co-authors Terry Anderson and Donald Leal argued that regulation was the product of a neo-Malthusian fear that competition over resources would lead to degradation and exploitation. While regulation did curb competition, the bureaucrats

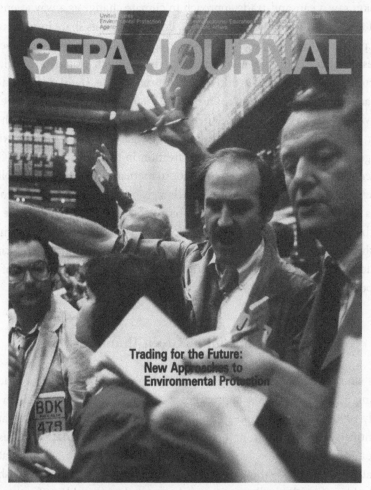

Figure 6.1 The SO₂ trading program was the centerpiece of the EPA's promotion of market-based alternatives in the 1990s, including this cover of the *EPA Journal* in 1992. US EPA, *EPA Journal* 18, no. 2 (May/June 1992).

who ran federal agencies had neither the incentive nor the ability to act in the interests of the general welfare, instead following the direction of the environmental community in creating a heavy blanket of rules that the public would never have chosen to struggle under. In place of that system, Anderson and Leal offered markets as a more objective measure of social preference. By extending property rights as far as possible (from the land underneath the National Parks to the fish swimming in the ocean) and enforcing strong tort laws for wrongful encroachment on neighbors' rights, this market model would capture actual environmental values as people showed their real preferences in what they were willing to pay for. Environmentalists who wanted to protect wilderness or conserve species would simply buy them.[126]

As Anderson and Leal pointed out, the underlying ideas of free market environmentalism were not new. Ronald Coase and Tom Crocker had theorized the substitution of property rights for regulatory interventions back in the 1960s. And a faith in the supremacy of markets when it came to elucidating value had often been accompanied by the accusation that elitist environmentalists had hijacked federal policy. Think tanks and foundations had drawn on business funding to sponsor the promulgation of these libertarian ideas—including the Pacific Research Institute for Public Policy, which supported the publication of *Free Market Environmentalism*. What was new was that Anderson and Leal and their followers saw themselves as environmentalists. Theirs was not an attack on environmental activism, they argued, but a new way forward.

Though Bush had presided over the creation of the nation's most expansive market-based model and the first expansion of the Clean Air Act in thirteen years, the 1992 election saw him unable to claim a place in this new environmentalism. Much of this was Bush's own doing, as he reacted to a worsening recession by appealing to the old protection versus prosperity paradigm. Across the country, Bush and the Republican Party appealed to working-class voters by portraying environmental protection as the domain of out-of-touch elites, including their support of issues such as whether to conserve the Pacific Northwest habitat of the endangered Spotted Owl at the expense of the timber industry.[127] In January 1992, Bush issued a moratorium on any non-essential new rules and asked the EPA and other agencies to bring forward recommendations for cuts.[128] For many of Bush's environmental supporters, including the EDF's Fred Krupp, the regulatory freeze harkened back to the blunt disregard shown by the Reagan administration and came as a betrayal from a president who had insisted that he was committed to environmental protection.[129] Perhaps most consequentially for Bush's record among environmentalists, the president prevented US negotiators from making binding commitments to reduce greenhouse gas emissions when the world's nations met for the first time to consider an international treaty to address climate change at the 1992 Earth Summit in Rio de Janeiro. For environmental advocates, Bush's "go-slow" approach revealed his real disinterest in environmental protection.[130]

Bill Clinton, the Democratic nominee in 1992, capitalized on Bush's growing environmental vulnerabilities. Though Clinton had not had a particularly strong record on environmental protection as governor of Arkansas, his running mate, Senator Al Gore, was one of Congress's environmental champions, so environmental voters flocked to the Democratic ticket. Meanwhile, Clinton worked to reframe the jobs versus environment paradigm. Speaking at an Earth Day event in 1992, Clinton declared, "I believe it is time for a new era in environmental protection, which uses the market to help us get our environment back on track—to recognize that Adam Smith's invisible hand can have a green thumb."[131] Dogged by the recession, Bush failed to articulate a compelling response, and Clinton became the nation's forty-second president. Moderate Republicans looking at the outcome could be forgiven for seeing little political benefit from prioritizing environmental protection.

The partisan lines traced by the 1992 election deepened during Clinton's eight years in office. Gore oversaw much of Clinton's environmental agenda, including the appointment of Gore's former legislative director Carol Browner as EPA administrator. Serving throughout Clinton's two terms, Browner introduced reforms to give industry more flexibility and autonomy in meeting environmental objectives as well as to tailor the EPA's regulations to the particular governance challenges in different areas around the country. At the same time, Browner aggressively pursued emission reductions, introducing a new National Ambient Air Quality Standard for the smallest (and thus most dangerous) particulate matter and tightening loopholes that had allowed electric utilities to increase capacity without installing the newest control technologies. Reversing Bush's position, Clinton endorsed the Framework Convention on Climate Change that had come out of the Rio Summit, though he insisted that cuts in United States emissions could only come from voluntary reductions until a binding international agreement was reached. The 1994 midterms swept into office a group of conservative Republican lawmakers who seemed to oppose environmental protections as a matter of principle. With his presidency bogged down by allegations of scandal, Clinton struggled to pursue his environmental agenda. Congress refused to fund a Clinton initiative designed to support the development of clean air technology and refused the president's request to make the EPA administrator an official cabinet position. In 1995, Republicans' attempts to limit the EPA's enforcement power contributed to a bitter fight over the budget that culminated in what was then the longest government shutdown in history.[132]

Amid that growing acrimony, the Acid Rain Program proved to be an even greater success than its supporters had imagined. By 2000, the country had achieved the 50 percent reduction in SO_2 emissions. Economists estimated that over this first period, permitting emission sources to buy and sell allowances saved electric utilities and other businesses between $1 billion and $2 billion in annual compliance costs compared to what they would have spent if the EPA had adopted uniform technology standards that every firm was required to meet.[133] Furthermore, the reduction of SO_2 led to a reduction in small particulates derived from SO_2 that are a primary cause of respiratory illnesses, with dramatic public health benefits. According to a 2012 study, the Clean Air Act Amendments of 1990 generated approximately $50 billion in annual public health benefits by 2012 against roughly $500 million in annual costs to industry.[134]

At the state and local levels, however, controversy was brewing about the Acid Rain Program and the larger emissions trading model. While the amendments were being drafted, some critics of trading had pointed out that a national market could leave some areas with harmful pollution levels even if the country as a whole succeeded in reducing SO_2 by 50 percent. These critics warned that trading could even exacerbate local pollution issues because existing sources could theoretically buy emission rights to expand current emissions. A solution was offered to zone the country according to the critical pollutant load a particular area could tolerate (which would become in effect a local cap on emissions in that area), but Bush's bill stuck with the national aggregate limit.[135] As well, the interstate transfer of SO_2 persisted. In New York, where the acidification of lakes and streams in the Adirondacks had helped dramatize the problem of acid rain nearly two decades before, environmental advocates complained that trading allowed Midwestern utilities, who were the major buyers of SO_2 allowances, to continue poisoning their state's waters. Governor Mario Cuomo threatened to prevent New York sources from selling their allowances and eventually sued the EPA over the failure to reduce emissions from Ohio's electric utilities.[136] Though the Adirondacks Council in New York managed in a separate lawsuit to get the EPA to monitor the contributions of trading to acidification, New York continued to suffer.[137]

At the local level, grassroots organizations that were in the midst of coalescing into the environmental justice movement argued that trading threatened to maintain or worsen pollution patterns that had long subjected poor neighborhoods and communities of color to a disproportionate share of environmental risks. Activists noted that power plants emitted toxic pollutants besides SO_2 and that by paying for the right to continue emitting SO_2, a local utility might also be maintaining higher levels of these toxins. Beyond such technical issues, many environmental justice advocates mistrusted any scheme that returned power over the allocation of pollution to businesses, fearing that polluters would do as they had done before and concentrate emissions in the marginalized communities where they were least likely to face resistance. The EPA was increasingly sensitive to such fears, monitoring the results of the trading program and opening new channels for environmental justice concerns with the creation of the Office of Environmental Equity in 1992 and the National Environmental Justice Advisory Council in 1993. But the critique persisted. In 1999, the council warned that trading was in fact creating "hot spots" of pollution in poor neighborhoods and communities of color.[138] In an exhaustive 2011 review of sulfur dioxide allowance trading over the first fourteen years of the program, public policy scholar Evan Rinquist found no indication that trading led to elevated levels of sulfur dioxide in poor neighborhoods or communities of color. But Ringquist did find that emissions trading appeared to be concentrating pollutants in communities where large percentages of adults lacked a high school diploma.[139] Today, the scholarly debate over the distribution of the benefits and costs of emissions trading programs continues and the notion of selling the right to pollute remains a potent issue among environmental justice activists.[140]

In opposing emissions trading as a perversion of the EPA's mandate to protect all Americans from the dangers of pollution, environmental justice advocates were tapping into a long line of skepticism toward the supposed neutrality of economists and their preferred market-based tools. Like the early environmental advocates in the 1970s, environmental justice advocates in the 1990s believed that market allocation and market valuation inherently favored the powerful. Though most national environmental organizations had come to embrace economic tools for evaluating policy and market approaches for easing compliance, doubts about such models persisted, including within the EPA itself. Speaking at a celebration of the thirtieth anniversary of Earth Day in 2000, Administrator Browner staked her opposition to the expansion of cost/benefit analysis in environmental policy, which she believed represented a "poisoning of the well." To rely on economics as a compass threatened to sap the moral urgency that had driven the EPA's greatest successes, Browner warned. Instead, policymakers ought to remember that "the historic commitment that was the foundation for our success in conquering environmental degradation was based on a simple premise—protect public health first, and then figure out how to deal with the costs."[141]

* * *

Environmental historian Samuel Hays was one of the first to call out the fetishization of markets in environmental policymaking in the 1990s. Referring specifically to the 1990 Amendments, Hays pointed out that it was the mandate of a 50 percent reduction in SO_2 that brought all the benefits associated with tackling acid rain, not the allowance market—in other words, the cap rather than trading.[142] Hays was right that the clamor around market-based approaches was louder than any actual changes. But what Hays could not see yet in 1998 was that the clamor captured the crumbling of people's faith in the government's capacity and thus sounded the closing of an era. The Bush administration and many members of Congress predicated their support for acid rain intervention on minimizing compliance costs, and the resulting market-based program proved to be a remarkable success in achieving its objectives with minimal problems for industry. Rather than the harbinger of a new era of bipartisan action, the Clean Air Act Amendments of 1990 proved to be the last time that Republicans supported a major expansion of the EPA's mandate. The years that followed saw Republicans open a deep partisan divide on the legitimacy of the state to intervene for the protection of the public welfare, rupturing what had been a wide base for environmental action. By the 2000s, even a cap-and-trade approach to climate change faced major resistance from a growing libertarian strain within the Republican Party. Blanket denunciations of regulation have been a part of Republican politics since the Reagan administration, but the 1990s saw these sentiments move from rhetoric into the heart of the party's policies.

Critically, the changes were not merely partisan. The turn toward market approaches reflected a deeper shift toward seeing government management as inherently less efficient than decisions made by private actors. Even as the

EPA recovered from the trauma of the Gorsuch years, growing wisdom held that the government's responsibility was to optimize markets and to make sure that social objectives were properly valued by transactions. This shift was and is far from complete. But by the 1990s, the idea of inalienable rights to clean air to be secured through robust government programs was losing purchase to a neoliberal approach that tended to regard public welfare as best served with a minimum of government interference.

The EPA played several roles in this shift—helping to lead the ascent of cost/benefit analysis in policymaking that lent support to environmental programs but created a situation in which the justifications for intervention hinged on technical determinations that could be overturned or manipulated. The EPA's pioneering market-based approaches reduced compliance costs and made new interventions possible in an increasingly difficult political climate but contributed to the notion that government directives were inherently less efficient and to be avoided wherever possible. In practicing a politics of the possible, the EPA creating lasting value in clean air. But with climate change beckoning, the challenge of rallying the public to meet a new scale of environmental challenge from this neoliberal foundation would become abundantly clear.

Epilogue

The EPA and a Changing Climate

The year 2020 marks the fiftieth anniversary of the formation of the Environmental Protection Agency (EPA) and the passage of the Clean Air Act Amendments of 1970. Looking back over the past half century, the EPA's accomplishments under that legislation have been remarkable. Even as the population expanded by 128 million and GDP grew by over $13 trillion, the EPA's programs drove down aggregate emissions of the six major air pollutants targeted by the National Ambient Air Quality Standards by over 75 percent. Since 1980, ambient levels of sulfur dioxide have declined by 92 percent, nitrogen dioxide by 65 percent, carbon monoxide by 85 percent, ozone by 35 percent, particulate matter by 44 percent and lead by 98 percent. In 2020 alone, the EPA's regulations prevented more than 230,000 premature deaths per year and reduced the rates of asthma, bronchitis, and other respiratory illnesses. Beyond human health, the benefits of improved air quality include significant gains in the health of forests and rivers, higher agricultural yields, and increased visibility across the country, from New York City to the Grand Canyon. The monetary costs of these gains have been substantial, with approximately $1.2 trillion spent to comply with the EPA's air pollution rules from 1970 to 2020. But the benefits have been astounding, totaling at least $50 trillion over that same period.[1]

The one glaring outlier is carbon dioxide (CO_2). In its last report in 2018, the United Nations Intergovernmental Panel on Climate Change warned that if emissions of CO_2 and other greenhouse gases continue at the current rate, the climate will warm by 1.5 degrees Celsius by 2040, flooding will displace some 50 million people, coral reefs will decline by as much as 90 percent, famines and fires will increase in intensity, and a host of other perils will collectively cause approximately $54 trillion in monetary damages worldwide.[2] A report published by the EPA and a dozen other United States agencies the next year found that climate change could reduce the country's GDP by 10 percent by the end of the century if the United States does not take

Valuing Clean Air. Charles Halvorson, Oxford University Press (2021). © Oxford University Press.
DOI: 10.1093/oso/9780197538845.003.0008

action.[3] Global GDP could fall by 25 percent.[4] While there is considerable uncertainty around this unprecedented problem, the investments required to avoid that damage seem likely to net out, or produce a positive boost to overall output.[5] But despite the devastation portended and the likely monetary benefits of an immediate and forceful response, the United States has been slow to act. Why?

The most obvious reason for America's inaction is the Republican Party. Over the past three decades, Republican politicians and voters have grown more and more hostile toward federal intervention on the environment, shattering the bipartisan base for environmental protection that had underpinned the EPA's expansive responsibilities since the agency's formation. As this book has shown, the seeds of this Republican turn were sown back in the 1970s, when business-financed political organizations such as the Mountain States Legal Foundation laid out a legal and intellectual framework for the deregulatory politics pursued by free enterprise evangelists such as Ronald Reagan. More recently, as Sagebrush politics moved from campaign rhetoric to the heart of Republican policy and ideology, opponents of a strong regulatory state have tapped into and fostered hostility toward liberalism and its expert-led public policy programs. Oil, coal, and petrochemical companies eagerly funded suspicion among conservative voters about the urgency and even the existence of climate change and other major environmental issues.[6] In a recent ethnographic study, sociologist Arlie Hochschild set out to understand why so many working-class Louisianans oppose regulations that would protect them from the public health risks and severe environmental degradation caused by the oil refineries and petrochemical industry. Rejecting regulation, Hochschild found, has become an article of faith, even for those with a personal bond to the physical landscape or firsthand experience with the ravages of industrial toxicity.[7] Given the advantage that Republicans enjoy in the Senate and the Electoral College, the result of this Republican turn has been a block on a legislative response to climate change at the federal level, despite the fact that a majority of voters nationwide support action.

But the inability to act in the face of unfolding cataclysm also owes to a failure of political imagination on the left. The Democratic Party, while acknowledging the existence of the problem, has proven incapable of mobilizing public support for the kind of expansive environmental policies that climate change demands. Here too, the reasons for inaction are rooted in the transformations over the past half-century. Since the Carter presidency, Democrats have too often played the Republicans' game in portraying government as a necessary evil, embracing the idea that government interventions should be kept as spare as possible and should ideally direct markets to solve environmental problems in place of direct federal mandates. For example, the rapid growth of solar power during Obama's presidency came from subsidies for renewable energy projects under the American Recovery and Reinvestment Act, not a mandate for fuel switching. Climate legislation that was proposed but not passed was built around a cap-and-trade model. The problem is not with these policies, per se—market-based programs can be elegant ways of meeting politically determined goals, from the bubble policy to sulfur dioxide emissions trading. Rather, the problem is that Democrats have grown chary of putting the federal government forward as a force for systemic change, depriving national political discourse of what should be a constant reminder of all that government mandates have done and can accomplish. Democrats have also grown too reliant on economics to make the case for what interventions they do put forth, forgetting that costs and benefits are only one part of articulating a shared responsibility for action.

Faith in markets and a cost/benefit approach to value run deep in popular environmental discourse today. Corporations pledge their commitment to the circular economy. Investment funds describe themselves as capitalizing the green revolution. And consumers flock to brands that promise to make an impact, or to reduce their impact, or impact change. While being more "environmentally conscious," as it is often put, does not by necessity preclude agitating for state intervention, market environmentalism offers a shift in individual behavior as a substitute for collective action, which it most decidedly is not. In a parody of the old Coasian idea of addressing pollution through market transactions, airlines invite their environmentally conscious customers to buy carbon credits to offset the emissions of jet travel. In this cultural milieu, there is still popular support for government action on climate change but little of the urgency that the threat demands and a distressing lack of demand for bold mandates of the sort that characterized the environmental movement a half century ago.

Unable or unwilling to put forth a strong legislative platform on climate change, the Democratic Party has increasingly come to rely on executive action and administrative policymaking. As a result, environmental protection has become increasingly vulnerable to dramatic shifts when control of the White House changes. In 1997, in the run-up to the international negotiations in Kyoto, the Senate voted 95–0 to approve a nonbinding resolution preemptively rejecting any agreement on climate change that committed the United States but not developing countries to binding reductions in greenhouse gases. Clinton went ahead and signed the resulting Kyoto Protocol but held the agreement back from the Senate, where it was unlikely to be confirmed. His successor, George W. Bush, promptly retracted Clinton's commitment and withdrew the United States from implementation negotiations.[8] In 2007, the Supreme Court found that the EPA had a responsibility and the authority to regulate CO_2 and greenhouse gases as pollutants under the Clean Air Act.[9]

In 2009, with Obama's support, the House of Representatives passed the American Clean Energy and Security Act, which would have created a cap-and-trade program to control greenhouse gas emissions from the energy sector. Business interests including the Heritage Foundation and Americans for Prosperity fiercely opposed the legislation and tapped into the anti-government Tea Party protests to prevent the bill from reaching a vote in the Senate. Six years later, Obama turned to administrative policymaking to reduce carbon emissions, issuing the Clean Power Plan in 2015, which expanded on the EPA's existing regulation of electric utilities, but without a new mandate from Congress. Later that year, Obama helped to negotiate the landmark international agreement in Paris to limit global warming to 2 degrees Celsius above pre-industrial levels. Like Clinton with the Kyoto Protocol, Obama chose not to submit the Paris Agreement to the Senate, where it faced little chance of confirmation. In 2017, the newly elected Republican president Donald Trump promptly announced that he was withdrawing the United States from the Paris Agreement and ending the Clean Power Plan.[10]

For now, the courts have tended to block the efforts of Republican presidents to weaken environmental protection through administrative action. Shortly after George W. Bush took office in 2001, the Supreme Court ruled that the EPA could not take economic costs into account in setting the National Ambient Air Quality Standards.[11] Soon thereafter, Bush tried to expand the emissions trading model of the Acid Rain Program to other pollutants and industries through the proposed Clear Skies Act. Stymied by environmental and Democratic opposition in Congress, Bush attempted to implement key parts of the plan through the EPA, issuing the Clean Air Interstate Rule and the Clean Mercury Rule. Both rules used a cap-and-trade system in place of technology standards, raising complaints from environmental advocates that the market model would surrender the government's ability to govern specific facilities and result in fewer improvements in environmental quality than would have been achieved under the old, proscriptive standards. The rules also ran afoul of the courts, which found that the statutory mandates to control pollution through standards were clear, and thus that the rules violated the Clean Air Act.[12]

Public support for the EPA has continued to make overt challenges to the agency's capacity politically hazardous. George W. Bush, eager to avoid the mistakes of the Reagan administration, appointed a moderate Republican in Christine Todd Whitman as EPA administrator. At the same time, he introduced new restrictions that limited public participation in and oversight over environmental policymaking, citing, among other things, national security concerns after the 9/11 terrorist attacks. Meanwhile, the administration also tried to undermine the scientific foundation of the EPA and other environmental agencies, intervening to remove or alter information in reports and seeking to introduce political litmus tests into the hiring and appointment process for scientific staff and advisors. In both cases, environmental advocates identified and raised alarms about the changes, preventing the full implementation of either plan but nonetheless leaving policymaking more difficult to access and the scientific foundation more contentious than before.[13]

Trump initially pursued a far more aggressive agenda at the EPA. Proposing dramatic budget and staffing cuts, Trump chose a prominent critic of the EPA to lead the agency in Scott Pruitt, who had frequently sued and derided the EPA as Oklahoma's attorney general. Like Anne Gorsuch before him, Pruitt managed the EPA at a remove from its staff, infamously installing a $43,000 soundproof booth in his office to keep his conversations secure from the EPA's career employees.[14] As under Gorsuch, EPA staff found themselves butting up against political appointees who seemed intent on preventing them from doing their jobs. Once again, many of those career staff turned to the volunteer groups that sprang up around the agency to collect and disseminate information about the damage that Pruitt was doing, including the Environmental Protection Network (formed by alumni of Save EPA) and the Environmental Data and Governance Initiative (formed by researchers and historians).[15] As information leaked out from the EPA, Pruitt's many ethical violations forced a Republican-controlled Congress to open multiple investigations into his conduct. In July 2018, Pruitt was forced to resign after just fourteen months as administrator.[16] Andrew Wheeler, Pruitt's successor and a former lobbyist for the coal industry, has proven more successful in pursuing the Trump administration's agenda without attracting major scandal. So far, Congress has refused to make the budget cuts to the EPA that Trump has proposed, but the administration continues to constrain the agency in other ways.

Under both Pruitt and Wheeler, the Trump administration has attempted to undercut the basis for environmental intervention under the pretense of improving the policymaking process. This moving of the goalposts includes a proposal (still under consideration as of December 2020) to give preference in rulemakings to research with publicly available data. Seemingly innocuous, this proposal would in reality prevent the EPA from using most public health research in determining safe levels of pollutants, since standard safeguards around the anonymity of subjects in such research makes full public accessibility of the underlying data impossible.[17] Another rule change, finalized in April 2020, excludes from cost/benefit considerations the often sizable co-benefits that result when the measures taken to reduce one pollutant end up also reducing another.[18] The monetary value of such co-benefits can often be higher than the targeted pollutant, as was the case with acid rain, which saw its greatest payoff in the decline in particulate matter that resulted from reducing sulfur dioxide. On the surface, the significance of those policy changes can be hard to grasp, which is exactly the intent. Under the pretense of technical tweaks, the Trump administration has been attempting to undermine the EPA's basis for intervention, betting that most people will never understand what is happening. The exclusion of co-benefits also highlights the risks of Democrats' reliance on executive action and the monetary benefits of regulation in protecting the environment.

Facing hostility and stalemate in Washington, environmental advocates have increasingly shifted their focus to state and local policies, reversing the consolidation of governance at the federal level over the past half century that this book traces. Other trends are also contributing to this pivot toward the states. Local leaders are increasingly confronted with the effects of a changing and warming climate, including worsening flooding and wildfires, pushing them by necessity to the forefront in responding to the threat. The country's growing concentration of population and economic activity along the coasts and in metropolitan areas means that a relatively small set of local and state leaders have come to oversee a large portion of the country's carbon footprint. High levels of public support for progressive policies in many of those same places combined with the abdication of responsibility at the federal level has resulted in local and state leaders assuming what are often national or even international leadership roles.[19] The same day that Trump declared that he would withdraw from the Paris agreement, a group of governors representing almost half the country's population and 60 percent of its GDP announced the formation of the United States Climate Alliance, which uses state-level policies to continue pursuing the emission reductions that the United States agreed to in Paris. In one of the many ironies of the current political moment, the success of this turn toward the states pushed Trump and other Republicans, historically the party of states' rights, to try to revoke the ability of California and other states to set their own emissions and fuel economy standards. Though this Republican gambit appears to have failed this time, the possibility that Republicans will succeed in the future should caution against relying too heavily on state and local leadership. Ultimately, the sheer magnitude of the climate problem ultimately demands a comprehensive federal response.

Much of the urgency in the current conversation around climate change is directed toward what has happened and what will happen if we fail to act. And for good reason: the results of inaction are already damaging and the consequences of continuing on the present path will be disastrous. The first book about climate change that I can remember reading, Elizabeth Kolbert's *Field Notes from a Catastrophe: Man, Nature, and Climate Change*, was published in 2006 when CO_2 concentration in the atmosphere measured 381 ppm. The most recent book I have read, David Wallace-Wells's *The Uninhabitable Earth: Life after Warming*, was published in 2019 when CO_2 levels are about 415 ppm. In the thirteen years between those books, the worst-case scenarios for sea-level rise, intensified drought and wildfires, biodiversity loss, and a host of other ills have instead become our likely trajectory. As this book was being prepared for publication, Australia burned. Then the Covid-19 pandemic hit. As carbon emissions fell amid severe restrictions on commerce, many commentators declared that the pandemic was proof that the United States and other countries could meet the challenge of climate change if leaders wished.[20] Ignoring for a moment the unsustainability of crippling reductions in trade, this optimistic perspective also missed the fact that the pandemic has revealed a disheartening failure to mobilize around public welfare across much of the United States and around the world. Public health experts have chillingly little authority these days, which should make us nervous about the prospects of experts leading us toward the necessary transformations in our economy, society, and culture when it comes to climate change, unless there are important changes in how we understand the value of expert governance. The election of Joe Biden in November 2020 promises an end to outright hostility to expert-led interventions from the White House, but the new administration will face deep and enduring cynicism toward state interventions as it seeks to act on climate change.

But we can take heart in the revival of an expansive understanding of the government's responsibility, authority, and capacity to protect the environment among young people across the world. Theirs is an environmentalism founded on the legitimacy and necessity of large-scale, proscriptive intervention. In the United States, this activism has centered around the Green New Deal, which finds its popularity among young Americans by offering a solution at a scale equal to the challenge. As the very name of the Green New Deal illustrates, history is a powerful tool for these young activists in demonstrating what the federal government is capable of accomplishing.

The history of the EPA is likewise a story of the state's potential. In 1970, the EPA set out with an audacious mandate to protect the environment from the ill effects of industrial society. By practicing the art of the possible without losing sight of that responsibility, the EPA managed to dramatically improve environmental quality. Fifty years later, the fire of the new generation could launch another collective effort. The climate challenges ahead are monumental. But they can be met if we have the will to do so, because the story of the EPA's power, the agency's agency, is ultimately the unfinished story of our power, our agency.

Notes

Abbreviations

CSF	Charles L. Schultze's Subject Files, Staff Office—CEA, Jimmy Carter Presidential Library
DBF	Danny J. Boggs Files, Ronald Reagan Library
DCP	Doug Costle Papers, Jimmy Carter Presidential Library
EHF	Edwin L. Harper Files, Ronald Reagan Library
	EMP Edmund S. Muskie Papers, Edmund S. Muskie Archives and Special Collections Library, Bates College, Lewiston, Maine
EPA Admin. Correspondence	Office of the Administrator, General Correspondence, 1971–1982, RG 412, Records of the Environmental Protection Agency, National Archives and Records Administration, College Park.
EPA Intra-Agency Memos	Office of the Administrator, Intra-Agency Memorandums, 1977–1983, RG 412, Records on the Environmental Protection Agency, National Archives and Records Administration, College Park, Maryland
ESF	Edward C. Schmults Files: 1974–77, Gerald R. Ford Library
ESP	Edward C. Schmults Papers: 1973–77 (1978–81), Gerald R. Ford Library
FFF	Fred Fielding Files, 1981–1986, Ronald Reagan Library
GHF	George Humphreys Files 1975–1977, Domestic Council, Gerald R. Ford Library.
Gray Presidential Files	C. Boyden Gray Files, White House Counsel's Office, George H. W. Bush Presidential Library
Gray VP Files	C. Boyden Gray Files, Vice Presidential Records, Counsellor's Office, George H. W. Bush Presidential Library
GSF	Glenn R. Schleede Files, Gerald R. Ford Library
JHF	Jeffrey Holmstead Files, White House Counsel's Office, George H. W. Bush Presidential Library
JWF	White House Central Files, Staff Member and Office Files, John C. Whitaker Files, Richard Nixon Presidential Library, Yorba Linda, California

KHF	Khristine Hall, Sub-group II.1 Toxic Chemicals Program—Staff Files, Washington, DC Office, Environmental Defense Fund Archive, Stony Brook University
MBF	Michael Boskin Files, Council of Economic Advisors, George H. W. Bush Presidential Library
MLP	Michael Levin Private Papers
NRDC Records	Board of Directors, 1970–1977, MS 1965, Accession 2013-M-064, Administrative, Natural Resources Defense Council Records, Yale University
RSF	Richard Schmalensee Files, Council of Economic Advisers, George H. W. Bush Presidential Library
RTP	Robert M. Teeter Papers, 1967–2004, Gerald R. Ford Library
SEF	Domestic Policy Staff, Stuart Eizenstat Subject Files, Jimmy Carter Library
WGF	William Gorog Files, 1975–76, Office of Economic Affairs, Gerald R. Ford Library
WSF	L. William Seidman Files, 1974–77, Office of Economic Affairs, Gerald R. Ford Library

Introduction

1. Gary Trudeau, *Doonesbury*, January 25–31, 1982.
2. A classic account of this evolution remains one of the best: Tom McCraw, *Prophets of Regulation* (Cambridge, MA: Harvard University Press, 1986).
3. Brian Balogh, *Chain Reaction: Expert Debate and Public Participation in American Commercial Nuclear Power, 1945–1975* (New York: Cambridge University Press, 1991).
4. Kim Philips-Fein, *Invisible Hands: The Businessmen's Crusade against the New Deal* (New York: W.W. Norton, 2009).
5. Paul Sabin, "Environmental Law and the End of the New Deal Order," *Law and History Review* 33, no. 4 (2015): 965–1003.
6. Elizabeth Popp Berman, *Thinking Like an Economist: How Economics Became the Language of U.S. Public Policy* (Princeton, NJ: Princeton University Press, 2020).
7. See, for example, Dan Carpenter, *Reputation and Power: Organizational Image and Pharmaceutical Regulation at the FDA* (Princeton, NJ: Princeton University Press, 2010).
8. See, for example, David Rosner and Gerald Markowitz, *Lead Wars: The Politics of Science and the Fate of America's Children* (Berkeley: University of California Press, 2013).
9. See, for example, Sarah Vogel, *Is It Safe? BPA and the Struggle to Define the Safety of Chemicals* (Berkeley: University of California Press, 2012).
10. Thus far, this scholarly turn has focused on the deregulation of particular industries and the rising power of finance. See, for example, Judith Stein, *Pivotal Decade: How*

the United States Traded Factories for Finance in the Seventies (New Haven, CT: Yale University Press, 2011), Gretta Krippner, *Capitalizing on Crisis: The Political Origins of the Rise of Finance* (Cambridge, MA: Harvard University Press, 2011), and Shane Hamilton, *Trucking Country: The Road to America's Wal-Mart Economy* (Princeton, NJ: Princeton University Press, 2008).

11. Over the past half century, as the country added 128 million people and $13 trillion in GDP, the EPA's regulations drove down sulfur dioxide levels by 93 percent, nitrogen oxides by 71 percent, volatile organic compounds by 60 percent, carbon monoxide by 83 percent, particulate matter by 81 percent, and lead by over 99 percent. GDP gains calculated from 1970 to 2018 (the last year for which there are data) in 2010 dollars, https://data.worldbank.org/indicator/NY.GDP.MKTP. KD?locations=US; air quality improvement from 1970 to 2018 (the last year for which there are data); estimates of monetary costs and benefits of improved air quality calculated from 1970 to 2020 in 2006 dollars. US Environmental Protection Agency, "The Benefits and Costs of the Clean Air Act, 1970 to 1990," October 1997. US Environmental Protection Agency, "The Benefits and Costs of the Clean Air Act from 1990 to 2020, April 2011.

12. Dennis Williams interview with Douglas Costle, August 4–5, 1996, EPA Oral Histories, EPA 202-K-01-002.

Chapter 1

1. Crocker's story was assembled from Thomas Crocker, "The Structuring of Atmospheric Pollution Control Systems," in *The Economics of Air Pollution, A Symposium*, ed. Harold Wolozin (New York: W. W. Norton, 1966); he later elaborated on his story in a conference paper, Thomas Crocker, "Trading Access to and Use of the Natural Environment: On the Origins of a Practical Idea from the Dismal Science," paper presented at the ASEH Annual Meeting in Boise, ID 2008 (session canceled, paper in my personal possession); Crocker expanded on those accounts in two interviews that I conducted with him on May 1, 2015, and November 18, 2015.

2. David Stradling, *Smokestacks and Progressives: Environmentalists, Engineers, and Air Quality in America, 1881–1951* (Baltimore: Johns Hopkins University Press, 1999).

3. Stradling, *Smokestacks and Progressives*.

4. S. Smith Griswold, "What Pollution Costs," *Bulletin of the Atomic Scientists* 21, no. 6 (1965): 12–16.

5. Stradling, *Smokestacks and Progressives*.

6. A. C. Pigou, *The Economics of Welfare* (London: Macmillan, 1920).

7. Griswold, "What Pollution Costs."

8. Stradling, *Smokestacks and Progressives*.

9. Christopher Sellers, *Crabgrass Crucible: Suburban Nature and the Rise of Environmentalism in Twentieth-Century America* (Chapel Hill: University of North Carolina Press, 2012).

10. Stradling, *Smokestacks and Progressives*.

11. Scott Dewey, *Don't Breathe the Air: Air Pollution and U.S. Environmental Politics, 1945–1970* (College Station: Texas A&M University Press, 2000).

12. Scott Dewey, "'Is This What We Came to Florida For?' Florida Women and the Fight against Air Pollution in the 1960s," *Florida Historical Quarterly* 77, no. 4 (1999): 503–531.

13. Dewey, "'Is This What We Came to Florida For?'"

14. H. Scott Gordon, "The Economic Theory of a Common-Property Resource: The Fishery," *Journal of Political Economy* 62, no. 2 (1954): 124–142.

15. Elizabeth Blackmar, "Peregrinations of the Free Rider: The Changing Logics of Collective Obligation," in *Transformations in American Legal History: Essays in Honor of Professor Morton J. Horwitz*, ed. Daniel W. Hamilton and Alfred L. Brophy, 267–297 (Cambridge, MA: Harvard University Press, 2009).

16. In 1951, President Truman appointed William Paley, chairman of the Columbia Broadcasting System, to chair a Materials Policy Commission to assess national demand and supply of natural resources, from copper to silk and even clean water. At Paley's recommendation, the Ford Foundation helped found Resources for the Future in 1952 as a center for research on the nation's natural resource supplies. Resources for the Future, *1954 Annual Report*.

17. As RFF's annual report put it in 1954, the organization aimed to strengthen the national economy by determining the most efficient use of "land, water, energy, timber, metals, living space, outdoor recreational facilities, and so forth." If earlier conservationists contented themselves with ensuring that a lumber company made use of all the trees it cut from a Forest Service lease, RFF would use benefit-cost analysis and other techniques to determine how the federal government could best price that concession to increase its contribution to the national coffers as well as its value to the overall economy. Resources for the Future, *1954 Annual Report*.

18. This position identified through a survey of Resources for the Future's Annual Reports, 1953–1960.

19. Paul Samuelson, "The Pure Theory of Public Expenditure," *Review of Economics and Statistics*, 36, no. 4 (1954): 387–389.

20. John Kenneth Galbraith, *The Affluent Society* (Boston: Houghton Mifflin Harcourt, 1958).

21. Lynne Snyder, "'The Death-Dealing Smog over Donora, Pennsylvania': Industrial Air Pollution, Public Health, and Federal Policy, 1915–1963" (PhD diss., University of Pennsylvania, 1994).

22. The conference proceedings were published as US Public Health Service, *Proceedings—National Conference on Air Pollution*, Washington, DC, November 18–20, 1958.

23. Reuben Gustavson, "What Are Air Pollution's Costs to Society," US Public Health Service National Conference on Air Pollution, Washington, DC, November 18, 1958.

24. Such research was to create new "techniques for the measurement of economic losses due to corrosion and other damage to materials, soiling, and reduced visibility," as well as "reliable cost estimates on both local and national bases." Further research could explore "potential by-product use, economic motivation techniques (such as

rapid tax amortization), and the social effects of polluted air on people and communities." United States, Surgeon General's Ad Hoc Task Group on Air Pollution Research Goals, *National Goals in Air Pollution Research* (Washington, DC: Public Health Service, 1960).

25. "New PHS Divisions in Reorganization," *Public Health Reports* 75, no. 10 (1960): 924

26. "National Conference on Air Pollution," *Public Health Reports* 78, no. 5 (1963): 423–429). PHS's expanding interest in the economics of air pollution is also evident in the research described in the semi-annual *Guides to Research in Air Pollution*. By 1966, the guide listed PHS-funded economics research on a variety of air pollution subjects from "Air Pollution and Effects on Property—Corrosion Studies," to "Air Pollution and Effects on Property—Dyed Fabric Fading." Public Health Service, *Guide to Research in Air Pollution for Projects Active in Calendar Year 1966* (Washington, DC: Public Health Service and American Society for Mechanical Engineers, 1966).

27. Ronald Coase, "The Problem of Social Cost," *Journal of Law and Economics* 3 (1960): 1–44.

28. Rachel Carson, *Silent Spring* (New York: Houghton Mifflin, 1962).

29. Dewey, "'Is This What We Came to Florida For?'"

30. Charles Jones, "The Limits of Public Support: Air Pollution Agency Development," *Public Administration Review* 32, no. 5 (1972): 502–508.

31. Dewey, *Don't Breathe the Air*.

32. Marc Landy, Marc Roberts, and Stephen Thomas. *The Environmental Protection Agency: Asking the Wrong Questions* (New York: Oxford University Press, 1990). Despite the polemical title, this account of the EPA's history, which emerged from a public policy executive training at Harvard University's School of Public Health, is one of the best books on the agency, thoroughly researched and carefully argued.

33. The field hearings are described in Series V.C. US Senate, Senate office staff and committee staff files, Boxes 56–58, Edmund S. Muskie Papers, Edmund S. Muskie Archives and Special Collections Library, Bates College, Lewiston, Maine (hereafter EMP).

34. Witness Schedule, Tampa Hearings, February 20, 1964, Subcommittee on Air and Water Pollution, Senate Office Staff and Committee Staff Files, Series V.C. US Senate, Box 58, Folder 1, EMP.

35. E.N. Lightfoot to John Mutz, February 16, 1964, Subcommittee on Air and Water Pollution, Senate Office Staff and Committee Staff Files, Series V.C. US Senate, Box 58, Folder 1, EMP.

36. Paul Huff to Senator Edmund Muskie, March 2, 1964, Subcommittee on Air and Water Pollution, Senate Office Staff and Committee Staff Files, Series V.C. US Senate, Box 58, Folder 1, EMP.

37. Jane May to Senator Muskie, February 23, 1964, Subcommittee on Air and Water Pollution, Senate Office Staff and Committee Staff Files, Series V.C. US Senate, Box 58, Folder 1, EMP.

38. Edmund Muskie to Jane May, March 4, 1964, Subcommittee on Air and Water Pollution, Senate Office Staff and Committee Staff Files, Series V.C. US Senate, Box 58, Folder 1, EMP.

39. Dewey, "'Is This What We Came to Florida For?'

40. Hedonics identifies distinct characteristics (or "price factors") that contribute to the overall price of a good or service—in this case, Tampa area agricultural land—allowing an economist like Crocker to isolate the degradation of air quality as an independent variable on the price of agricultural land. Thomas Crocker, "Externalities, Property Rights, and Transactions Costs: An Empirical Study," *Journal of Law & Economics* 14, no. 2 (1971): 451–464.

41. See footnote 1, this chapter.

42. By the 1950s, participants in the field of land economics had begun describing the economic impact of pollution using the monetary values of crops damaged by smog or fisheries destroyed by agricultural runoff. See, for example, Howard Gregor, "Urban Pressures on California Land," *Journal of Land & Public Utility Economics* 33, no. 4 (November 1957): 311–325; and Lawrence Hines, "Measurement of Recreation Benefits: A Reply," *Journal of Land & Public Utility Economics* 34, no. 4 (November 1958): 365–367.

43. David Harvey, *A Brief History of Neoliberalism* (New York: Oxford University Press, 2005).

44. Thomas Crocker, "The Structuring of Atmospheric Pollution Control Systems," in *The Economics of Air Pollution, A Symposium*, edited by Harold Wolozin (New York: W. W. Norton, 1966).

45. Thomas Crocker, "Externalities, Property Rights, and Transaction Costs: An Empirical Study," *Journal of Law & Economics* 14, no. 2 (1971): 451–464.

46. As Dales put it, "If it is feasible to establish a market to implement a policy, no policymaker can afford to do without one. Unless I am very much mistaken, markets *can* be used to implement any anti-pollution policy that you or I can dream up." J. H. Dales, *Pollution, Property, & Prices: An Essay in Policy-Making and Economics* (Toronto: University of Toronto Press, 1968), 100.

47. Thomas Crocker, "In Polk & Hillsborough Counties, Florida," *Bulletin of the Atomic Scientists* 21, no. 6 (1965): 17–19.

48. Resources for the Future, *1961 Annual Report*.

49. The rise of pollution as a research concern at RFF resulted from and helped cause the diminishment of natural resources as a concern at the organization. As early as 1962, RFF economists Harold Barnett and Chandler Morse argued that conservation had allowed society to escape the resource trap about which Malthus and his latter day counterparts had long warned. Since the resource base appeared secure, RFF could worry about pollution. Resources for the Future, *1962 Annual Report*: 27–34.

50. Resources for the Future, *1963 Annual Report*.

51. Resources for the Future, *1965 Annual Report*.

52. Kenneth Boulding, "Economics of the Coming Spaceship Earth," *1966 Resources for the Future Forum on Environmental Quality*, Washington, DC, March 8–9, 1966.

53. Erhun Kula, *History of Environmental Economic Thought* (London: Routledge, 1997).

54. Garrett Hardin, "The Tragedy of the Commons," *Science* 162, no. 3859 (1968): 1243–1248.

55. Paul Sabin, *The Bet: Paul Ehrlich, Julian Simon, and Our Gamble over Earth's Future* (New Haven, CT: Yale University Press, 2013).

56. Christopher Sellers, *Crabgrass Crucible: Suburban Nature and the Rise of Environmentalism in Twentieth-Century America* (Chapel Hill: University of North Carolina Press, 2012).

57. Dewey, *Don't Breathe the Air.*

58. *Air Quality Act of 1967,* Public Law 90–148, *U.S. Statutes at Large* 81 (1967): 485–507.

59. Edmund Muskie to Linda Baer, July 7, 1969, V.A.7 91st Congress, Box 819, Folder 5, EMP; Edmund Muskie to Perry Walper, May 27, 1969, V.A.7 91st Congress, Box 821, Folder 5, EMP.

60. Eliot Cutler to Senator Muskie, February 17, 1969, V.A.7 91st Congress, Box 819, Folder 4, EMP.

61. John Esposito and Larry Silverman, *Vanishing Air: The Ralph Nader Study Group Report on Air Pollution* (New York: Grossman, 1970).

62. R. P. White to Mayor Joseph M. Barr, July 10, 1968, V.A. 7, 91st Congress, Box 821, Folder 5, EMP.

63. The description of particulate matter emissions from aluminum can manufacturing is based on the EPA Office of Compliance Sector Notebook Project, "Profile of the Nonferrous Metals Industry," September 1995. US EPA 310-R-95-010; Continental Can Company had manufacturing plants in Mankato and Stockton in 1960 according to a list compiled by former employees. Scott Rollert, "Master list of Continental Can Co. cities and plant numbers," May 1, 2011, accessed January 26, 2017, http://www.therustybunch.com/phpBB3/viewtopic.php?t=17844.

64. Historians of regulation long ago noted the willingness of business executives to support a unified set of regulations once they become convinced that some sort of intervention is inevitable. See, for example, Samuel Huntington, "The Marasmus of the ICC: The Commission, the Railroads, and the Public Interest," *Yale Law Journal,* 61, no. 4 (1952): 467–509; and Gabriel Kolko, *Railroads and Regulation, 1877–1916* (Princeton, NJ: Princeton University Press, 1965).

65. Adam Rome, *The Genius of Earth Day* (New York: Hill and Wang, 2013).

66. Christopher Sellers, *Crabgrass Crucible: Suburban Nature and the Rise of Environmentalism in Twentieth-Century America* (Chapel Hill: University of North Carolina Press, 2012).

67. J. Brooks Flippen, *Nixon and the Environment* (Albuquerque: University of New Mexico Press, 2000).

68. John C. Whitaker with Charles Wilkinson and Patty Limerick, interview, November 19, 2003, accessed February 24, 2016, http://centerwest.org/wp-content/uploads/2011/01/whitaker.pdf.

69. J. Brooks Flippen, *Nixon and the Environment* (Albuquerque: University of New Mexico Press, 2000).

70. Richard Nixon, "Statement about the National Environmental Policy Act of 1969," January 1, 1970. Archived at the American Presidency Project, University of California, Santa Barbara, accessed February 14, 2017, http://www.presidency.ucsb.edu/ws/?pid=2557.

71. Statement by Edmund S. Muskie, News Conference, May 13, 1970, Folder 1, Box 73A, Senate office staff and committee staff files, Billings, Leon, Series V.C. US Senate, EMP.

72. Leon Billings to Richard Royce, August 8, 1968, Folder 5, Box 819, V.A. 7, 91st Congress, EMP.

73. Eliot Cutler to File, "Outline of Proposed Air Pollution Legislation," undated; Don Nicoll to Senator Muskie, June 2, 1970; Eliot Cutler to Senator Muskie, June 3, 1970; Eliot Cutler to Senator Muskie, June 4, 1970; all documents in Folder 5, Box 974, V.A. 7, 91st Congress, EMP.

74. National Air Quality Standards Act of 1970, S. Res. 4358, 91st Cong. (1970).

75. National Air Quality Standards Act of 1970, S. Res. 4358, 91st Cong. (1970).

76. Chris DeMuth to John Whitaker, July 2, 1970, folder, "Clean Air Act—1970 [from OA 8182] [1 of 2]," Box 34, John C. Whitaker Files, Richard Nixon Presidential Library (hereafter JWF).

77. Adam Rome, *The Genius of Earth Day* (New York: Hill and Wang, 2013).

78. National Air Quality Standards Act of 1970, S. Res. 4358, 91st Cong. (1970).

79. Senator Muskie, speaking on S. 4358, 91st Cong., 2nd sess., *Congressional Record* 116 (September 22, 1970): S 33099.

80. *Air Quality Act of 1967*, Public Law 90–148, *U.S. Statutes at Large* 81 (1967): 503.

81. Senator Randolph, speaking on S. 4358, 91st Cong., 2nd sess., *Congressional Record* 116 (September 22, 1970): S 33074.

82. See, for example, Edmund Muskie to Sumner Thompson, March 14, 1969, Folder 5, Box 821, V.A.7 91st Congress, EMP.

83. Edmund Muskie to David MacNeill, February 18, 1969, Folder 4, Box 819, V.A.7 91st Congress, EMP.

84. Senator Nelson, speaking on S. 4358, 91st Cong., 2nd sess., *Congressional Record* 116 (September 21, 1970): S 33114–33115.

85. Ozone is the most prevalent of the photochemical oxidants and researchers and regulators often used it as a proxy for other oxidants. Ground level, or tropospheric, ozone is the same compound that protects living organisms from harmful ultraviolet rays in the stratosphere. Ozone's propensity to split off an oxygen molecule, the property that allows it to absorb ultraviolet rays in the stratosphere, makes it highly reactive at ground level.

86. According to historian Hugh Gorman, a 1954 Stanford study found that automobiles released 1,000 tons of hydrocarbons per day while refineries, gasoline transportation, and filing stations released just 440 tons daily. Hugh Gorman, *Redefining Efficiency: Pollution Concerns, Regulatory Mechanisms, and Technological Change in the U.S. Petroleum Industry* (Akron, OH: University of Akron Press, 2001), 236–237.

87. Gary Bryner, *Blue Skies, Green Politics: The Clean Air Act of 1990* (Washington, DC: CQ Quarterly Press, 1993.

88. In fact, General Motors, the largest automobile manufacturer in the world, was directly deterred from such investment as a result of its ownership of the Ethyl Corporation, producer of lead additives that ruined such converters, until 1962. Gorman, *Redefining Efficiency*, 311.

89. Many historians have chronicled the jockeying and lobbying of automobile manufacturers around the Clean Air Act. One of the best accounts is Tom McCarthy, *Auto Mania: Cars, Consumers, and the Environment* (New Haven, CT: Yale University Press, 2007).

90. Senator Griffin, speaking on S. 4358, 91st Cong., 2nd sess., *Congressional Record* 116 (September 22, 1970): S 33081–33083.

91. See, for example, Senator Muskie and Senator Griffin, speaking on S. 4358, 91st Cong., 2nd sess., *Congressional Record* 116 (September 21, 1970): 32904–32907; and Exhibit 2, entered into record on S. 4358, 91st Cong., 2nd sess., *Congressional Record* 116 (September 21, 1970): 32915.

92. Senator Griffin, speaking on S. 4358, 91st Cong., 2nd sess., *Congressional Record* 116 (September 22, 1970): 33081.

93. Voting toll on H.R. 17255, passed in lieu of S. 4358, *Congressional Record* 116 (September 22, 1970): S 33120; E. W. Kenworthy, "A Clean-Air Bill," *New York Times,* June 11, 1970.

94. James F. C. Hyde, Jr. to Don Rice, November 5, 1970, folder, "Air Pollution Bill (Air Quality Control Bill) [from OA 8182] [4 of 4]," Box 24, JWF.

95. Maurice Stans to John Ehrlichman, undated. Richard Nixon Library, folder, "Air Pollution Bill (Air Quality Control Bill) [from OA 8182] [2 of 4]," Box 24, JWF.

96. Muskie acknowledged the "badly timed" letter from the Nixon administration to the House and Senate conferees and stated that Nixon's implementation of the Clean Air Act should be reviewed by the Senate in 1971 to make sure that the regulations issued under the act did not "water down the strong policy which the Senate is adopting." Senator Muskie, speaking on Conference Report for H.R. 17255, passed in lieu of S. 4358, 91st Cong., 2nd sess., *Congressional Record* 116 (December 18, 1970): S 42387.

97. The two major changes pertained to easing statutory deadlines for the automobile industry. Senator Muskie, speaking on Conference Report for H.R. 17255, passed in lieu of S. 4358, 91st Cong., 2nd sess., *Congressional Record* 116 (December 18, 1970): S 42386–42387.

98. Ken Cole to Dwight Chapin, December 18, 1970, folder, "Clean Air Act—1970 [from OA 8182] [1 of 2]," Box 34, JWF.

99. Richard Nixon, "Remarks on Signing the Clean Air Amendments of 1970," December 31, 1970. Archives at the American Presidency Project, University of California, Santa Barbara, accessed February 24, 2016, http://www.presidency.ucsb.edu/ws/?pid=2874.

100. For example, the Clean Water Act of 1972 famously charged the EPA with reducing water pollution such that the rivers and waterways would become "fishable and swimmable within a decade. 33 U.S.C. §1251 et seq. (1972).

Chapter 2

1. An early and influential articulation of the layering phenomenon comes from Karen Orren and Stephen Skowronek, "'Beyond the Iconography of Order: Notes for a 'New Institutionalism,'" in *The Dynamics of American Politics*, ed. L. Dodd and C. Jillson (Boulder CO: Westview Press, 1994): 311–330. Layering has been subsequently analyzed across the federal government, including in environmental policy; see, for example, Christopher Klyza and David Sousa, *American Environmental Policy, 199–2006: Beyond Gridlock* (Cambridge, MA: MIT Press, 2007).

2. As historian J. Brooks Flippen explains, the Council on Environmental Quality replaced the short-lived and ineffective Environmental Quality Council. J. Brooks Flippen, *Nixon and the Environment* (Albuquerque: University of New Mexico Press, 2000), 35-36.

3. *National Environmental Policy Act of 1969*, Public Law 91-190, *U.S. Statutes at Large* 83 (1970): 852-856.

4. Christopher DeMuth to John Whitaker, January 16, 1970, folder, "CEQ [Council on Environmental Quality]—Sept. 69-June 70 [from OA 8120] [3 of 3]," Box 41, John C. Whitaker Files, Richard Nixon Presidential Library (hereafter JWF).

5. Aldo Leopold had published his seminal conservationist meditation two decades before. Aldo Leopold, *A Sand County Almanac: And Sketches Here and There* (New York: Oxford University Press, 1949).

6. John C. Whitaker to the President, January 20, 1970, folder, "CEQ [Council on Environmental Quality]—Sept. 69-June 70 [from OA 8120] [2 of 3]," Box 41, JWF.

7. Biographical detail taken from the Biographical Note section of finding aid for the Library of Congress' Russell E. Train Papers collection, accessed February 26, 2016, http://rs5.loc.gov/service/mss/eadxmlmss/eadpdfmss/2009/ms009069.pdf.

8. Elly Peterson to John Whitaker, January 22, 1970, folder, "CEQ [Council on Environmental Quality]—Sept. 69-June 70 [from OA 8120] [3 of 3]," Box 41, JWF.

9. John C. Whitaker to Russell Train, February 27, 1970, folder, "CEQ [Council on Environmental Quality]—Sept. 69-June 70 [from OA 8120] [2 of 3]," Box 41, JWF.

10. Whitaker, for one, believed reports written by the council not worth Nixon's time, "even in summary form." John Whitaker to John Campbell, July 23, 1970, folder, "WHCF: Subject Categories EX FG 278 National Industrial Pollution Control Council [1970]," Box 1, FG 278 National Industrial Pollution Control Council, Richard Nixon Presidential Library, Yorba Linda, California. In other records the council's role is revealed to be primarily a stage for Nixon to make a show of his concern about the business community's complaints about the costs of new regulations.

11. Marc Landy, Marc Roberts, and Stephen Thomas, *The Environmental Protection Agency: Asking the Wrong Questions* (New York: Oxford University Press, 1990).

12. Landy, Roberts, and Thomas, *The Environmental Protection Agency.*

13. Russell Train to John D. Ehrlichman, April 27, 1970, folder, "[Environmental Protection Agency, Creation of by Reorganization Plan No. 3 of 1970] [from OA 8181] [3 of 3]," Box 64, JWF.

14. John C. Whitaker, Memorandum for the Record, November 9, 1970, folder, "Chron, Sept.—Dec. 1970, J. C. Whitaker [3 of 4, November 1970]," Box 3, JWF.

15. Bureau of National Affairs, Inc., "President to Propose Changes in Environmental, Oceanic Programs," *Environment Reporter* 1, no. 7 (June 12, 1970): 136.

16. Walter C. Bornemeier to the president, July 27, 1970, folder, "[Environmental Protection Agency, Creation of by Reorganization Plan No. 3 of 1970] [from OA 8181] [2 of 3]," Box 64, JWF; Sydney Howe to Charles W. Colson, April 10, 1970, folder, "Interest Groups," Box 88, Doug Castle's Ash Council Files, Doug Costle Papers, Jimmy Carter Library (hereafter DCP).

17. David Vogel, *Fluctuating Fortunes: The Political Power of Business in America* (New York: Basic Books, 1989).

18. George T. Bell to H. R. Haldeman, August 6, 1970, folder, "[Environmental Protection Agency, Creation of by Reorganization Plan No. 3 of 1970] [from OA 8181] [2 of 3.]," Box 64, JWF.

19. Edison Electric Institute's monthly *EEI Bulletin* made space for articles on catfish thriving in rivers where the thermal discharge of power plants had artificially raised the temperature and on how the industry might meet the current "environmental crisis." But the trade journal included no discussion of the EPA's creation or effect on the industry until 1972. Loren D. Jensen, "Cooling Water Discharge Project," *EEI Bulletin* 38, no. 7 (1970): 225–228; Earl Ewald, "Energy Alternatives—Now and in the Future," *EEI Bulletin* 39, no. 2 (1971): 61–63; Shearon Harris, "Harris Warns that Environmental Regulations May Dim Power Supply Outlook," *EEI Bulletin* 40, no. 1 (1972): 2–3.

20. Richard Nixon, "Special Message to the Congress about Reorganization Plans to Establish the Environmental Protection Agency and the National Oceanic and Atmospheric Administration, July 9, 1970, accessed February 26, 2016, http://www.presidency.ucsb.edu/ws/index.php?pid=2575&st=environmental+protection+agency&st1.

21. Ed Hanley interview with Chuck Elkins, "Behind the Scenes at the Creation of EPA," EPA Alumni Association Oral History Project, 2013.

22. Timothy Conlan, *New Federalism: Intergovernmental Reform from Nixon to Reagan* (Washington, DC: Brookings Institution, 1988).

23. Organization Chart, folder, "Environmental Protection Agency [from CFOA 771] [6 of 7]," Box 134, JWF.

24. Richard Corrigan, "Environment Report/Success of New Agency Depends on Ruckelshaus' Direction," *National Journal* (November 28, 1970): 2591–2595.

25. Doug Costle, "Notes for Whitaker Briefing," August 26, 1970, folder, "Implementation—Organization (2) [1]," Box 87, DCP.

26. Corrigan, "Environment Report/Success of New Agency Depends on Ruckelshaus' Direction," 2593.

27. Kerrigan Clough interview with author, July 25, 2015.

28. Ed Hanley interview with Chuck Elkins, "Behind the Scenes at the Creation of EPA," EPA Alumni Association Oral History Project, 2013.

29. Andrew M. Rouse to John Whitaker, November 12, 1970, folder, "EPA—Nov. 6 to Dec., 1970 [from OA 8181]," Box 64, JWF.

30. John C. Whitaker to John D. Ehrlichman, November 5, 1970, folder, "Chron, Sept.—Dec. 1970, J. C. Whitaker [3 of 4, November 1970]," Box 3, JWF.

31. John C. Whitaker, Memorandum for the Record, November 9, 1979, folder, "Chron, Sept.–Dec. 1970, J.C. Whitaker [3 of 4, November 1970]," Box 3, JWF.

32. John C. Whitaker to Richard Nixon, November 5, 1970, folder, "Chron, Sept.—Dec. 1970, J. C. Whitaker [3 of 4, November 1970]," Box 3, JWF.

33. John C. Whitaker to Dwight Chapin, November 30, 1970, folder, "Chron, Sept.—Dec. 1970, J. C. Whitaker [3 of 4, November 1970]," Box 3, JWF.

34. William D. Ruckelshaus, "A Breath of Fresh Air," Second International Clean Air Congress, Washington, DC, December 7, 1970, folder, "EPA—Nov. 6 to Dec., 1970 [from OA 8181]," Box 64, JWF.

35. Ruckelshaus, "A Breath of Fresh Air," December 7, 1970.

36. William Ruckelshaus interview with author, May 13, 2016.

37. Samuel Hays, "The Politics of Clean Air," in *Explorations in Environmental History: Essays* by Samuel P. Hays, 219–312 (Pittsburgh: University of Pittsburgh Press, 1998).

38. *Clean Air Act, U.S. Code* 42 (1970), § 7409 (b)(1) and § 7409 (a)(1).

39. Samuel Hays, "The Politics of Clean Air," in *Explorations in Environmental History: Essays* by Samuel P. Hays, 219–312 (Pittsburgh: University of Pittsburgh Press, 1998).

40. *Clean Air Act, U.S. Code* 42 (1970), § 7409 (b)(1) and § 7409 (a)(1).

41. US Environmental Protection Agency, "Notice of Proposed Standards for Sulfur Oxides, Particulate Matter, Carbon Monoxide, Photochemical Oxidants, Hydrocarbons, and Nitrogen Oxides," *Federal Register* 36, no. 21 (January 30, 1971): 1502–1515.

42. The standard for carbon monoxide called for emissions to be kept below a maximum hourly concentration of thirty-five parts per million and an eight-hour averaged concentration of nine parts per million. Each state would be responsible for meeting that standard in each of the air pollution control regions within its borders and would be considered in compliance if those regions managed to avoid exceeding those limits more than once per year. US Environmental Protection Agency, "Table of Historical CO NAAQS," accessed November 18, 2015. http://www3.epa.gov/ttn/naaqs/standards/co/s_co_history.html; US Environmental Protection Agency, "Data Table of Ambient Air Levels, 1970–1999," provided by Nick Magnus, US EPA Air Quality Standards, to author on November 18, 2015. Los Angeles exceeded the eight-hour averaged standard of nine carbon monoxide parts per million 1,015 times in 1972, with the four highest recorded levels each topping 26 ppm, nearly three times the national standard. St. Louis exceeded the same standard four times in 1972, recording eight-hour averages of 10.5 ppm, 10.4 ppm, 10.1 ppm, and 9.9 ppm.

43. Ruckelshaus paraphrased Ehrlichman's reaction in William Ruckelshaus interview with author, May 13, 2016.

44. "EHS Staff Functions," undated, folder, "EPA Taskforce, 1970 [3]," Box 85, DCP.

45. President's Advisory Council on Executive Organization to the president, April 29, 1970, folder, "EPA Briefing Book, 1970 [1]," Box 83, DCP.

46. US Environmental Protection Agency, *The Economics of Clean Air, Report of the Administrator of the Environmental Protection Agency to the Congress of the United States in Compliance with Public Law 90-148, The Clean Air Act, as Amended*, Washington, DC, 1971.

47. William Ruckelshaus interview with author, May 13, 2016; Sansom was confirmed as deputy administrator for Policy, Planning, and Evaluation in October. Bureau of National Affairs, Inc., "Planning and Evaluation Chief Named for Environmental Protection Agency," *Environment Reporter* 2, no. 23 (October 8, 1971): 679.

48. Robert W. Fri to John Whitaker, July 20, 1971, folder, "Environmental Protection Agency, 1971 [from OA 8143] [2 of 4]," Box 64, JWF.

49. EPA, Office of Planning and Management, June 24–25, 1972, folder, "Environmental Protection Agency [from CFOA 771] [2 of 7]," Box 133, JWF.

50. Alan Carlin, "History of Economic Research at the EPA," US EPA, National Center for Environment Economics, accessed December 9, 2015, http://yosemite.epa.gov/ee/epa/eed.nsf/00000000000000000000000000000000/2f68aa9ffb75364b852577970 0781a24!OpenDocument.

51. Environmental Protection Agency, "Organization and Functions—Organization," July 14, 1972, folder, "Organization and Functions [1972]," Box 1, Papers of Dr. Robert L. Sansom, 1972–74, Richard Nixon Presidential Library, Yorba Linda, California.

52. Robert W. Fri to John Whitaker, July 20, 1971, folder, "Environmental Protection Agency, 1971 [from OA 8143] [2 of 4]," Box 64, JWF.

53. Speaking on the floor of the Senate, Senator J. Caleb Boggs, a Republican from Delaware and a member of the subcommittee, described the proposed act as aligned with both the spirit and many of the specific objectives of Nixon's Environmental Message to Congress in 1970; another member of the subcommittee, Senator Cooper, noted that Nixon himself had recommended important features in the proposed act, including the NAAQS. Senator Boggs speaking on S. 4358, 91st Cong., 2nd sess., *Congressional Record* 116 (September 22, 1970): S 32907; Senator Cooper speaking on S. 4358, 91st Cong., 2nd sess., *Congressional Record* 116 (September 22, 1970): S 32918.

54. So figured legislators like Representative Ken Hechler, a Democrat from West Virginia, who harshly critiqued earlier failures in an implicit challenge to Nixon and the EPA. "We can no longer afford the pussyfooting, artful dodging, delays, end runs, and outright flouting of the intent of the legislation which has characterized the history of air pollution control," Hechler declared, continuing on, "I trust that the President and the Environmental Protection Agency will seize this challenge and thus protect the right of every citizen to breathe clean air." December 18, 1970, the House agreed to conference report, 42521; Muskie tempered warnings such as these with an insistence that neither Nixon nor the Republican Party more generally had interfered in any way with the act's passage. Dismissing speculation in December 1970 that the Nixon administration had attempted to undercut the act when it was in conference, Muskie declared on the Senate floor that such insinuations were especially unfortunate "because the Republican side of this subcommittee and this committee has cooperated so wholeheartedly over so many years in this legislation.... There has never been the slightest bit of partisanship in any of our committee deliberations or in our conference work. Representative Hechler, speaking on Conference Report for H.R. 17255, passed in lieu of S. 4358, 91st Cong., 2nd sess., *Congressional Record* 116 (December 18, 1970): H 42521.

55. Senator Muskie, speaking on Conference Report for H.R. 17255, passed in lieu of S. 4358, 91st Cong., 2nd sess., *Congressional Record* 116 (December 18, 1970): S 42387.

56. US Environmental Protection Agency, "National Primary and Secondary Ambient Air Quality Standards," *Federal Register* 36, no. 84 (April 30, 1971): 8186–8201.

Announcing the final NAAQS in April 1971, Ruckelshaus publicly underscored how difficult they would be to achieve. On carbon monoxide, Ruckelshaus declared: "Of seven major cities where we have good enough data to make accurate predictions, only one—Cincinnati, Ohio—will come close with the presently contemplated automobile controls in the time allowed." The other six cities (Chicago, Denver, Los Angeles, New York, Philadelphia, and Washington, DC) would not achieve the standard until sometime in the 1980s. "Environmental Protection Agency Sets National Air Quality Standards," *Journal of the Air Pollution Control Association* 21, no. 6: 352–353.

57. Bureau of National Affairs, Inc., "NIPCC Environmental Cost Council Suggested by Secretary of Commerce," *Environment Reporter* 2, no. 25 (October 22, 1971): 722.

58. Bureau of National Affairs, Inc., "Commerce Secretary Stans Advocates Consideration of Environmental Costs," *Environment Reporter* 2, no. 26 (October 29, 1971): 759.

59. Other studies under way within the agency's first year included a review of the Water Office's requirement that all cities develop secondary water treatment facilities, an estimation of the costs of the EPA's vessel waste standards, economic analysis to support the agency's report to Congress about progress toward the automobile standards, and a study of the economics of recycling. Robert W. Fri to John Whitaker, July 20, 1971, folder, "Environmental Protection Agency, 1971 [from OA 8143] [2 of 4]," Box 64, JWF.

60. Samuel Hale Jr. to Assistant Administrator for Planning and Management, April 1971, folder, "Economics, Materials—Vol. II [from OA 10144] [3 of 4]," Box 132, JWF.

61. The National Air Pollution Control Administration had created 150 of these Air Quality Control Regions across the country.

62. Henry L. Diamond to John C. Whitaker, September 4, 1970, folder, "[Environmental Protection Agency, Creation of by Reorganization Plan No. 3 of 1970] [from OA 8181] [1 of 3]," Box 64, JWF.

63. Bureau of National Affairs, Inc., "Private Contractors Available for EPA Aid to State Air Programs," *Environment Reporter* 2, no. 11 (July 16 1971): 308.

64. Summarizing general themes from the comments, *Environment Reporter* noted that several states and industry groups challenged the EPA's authority to prescribe control plans that should have been the responsibility of the states—a further testament to the widespread conviction that the EPA's guidelines were more like requirements. These critics took special issue with Appendix B, in which the EPA laid out how a control system based on emission limitations might function. Bureau of National Affairs, Inc., "EPA Receives Critical Comments on Proposed Implementation Plans," *Environment Reporter* 2, no. 1 (July 16, 1971): 306–307.

65. William N. Letson to John C. Whitaker and Donald B. Rice, July 19, 1971, folder, "Environmental Protection Agency, 1971 [from OA 8143] [2 of 4]," Box 64, JWF.

66. California Proposition 9, "Mandates on Internal Combustion Fuels," California statewide ballot, June 6, 1972, Defeated.

67. Kenneth W. Wade to C. D. Ward, May 30, 1971, folder, "Environmental Protection Agency [from CFOA 771] [3 of 7]," Box 134, JWF.

68. Memorandum for the Record, November 3, 1971, folder, "Chron, Nov.–Dec. 1971, J. C. Whitaker [1 of 2, November 1971]," Box 4, JWF.

69. At least one environmentalist critic of the final SIP guidelines singled out this substitution of operational controls for emission limits in the copper industry as an especially destructive implication of the guideline revisions. Copper smelters, on the other hand, had professed to be unable to control emissions solely through stack scrubbers, claiming in a Bureau of Mines report in October 1971 that existing control technology was simply inadequate. John C. Whitaker to William H. Rodgers Jr., September 14, 1971, folder, "Chron, July—Oct. 1971, J. C. Whitaker [3 of 4, September 1971]," Box 4, JWF; Bureau of National Affairs, Inc., "Mines Bureau Reports Some Smelters Cannot Meet Sulfur Oxides Standards," *Environment Reporter* 2, no. 27 (November 5, 1971): 801.

70. Notes for Conversation with Ruckelshaus," December 28, 1971, folder, "Environmental Protection Agency, 1971 [from OA 8143] [4 of 4]," Box 64, JWF.

71. "Notes for Conversation with Ruckelshaus," December 28, 1971, folder, "Environmental Protection Agency, 1971 [from OA 8143] [4 of 4]," Box 64, JWF.

72. John A. Green to Mrs. John C. Sheehy, January 6, 1972, folder, "EPA [Environmental Protection Agency]—1971 [from CFOA 1139] [3 of 3]," Box 63, JWF.

73. Environmentalists gained that standing in the Scenic Hudson Preservation Conference v. Federal Power Commission decision of 1965, when the United States Court of Appeals for the Second Circuit allowed an environmentalist organization to intervene in hearings of the Federal Power Commission regarding an electric utility project despite the organization having no financial interests in the landscape in question. Robert Lifset, *Power on the Hudson: Storm King Mountain and the Emergence of Modern American Environmentalism* (Pittsburgh: University of Pittsburgh Press, 2014).

74. "*Clean Air Act Amendments of 1970*, Public Law 91–604, *U.S. Statutes at Large* 84 (1970): 1706–1707; in suing a polluter, citizens effectively acted as the government and courts had the power to issue penalties and injunctions. Adam Babich, "Citizen Suits: The Teeth in Public Participation," *Environmental Law Review* 25 no. 3 (1995): 10141–10151.

75. The Ford Foundation supplied NRDC with an initial grant of $410,000 for the first fifteen months of operations, with continued support promised for at least five years. Several other foundations contributed another $43,000 in NRDC's first year. "Results of Fund-Raising Activities," December 17, 1970, folder, "Board Meeting—December 17, 1970," Box 4, Board of Directors, 1970—1977, MS 1965, Accession 2013-M-064, Administrative, Natural Resources Defense Council Records, Yale University (hereafter NRDC Records).

76. "Proposed Guidelines for Taking Cases," December 19, 1970, folder, "Board Meeting—December 17, 1970," Box 4, NRDC Records.

77. Ed Strohbehn to Executive Committee, July 28, 1971, folder, "EXCHE August 12, 1971," Box 4, NRDC Records.

78. "Note re Membership Figures," folder, "June 5, 1975 Annual Meeting," Box 2, NRDC Records.

79. David Hawkins interview with author, September 18, 2015; Doug Costle, who had helped to design the EPA, echoed Hawkins's depiction of this strategy as well as his assessment of its success in an oral history he gave in 1996. Dennis Williams interview with Doug Costle, August 4–5, 1996, EPA Oral History Project, EPA 202-K-01-002.

80. Physical proximity to federal policymaking also allowed NRDC's Washington, DC, office to collaborate with environmentalist organizations such as the Sierra Club that were also interested in national environmental laws. "NRDC Washington D.C. Office," folder, "EXCHE May 6, 1971," Box 4, NRDC Records.

81. David Hawkins interview with author, September 18, 2015.

82. Ruckelshaus mentioned NRDC's 1972 Senate testimony against granting extensions to automobile manufacturers as the principal factor in his decision to reverse course and deny the extension request, having been convinced by NRDC that the manufacturers could in fact meet the 1975 deadline. William Ruckelshaus interview with author, May 13, 2016.

83. Daniel Carpenter, *Reputation and Power: Organizational Image and Pharmaceutical Regulation at the FDA* (Princeton, NJ: Princeton University Press, 2010).

84. David Hawkins interview with author, September 18, 2015.

85. John C. Whitaker to Larry Young, September 13, 1971, folder, "Chron, July–Oct. 1971, J. C. Whitaker [3 of 4, September 1971]," Box 4, JWF.

86. Richard Ayres, Julie Copeland, and James Miller to NRDC Board of Trustees," May 1972, folder, "May 11, 1972 Board," Box 3, NRDC Records; United States territorial possessions like Puerto Rico submitted SIPs along with the fifty states.

87. Richard Ayres, speaking on Implementation of the Clean Air Act Amendments of 1970—Part 1 (Title I), Hearings before the Subcommittee on Air and Water Pollution of the Committee on Public Works, United States Senate, Ninety-Second Congress, Second Session, February 16, 17, 18, and 23, 1972. Serial No. 92-H31, February 16, 1972.

88. Richard Ayres, speaking on Implementation of the Clean Air Act Amendments of 1970, Hearings before the Subcommittee on Air and Water Pollution of the Committee on Public Works, February 16, 1972.

89. Richard Ayres, speaking on Implementation of the Clean Air Act Amendments of 1970, Hearings before the Subcommittee on Air and Water Pollution of the Committee on Public Works, February 16, 1972.

90. These advocates included Dr. Arthur Atkisson of the National Tuberculosis & Respiratory Disease Association's Air Conservation Commission, David Calfee of the Public Interest Group, and Jacob Kreshtool of Delaware Citizens for Clean Air. Alphabetical List of Witnesses, Implementation of the Clean Air Act Amendments of 1970—Part 1 (Title I), Hearings before the Subcommittee on Air and Water Pollution of the Committee on Public Works, United States Senate, Ninety-Second Congress, Second Session, February 16, 17, 18, and 23, 1972. Serial No. 92-H31, February 16, 1972.

91. William Ruckelshaus, speaking on Implementation of the Clean Air Act Amendments of 1970—Part 1 (Title I), Hearings before the Subcommittee on Air

and Water Pollution of the Committee on Public Works, United States Senate, Ninety-Second Congress, Second Session, February 16, 17, 18, and 23, 1972, Serial No. 92-H31, February 17, 1972.

92. William Ruckelshaus, Testimony on Implementation of the Clean Air Act Amendments of 1970, Hearings before the Subcommittee on Air and Water Pollution of the Committee on Public Works, February 17, 1972.

93. William Ruckelshaus, "Reality Before Rhetoric in the Environmental Movement," An Address by William D. Ruckelshaus to the Audubon Society, Milwaukee, Wisconsin, May 22, 1971, folder, "Environmental Protection Agency, 1971 [from OA 8143] [3 of 4]," Box 64, JWF.

94. Bureau of National Affairs, Inc., "Current Developments," Environment Reporter 2, no. 15 (August 13, 1971): 419.

95. Bureau of National Affairs, Inc., "Benefits Will Outweigh Control Costs, CEQ Chief Tells Soft Drink Association," Environment Reporter 2, no. 30 (November 26, 1971): 888.

96. Bureau of National Affairs, Inc., "Ruckelshaus Says Tough Approach to Environment Not Always Wise Course," Environment Reporter 2, no. 34 (December 24, 1971): 1031.

97. Rising prices for new automobiles and electric power plants would be among the more discernible costs for consumers, according to the agency. Allowing that existing benefits research was insufficient in many cases to quantify monetary benefits, the EPA nonetheless argued that a crude estimate for 1977 showed $14.2 billion in benefits to be obtained from $12.3 billion in spending on emissions control. More precise figures, the EPA stated, would have to await newly begun benefits research. Bureau of National Affairs, Inc., "EPA Says Private Outlays for Control to Exceed Estimates Made in 1971 Report," Environment Reporter 2, no. 45 (March 10, 1972): 1353–1354.

98. "Environmental Protection Agency Review System for State Implementation Plans," January 10, 1971, folder, "EPA [Environmental Protection Agency]—1971 [from CFOA 1139] [3 of 3]," Box 63, JWF.

99. Robert W. Fri to John Whitaker, July 20, 1971, folder, "Environmental Protection Agency, 1971 [from OA 8143] [2 of 4]," Box 64, JWF.

100. Natural Resources Defense Council Inc. v. Environmental Protection Agency, 529 F. 755 (2d Cir. 1976).

101. City of Riverside v. Ruckelshaus, Civil No. 72-2122-IH (C.D. Cal. 1972).

102. Natural Resources Defense Council Inc. v. Environmental Protection Agency, 475 F. 968 (2d Cir. 1973).

103. R. L. Samson to John Whitaker and William A. Morrill, May 9, 1972, folder, "EPA [Environmental Protection Agency]—1971 [from CFOA 1139] [3 of 3]," Box 63, JWF.

104. The eleven states with fully approved SIPs were Alabama, American Samoa, Colorado, Connecticut, Florida, Guam, Mississippi, New Hampshire, North Carolina, North Dakota, Oregon, Puerto Rico, South Dakota, and West Virginia. Bureau of National Affairs, Inc., "Ruckelshaus Announces EPA Approval of State Plans to Meet Air Standards," Environment Reporter 3, no. 5 (June 2, 1972): 123.

105. John C. Whitaker to Bill Ruckelshaus, July 27, 1971, folder, "Chron, July–Oct. 1971, J. C. Whitaker [1 of 4, July 1971]," Box 4, JWF.
106. Peter Blake, "EPA Telethon Gets 'R' Rating," *Rocky Mountain News*, January 1972, folder, "Environmental Protection Agency [from CFOA 771] [3 of 7]," Box 134, JWF.
107. Ken Cole to John Whitaker, February 28, 1972, folder, "EPA [Environmental Protection Agency]—1971 [from CFOA 1139] [3 of 3]," Box 63, JWF.

Chapter 3

1. President's Advisory Council on Executive Organization to the President, April 29, 1970, folder, "EPA Briefing Book, 1970 [1]," Box 83, Doug Costle Papers, Jimmy Carter Presidential Library (hereafter DCP).
2. Carl E. Bagge to John C. Whitaker, September 21, 1972, folder, Council on Environmental Quality, "Clean Air Act—1971 [from CFOA 764," Box 35, White House Central Files, Staff Member and Office Files, John C. Whitaker Files, Richard Nixon Presidential Library (hereafter JWF).
3. Steve Jellinek to George Humphreys, September 1975, folder, Council on Environmental Quality "Domestic Policy Review (2)," Box 6, George Humphreys Files 1975–1977, Domestic Council, Gerald R. Ford Library (hereafter GHF).
4. William Nordhaus to the Economic Policy Group, January 15, 1979, attached to Si Lazarus, Memo to Regulatory Process Bill File, February 16, 1979, folder, "1 Regulation," Box 73, Charles L. Schultze's Subject Files, Staff Office—CEA, Jimmy Carter Presidential Library (hereafter CSF).
5. Richard Corrigan, "Environment Report: Success of New Agency Depends on Ruckelshaus' Direction," *National Journal*, November 28, 1970.
6. Marc Landy, Marc Roberts, and Stephen Thomas. *The Environmental Protection Agency: Asking the Wrong Questions* (New York: Oxford University Press, 1990).
7. See, for example, the Council on Environmental Quality's Russell Train being told to clear his environmental message speech with OMB before delivering it to Congress as well as OMB editing the CEQ's annual report. John C. Whitaker to Russ Train, September 3, 1971, folder, "Chron, July–Oct. 1971, J. C. Whitaker [3 of 4, September 1971]," Box 4, JWF; John C. Whitaker to Al Alm, June 2, 1972, folder, "Annual Report '72, Council on Environ. Quality [from CFOA 249]," Box 43, JWF.
8. OMB Director to William Ruckelshaus, May 21, 1971, v, "Environmental Protection Agency, 1971 [from OA 8143] [1 of 4]," Box 64, JWF.
9. Memo to Train, Ruckelshaus, Peter Peterson, and Virginia Knauer, Subject was "Quality of Life Balance—Consumer/Environment/Industry/Safety," folder, "WHCF: Subject Categories GEN EX FG 298 Environmental Protection Agency 1/1/71—[1972, Folder 1 of 3]," Box 1, FG 298, Richard Nixon Presidential Library.
10. Nixon advisors had recognized from the outset that this review would be controversial, treading as it did on the autonomy of a new and popular agency. Don Rice to George Shultz and Weinberger, May 10, 1971, folder, "Environmental Protection Agency, 1971 [from OA 8143] [1 of 4]," Box 64, JWF; In a testament to the continued sensitivity of such review, some advisors debated announcing the formal Quality of

Life Review orally to agency heads to slow leaks to the press before ultimately deciding that the review would be announced quietly in a memo. James C. Whitaker to Don Rice, July 16, 1971, folder, "WHCF: SMOF: John C. Whitaker Subject File. Quality of Life—1971 [from OA 8146] [1 of 4]," Box 96, JWF.

11. Memo to Train, Ruckelshaus, Peter Peterson, and Virginia Knauer, folder, "WHCF: Subject Categories GEN EX FG 298 Environmental Protection Agency 1/1/71—[1972, Folder 1 of 3]," Box 1, FG 298, Richard Nixon Presidential Library.

12. John C. Whitaker to Ken Cole, February 29, 1972, folder, "EPA [Environmental Protection Agency]—1971 [from CFOA 1139] [3 of 3]," Box 63, JWF.

13. Hubert Heffner memo to John Ehrlichman, July 9, 1971, folder, "Quality of Life—1971 [from OA 8146] [1 of 4]," Box 96, JWF.

14. John C. Whitaker to Ken Cole, February 29, 1972, folder, "EPA [Environmental Protection Agency]—1971 [from CFOA 1139] [3 of 3]," Box 63, JWF.

15. Jim Tozzi to Frank Zarb, June 6, 1974. Digitized online at http://thecre.com/ombpapers/QualityofLife5.htm.

16. Bureau of National Affairs, Inc., "Office of Management and Budget Plays Critical Part in Environmental Policymaking, Faces Little External Review," *Environment Reporter* 7, no. 18 (September 3, 1976): 693.

17. Richard Ayres, speaking on Implementation of the Clean Air Act Amendments of 1970, Hearings before the Subcommittee on Air and Water Pollution of the Committee on Public Works, February 16, 1972.

18. David Hawkins interview with author, September 18, 2015.

19. William Ruckelshaus interview with author, May 13, 2016.

20. Roy Gamse interview with author, May 4, 2015.

21. Bud Ward interview with author, April 24, 2015; Tozzi, for his part, seems to have given the EPA analysis a pretty fair shake, at least in the first few years of regulatory review. Often asked to evaluate the EPA's own analysis for advisors in the Nixon and Ford administrations, Tozzi typically offered suggestions for improving the EPA's analysis but noted that the agency's internal review was generally quite good. Tozzi memos, folder, "FG 298 5/1/75—10/31/75," Box 187, FG 298, Gerald R. Ford Library.

22. Kerry Clough interview with author, July 26, 2015.

23. Kerry Clough interview with author, July 26, 2015.

24. Peter Flanigan to John Ehrlichman, October 16, 1972, folder, "WHCF: Subject Categories GEN EX FG 298 Environmental Protection Agency 1/1/71—[1972, folder 3 of 3]," Box 2, FG 298, Richard Nixon Presidential Library.

25. At one point, Nixon advisors were so concerned about such leaks that Whitaker sent a chastising note about a lead removal proposal to Ruckelshaus at his home address, explaining that "I have lost confidence that there is such a thing as private communication in your shop." Whitaker demanded Ruckelshaus take disciplinary action if he found the leak, noting that "big issues," must remain in confidence so that they could be rejected by the White House without fear of political blowback. John C. Whitaker to Bill Ruckelshaus, January 21, 1972, folder, "EPA [Environmental Protection Agency]—1971 [from CFOA 1139] [3 of 3]," Box 63, JWF.

26. Peter Flanigan to John Ehrlichman, October 16 1972, folder, "WHCF: Subject Categories GEN EX FG 298 Environmental Protection Agency 1/1/71—[1972, folder 3 of 3]," Box 2, FG 298, Richard Nixon Presidential Library.

27. "A Layoff Warning Issued by Carbide," January 20, 1971, Folder 2, Box 73A, EMP.

28. Ralph Nader to Edmund Muskie, January 20, 1971; Edmund Muskie to Ralph Nader, undated; Edmund Muskie to Birny Mason, undated; Edmund Muskie to William Ruckelshaus, undated. All letters in Folder 2, Box 73A, EMP.

29. In 1975, the AFL-CIO announced that thirty-nine firms had blamed plant closings on environmental regulations between 1970 and 1974 and that local unions in each case had found no evidence that regulations were primarily responsible. Bureau of National Affairs, Inc., "AFL-CIO Department Rejects Claims that Environmental, Safety Rules Close Plants," *Environment Reporter* 6, no. 21 (September 19, 1975): 872.

30. John C. Whitaker to James Lynn, Russell Train, and William Ruckelshaus, July 12, 1971, folder, "Chron, July–Oct. 1971, J. C. Whitaker [1 of 4, July 1971]," Box 4, JWF, emphasis in original.

31. Malcolm R. Lovell Jr. to William Ruckelshaus, November 9, 1971, folder "Laa-Lac," Box 66, Office of the Administrator, General Correspondence, 1971–1982, RG 412, Records of the Environmental Protection Agency, National Archives and Records Administration, College Park (hereafter EPA Admin. Correspondence).

32. Bureau of National Affairs, Inc., "Labor Department, EPA to Cooperate on Economic Dislocation of Control," *Environment Reporter* 2, no. 30 (November 30, 1971): 884–885.

33. US EPA, Economic Dislocation Early Warning System, Second Quarterly Report— January–March 1972." Included in William Ruckelshaus to James Hodgson, July 21, 1972, folder "Laa-Lac," Box 66, EPA Admin. Correspondence.

34. Roy Gamse, "The Impact of the Environmental Program on Jobs," Outline of Comments by Roy N. Gamse, Director EPA Economic Analysis Division at the Environmental Study Conference on Jobs and the Environment, February 23, 1976, folder "Labor and Environment," Box 22, Carlton Neville Collection, Donated Historical Material, Jimmy Carter Presidential Library.

35. Roy Gamse interview with author, May 4, 2015.

36. William Ruckelshaus, "The Costs and Benefits of Pollution Control," presented to the Los Angeles Chamber of Commerce Symposium, March 30, 1972, folder, "Mar. 30, 1972—Los Angeles Cham. of Commerce Symposium, L.A., Cali," Box 5, Papers of William D. Ruckelshaus, Speeches 1970–72, Richard Nixon Presidential Library.

37. William Ruckelshaus, "The Costs and Benefits of Pollution Control," presented to the Los Angeles Chamber of Commerce Symposium, March 30, 1972, folder, "Mar. 30, 1972—Los Angeles Cham. of Commerce Symposium, L.A., Cali," Box 5, Papers of William D. Ruckelshaus, Speeches 1970–72, Richard Nixon Presidential Library.

38. From the beginning, the Quality of Life Review Committee had found itself consumed with the basic problem of "how to get the facts." John Whitaker to John Ehrlichman, July 20, 1971, folder, "WHCF Subject Files [EX] FG 6-17 1/1/71–7/31/71," Box 1, FG 6-17 Council on Environmental Quality, Richard Nixon Presidential Library.

39. Sometimes, individual entities coordinated this research and lobbying, as when the Tennessee Valley Authority's Aubrey Wagner sent Nixon's administration a report it had commissioned on the extent of its own compliance cost burden in 1972. In words that must have seemed promising, Nixon advisor Peter Flanigan thanked Wagner for sending the report, noting "although we are becoming increasingly aware of industry resistance to mounting costs, seldom is sufficient detail available to provide a compelling case for possible reassessment." Peter Flanigan to Aubrey Wagner, November 30, 1972, folder, "WHCF: Subject Categories GEN EX FG 298 Environmental Protection Agency 1/1/71—[1972, Folder 3 of 3]," Box 2, FG 298, Richard Nixon Presidential Library.

40. John Whitaker to John Ehrlichman, March 28, 1973, folder, "[CF] FG 298 Environmental Protection Agency [1971–74]," Box 26, Subject Files: Confidential Files, 1969–1974, Richard Nixon Presidential Library.

41. Memos between Kenneth Cole and Chuck Perry, December 1971, folder, "WHCF: Subject Files (BE) Business-Economics. EX BE 5-2 Cost of Living. [4 of 9] March 1971–February 1972," Box 60, Subject Files, EX BE 5-2, Richard Nixon Presidential Library.

42. Donald Crabill, deputy associate director for Natural Resources within the OMB put together a report for Richard Fairbanks (an advisor to John Whitaker) on accounting for consumer satisfaction in calculating the costs of auto emission standards. Donald Crabill to Richard Fairbanks, April 25, 1973, folder, "WHCF: SMOF: Whitaker Subject File, Auto Emissions [from CFOA 1140] [1 of 2]," Box 29, JWF.

43. John Whitaker to Tod Hullin, September 29, 1971, folder, "WHCF: SMOF Fairbanks Subject File, Environmental Economics, 3. Materials [from OA 10144] [1 of 3]," Box 132, JWF.

44. John C. Whitaker to Tod Hullin, September 29, 1971, folder, "WHCF: SMOF: Fairbanks Subject File, Environmental Economics, 3. Materials [from OA 10144] [1 of 3]," Box 132, JWF.

45. Dick Fairbanks to John Whitaker, July 27, 1971, folder, "Environmental Economics, 3. Materials [from OA 10144] [2 of 3]," Box 132, JWF.

46. McCracken Report, 1972, folder, "WHCF: SMOF: Whitaker Subject Files Economics [from CFOA 822]," Box 54, JWF.

47. Bureau of National Affairs, Inc., "No Industry to Be Severely Affected by Control Costs, Government Reports," Environment Reporter 2, no. 46 (March 17, 1972): 1391–1392.

48. McCracken Report, 1972, folder, "WHCF: SMOF: Whitaker Subject Files Economics [from CFOA 822]," Box 54, JWF.

49. Bureau of National Affairs, Inc., "White House Report Concludes Cost of Controls Will Outweigh Benefits," Environment Reporter 2, no. 47 (March 24, 1972): 1417.

50. John Whitaker to John Ehrlichman, March 28, 1973, folder, "[CF] FG 298 Environmental Protection Agency [1971–74]," Box 26, Subject Files: Confidential Files, 1969–1974, FG 298, Richard Nixon Presidential Library.

51. Senator Ed Muskie Speech to Florida State Senate, April 27, 1971, Folder 1, Box 76, Edmund S. Muskie Papers, Edmund S. Muskie Archives and Special Collections Library, Bates College (hereafter EMP).

52. Senator Eagleton, responding to testimony from NRDC's Richard Ayres, declared that "on this question of an economic factor, I am as positive about this as a mortal can be, that was specifically written out of the bill." Senator Eagleton, speaking on Implementation of the Clean Air Act Amendments of 1970—Part 1 (Title I), Hearings before the Subcommittee on Air and Water Pollution of the Committee on Public Works, United States Senate, Ninety-Second Congress, Second Session, February 16, 17, 18, and 23, 1972. Serial No. 92-H31, February 16, 1972; Senator Boggs, speaking on speaking on Implementation of the Clean Air Act Amendments of 1970—Part 1 (Title I), Hearings before the Subcommittee on Air and Water Pollution of the Committee on Public Works, United States Senate, Ninety-Second Congress, Second Session, February 16, 17, 18, and 23, 1972. Serial No. 92-H31, February 23, 1972.

53. Maria Grimes and Robert Want to Leon Billings, March 16, 1973, Folder 1, Box 102, EMP; In subsequent hearings on the Clean Air Act, the subcommittee continued to collect information on such subjects as the "implications of environmental controls on national growth policy," as well as the "implication of environmental controls on energy policy and fuels availability." Leon Billings to Edmund Muskie, February 5, 1973, Folder 7, Box 74, EMP.

54. Leon Billings, undated memo, Folder 10, Box 74, EMP.

55. Edmund Muskie, "Government in the Sunshine," Remarks at the Tiger Bay Club, Tallahassee, Florida, January 7, 1972, Folder 4, Box 73A, EMP.

56. Leon Billings to files, February 9, 1972, Folder 10, Box 74, EMP.

57. Leon Billings to L. Street Research, January 20, 1972, Folder 1, Box 76, EMP.

58. Ruckelshaus first encountered Teeter in Ruckelshaus's run for a US Senate seat in Indiana in the 1960s and brought the pollster into the EPA's planning process. William Ruckelshaus interview with author, May 13, 2016.

59. John C. Whitaker to John D. Ehrlichman, June 14, 1971, folder, "Chron, April–June 1971, J. C. Whitaker [3 of 3, May 1971]," Box 4, JWF. As Teeter wrote in January 1972 memo to the Nixon campaign, the environment figured as an important secondary issue that would likely rise in importance. Teeter also noted that the environment was a key concern for the young affluent voters who often voted a split Republican and Democratic ticket and whose vote had proved crucial in swing states. Indeed, Teeter continued, the environment might be the only issue on which Nixon could appeal to these voters. Robert Teeter to H. R. Haldeman, January 6, 1972, folder, "January 6, 1972—H.R. Haldeman—The Environment," Box 64, Teeter Papers, Richard Nixon Presidential Library.

60. John C. Whitaker to John D. Ehrlichman, July 9, 1971, folder, "Chron, July–Oct. 1971, J. C. Whitaker [1 of 4, July 1971]," Box 4, JWF.

61. John C. Whitaker to Ed Harper, July 9, 1971, folder, "Chron, July–Oct. 1971, J. C. Whitaker [1 of 4, July 1971]," Box 4, JWF.

62. Opinion Research Corporation, "U.S. Voters Appraise Candidates and Issues," January 1972, pp. 32–33, 57, folder, "US Voters Appraise Candidates and Issues Jan. 1972 (1)," Box 2, 1972 Presidential Campaign: National Polls, Robert Teeter Papers, 1967–77, Gerald R. Ford Library.

63. Opinion Research Corporation, "1972 Presidential Campaign: National Polls, September 1972," folder, "National Survey, Sept. 1972 (1)," Box 4, 1972 Presidential Campaign: National Polls, Robert Teeter Papers, 1967–77, Gerald R. Ford Library.

64. Miller Center of Public Affairs, University of Virginia. "Richard Nixon: Campaigns and Elections," accessed December 23, 2015, http://millercenter.org/president/biography/nixon-campaigns-and-elections.

65. Conrad Black, *Richard M. Nixon: A Life in Full* (New York: Public Affairs, 2007).

66. Mike Duval to Ken Cole, September 10, 1974, folder, "WE Welfare 8/9/74–9/30/74 Executive," Box 1, Subject File WE Welfare, White House Central File, Gerald R. Ford Library.

67. Allan Pulsipher to Glenn Schleede, September 18, 1974, and September 26, 1974, folder, "Economic Impact of Environmental Programs, 1974: General (2)," Box 9, Glenn R. Schleede, Files: 1974–1977, Domestic Council, Gerald R. Ford Library.

68. Meeting Notes and Memo, "President's Meeting with Dr. Stever," September 18, 1974, folder "6. Presidential Meeting 9/19/74: Mtg. w/ Guy Stever re National Science Foundation programs," Box 3, Kenneth R. Cole Jr. Files, 1974–1975, Gerald R. Ford Library.

69. Glenn Schleede, draft of "Analyses Directed toward Achieving Balancing among National Objectives," folder, "WE Welfare 8/9/74–9/30/74 Executive," Box 1, Subject File WE Welfare, White House Central Files, Gerald R. Ford Library.

70. According to the report, the EPA undercounted the capital expenditures forced on the industry by pollution controls, which had risen 18 percent in the previous five years. An additional 28 percent increase in capital costs could be attributed to pollution control requirements in other industries that supplied materials for the paper manufacturers. Jim Cavanaugh to George Humphreys, October 9, 1975, folder, "BE 4-26 Paper and allied products 8/9/74–1/20/77 Executive," Box 13, Subject File, BE, White House Central Files, Gerald R. Ford Library.

71. Jim Cavanaugh to George Humphreys, October 9, 1975, folder, "BE 4-26 Paper and allied products 8/9/74–1/20/77 Executive," Subject File, BE, White House Central Files, Gerald R. Ford Library.

72. Notes from meeting between Russell Train and Gerald Ford, September 4, 1974, folder, "3. Presidential Meeting 9/4/74: w/ Russell Train re EPA matters," Box 3, Kenneth R. Cole Jr. Files, 1974–1975, Domestic Council, Gerald R. Ford Library.

73. In one letter, Train detailed changes the agency had made to its rulemaking process to ensure that its regulations were not "overly burdensome." Russell Train to Gerald Ford, October 2, 1975, folder, "BE 2 9/1/75–10/6/75 Executive," Box 2, Subject File BE, White House Central Files, Gerald R. Ford Library. In another missive, Train passed on a letter from the Bay Area Council (the San Francisco business advocate) thanking him for a lecture he had delivered on the possibility of finding "accommodation . . . between environmental and economic goals." Russell Train to William J. Barody Jr., folder, "WE 9/22/75–10/31/75 Executive," September 22, 1975, Subject File WE, White House Central Files, Gerald R. Ford Library.

74. Glenn Schleede to Mike Duval and Jim Cavanaugh, October 1, 1974, folder, "FG 298 Environmental Protection Agency, 8/9/74–10/31/74 Executive," Box 187, Subject File

FG 298 United States Environmental Protection Agency, White House Central Files, Gerald R. Ford Library.

75. Bureau of National Affairs, Inc., "Arguments For and Against 'Scrubbers' Largely Ignore Possible Economic Effects," *Environment Reporter* 5, no. 28 (November 8, 1974): 1109–1110; AEP CEO Donald Cook's aggressive hostility to the EPA was noteworthy, attracting articles like E. W. Kenworthy, "Donald Cook vs. E.P.A.," *New York Times,* November 24, 1974.

76. For instance, less than a month before AEP ran its tombstone ads, an internal EPA study found nearly 100 scrubbers already in use at over 50 electric power plants. Bureau of National Affairs, Inc., "EPA Reports in Use, Reliability of Scrubbers Installed by Power Plants," *Environment Reporter* 5, no. 22 (September 27, 1974): 793.

77. Mike Duval to the president, October 31, 1974, folder, "FG 298 Environmental Protection Agency, 8/9/74–10/31/74 Executive," Box 187, FG 298, White House Central Files, Subject File, Gerald R. Ford Library.

78. The court cited analysis provided by the industry that scrubbers would raise the utility bills 23 to 35 percent. Bureau of National Affairs, Inc., "Third Circuit Tells EPA to Reconsider Economic Implications of 'Scrubber' Use," *Environment Reporter* 6, no. 19 (September 5, 1975): 758–759.

79. Edwin Clark to Glenn Schleede, September 9, 1974, folder, "Economic Impact of Environmental Programs, 1974: Council on Environmental Quality Summary (1)," Box 9, Glenn R. Schleede Files, Gerald R. Ford Library (hereafter GSF).

80. Expertise in evaluating compliance costs seems to have been coalescing in this period in the discipline of economics. One memo unrelated to the CEQ survey suggests that compliance costs conducted by economists appear to have been valued over those done by engineers. George Humphreys to Jim Cavanaugh, November 12, 1975, folder, "FG 6-17 7/1/75–2/29/76," Box 65, FG 6-17, Council on Environmental Quality, Gerald R. Ford Library.

81. Council on Environmental Quality, "Studies Relating to the Economic Impact of Environment Programs," September 1974, folder, "Economic Impact of Environmental Programs, 1974: Council on Environmental Quality Summary (4)," Box 9, GSF.

82. Alan Carlin, "History of Economic Research at the EPA," US EPA, National Center for Environment Economics, accessed December 9, 2015. http://yosemite.epa.gov/ ee/epa/eed.nsf/00000000000000000000000000000000/2f68aa9ffb75364b852577970 0781a24!OpenDocument; EPA Grant # CPA 22-69-52. http://yosemite.epa.gov/ee/ epa/eerm.nsf/vwRepNumLookup/EE-0206!OpenDocument&ExpandSection=3#_ Section3; EPA Grant # CPA 22-69-52. http://yosemite.epa.gov/ee/epa/eerm.nsf/ vwRepNumLookup/EE-0206!OpenDocument&ExpandSection=3#_Section3

83. See, for example, Kenneth Boulding, "Economics of the Coming Spaceship Earth," address at the 1966 Resources for the Future Forum on Environmental Quality, Washington, DC, March 8–9, 1966.

84. E. F. Schumacher, *Small Is Beautiful: A Study of Economics as if People Mattered* (London: Blond and Briggs, 1973), critiqued the prevailing assumptions about the connections between economic growth and human happiness; Paul Sabin,

The Bet: Paul Ehrlich, Julian Simon, and Our Gamble over Earth's Future (New Haven, CT: Yale University Press, 2013), describes how Ehrlich became a public luminary in the 1970s with his pronouncements that the earth faced a Malthusian population bomb.

85. Exemplifying this trend, the first issue of the *Journal of Economics and Management* (edited by Allen Kneese and Ralph D'Arge) featured articles like W. Beckerman and A. Markandya, "Pollution Control and Optimal Taxation: A Static Analysis," *Journal of Economics and Management* 1, no. 1 (1974): 43–52, and A. Myrick Freeman, "On Estimating Air Pollution Control Benefits from Land Value Studies," *Journal of Economics and Management* 1, no. 1 (1974): 74–83.

86. A. Myrick Freeman, Robert Haveman, and Allen Kneese, *The Economics of Environmental Policy* (New York: John Wiley, 1973). Two other early practitioners in the field listed the first textbooks in email exchanges with me. Tom Tietenberg, email message to author, September 17 and 20, 2015; Lynne Lewis, email message to author, September 20, 2015.

87. See, for example, EPA Research Grant Number R805059010, "Methods Development for Assessing Tradeoffs in Environmental Management," $690,000, for which Crocker served as project director.

88. Frank L. Cross Jr. and Susan M. Hennigan, *National Directory of Environmental Impact Experts, Consultants, Regulatory Agencies* (Westport, CT: Technomic Publishing, 1974).

89. Michael Levin interview with author, March 16, 2015.

90. Richard Morgenstern interview with author, May 5, 2015.

91. Executive Order 11821 of November 27, 1974, Inflation Impact Statements. http://www.presidency.ucsb.edu/ws/?pid=23905.

92. A statement would be triggered by any of the following criteria: over $100 million in additional annual compliance costs, an increase in a product's price by more than 5 percent, an increase in national oil consumption of more than 25,000 barrels per day, and a 3 percent increase in national demand for steel (or a commensurate reduction in the national supply). Bureau of National Affairs, Inc., "OMB Approves EPA Guidelines on Inflation Impact Statements," *Environment Reporter* 6, no. 33 (December 12, 1975): 1386–1387.

93. Executive Order 11949 of December 31, 1976, Economic Impact Statements. http://www.presidency.ucsb.edu/ws/?pid=23684.

94. Paul to Roderick Hills, folder, "EPA (2)," Box 31, Edward C. Schmults Files, Gerald R. Ford Library.

95. "Transition Memo for the Carter Administration," 1976, folder, "6 [COWPS] [18]," Box 102, CSF.

96. Testimony of W. Howard Winn on Behalf of Kennecott Copper Corporation before Administrative Law Judge Paul N. Pfeiffer, Ely, Nevada, March 12, 1974. Docket No. CAA-2, folder, "Sec 110(f) Hearing [Clean Air Act]," Region IX Enforcement Div., Hearing Officer's Records 1972–1976, P to S. (18), RG 412 EPA, National Archives and Records Administration, San Bruno.

97. G. P. Etcheverry (Mayor), Joaquin Gomez (Councilman), Garey A. Harrison (Councilman), and Floyd O. Ricketts (Councilman) to Administrative Law Judge Paul N. Pfeiffer, March 8 1974; James J. Mahoney (County Auditor) to Paul N. Pfeiffer, March 12 1974; Morris Sundrick (chairman, Board of County Commissioners) to Paul N. Pfeiffer, March 11, 1974; R. B. Scott (Deputy Assessor) to Administrative Law Judge Paul N. Pfeiffer, March 11 1974; Lloyd Williams (Recording Secretary, Central Labor Council) to Paul Pfeiffer, March 1974; James Chacas (President, White Pine Jaycees) to Paul Pfeiffer; Clare Olsen (General Manager, Mt. Wheeler Power, Inc.) to Paul N. Pfeiffer, March 12 1974. All letters in folder, "Sec 110(f) Hearing [Clean Air Act]," Region IX Enforcement Div., Hearing Officer's Records 1972–1976, P to S. (18), RG 412 EPA, National Archives and Records Administration, San Bruno.

98. Ford advisors had concluded from a survey of existing pollution control technology in the smelter industry that such an exemption was needed to avoid major shutdowns and had helped to work out the compromise with the EPA before the agency announced its final rules on smelters. Unknown to Mike Duval, October 17, 1974, folder, "HE 9-1 Air Pollution 8/9/74–12/31/74," Box 13, HE 9-1, Gerald R. Ford Library.

99. Robert List to Gerald Ford, July 30, 1976; James Santini to Gerald Ford, July 2, 1976; Mike O'Callaghan to Gerald Ford, September 4, 1976; Larry Dunton to Gerald Ford, June 16, 1976. All letters in folder, "HE 9-1 6/1/76–7/3076 Executive," Box 13, White House Central Files, Subject File, Gerald R. Ford Library.

100. George Humphreys to Congressman James Santini, August 9, 1976, folder, "HE 9-1 6/1/76–7/3076 Executive," Box 13, White House Central Files, Subject File, Gerald R. Ford Library.

101. In January 1977 Kennecott successfully appealed the EPA administrative judge's decision and quickly reopened the smelter, only to have an appeals court rule in the EPA's favor and once again close operations at McGill in April 1977. G. William Frick to administrator, April 27, 1977, folder, "Region 9," Box 16, Office of Regional and Intergovernmental Operations, Regional Correspondence, RG 412: Records of the Environmental Protection Agency, National Archives and Records Administration.

102. William Trombley, "Battered Nevada Town Finally Feels a Hint of Shifting Economic Winds," LA Times November 30, 1986, accessed August 20, 2015, http://articles.latimes.com/1986-11-30/news/mn-515_1_nevada-town.

103. Kennecott Copper Corporation, 1976 Annual Report.

104. R. Shep Melnik and other commentators have described Kennecott's strategy to forgo investment in pollution control and invest instead in court challenges to delay enforcement actions as a common ploy used by corporations with already declining productivity. R. Shep Melnik, Regulation and the Courts: The Case of the Clean Air Act (New York: Brookings Institution Press, 1983).

105. Already by 1971, the EPA had concluded that the automobile manufacturers could not produce a technological solution (such as the catalytic converter) in time to meet emissions standards deadlines set for the industry. Even with the catalytic converter, however, cities like Los Angeles had no hope of meeting the 1975 deadlines, since only new cars would have the controls. John Whitaker to John

Ehrlichman, June 25, 1971, folder, "WHCF: Subject Files: EX FG 6-16 OMB. EX FG 6-16 Office of Management and Budget [6/16/71]–6/30/71," Box 2, FG 6–16, Office of Management and Budget, White House Central Files, Gerald R. Ford Library; a subsequent EPA study concluded that gasoline consumption would have to be cut by over 80 percent in Los Angeles to meet the 1975 deadline. Tom McCarthy, *Auto Mania: Cars, Consumers, and the Environment* (New Haven, CT: Yale University Press, 2007).

106. Unwilling to propose draconian restrictions on driving that were politically untenable to enforce, California's Air Resources Board submitted a plan in January 1972 that they knew did not provide a viable path to meeting the 1975 deadline. Under the watchful eye of organizations like the Natural Resources Defense Council, the EPA rejected California's implementation plan in May 1972, thus compelling the agency to promulgate its own plan for the state. The EPA did so in September 1972 but found itself promptly sued by a local environmental group for failing to include the transportation controls—the only means by which the photochemical standard might conceivably be met by the 1975 deadline. Litigating on behalf of the cities of Riverside and San Bernardino, the Center for Law in the Public Interest filed a civil suit in September 1972 to compel Ruckelshaus to create a transportation control plan for the South Coast Air Basin. Despite the EPA's argument that an adequate plan was forthcoming, the US Central District of California Court held that the EPA was obligated under the Clean Air Act to produce a plan capable of achieving the standards by the 1975 deadline. The court gave Ruckelshaus until January 15, 1973, to promulgate a plan with the necessary transportation controls. Simultaneously, NRDC won a decision against the EPA in the US Court of Appeals for the District of Columbia Circuit that compelled the agency to insist that the states include land-use and transportation controls if that was the only means of attaining the standards by the 1975 deadline. Tom McCarthy, *Auto Mania: Cars, Consumers, and the Environment* (New Haven, CT: Yale University Press, 2007).

107. Ken Cole to Richard Nixon, January 15, 1973, folder, "WHCF: Subject Categories EX FG 298 Environmental Protection Agency 1/1/73–4/30/73," Box 2, FG 298, White House Central Files, Richard Nixon Presidential Library.

108. The EPA's senior management openly questioned the viability of the controls and echoed Ruckelshaus in depicting their own hands as tied by the court and congressional mandates. The EPA's chief counsel John R. Quarles Jr. cast a hopeful image of the Los Angeles community coming together to achieve the reductions in an interview with *Environment Reporter* in January 1973 before admitting that even if the EPA had internally decided that such reductions were not realistic, the agency was still compelled to make every effort to achieve the deadlines in the act. The EPA would not appeal to Congress for relief, Quarles claimed, but he allowed that state legislators might do so. Bureau of National Affairs, Inc., "EPA Proposes Gasoline Rationing Plan for Los Angeles Area," *Environment Reporter* 3, no. 38 (January 19, 1973): 1097–1098; Robert Sansom, the head of EPA's air program, told a group in New York City in June that the EPA would soon ask Congress to reconsider the feasibility of the 1975 deadline. Sansom cited the drastic reductions needed in Los

Angeles as a prime example of the difficulties that Congress had not foreseen in setting the 1975 deadline. Bureau of National Affairs, Inc., "Sansom Says EPA to Request Congress to Establish Realistic Clean Air Goals," *Environment Reporter* 4, no. 12 (July 20, 1973): 461–462; Robert Fri, who succeeded Ruckelshaus as acting administrator when Ruckelshaus left to head the Federal Bureau of Investigation, was blunter. Speaking with *Environment Reporter* in June 1973, Fri declared that the EPA would "play out," the Clean Air Act, "no matter what the outcome, and then ask Congress if that's what it wanted." Fri continued that he was "not so sure these are the results the Congress intended," adding "nor do I consider them reasonable." Fri said he would ask Congress in September to extend California's deadline for at least five years. Bureau of National Affairs, Inc., "Fri Calls for Clean Air Act Changes to Avoid Extreme Automobile Controls," *Environment Reporter* 4, no. 8 (June 22, 1973): 266–269; based on interviews concerning the transportation control plans, historian Tom McCarthy has drawn the same conclusion—that Ruckelshaus and the EPA intended the plans in part to shock the public into "send[ing] a message to Congress about amending the law." Tom McCarthy, *Auto Mania: Cars, Consumers, and the Environment* (New Haven, CT: Yale University Press, 2007).

109. William Ruckelshaus interview with author, May 13, 2016.

110. John Ehrlichman to Richard Nixon, March 1, 1973, folder, "WHCF: Subject Categories EX FG 298 Environmental Protection Agency 1/1/73–4/30/73," Box 2, FG 298, White House Central Files, Richard Nixon Presidential Library. Ever one to appreciate a bit of crafty politics, Nixon sent along a note reading "well done" to Ruckelshaus for his ploy. Bruce Kehrli to John Ehrlichman, March 10, 1973, folder, "WHCF: Subject Categories EX FG 298 Environmental Protection Agency 1/1/73–4/30/73," Box 2, FG 298, White House Central Files, Richard Nixon Presidential Library.

111. William Ruckelshaus interview with author, May 13, 2016.

112. R. E. Pentz to Richard Nixon, December 17, 1973, folder, "WHCF: Subject Categories GEN FG 298 [1973–1974]," Box 2, RG 298, Richard Nixon Presidential Library.

113. Frederick Llewellyn to EPA Region 9, March 5, 1973, folder, "Air Quality [from CFOA 1140]," Box 24, JWF.

114. Bureau of National Affairs, Inc., "EPA Transportation Control Plans Seen Causing 'Complete Paralysis'" *Environment Reporter* 5, no. 27 (November 1, 1974): 1053.

115. Jerry M. Patterson to President Richard M. Nixon, December 5, 1973, folder, "WHCF: Subject Categories EX FG 298 1/1/74–5/30/74," Box 2, RG 298, Richard Nixon Presidential Library.

116. Petition Regarding the Environmental Protection Agency Rules and Regulations to be implemented July 1, 1974, in the City of Sunnyvale. December 3 1973, folder, "WHCF: Subject Categories GEN FG 298 [1973–1974]," Box 2, FG 298, White House Central Files, Richard Nixon Presidential Library.

117. McCarthy, *Auto Mania*, 199–200.

118. Nixon Advisor Glenn Schleede warned that the Boston plan represented a harbinger of federal intrusions into "the business of others." The EPA withdrew the Boston

proposal shortly thereafter. Glenn Schleede to Ken Cole, August 13, 1974, folder, "Environmental Protection Agency, 1974: Air Quality Transportation Control Plans," Box 17, GSF.

119. *Energy Supply and Environmental Coordination Act of 1974*, Public Law 93–319, *U.S. Statutes at Large* 88 (1974): 246–265.

120. Over the next few years, various court rulings and the Clean Air Act amendments of 1977 vacated most of the EPA's statutory mandates to require transportation controls and gun-shy agency officials backed away from any further mandatory programs. McCarthy, *Auto Mania*.

121. One angry pamphlet denounced the parking lot controls as the work of environmentalist organizations like NRDC that had effectively captured the EPA and called for an FBI investigation into the "leftist subversive presence or pressure [that] has crept into that agency." Though such accusations sounded intemperate in 1974, by the end of the decade they provided the ideological basis for the Republican Party's attacks on federal regulatory agencies. W. S. McBirnie, "E.P.A. Destroyer of America!" Attached to David Hawkins to Staff and Board of Trustees, March 7, 1974, folder, "March 7, 1974 Executive Committee," Box 3, NRDC Records.

122. Bureau of National Affairs, Inc., "Train Delivers Far-Ranging Defense of Economic Role of Pollution Control," *Environment Reporter* 5, no. 23 (October 4, 1974): 845–846; Bureau of National Affairs, Inc., "Sawhill Sees Environmental Benefits Offsetting Economic, Energy Costs," *Environment Reporter* 5, no. 30 (November 22, 1974): 1180–1182; Bureau of National Affairs, Inc., "EPA, CEQ Release Final Chase Report on Pollution Controls' Economic Impact," *Environment Reporter* 5, no. 39 (January 24, 1975): 1477.

123. Memos on $2,000 claim are in folder, "Regulatory Reform May 1975 (2)," Box 28, James Canon Papers, Gerald R. Ford Library.

Chapter 4

1. Conference program, registration list, and introduction all in folder, "Regulatory Reform: Economic Policy Review," Box 30, Edmund S. Muskie Papers, Edmund S. Muskie Archives and Special Collections Library, Bates College, Lewiston, Maine (hereafter EMP).

2. US Environmental Protection Agency, "Controlled Trading: Putting the Profit Motive to Work for Pollution Control" (Washington, DC, 1980), Box W, Papers in Personal Collection of Michael Levin (hereafter MLP).

3. David Vogel, *Fluctuating Fortunes: The Political Power of Business in America* (New York: Basic Books, 1989). Vogel derived his data from two periodicals, "The Surprisingly High Cost of a Safer Environment," *Business Week*, September 14, 1974, and Steven Rattner, "Productivity Lag Causes Worry," *New York Times*, May 8, 1979.

4. Carl Biven, *Jimmy Carter's Economy: Policy in an Age of Limits* (Chapel Hill: University of North Carolina Press, 2002).

5. Michael Gorn interview with William Ruckelshaus, January 1993, EPA Oral History Series, https://archive.epa.gov/epa/aboutepa/william-d-ruckelshaus-oral-history-interview.html.

6. A 1973 report from the Council on Economic Priorities lauded Armco Steel Corporation as the nation's cleanest steel manufacturer, averaging just 4.1 pounds of particulate emissions and 2.1 pounds of sulfur dioxide emissions for each ton of steel produced. Armco's efforts toward compliance stood in stark contrast to those of National Steel Corporation, which emitted some 21.9 pounds of particulates and 15.2 pounds of sulfur dioxide for each ton. Bureau of National Affairs, Inc., "CEP Report says Steel Industry Fails to Meet Pollution Control Requirements," *Environment Reporter* 4, no. 4 (May 25, 1973): 134–135.

7. See, for example, Bureau of National Affairs, Inc., "U.S. Steel to Close Gary Furnaces Rather Than Pay $2,300 Daily Fine," *Environment Reporter* 5, no. 36 (January 3, 1975): 1375

8. Bureau of National Affairs, Inc., "Steel Industry Will Need up to $14 Billion to Meet Environmental Rules, Study Says," *Environment Reporter* 6, no. 5 (May 16, 1975): 134–135.

9. In calling for the EPA to closely review the report, Alm noted that the compliance cost predictions were within 30 percent of the EPA's own estimates. Bureau of National Affairs, Inc., "EPA Review of Steel Study Suggested; Battelle Reports on Clean Coal Process," *Environment Reporter* 6, no. 9 (June 27, 1975): 390.

10. Bureau of National Affairs, Inc., "Train Cites Progress, Problems in Meeting Air Quality Deadline," *Environment Reporter* 6, no. 6 (May 16, 1975): 305–306.

11. Marc Landy, Marc Roberts, and Stephen Thomas, *The Environmental Protection Agency: Asking the Wrong Questions* (New York: Oxford University Press, 1990).

12. Benjamin Waterhouse, *Lobbying America: The Politics of Business from Nixon to NAFTA* (Princeton, NJ: Princeton University Press, 2014).

13. David Vogel, *Fluctuating Fortunes: The Political Power of Business in America* (New York: Basic Books, 1989).

14. Waterhouse, *Lobbying America*.

15. Paul Sabin, "Environmental Law and the End of the New Deal Order," *Law and History Review* 33, no. 4 (2015): 965–1003.

16. Myrick Freeman and Robert A. Haveman, "Clean Rhetoric and Dirty Water," *Public Interest* 28 (Summer 1972): 51–85.

17. Kneese and Schultze reported on the preliminary results of the study in Resources for the Future, *1973 Annual Report*.

18. Arthur Burns to Staff Secretary, January 8, 1970, folder, "WHCF Subject Files [EX] FG 6–17 Council on Environmental Quality, Begin [6/24/69]–4/31/70 1," Box 1, FG 6–17, Richard Nixon Presidential Library.

19. Council on Environmental Quality, "Decision Paper: Sulfur Oxides," November 27, 1970, attached to Alvin Alm to Bruce Segal et al., December 2, 1970, folder, "EPA Start-Up Issues [1]," Box 84, Doug Costle's Ash Council Files, Doug Costle Papers, Jimmy Carter Library (hereafter DCP).

20. Bureau of National Affairs, Inc. "Sulfur Emissions Tax Recommended by Walter Heller, Other Economists," *Environment Reporter* 3, no. 4 (May 26, 1972): 104.

21. William Ruckelshaus interview with author, May 13, 2016.

22. Roy Gamse interview with author, May 4, 2015.

23. Explaining his support for a tax, Train stated that it would encourage firms to invest in control technology research and development—of the sort that electric power executives had declared nonexistent in testifying during the same hearings. Bureau of National Affairs, Inc., "Train Recommends Air Pollution Tax as Valuable Supplement to Regulations," *Environment Reporter* 4, no. 22 (September 28, 1973): 857–858.

24. Bureau of National Affairs, Inc. "Pollution Taxes Self-Defeating Petroleum Institute Spokesman Says," *Environment Reporter* 2, no. 24 (October 16, 1971): 701–702.

25. Alan Pulsipher to Gary Seevers, September 17, 1974, attached to Alan Pulsipher to Alan Greenspan, April 24, 1975, folder, "Environment, April 15–June 30, 1975," Box 14, James Cannon Files, Gerald R. Ford Library.

26. Russell Train to Gerald Ford, October 2, 1975, attached to George Humphreys to Rod Hills, October 15, 1975, folder, "EPA (1)," Box 31, Edward C. Schmults Files: 1974-77, Gerald R. Ford Library (hereafter ESF).

27. Vance Hartke to Gerald Ford, January 22, 1975, folder, "HE 9-1 1/1/75–6/30/75," Box 13, HE 9-1, Gerald R. Ford Library.

28. Andrew Needham, *Power Lines: Phoenix and the Making of the Modern Southwest* (Princeton, NJ: Princeton University Press, 2015).

29. As early as 1971, a senior official in the Department of the Interior warned the Senate that new protections were likely needed to protect national parks against the pollutants created by proliferating electric power facilities, particularly around the Four Corners region, where a pair of massive plants was under construction. Countering that claim, the chairman of the Federal Power Commission testified at the same hearings and urged instead that Congress avoid any new pollution controls in order to ensure that the region's growing metropolises received the power they required. Bureau of National Affairs, Inc., "Pecora Says Legislation to Protect Recreational Values May Be Needed," *Environment Reporter* 2, no. 28 (November 12, 1971): 826–828.

30. Thomas Disselhorst, "Sierra Club v. Ruckelshaus: On a Clear Day . . . ," *Ecology Law Quarterly* 4, no. 3 (1975): 739–780.

31. The EPA's classification system consisted of three classes. No deterioration would be allowed in pristine Class I areas, which the EPA defined as areas of "exceptional scenic, recreational, or ecological value, or where no further major industrial growth is desired." Moderate deterioration would be allowed in Class II areas, and Class III areas could add emissions all the way up to limits imposed by the national air quality standards. Bureau of National Affairs, Inc., "EPA to Repropose Rules to Prevent Significant Air Quality Deterioration," *Environment Reporter* 5, no. 5 (May 31, 1974): 131–132.

32. In October 1975, for instance, NRDC's Dave Hawkins proposed bringing a contempt action against EPA Administrator Russell Train over his failure to prevent air

quality degradation. NRDC's Board of Directors affirmed the lawsuit as a last resort but asked about more collegial means of getting Train to issue sufficient regulations that might be pursued before that final resort—a strategy in keeping with NRDC's well-honed model of suggesting policy to EPA staffers before bringing lawsuits. Folder, "Minutes of a Regular Meeting of the Board of Trustees," October 30, 1975, Box 2, folder, "Oct. 30, 1975 Board Meeting," Natural Resources Defense Council Records, Yale University (hereafter NRDC Records). Meanwhile, Muskie and other legislators insisted that they had intended to prevent significant deterioration in the Clean Air Act and they repeatedly dragged EPA officials in to rebuke them for the agency's various failures to uphold this mandate, including attempting to transfer authority to the states. Bureau of National Affairs, Inc., "Muskie Says Congress Intended Act to Prohibit Significant Deterioration," *Environment Reporter* 4, no. 13 (July 27, 1973): 527–528; Bureau of National Affairs, Inc., "EPA Rules Would Give States Authority to Determine 'Significant Deterioration,'" *Environment Reporter* 5, no. 17 (August 23, 1974): 507–508.

33. Bureau of National Affairs, Inc., "NAM says Nondegradation Regulations Will Have 'Negative Effect' on Growth," *Environment Reporter* 6, no. 18 (August 29, 1975): 697–698.

34. Phoenix Chamber of Commerce, "Dynamic Phoenix," 1976, attached to Charles Leppert Jr. to Jim Cannon, January 20, 1976, folder, "Clean Air Strategy (2)," Box 9, George Humphreys Files 1975–1977, Domestic Council, Gerald R. Ford Library (hereafter GHF).

35. Reports contained in folder, "5003 Clean Air Act Amendments—Significant Deterioration—Electric Utilities December 1975–February 1976," Box 6, William Gorog Files, 1975–76, Office of Economic Affairs, Gerald R. Ford Library (hereafter WGF).

36. Richard Ayres to Russell Train, September 26 1975, attached to Richard Ayres to George Humphreys, October 16, 1975, folder, "Clean Air Strategy (1)," Box 9, GHF.

37. Richard Ayres to Russell Train, September 26, 1975, folder, "Clean Air Strategy (1)," Box 9, GHF.

38. Judith Hope, "The Scope of the Writ of EPA," October 13, 1975, memorandum for James Cannon, page 6, underlined for emphasis in original, folder, "EPA (2)," Box 31, ESF.

39. Judith Hope, "The Scope of the Writ of EPA," October 13, 1975, memorandum for James Cannon, folder, "EPA (2)," Box 31, ESF.

40. Allen Kneese and Charles Schultze, *Pollution, Prices, and Public Policy* (Washington, DC: Brookings Institution, 1975).

41. Kneese and Schultze, *Pollution, Prices, and Public Policy*, 2.

42. At the time, Mark Green was director of Nader's Corporate Accountability Research Group. Mark Green and Ralph Nader, "Economic Regulation vs. Competition: Uncle Sam the Monopoly Man," *Yale Law Journal* 82, no. 5 (April 1973): 871–889. Responding to a critique in the same issue of the journal, Green and another legal advocate expanded the distinction between economic regulation and health and safety

regulation. Mark Green and Beverly Moore, "Winter's Discontent: Market Failure and Consumer Welfare," *Yale Law Journal* (April 1973): 903–919.

43. Ralph Nader, speaking to Symposium on Regulatory Myths, Hearing before the Subcommittee for Consumers and the Subcommittee on the Environment of the Committee on Commerce, United States Senate, Ninety-Fourth Congress, First Session, June 23, 1975. Serial No. 94–26, 21.

44. Ralph Nader and Mark Green, "Nader: Deregulation Is Another Consumer Fraud," *New York Times*, June 29, 1975.

45. Summary of Meeting between Russell Train and James Cannon, September 2, 1975, folder, "Domestic Policy Review (2)," Box 6, GHF.

46. For Naisbitt's biography, see Sandra Salmans, "'Megatrends' Author's Rise," *New York Times*, October 11, 1983.

47. Connecticut Enforcement Project, *Economic Law Enforcement*, vol. 1, *Overview* (Washington, DC: US Environmental Protection Agency, September 1975).

48. Connecticut State Library, *S-97 Connecticut Gen. Assembly, Senate Proceedings 1973* Vol. 16 Part 8 3473–4003; Connecticut State Library *H-145 Connecticut Gen. Assembly, House Proceedings 1973 Spec. Sess.* Vol. 16 Part 15 (July): 7447–7910.

49. Bureau of National Affairs, Inc., "Environmental Protection Unit Moves to Eliminate 'Profits of Pollution,'" *Environment Reporter* 5, no. 40 (January 31, 1975): 1512.

50. Larry White to Charles Schultze, undated, folder 3, Box 74, Charles L. Schultze's Subject Files, Staff Office—CEA, Jimmy Carter Presidential Library (hereafter CSF).

51. It is difficult to determine the exact genealogy of the offset policy. The limited scholarship on California's offset program credits Region IX administrator Paul DeFalco Jr. with having "ginned up" the idea largely on his own. In the most sustained historical account, Hugh Gorman and Barry Solomon discuss the theoretical origins of the trading idea among Thomas Crocker and other economists but conclude that DeFalco devised the applied policy with little influence from such theories. Hugh Gorman and Barry Solomon, "The Origins and Practice of Emissions Trading," *Journal of Policy History* 14, no. 3 (2002): 293–320. Other published accounts echo that sui generis narrative. See, for example, the description of the first trading programs from two advocates of such policies in Daniel Dudek and John Palmisano, "Emissions Trading: Why Is this Thoroughbred Hobbled?" *Columbia Journal of Environmental Law* 13 (1988): 217–255; or in the more ambivalent depiction of trading policies, Carol Neves, *The Environment Goes to Market: The Implementation of Economic Incentives for Pollution Control* (Washington, D.C.: National Academy of Public Administration, 1994); or in the popular history recounted in Michael Weisskopf, "Buying and Selling U.S. Licenses to Pollute Air," *Washington Post*, December 26, 1989. John Wise, who was a member of the regulatory staff at Region 9 at the time and later became deputy regional administrator under DeFalco, recounted that the policy was "ginned up" by DeFalco. Pressed about the possible contributions of economic theory or any outside influence, Wise maintained, "I think it was pretty much on his own gut instinct." John Wise interview with author, July 28, 2015. DeFalco himself is deceased and the records of the Region IX office in the National Archives in San

Bruno, California, do not include any from the California program. We may never know whether DeFalco ever read Crocker or Dales or any of the by-then voluminous literature on market approaches to pollution control.

52. US Environmental Protection Agency, "New Source Review in Non-Attainment Areas (Tradeoff Policy)," in *Environmental Protection Agency Transition Papers to Incoming Carter Administration on Areas of Agency Jurisdiction*, 1302–1303, published in Bureau of National Affairs, *Environment Reporter* 7, no. 36 (January 7, 1977): 1288–1334.

53. Bureau of National Affairs, Inc., "EPA April Guidance Paper Details Agency Policy on New Source Review," *Environment Reporter* 7, no. 1 (May 7, 1976): 4–5.

54. See, for example, Hugh Gorman and Barry Solomon, "The Origins and Practice of Emissions Trading," *Journal of Policy History* 14, no. 3 (2002): 293–320.

55. Bureau of National Affairs, Inc., "Industry, Environmental Groups Criticize EPA Draft Tradeoff Policy," *Environment Reporter* 7, no. 29 (November 19, 1976): 1043–1045.

56. Bureau of National Affairs, Inc., "EPA Policy on Growth in Dirty Areas Rapped by State, Local, Industry Groups," *Environment Reporter* 7, no. 44 (March 4, 1977): 1683–1685.

57. The Air Pollution Control Association represented businesses involved in pollution control—polluters as well as pollution control equipment manufacturers and environmental consultancies that sold goods and services to emission sources. Bureau of National Affairs, Inc., "APCA Board Recommends EPA Withdraw Development Policy for Polluted Areas," *Environment Reporter* 7, no. 49 (April 8, 1977): 1862

58. Bureau of National Affairs, Inc., "Industry, Environmental Groups Criticize EPA Draft Tradeoff Policy."

59. Bureau of National Affairs, Inc., "EPA Policy on Growth in Dirty Areas Rapped by State, Local, Industry Groups."

60. Sean Wilentz, *The Age of Reagan: A History, 1974–2008* (New York: Harper Collins, 2008). At that national convention, delegates voted to include a plank calling for environmental protection to be brought into "balance" with economic growth into the official party platform. Bureau of National Affairs, Inc., "Republican Platform Calls For 'Balance' between Environmental Concerns, Growth," *Environment Reporter* 7, no. 16 (August 20, 1976): 633–634.

61. For instance, a Ford advisor reported on Carter's speech at a consumer protection luncheon hosted by Ralph Nader, noting where he was applauded and the questions he received. Ed Schmults to Dave Green, August 31, 1976, folder, "Reg. Ref.—Gen. 8/76–10/76," Box 35, ESF. That same advisor kept a clippings file full of Carter's pronouncements on regulatory reform, folder, "Regulatory Reform: Carter, Jimmy," Box 29, ESF.

62. Carlton Neville, who ran Conservationists for Carter, compiled a long list of Ford's failures in environmental protection, including his vetoing of several important pieces of legislation and his erosion of the EPA's independence, folder, "Ford's Environmental Record," Box 19, Carlton Neville Collection, Donated Historical Material, Jimmy Carter Library.

63. Bureau of National Affairs, Inc., "Carter Record on Environment, Energy Praised by Conservationists, Businessmen," *Environment Reporter* 7, no. 11 (July 16, 1976): 459–462.

64. While reform proponents presented the papers, the discussants chosen for each panel included environmental activists like Joseph Sax, the University of Michigan scholar who had pioneered the legal notion of a public trust in development projects, and Edwin Clark of the Council on Environmental Quality. Massachusetts Institute of Technology Economics Department, "Program for MIT Conference on Air Pollution and Administrative Control" (Cambridge, MA, December 2–3, 1976), Folder 2, Box 96, EMP.

65. Karl Braithwaite to Files, February 18, 1977, Folder 2, Box 96, EMP.

66. The prestigious Godkin Lectures at Harvard's John F. Kennedy School of Government featured an annual set of talks on the theme of the Essentials of Free Government and the Duties of the Citizen and served as a prominent platform for introducing new ideas to a wide audience of policymakers. Thomas Mullen, "Schultze Delivers Godkin Lecture on Tax Incentives," *The Crimson*, November 30, 1976.

67. Charles Schultze, *The Public Use of Private Incentives*, draft of lecture given as Godkin Lectures, November 1976, Folder 2, Box 96, EMP.

68. US Environmental Protection Agency, "Non-Regulatory (Economic) Approaches to Environmental Programs," in *Environmental Protection Agency Transition Papers to Incoming Carter Administration on Areas of Agency Jurisdiction*, 1298–1299, published in Bureau of National Affairs, *Environment Reporter* 7, no. 36 (January 7, 1977): 1288–1334.

69. US Environmental Protection Agency, "Non-Regulatory (Economic) Approaches to Environmental Programs."

70. US Environmental Protection Agency, "Non-Regulatory (Economic) Approaches to Environmental Programs."

71. US Environmental Protection Agency, "Non-Regulatory (Economic) Approaches to Environmental Programs."

72. Bureau of National Affairs, Inc., "Senate Filibuster Kills S 3219, Fanning Controversy over Auto Rules," *Environment Reporter* 7, no. 23 (October 8, 1976): 835–836.

73. Samuel Hays, "The Politics of Clean Air," in *Explorations in Environmental History: Essays* by Samuel P. Hays, 219–312 (Pittsburgh: University of Pittsburgh Press, 1998).

74. Samuel Hays, "The Politics of Clean Air."

75. Allen V. Kneese and F. Lee Brown, *The Southwest under Stress: National Resource Development Issues in a Regional Setting* (Baltimore: Johns Hopkins University Press for Resources for the Future, 1981).

76. *Clean Air Act Amendments of 1977*, Public Law 95-95, *U.S. Statutes at Large* 91 (1977): 685–796.

77. Bureau of National Affairs, Inc., "Clean Air Act Requires Studies to Analyze Economic Incentives," *Environment Reporter* 8, no. 16 (August 19, 1977): 594–595.

78. Douglas Costle memo to the president, September 2, 1977, folder, "Weekly Reports to the President, 1977," Box 64, DCP.

79. Douglas Costle memo to the president, September 30, 1977, folder, "White House Memos, 1977," Box 65, DCP.

80. Bureau of National Affairs, Inc., "Steel Industry Seen Progressing in Improving Pollution Control," *Environment Reporter* 8, no. 24 (October 14, 1977): 906–907.

81. Bureau of National Affairs, Inc., "Court's Upholding of EPA Petition Denial Clears Way for Birmingham Steel Shutdown," *Environment Reporter* 7, no. 48 (April 1, 1977): 1826–1827.

82. Douglas Costle memo to the president, September 30, 1977, folder, "White House Memos, 1977," Box 65, DCP.

83. Charles Schultze to Stuart Eizenstat, September 1980, folder, "Steel [2]," Box 58, Doug Costle Papers, Jimmy Carter Library, Atlanta, GA (hereafter DCP).

84. The Sierra Club's challenge was consolidated in Asarco Incorporated v. Environmental Protection Agency, 578 F.2d 319 (D.C. Cir. 1978).

85. Bureau of National Affairs, "Steel Industry Seen Progressing in Improving Pollution Control," *Environment Reporter* 8, no. 24 (14 October 1977): 906–907.

86. Richard Liroff, *An Issue Report: Reforming Air Pollution Regulation: The Toil and Trouble of EPA's Bubble* (Washington, DC: Conservation Foundation, 1986).

87. William Drayton to Jodie Bernstein, Marvin Durning, Thomas Jorling, David Hawkins, and Steven Jellinek, May 5, 1978, folder, "Issue Memos Policies [2]," Box 45, DCP.

88. John E. Barker to Roy Gamse, May 4, 1978, folder, "Issue Memos Policies [2]," Box 45, DCP; Bureau of National Affairs, "Offset Policy Revision Delayed as EPA Considers Industry Petition," *Environment Reporter* 9, no. 28 (10 November 1978): 1277.

89. Paul Sabin, "'Everything Has a Price: Jimmy Carter and the Struggle for Balance in Federal Regulatory Policy,'" *Journal of Policy History* 28, no. 1 (2016): 1–47.

90. Douglas M. Costle, "Efficiency and Compassion: The Carter Regulatory Program," Speech in Los Angeles, California, October 17, 1979, folder, "EPA—Memos, Reports, and Speeches," Box 31, DCP.

91. Executive Order 12044 of March 23, 1978, Improving Government Regulations. http://www.presidency.ucsb.edu/ws/?pid=30539; as with the Nixon and Ford reviews, Carter's advisors hoped that their review would prompt regulatory agencies to incorporate better cost/benefit assessment into their own rulemaking. Stuart Eizenstat to the president, November 20, 1978, folder, "5 Government Regulations—Reform [O/ A 6243] [1]," Box 211, Domestic Policy Staff, Stuart Eizenstat Subject Files, Carter Library.

92. In 1976, every air quality region that included a major city (above 100,000 residents) had at least one day in which levels of photochemical oxidants rose higher than the 0.08 ppm standard (an exceedance in the EPA's terminology). Many of these cities notched far more than a single exceedance. Los Angeles faced the worst smog problem in the country, recording 135 exceedances in 1976. But New York (59 exceedances), Dallas (65), Chicago (17) and most other cities also went far beyond the national limits. Many smaller cities like Baton Rouge, Louisiana (71), and Steubenville, Ohio (97), greatly surpassed the standard because of their oil refining operations. Larry White to Charles Schultze, undated, Folder 3, Box 74, CSF.

93. Regulatory Analysis Review Group, "Environmental Protection Agency's Proposed Revisions to the National Ambient Air Quality Standards for Photochemical Oxidants," Folder 2, Box 74, Charles L. Schultze's Subject Files, Staff Office—CEA, Jimmy Carter Presidential Library.

94. Larry White to Charles Schultze, December 28, 1978, Folder 2, Box 74, Charles L. Schultze's Subject Files, Staff Office—CEA, Carter Library

95. Bureau of National Affairs, Inc., "EPA's Relaxing Ozone Standard 'A Wrong Decision,' Muskie Says," *Environment Reporter* 9, no. 40 (February 2, 1979): 1820.

96. Landy, Roberts, and Thomas, *The Environmental Protection Agency*.

97. David Hawkins to Regional Administrator, Regions I–X, attached to Dave Hawkins to Doug Costle, 1 Sept. 1978, folder, "Air & Waste (July–September)," Box 26, EPA Intra-Agency Memos, Office of the Administrator, Records of the Environmental Protection Agency, RG 412, National Archives and Records Administration, College Park, MD (hereafter EPA Intra-Agency Memos).

98. David Hawkins to the Administrator, 10 October 1978, folder, "Air & Waste (October–December)," Box 28, EPA Intra-Agency Memos.

99. David Hawkins to Administrator, November 1978, folder, "Issue Memos Policies [2]," Box 45, DCP.

100. David Hawkins interview with author, September 18, 2015.

101. George Ferreri to David Hawkins, December 11, 1978, attached to Dave Hawkins to Bill Drayton, Devember 14, 1978, folder, "Air & Waste (October–December)," Box 28, EPA Intra-Agency Memos.

102. J. Edward Roush to William Drayton, December 15, 1978, folder, "Bubble Concept," Box 5, DCP.

103. Liroff, *An Issue Report: Reforming Air Pollution Regulation*.

104. John Wise interview with author, July 28, 2015.

105. Bill Becker interview with author, May 1, 2015.

106. Liroff, *An Issue Report: Reforming Air Pollution Regulation*. ·

107. Endorsements in folder, "Orig. Bubble Policy—Press Conf. + Endorsements—Proposal," Box P, MLP.

108. US EPA, "Air Pollution Control; Recommendation for Alternative Emission Reduction Options within State Implementation Plans," *Federal Register* 44, no. 13 (1979): 3740–3744.

109. Bureau of National Affairs, "Industry Group Challenges Offset Rule in Petition Filed in D.C. Appeals Court," *Environment Reporter* 9, no. 42 (1979): 1958; AISI Position Paper, "The Bubble Concept," attached to AISI—EPA Meeting, February 28, 1979, folder, "Steel [2]," Box 58, DCP.

110. William Drayton interview with author, March 31, 2017.

111. Rick Tropp to Bill Drayton, December 12, 1979, folder, "Innovation—Carter Policies, OPE Work Group, etc. 1979–81," Box P, MLP.

112. See, for example, William Drayton, "Beyond Effluent Fees," in *Approaches to Controlling Air Pollution*, ed. Ann F. Friedlaender (Cambridge, MA: MIT Press, 1978); and William Drayton, "Speech to New York Environmental Planning

Lobby," Albany, NY, October 18, 1980, folder, "EPA Conference on Innovation on Environmental Technology, 11/15/80," Box 32, DCP.

113. For the airline and trucking stories, see David Vogel, *Fluctuating Fortunes: The Political Power of Business in America* (New York: Basic Books, 1989).

114. Liroff, *An Issue Report: Reforming Air Pollution Regulation.*

115. Liroff, *An Issue Report: Reforming Air Pollution Regulation.*

116. Bureau of National Affairs, "Steel Companies Say Bubble Policy Not Beneficial, Impossible to Use," *Environment Reporter* 10, no. 43 (1980): 2041.

117. Liroff, *An Issue Report: Reforming Air Pollution Regulation.*

118. Michael Levin interview with author, May 7, 2015; slides reproduced in US Environmental Protection Agency (US EPA), "Controlled Trading: Putting the Profit Motive to Work for Pollution Control" (Washington, DC, 1980), Box W, Papers in Personal Collection of Michael Levin (hereafter MLP).

119. Walter Stahr to Mike Levin, July 17, 1980, folder, "ET—Pre '82 Additional Material," Box P, MLP.

120. Bubble Project Staff, "The Bubble Clearinghouse, Volume 1," July 1980, folder, "Bubble Issues—General Issues, Memos, Policies—Post Promulgation" (hereafter "Bubble Issues") box 6, DCP.

121. "Talking Points for Meeting with the Environmental Coalition of the Council of Industrial Boiler Owners," June 17, 1980, folder, "Bubble Issues—General Issues, Memos, Policies—Post Promulgation," Box 6, DCP.

122. Barbara Blum to the president, August 29, 1980, folder, "Bubble Issues," Box 6, DCP.

123. Roy Gamse to William Drayton, n.d., folder, "Bubble Issues," Box 6, DCP.

124. Bill Drayton to the administrator, July 28, 1980, folder, "Bubble Issues," Box 6, DCP.

125. Rick Tropp to Frans Kok, Mike Levin, and Roy Gamse, August 5, 1980, folder, "Bubble Issues," Box 6, DCP.

126. Douglas Costle to Stuart Eizenstat, July 29, 1980, folder, "2 EPA [3]," Box 29, Charles L. Schultze's Subject Files, Staff Office—CEA, Jimmy Carter Presidential Library, Atlanta, GA.

127. William Drayton to Assistant Administrators, n.d., folder, "Reg. Reform Conf.— Original 9/80—D.C.," Box P, MLP.

128. Liroff, *An Issue Report: Reforming Air Pollution Regulation.*

129. Douglas Costle to Stu Eizenstat, October 3, 1980, folder, "Bubble Concept," Box 5, DCP.

130. John Palmisano to William Drayton, October 16, 1980, folder, "Bubble Issues," Box 6, DCP.

131. US EPA, "EPA Approves 'Bubble' for R.I. Power Plant," October 22, 1980, folder, "Bubble Issues," Box 6, DCP.

132. US EPA, "EPA Plans to Approve Armco Steel 'Bubble' in Ohio," October 20, 1980, folder, "Bubble Issues," Box 6, DCP.

133. William Drayton to Dick Cavanaugh and Sandy Apgar, November 12, 1980, folder, "Bubble Issues," Box 6, DCP.

134. See, for example, M. T. Maloney and Bruce Yandle, "Bubbles and Efficiency: Cleaner Air at Lower Cost," *Regulation* (May/June 1980): 49–52; Jack Landau, "Economic

Dream or Environmental Nightmare? The Legality of the 'Bubble Concept' in Air and Water Pollution Control," *Boston College Environmental Affairs Law Review* 8, no. 4 (1980): 741–81; and Laurens H. Rhinelander, "The Bubble Concept: A Pragmatic Approach to Regulation under the Clean Air Act," *Virginia Journal of Natural Resources Law* 1, no. 2 (1981): 177–228.

135. Thomas McCraw. *Prophets of Regulation: Charles Adams, Louis Brandeis, James Landis, and Alfred Kahn.* Cambridge, MA: Belknap Press of Harvard University Press, 1984.

136. The Comprehensive Environmental Response, Compensation, and Liability Act (better known as Superfund) charged the EPA with cleaning up the nation's most polluted hazardous waste sites. Meanwhile, the Paperwork Reduction Act created a new body, the Office of Information and Regulatory Affairs, that gave the White House a new set of tools for reviewing (and rejecting or changing) regulations put forward by the EPA and other agencies. Paul Sabin, "'Everything Has a Price,' Jimmy Carter and the Struggle for Balance in Federal Regulatory Policy," *Journal of Policy History* 28, no. 1 (2016): 1–47.

137. United States Environmental Protection Agency, "1980 Ambient Assessment—Air Portion," Office of Air Quality Planning and Standards, February 1981.

138. James Turner and Andrew Isenberg, *The Republican Reversal: Conservatives and the Environment from Nixon to Trump* (Cambridge, MA: Harvard University Press, 2018).

Chapter 5

1. Gorsuch changed her name to Anne Burford after her wedding in February 1983, nineteen days before resigning from the EPA. To avoid confusion, I refer to her as Anne Gorsuch throughout. Anne M. Burford and John Greenya, *Are You Tough Enough? An Insider's View of Washington Power Politics* (New York: McGraw-Hill, 1986).

2. On the energy crisis as a key issue in the 1980 election, see Meg Jacobs, *Panic at the Pump: The Energy Crisis and the Transformation of American Politics in the 1970s* (New York: Hill and Wang, 2016).

3. See, for example, Douglas Costle, "Steel and the Clean Air Act," Los Angeles, August 1, 1980, folder, "Steel," Box 57, DCP; Marlin Fitzwater to the Administrator, July 3, 1980, folder, "Acid Rain [2]," Box 1, DCP.

4. For Reagan's environmental policy positions as a candidate, see James Turner and Andrew Isenberg, *The Republican Reversal: Conservatives and the Environment from Nixon to Trump* (Cambridge, MA: Harvard University Press, 2018).

5. Ronald Reagan, Inaugural Address, January 20, 1981. Digitized as part of the American Presidency Project and online at https://www.presidency.ucsb.edu/documents/inaugural-address-11.

6. Kim Phillips-Fein, *Invisible Hands: The Making of the Conservative Movement from the New Deal to Reagan* (New York: W.W. Norton, 2009).

7. Turner and Isenberg, *The Republican Reversal.*

8. Brian Drake, *Loving Nature, Fearing the State: Environmentalism and Antigovernment Politics before Reagan.* Seattle: University of Washington Press, 2013.

9. Decker writes that these first claims were inspired by the writings of corporate attorney Lewis Powell. Jefferson Decker, "Lawyers for Reagan: The Conservative Litigation Movement and American Government, 1971–87" (PhD diss., Columbia University, 2009).

10. Jonathan Lash, Katherine Gillman, and David Sheridan, *A Season of Spoils: The Reagan Administration's Attack on the Environment* (New York: Pantheon, 1984). One of the most prominent books to challenge Reagan's environmental policies, this book is also one of the most reliable, drawing on the expertise and reputation of nearly all the major environmental advocacy groups, the fact checking of a congressional subcommittee, and the cross referencing of over 400 interviews.

11. Caroline Mayer, "EPA Head Drives Costly Air Polluter," *Washington Post*, November 21, 1981.

12. In a sign that that commitment might not extend very deep into the new administration, someone in Reagan's office went through the transition report putting check marks next to points and policies with which they agreed. Devolution to the states, economic incentives, marketable rights, and nearly every other point pertaining to a scaling back of federal authority received an affirming check. The proposed commitment to environmental protection did not. Dan W. Lufkin and Henry Diamond to the President-Elect, undated, folder, "Environment— Reagan Task Force," Box 75, Danny J. Boggs Files, Ronald Reagan Library (DBF hereafter).

13. The new administration's centralization is described in David Wimer to Stanton Anderson, December 19, 1980, folder, "[Transition Reports on]: Wage and Price Stability (1)," Box 8, Edwin L. Harper Files, Ronald Reagan Library (EHF hereafter); and "The Council's Effectiveness in Regulatory Intervention," folder, "[Transition Reports on]: Wage and Price Stability (3)," Box 8, EHF.

14. Lash, Gillman, and Sheridan, *A Season of Spoils.*

15. Carl Bagge to Dave Stockman, January 13, 1981, Folder ID: 92043-005, C. Boyden Gray Files, Vice Presidential Records, Counsellor's Office, George H. W. Bush Presidential Library (Gray VP Files hereafter).

16. Office of the Press Secretary, "Fact Sheet: Memorandum to Executive Branch Agencies Ordering 60-Day Freeze on Regulations," January 29, 1981, Folder ID: 92016-004, Gray VP Files.

17. Environmental regulations made up the largest share of the 100 regulations that the OMB identified as the top deregulatory opportunities in February 1981, with the EPA's regulations accounting for sixteen of those thirty environmental regulations. Glenn Schleede to multiple recipients, "Regulatory Fact Sheet & 'List of 100,'" February 17, 1981, Folder ID: 92021-001, Gray VP Files; a preliminary survey of the regulatory relief program taken in April 1981 found that the biggest cost savings would likely come from the EPA and the Department of Transportation. The survey noted that the relief program had targeted twenty-seven EPA regulations for reform or elimination, with $3.4 billion in one-time savings and $1.3 billion in annual savings (not including the

relaxation of automobile regulations). Tom Hopkins and Tom Lenard to Jim Miller, April 24, 1981, folder, "Regulatory Reform Actions (1)," Box 7, Robert B. Carleson Files, Ronald Reagan Library.

18. For large businesses, the EPA and environmental regulations were the overwhelming focus of concern. For small businesses, the EPA shared top billing with the Department of Labor. Department of Commerce, "Business Responses on Regulatory Burdens: An Initial Report Submitted to the Task Force on Regulatory Relief," June 1981, Folder ID: 92029-009, Gray VP Files.

19. The response sent by the chemical manufacturer DuPont and Company was typical in offering a detailed plan for the easing of specific regulatory requirements. William G. Simeral to Malcolm Baldrige, James Miller, and C. Boyden Gray, April 30, 1981, Folder, "Environment—General [Emissions]," Box 72, DBF.

20. Of the large businesses that responded, 228 singled out the EPA as their primary concern, with the second place Health and Human Services topping the lists of only forty-six businesses. "Summary of Responses/Private Sector through May 20, 1981," May 22, 1981, Folder ID: 92030-004, Gray VP Files.

21. Paul Sabin, "'Everything Has a Price': Jimmy Carter and the Struggle for Balance in Federal Regulatory Policy," *Journal of Policy History* 28, no. 1 (2016): 1–47.

22. Brian Mannix interview with author, May 5, 2015.

23. Executive Order 12291 of February 17, 1981, Federal Regulation, https://www.archives.gov/federal-register/codification/executive-order/12291.html.

24. Michael Horowitz to Fred Fielding, March 17, 1981, Folder ID: 92020-001, Gray VP Files.

25. Chuck Ludlam to Executive Committee, June 16, 1981, Folder 9, Box 3, Series, Khristine Hall, Sub-group II.1 Toxic Chemicals Program—Staff Files, Washington, DC Office, Environmental Defense Fund Archive, Stony Brook University (KHF hereafter).

26. DeMuth's provocative claim that Reagan's regulatory reviewers would rely on "economic textbooks" to assess the public benefit of proposed environmental protections only alarmed the League's representatives further. Chuck Ludlam, Nancy Drabble, and Sandra Willett to Chris DeMuth, October 28, 1981, Folder ID: 92020-001, Gray VP Files.

27. For instance, in 1981 the Environmental Defense Fund began the process of hiring an economist "interested in the economics of environmental problems, of the cost of regulatory reform proposals, or tax incentive schemes, the federal environmental budget, cost-benefit analyses with respect to the environment," in a seeming recognition that now, more than ever before, the vitality of the EPA's rulemakings depended on their ability to stand up to the scrutiny of White House economists. Janet Brown to All Toxics staff, All Senior Program staff, Susan Butler, and Ted Anderman, "October 19, 1981," Folder 2, Box 2, Robert Rauch Files, Washington, DC Office, Sub-group II.1 Toxic Chemicals Program—Staff Files, Series 3, Environmental Defense Fund Archive, Stony Brook University.

28. Peter Passell, "The Editorial Notebook; Paying for Pollution Virtue," *New York Times*, October 13, 1982.

29. "Environment in the '80s—The Carter CEQ Says Farewell," September/October 1981, folder, "Environment—Council on Environmental Quality [1 of 3]," Box 71, DBF; Malcolm Baldwin to Frank Hodsoll, March 13, 1981, folder, "Environment—Council on Environmental Quality [1 of 3]," Box 71, DBF.

30. Caroline Isber interview with author, October 7, 2019.

31. Richard Andrews, "Economics and Environmental Decisions, Past and Present," in *Environmental Policy under Reagan's Executive Order: The Role of Benefit-Cost Analysis*, edited by V. Kerry Smith, 43–85 (Chapel Hill: University of North Carolina Press, 1984).

32. Lash, Gillman, and Sheridan, *A Season of Spoils*.

33. Lash, Gillman, and Sheridan, *A Season of Spoils*.

34. David Stockman memo to Ed Meese, undated. Folder, "Environmental Protection Agency—White House (1)," Box 10, Fred Fielding Files, Ronald Reagan Presidential Library, Simi Valley, California (FFF hereafter).

35. Lash, Gillman, and Sheridan, *A Season of Spoils*.

36. Lash, Gillman, and Sheridan, *A Season of Spoils*.

37. Caroline Isber interview with author, October 7, 2019.

38. Bill Drayton interview with author, October 23, 2019.

39. Joel Mintz, *Enforcement at the EPA: High Stakes and Hard Choices*, rev. ed. (Austin: University of Texas Press, 2012).

40. Bill Drayton interview with author, October 23, 2019.

41. US National Commission on Air Quality, *To Breathe Clean Air: Report of the National Commission on Air Quality*, (Washington, DC, 1981).

42. The amendments were especially vital to the steel industry, which had one of the worst records of compliance with the act and which by and large did not have the capital to both modernize to meet foreign competition and invest in the pollution controls that the 1977 act required by 1982. The EPA had worked out special arrangements with the industry before and the senior legal counsel wrote Reagan in his first month in office to urge him to resolve the industry's crisis by amending the Clean Air Act. Michele Corash to Boyden Gray, February 6, 1981, Folder ID: 92043-006, Gray VP Files.

43. Philip Shabecoff, "Industry Groups Seeking Changes in Clean Air Law," *New York Times*, March 21, 1981.

44. "General Principles," folder, "EPA: Issues (1)," Box 37, DBF.

45. "Issue Memo: Should the basis for setting the primary NAAQS be changed?" 1981, Folder ID: 92010-008, Gray VP Files.

46. Tom Hopkins to Boyden Gray, June 12, 1981, Folder ID: 92010-008, Gray VP Files.

47. The decision concerned a cotton dust standard created by the Occupational Health and Safety Administration to protect workers from respiratory damage. Charging that the cotton dust standard carried much higher costs to industry than benefits to workers' health, a textile trade association sued the Department of Labor (of which OSHA is a part) to overturn the standard, only to have the Supreme Court rule in OSHA's favor. While the specific standard upheld by the Supreme Court predated Reagan's EO 12291 and its cost/benefit test, the Court's decision called into question whether regulatory agencies could be compelled to comply with Reagan's order.

American Textile Manufacturers Institute, Inc. v. Donovan, Secretary of Labor 79 U.S. 1429 (1981).

48. Memos detailing the various proposals reveal an awareness of the acute political sensitivity of amending fundamental programs like the national air quality standards as well as a conviction that well-crafted amendments could pass. Anne Gorsuch, "Clean Air Act Amendments: Summary of the Clean Air Act Working Group Discussions," June 10, 1981, folder, "[Cabinet Council on Natural Resources and Environment 06/10/1981 (Case File 018845)]," Box 38, Richard G. Darman Files, Ronald Reagan Library; Cabinet Council on Natural Resources and Environment, "Agenda," June 19, 1981, folder, "[Cabinet Council on Natural Resources and Environment 06/10/1981 (Case File 018845)]," Box 38, Richard G. Darman Files, Ronald Reagan Library.

49. In late June, Representative Henry Waxman, who chaired the House subcommittee on the environment and supported strong regulations, obtained a copy of Gorsuch's plans and released them to the press. Philip Shabecoff, "Democrat Discloses Reagan Draft Document Easing Clean Air Standards," *New York Times*, June 20, 1981; Philip Shabecoff, "Clean Air Act: A Barometer of Changes," *New York Times*, July 1, 1981.

50. Philip Shabecoff, "Reagan Delaying Proposals for Clean Air Act," *New York Times*, July 28, 1981.

51. This account of Stockman and Reagan's plan is taken from two interviews with Bill Drayton. Bill Drayton interview with author, March 31, 2017; Bill Drayton interview with author, October 23, 2019.

52. Bill Drayton interview with author, October 23, 2019.

53. Caroline Isber interview with author, October 7, 2019.

54. Bill Drayton interview with author, October 23, 2019.

55. Since Reagan took over, the printouts listed fifty referrals to the Justice Department as compared to 230 the previous year during the Carter administration. Philip Shabecoff, "Environmental Cases Off Sharply under Reagan," *New York Times*, October 15, 1981.

56. Philip Shabecoff, "Funds and Staff for Protecting Environment May Be Halved," *New York Times*, September 29, 1981; Daniel Lazzare, "EPA Slashes Called 'Bomb in Basement,'" *Bergen Record*, October 15, 1981.

57. Tom Morganthau and Mary Hager, "The 'Ice Queen' at EPA," *Newsweek*, October 19, 1981.

58. Viewpoint, "We Need a Credible EPA . . . and Industry Can Help," *chemicalweek*, October 21, 1981.

59. Lash, Gillman, and Sheridan, *A Season of Spoils*.

60. Bill Drayton interview with author, October 23, 2019.

61. Dan Lufkin, "An Open Letter to the President," folder, "EPA—Miscellaneous," Box 31, DCP.

62. William Drayton, Speaking on Environmental Protection Agency: Private Meetings and Water Protection Programs, Hearings before the Environment, Energy, and Natural Resources Subcommittee of the Government Operations Committee, United States House of Representatives, Ninety-Seventh Congress, First Session, October 21 and November 4. Serial 97-474, October 21, 1981.

63. Samuel Hays, "The Politics of Clean Air," in *Explorations in Environmental History: Essays* by Samuel P. Hays, 219–312 (Pittsburgh: University of Pittsburgh Press, 1998).

64. "Pollster Lou Harris to Politicians: 'Hands Off' Environmental 'Sacred Cow,'" *Inside E.P.A. Weekly Report* 2, no. 43, October 23, 1981, folder, "EPA—Harris Poll," Box 30, DCP.

65. Doug Costle to Office of Senator Gary Hart, October 20, 1981, folder, "EPA—Harris Poll," Box 30, DCP; Doug Costle to Susan King, October 20, 1981, folder, "EPA—Harris Poll," Box 30, DCP.

66. Chamber of Commerce of the United States, "Poll Shows Most Americans Agree: Clean Air Act Should Be Revised," December 8, 1981, Folder ID: 92010-011, Gray VP Files; Opinion Research Corporation, "Public Attitudes Toward the Clean Air Act: A Report for the Chamber of Commerce of the United States," December 1981, Folder ID: 92010-011, Gray VP Files.

67. Resources and Environmental Quality Division, Chamber of Commerce of the United States, "Clean Air Act: Position Comparison Paper," December 1981, Folder ID: 92010-011, Gray VP Files.

68. Mintz, *Enforcement at the EPA*.

69. Philip Shabecoff, "U.S. Environmental Agency Making Deep Staffing Cuts," *New York Times*, January 3, 1982.

70. Bill Drayton to "Albert Gore Jr., Tom Grumbly, and My Co-members of the House Democratic Caucus Environment Advisory Group," December 28, 1981, folder, "Save EPA Campaign Material," Box 56, DCP.

71. Russell Train, "The Destruction of EPA," *Washington Post*, February 2, 1982.

72. Republican Study Committee, "Defending EPA Budget Cuts and Administrator Anne Gorsuch," February 12, 1982, attached to John Daniel to Assistant Administrators et al., February 17, 1982, folder, "OA JAN—MAR," Box 89, EPA Inter-Agency Memos.

73. Sending a copy to Costle, Drayton stated that the budget would provide the "necessary ammunition" that sympathetic legislators needed to attack Reagan. Bill Drayton to Doug Costle, February 12, 1982, folder, "Save EPA Campaign Material," Box 56, DCP.

74. Longtime Beltway interveners in regulatory policy like the Natural Resources Defense Council and the Environmental Defense Fund joined with more conservative organizations like the National Audubon Society to produce the report. *Indictment: The Case against the Reagan Environmental Record*, March 1982, folder, "Environment—Ozone," Box 74, DBF. The charge clearly registered for Reagan, with multiple advisors recording news of the report in their files, including Folder ID: 92010-009, Gray VP Files.

75. Gorsuch asked each of the EPA's program offices to provide responses to the charges leveled by *Indictment*, and then asked for more thorough rejoinders when those initial defenses failed to blunt the criticism. The Administrator to Assistant Administrators and Associate Administrators, June 11, 1982, folder, "Administrator April—June," Box 93, EPA Inter-Agency Memos.

76. Mintz, *Enforcement at the EPA*.

77. National Development Association's Clean Air Project included letters to the editor and a conference in Washington, DC. Materials located in Folder ID: 92011-003, Gray VP Files and Folder ID: 92011-004, Gray VP Files.

78. The Administrator to Kathleen Bennett, June 2, 1982, folder, "OPRM April—June," Box 93, EPA Inter-Agency Memos.

79. United Steel Workers Legislative Committee of Ohio wrote HR 5252 sponsor Tomas Lunken to tell him that they were "appalled" at his support for the bill. Rejecting the steel companies' efforts to portray amendments as necessary for preventing dislocating job losses, the committee secretary wrote "the reauthorization process for the Clean Air Act is *not* to be used as a scapegoat for a failing economic policy; jobs *are not lost* because of regulations to protect environment and occupational health and *are not created* if those laws are abandoned." Ghay Holcomb to Thomas A. Lunken, February 1, 1982, Folder ID: 92010-009, Gray VP Files.

80. Representative Henry Waxman, speaking on H.R. 5252 A bill to Amend the Clean Air Act, Hearings before the Subcommittee on Health and the Environment of the Committee on Energy and Commerce, House of Representatives, Ninety-Seventh Congress, Second Session. Serial 97–157, February 10, 1982.

81. US Congress, "Environment 1982: Overview," *Congressional Quarterly Almanac,* 97th Cong., 2nd sess., 1982, at 505.

82. In its March 1982 newsletter, the pro-business National Council for Environmental Balance, Inc. complained bitterly that environmentalists had tarred meaningful reforms through their "typical emotional propaganda technique of distortion and promotion of mass hysteria," Folder ID: 9201-009, Gray VP Files.

83. With increasing frustration, proponents of HR 5252 in the Reagan administration and Congress urged the bill's supporters to offer counternarratives. "Development of a Proper Focus for the Clean Air Act Debate," Folder ID: 9201-009, Gray VP Files; Martin Smith to James T. Broyhill, July 22, 1981," Folder ID: 9201-009, Gray VP Files.

84. Steven Roberts, "Administration Fails in Key Votes to Ease Pollution Standards," *New York Times,* August 12, 1982.

85. Office of Policy Development, "Gambling with Economic Recovery," November 3, 1982, folder, "[Environmental Protection Agency (EPA)—Acid Rain, Clean Air, Clean Water Issues] (1 of 2)," Box 6, Becky Norton Dunlop Files, Series IX: Subject File, Ronald Reagan Library. The EPA did not enforce sanctions when the deadline passed in 1982 and in June 1983, the Dannemeyer-Waxman amendment disallowed such sanctions.

86. Dan W. Lufkin and Henry Diamond to the President-Elect, n.d., folder, "Environment—Reagan Task Force," Box 75, DBF.

87. "Talking Points for Drayton Speech at Reg Reform Conference," November 1980, folder, "EPA Conference on Innovation on Environmental Technology, 11/15/80," Box 32, DCP.

88. Bill Drayton to Doug Costle, December 22, 1980, folder, "Bubble," Box 5, DCP.

89. Richard Liroff, *An Issue Report: Reforming Air Pollution Regulation: The Toil and Trouble of EPA's Bubble* (Washington, D.C., The Conservation Foundation, 1986).

90. Robert Martinott, "How to Limit the Rising Costs of Stricter Regulation," *Chemical Week*, January 21, 1981.

91. William Drayton, "Getting Smarter about Regulation," *Harvard Business Review* 59, no. 4 (1981): 38–53.

92. David Hawkins to the Administrator, December 18, 1980, folder, "Bubble," Box 5, DCP.

93. David G. Doniger, "Remarks at the Annual Meeting of the South Atlantic Section of the Air Pollution Control Association," January 9, 1981, folder, "ET—NRDC Comments 1982," Box CC, MLP.

94. The article also illustrated the challenge of using the EPA's offset policy in the absence of an active market. As the article described, a Chicago wood products manufacturer had spent two years seeking a buyer for the emission offsets it could generate by closing down its increasingly obsolete plant. Announcing the sale in a local newspaper attracted only charlatans and the confused. At the time of publication, the firm had finally found a buyer, but the sale remained tied up in regulatory uncertainty. Greg Johnson, "An Emerging Market for Pollution Rights," *Industry Week*, March 3, 1980.

95. Environmental Protection Agency, Emission Reduction Banking & Trading Project, "Conference for Potential Brokers of Emission Reduction Credits," folder, "ML Presentation—Brokers' Conf. 1/81," Box P, MLP.

96. Mike Levin, speech notes for "Brokers Conference: Opening Remarks," January 26, 1981, folder, "ML Presentation—Brokers' Conf. 1/81," Box P, MLP.

97. Among other things, the handbook instructed would-be brokers on how to identify profitable markets where industrial growth would soon run up against regulatory limits on air quality and where local regulators seemed likely to permit trading. US Environmental Protection Agency, *Brokering Emission Reduction Credits: A Handbook* (Washington, DC, 1981).

98. In 1982, Fred Singer, a senior fellow at the Heritage Foundation, explained the Foundation's growing support for measures that Singer described as yielding cleaner air and water in a cheaper and more equitable fashion than direct controls. Fred Singer to Clean Air Distribution, 1982, folder, "Environment—Market," Box 74, DBF.

99. Bruce Ackerman, Richard Stewart, and Robert Rabin to General Counsel, January 20, 1981; Steve Jellinek to Mike Farrell, January 23, 1981; memo for Peter McPherson, January 23, 1981, all in folder, "Environmental Protection Agency—White House (2)," Box 10, FFF.

100. Michael Levin to Walter Barber, April 14, 1981, folder, "OPM (APR–JUNE)," Box 75, EPA Inter-Agency Memos.

101. Lash, Gillman, and Sheridan, *A Season of Spoils*.

102. Lash, Gillman, and Sheridan, *A Season of Spoils*.

103. Liroff, *An Issue Report*.

104. Mike Levin, "Banking Update," 1981, folder, "ET—Pre '82 Additional Material," Box P, MLP.

105. If the local control authority could resolve remaining procedural issues, Levin offered to split the $36,000 needed to set up the bank and operate it in the first year.

Michael Levin to William Baker, October 28, 1982, folder, "Middlesex County," Box CC, MLP.

106. The regulations were finally issued in US Environmental Protection Agency, "Emissions Trading Policy Statement," *Federal Register* 51, no. 233 (December 4, 1986): 43814.

107. US EPA, *The Bubble and Its Use with Emissions Reduction Banking* (Washington, DC, April 1982).

108. US EPA, Minnesota Mining and Manufacturing Co., and Citizens for a Better Environment, "Regulatory Reform at EPA: Cost Saving Approaches to Controlling Pollution," April 29, 1982, folder, "Regulatory Reform at EPA," Box P, MLP. For 3M's reputation in this regard, see Andrew Winston, "3M's Sustainability Innovation Machine," *Harvard Business Review*, May 15, 2012.

109. Michael Levin interview with author, March 16, 2015.

110. Kevin Hopkins to Martin Anderson, December 8, 1981, folder "Regulation (1)," Box 1, Kevin R. Hopkins Files, Reagan Library.

111. To take one example, Marvin Kosters and Jeffrey Eisenach ("Is Regulatory Relief Enough?" *Regulation* 6 [March/April 1982]: 20–27) answered their title question with eight pages in the negative.

112. US EPA, "Emissions Trading Policy Statement," *Federal Register* 47 (April 7, 1982): 15076.

113. "Managing Resources and the Environment," June 22,1982, folder, "Environment—Smith Group," Box 75, DBF, Reagan Library.

114. Working Group on Alternatives to Federal Regulation, November 5, 1982, folder, "Working Group on Alternatives to Federal Regulation," Box 15, Robert B. Carleson Files, Reagan Library.

115. Working Group on Alternatives to Federal Regulation, November 5, 1982, folder, "Working Group on Alternatives to Federal Regulation [10/14/1982 Meeting] (1)," Box 16, Robert B. Carleson Files, Reagan Library.

116. Michael Levin, "Proposal for Establishment of a Standing Committee on Emissions Trading," September 30, 1982, folder, "ET Standing Committee '82 Substantive Results," Box P, MLP.

117. "Court Overturns Rule on Pollution: Easing of Factory Standards by Environmental Agency Held Not Permissible," *New York Times*, August 19, 1982.

118. Christopher DeMuth to the Vice President and Director Stockman, September 14, 1982, Folder ID: 92048-006, Gray VP Files.

119. See, for instance, in Illinois, Kevin Greene to Gary Gulezian, March 8, 1983, folder, "ET—Steel Ract," Box CC, MLP; and in Los Angeles, Bureau of National Affairs, "NRDC Blasts Proposed Sohio Bubble, Pushes Actual Emissions Baseline," *Environment Reporter*, August 24, 1984, copy in folder, "ET—NRDC Comments 1982," Box CC, MLP.

120. Kevin Hopkins to Martin Anderson, December 8, 1981, folder, "Regulation (1)," Box 1, Kevin R. Hopkins Files, Ronald Reagan Library.

121. These different complaints offered by various conference attendees were collected in *Environmental Policy under Reagan's Executive Order: The Role of Benefit-Cost*

Analysis, edited by V. Kerry Smith, 121–164 (Chapel Hill: University of North Carolina Press, 1984).

122. The number of enforcement cases fell from forty three in Carter's last year to three in Gorsuch's first year. Mintz, *Enforcement at the EPA.*

123. Mintz, *Enforcement at the EPA.*

124. Gorsuch was accused of withholding $6.1 million in Superfund money to avoid helping Democratic senate candidate Edmund Brown as well as fast tracking Superfund approval to help a Republican Indiana Senate candidate. Stuart Taylor Jr., "U.S. Will Sue Companies for Cost of Cleanup at Waste Site on Coast," *New York Times,* March 30, 1983.

125. Mintz, *Enforcement at the EPA.*

126. Philip Shabecoff, "EPA Chief Assailed on Lead Violation," *New York Times,* April 13, 1983.

127. Frank Newport, Jeffrey Jones, and Lydia Saad, "Ronald Reagan from the People's Perspective: A Gallup Poll Review," *Gallup News,* June 7, 2004, https://news.gallup.com/poll/11887/ronald-reagan-from-peoples-perspective-gallup-poll-review.aspx.

128. "Notes from Anne Gorsuch Telecon," February 7, 1983, folder, "FG 122 (Environmental Protection Agency) (124200–124999)," Box 45, FG 122—Environmental Protection Agency, Ronald Reagan Library.

129. Craig Fuller to Ed Meese, February 14, 1983, folder, "FG 122 (Environmental Protection Agency) (077799) (1 of 3)," Box 44, FG 122—Environmental Protection Agency, Ronald Reagan Library.

130. Charles P. Moraglia, "Correspondence Tracking Worksheet," folder, "FG 122 (Environmental Protection Agency) (125000–126799)," Box 45, FG 122—Environmental Protection Agency, Ronald Reagan Library.

131. Mintz, *Enforcement at the EPA.*

132. Ronald Reagan, "Letter Accepting the Resignation of Anne M. Burford as Administrator of the Environmental Protection Agency," archived at the American Presidency Project, University of California, Santa Barbara, http://www.presidency.ucsb.edu/ws/index.php?pid=41033.

133. Lash, Gillman, and Sheridan, *A Season of Spoils.*

134. Save EPA's continued watchdog role included the 1984 report *America's Toxic Protection Gap: The Collapse of Compliance with the Nation's Laws,* which Drayton used to pressure Ruckelshaus to reverse Gorsuch's toxics policies. Bill Drayton to William Ruckelshaus, August 17, 1984, folder, "EPA—Correspondence," Box 28, DCP; the report is the last that Save EPA published, shifting thereafter into a loose network that continues to keep tabs on the agency into the present.

135. Ruckelshaus's speech is attached to Patsy Faoro to Craig Fuller, March 21, 1983, folder, "FG 122 (Environmental Protection Agency) (118500–118569)," Box 44, FG 122—Environmental Protection Agency, Ronald Reagan Library.

136. Clyde Farnsworth, "Promise of Deregulation Proved Tough to Keep," *New York Times,* August 18, 1988.

137. Jim Tozzi to Doug Costle, May 6, 1983, folder, "EPA—Miscellaneous," Box 31, DCP.

138. No stranger to controversial remarks, Watt had evidently crossed a line when he celebrated the diversity of his coal advisory commission by remarking that "I have a black, I have a woman, two Jews and a cripple. And we have talent." Steven Weisman, "Watt Quits Post; President Accepts with 'Reluctance,'" *New York Times*, October 10, 1983.

139. Philip Shabecoff, "Questions Arise Not Just over Watt's Words," *New York Times*, October 2, 1983.

140. Philip Shabecoff, "Lavelle Verdict: E.P.A Trial Over, but Not Inquiries," *New York Times*, December 3, 1983.

141. Walt Barber to Jim Miller, February 11, 1981, folder, "EPA: Issues (1)," Box 37, DBF.

142. James Conant and Peter Balint, *The Life Cycles of the Council on Environmental Quality and the Environmental Protection Agency, 1970–2035* (New York: Oxford University Press, 2016).

143. Mintz, *Enforcement at the EPA*.

144. Marc Landy, Marc Roberts, and Stephen Thomas, *The Environmental Protection Agency: Asking the Wrong Questions* (New York: Oxford University Press, 1990).

145. Bill Drayton interview with author, March 31, 2017.

Chapter 6

1. Robert Hahn and Gordon Hester, "The Market for Bads: EPA's Experience with Emissions Trading," *Regulation* 11, no. 3 (1987): 48–53.

2. Gerald Markowitz and David Rosner, *Lead Wars: The Politics of Science and the Fate of America's Children* (Berkeley: University of California Press, 2013).

3. Richard Newell and Kristian Rogers, "The Market-Based Lead Phasedown," in *Moving to Markets in Environmental Regulation: Lessons from Thirty Years of Experience*, ed. Jody Freeman and Charles D. Kolstad, 171–193 (New York: Oxford University Press, 2007).

4. The EPA study found that moving to 0.01 g per leaded gallon standard would produce $36 billion (1983) in benefits, at a cost to the refining industry of $2.6 billion. Tom Tietenberg, "Ethical Influences on the Evolution of the US Tradable Permit Approach to Air Pollution Control," *Ecological Economics* 24 (1998): 241–257.

5. White House economist Brian Mannix included a trading approach in his proposal for the White House's phasedown recommendations in May 1982, indicating that the trading option was well covered by then. Brian Mannix to Chris DeMuth, May 21, 1982, Folder ID: 92010-009, Gray VP Files.

6. Two economists who investigated the program estimated that banking allowed firms to save "hundreds of millions" of dollars, based on even more lead rights being banked than in the EPA's estimate in rulemaking proposal that banking would save $226 million. Robert Hahn and Gordon Hester, "Marketable Permits: Lessons for Theory and Practice," *Ecology Law Quarterly* 361 (1989): 361–406.

7. Martin Murphy, "Alcohol Blenders Turn Lead Rights Trading into a Growth Industry," *Oil Daily*, July 9, 1985.

8. Richard Newell and Kristian Rogers, "The Market-Based Lead Phasedown," in *Moving to Markets in Environmental Regulation: Lessons from Thirty Years of Experience*, ed. Jody Freeman and Charles D. Kolstad (New York: Oxford University Press, 2007).

9. Alan Loeb, who worked as an attorney at the EPA on the lead phasedown team, recounted a process of continuous tinkering with an eye to keeping the lead rights attractive to refineries while steadily reducing emissions. Alan Loeb interview with author, March 16, 2015.

10. Fittingly, the EPA's first attempt to resolve the issue by amending California's State Implementation Plan to allow for Merck's generator upgrade ran into Reagan's ban on new rulemakings during the regulatory freeze. Mary Doyle to W. Ernst Minor, February 9, 1981, folder, "EPA: Issues (2)," Box 37, DBF.

11. The most important constraint was that a firm would receive no credits for plant shutdowns that would have occurred regardless of what happened with pollution controls. Daniel Manelli to Danny Boggs, February 16, 1983, folder, "Environment—'Banking' [Emissions Reduction Banking]," Box 70, DBF.

12. Barry Solomon and Russell Lee, "Emissions Trading and Environmental Justice," *Environment* 42, no. 8 (2000): 32–45.

13. Though many environmentalists came to accept market solutions under certain conditions, there were others who believed that pollution was a moral failure and saw emissions trading as a betrayal of the government's duty to address that failure. These attitudes were explored in works like M. Douglas and A. Wildavsky, *Risk and Culture* (Berkeley: University of California Press, 1982).

14. Joseph Cannon to the Administrator, April 25, 1983, folder, "OPRM APR—JUNE," Box 106, EPA Inter-Agency Memos.

15. Chevron U.S.A., Inc. v. Natural Resources Defense Council, 467 U.S. 837 (1984).

16. William Ruckelshaus interview with author, May 13, 2016.

17. Stephen Connolly et al., "Emissions Trading in Selected EPA Regions," September 30, 1984, folder, "ET Evaluations," Box P, MLP.

18. Darryl Tyler to Mike Levin, November 1, 1985, folder, "Final ET: AA Briefings—1985," Box CC, MLP.

19. See, for example, "Working Agenda: Meeting of Standing Committee on Emissions Trading," November 19, 1982, folder, "ET Standing Committee '82 Substantive Results," Box P, MLP.

20. See, for example, Michael Levin, "Building a Better Bubble at EPA: Statutes and Stopping Points," *Regulation* (March/April 1985): 33–42.

21. TCS Management Group, Inc. "Evaluation of the Impacts of Emission Bubbles," September 11, 1984, folder, "ET Evaluations," Box P, MLP.

22. William Ruckelshaus interview with author, May 13, 2016.

23. Richard Liroff, *An Issue Report: Reforming Air Pollution Regulation: The Toil and Trouble of EPA's Bubble* (Washington, DC: Conservation Foundation, 1986).

24. US Environmental Protection Agency, "Emissions Trading Policy Statement," 51 *Federal Register* 233 (December 4, 1986).

25. William Ruckelshaus interview with author, May 13, 2016.

26. For instance, the Brookings Institution decided in 1983 to devote its annual regulatory colloquium to risk assessment and management, drawing in part on the National Academy of Science's recent report. Robert Crandall and Lester Lave to Interested Participants in the Regulatory Colloquium, May 4, 1983, folder, "Environment—Risks," Box 75, DBF.

27. National Research Council, *Risk Assessment in the Federal Government: Managing the Process* (Washington, DC: National Academies Press, 1983).

28. Marc Landy, Marc Roberts, and Stephen Thomas, *The Environmental Protection Agency: Asking the Wrong Questions* (New York: Oxford University Press, 1990).

29. William Ruckelshaus, "Science, Risk, and Public Policy," *Science* 221, no. 4615 (1983): 1026–1028.

30. US Environmental Protection Agency, "Unfinished Business: A Comparative Assessment of Environmental Problems," February 1987.

31. Clyde Farnsworth, "Norse Seek Curb on Acid Rainfall," *New York Times*, November 27, 1970.

32. United Nations, *Report of the United Nations Conference on the Human Environment*, Stockholm, June 5–16, 1972, A. Conf. 48, 14, Rev. 1, accessed December 20, 2016, http://www.un-documents.net/aconf48-14r1.pdf.

33. Researchers in 1974 found that acidity in rain in the eastern United States had increased 100 to 1,000 times from normal levels, damaging forests and lakes as well as crops and buildings. Boyce Rensberger, "Acid in Rain Found Up Sharply in East; Smoky Curb Cited," *New York Times*, June 13, 1974.

34. Roger Raufer and Stephen Feldman, *Acid Rain and Emissions Trading: Implementing a Market Approach to Pollution Control* (Totowa, NJ: Rowman & Littlefield, 1987).

35. In 1979, the EPA's top air official declared that controlling acid rain within the twentieth century would require amendments to the Clean Air Act because the secondary sulfur oxide standard was incapable of making the necessary reductions. Bureau of National Affairs, Inc., "EPA Official Says Amending Act Only Way Now to Control Acid Rain," *Environment Reporter* 10, no. 24 (October 12, 1979): 1342–1343.

36. Costle's resignation letter as well as a series of talking points in which he denied threatening to resign are located in Costle's papers at the Carter Library, folder, "Confidential Correspondence—Miscellaneous [2]," Box 11, DCP. It is unclear whether Costle ever communicated his threat to the president or his advisors.

37. Coverage of acid rain in national media as represented by mention in articles in the *New York Times* soared from sixteen articles published through 1978 to eighteen in 1979, sixty-two in 1980 and then remained an object of great interest and concern for the next decade. Harold Faber, "Deadly Rain Imperils 2 Adirondacks Species," *New York Times*, March 28, 1977.

38. Armin Rosencranz, "The ECE Convention of 1979 on Long-Range Transboundary Air Pollution," *American Journal of International Law* 75, no. 4 (1981): 975–982.

39. Canadian Embassy, *No. 84*, March 4, 1980, folder, "Confidential Correspondence—Miscellaneous [2]," Box 11, DCP.

40. Henry Ginger, "Reagan Arrives in Canada to Heckling and Applause," *New York Times*, March 11, 1981.

41. Trudeau's supposed nefarious intent was revealed by a Canada expert advising Reagan's EPA along with the United States Chamber of Commerce. Richard Funkhouser, "How to Negotiate with the Canadians," August 25, 1981, folder, "OIA (JULY—SEPT)," Box 80, EPA Inter-Agency Memos.
42. For instance, in 1980 the Sierra Club announced plans to sue twenty of the nation's largest electric utilities for their contributions to and failure to address the problem of acid rain. "Sierra Club Plans to Sue 20 Utilities over Air Quality," New York Times, September 18, 1980.
43. Sixty percent of the nation's sulfur oxides emissions amounted to 14.4 million tons in 1983. As new control technology made its way into the nation's automobile fleet, utilities' share of nitrogen oxide emissions would only grow. Roger Raufer and Stephen Feldman, Acid Rain and Emissions Trading: Implementing a Market Approach to Pollution Control (Totowa, NJ: Rowman & Littlefield, 1987).
44. "One can see some signs of recent erosion of rocks in New Hampshire," Battelle reported to American Electric Power. "Some lakes and streams show apparent increases in acidity . . . [and] some crop damage has been claimed," the report also allowed, but acidic deposition had not yet been shown to cause "significant damage to the environment" nor could it be definitively attributed to SO_2 emissions from electric utilities. Joseph Oxley, "Research Report to American Electric Power Service Corporation," September 1, 1980. Battelle Columbus Laboratories, attached to Charles Carter to Daniel Boggs, March 9, 1981 folder, "Environment—Clean Air Act [4 of 4]," Box 71, DBF.
45. American Electric Power's report and the rest of Rhodes's acid rain mailing was sent to Reagan's senior environmental advisor via an attorney who probably worked as a Washington, DC, lobbyist. Joseph Oxley, "Research Report to American Electric Power Service Corporation," September 1, 1980. Battelle Columbus Laboratories. Attached to Charles Carter to Daniel Boggs, March 9, 1981, folder, "Environment—Clean Air Act [4 of 4]," Box 71, DBF.
46. For example, in 1981, Reagan's EPA carefully monitored an episode in which the National Academy of Sciences had been misquoted as calling for a 50 percent reduction in SO_2 emissions in a Washington Post editorial, cheerfully sending along the Academy's correction of the editorial to members of Congress. Denise Mitstifer to Bill Prendergast, January 4, 1982, folder, "OA JAN—MAR," Box 89, EPA Inter-Agency Memos.
47. Time, November 8, 1982.
48. Edison Electric Institute, Steering Committee of the Clean Air Act Issue Group, "Changing Administration Position on Acid Rain," May 23, 1983, folder, "FG 122 (Environmental Protection Agency) (151400-151999)," Box 47, FG 122—Environmental Protection Agency, Ronald Reagan Library. Identifying the Reagan administration as an ally, the Edison Electric Institute kept Gorsuch's EPA closely apprised of its fight against a new SO_2 control program. "EEI Status Report on Clean Air Act/Acid Rain Communications Activities—1981," attached to Anne Gorsuch to Al Hill et al., June 7, 1982, folder, "OPRM April—June," Box 93, EPA Inter-Agency Memos.

49. As with other matters during his second stint at the EPA, Ruckelshaus took considerable license in interpreting Reagan's public pronouncement as a mandate for regulatory intervention, spurring frustration among Reagan officials who were forced to tolerate stronger stances than they desired to avoid further politically damaging confrontations on environmental issues. Martin Smith to Edwin Harper, June 10, 1983, folder, "FG 122 (Environmental Protection Agency) (151400–151999)," Box 47, FG 122—Environmental Protection Agency, Ronald Reagan Library.

50. Michael Deland and Paul Keough, "Acid Rain: A Regional Report," December 12, 1983, folder, "Acid Rain, 1983," Box 1, Program Development Files, 1973–1989, Subject Files, A-FE, 1/1/1973–12/31/1989, Region I Regional Administrator, RG 412 Environmental Protection Agency, National Archives and Records Administration, Boston, Massachusetts.

51. Martin Smith to Roger Porter, August 8, 1983, folder, "Environment—Acid Rain [1 of 5]," Box 70, DBF.

52. William Clark to Edwin Harper, April 3, 1983, folder, "Environment—Acid Rain [1 of 5]," Box 70, DBF. Though the joint United States and Canada lake liming project failed to get off the ground, the trade group Electric Power Research Institute undertook a major demonstration project in 1984, continuing to present liming as a technological solution that would circumvent the need for any changes in electrical generation or consumption. Douglas Britt and James Fraser, "Adirondack Experimental Lake Liming Program," *Lake and Reservoir Management* 1, no. 1 (1984): 360–367.

53. Irvin Molotsky, "U.S. Identifies 23 Films Labeled as Propaganda," *New York Times*, March 5, 1983.

54. The Working Group on Energy, Natural Resources, and Environment to the Domestic Policy Council, November 9, 1987, Folder ID: 15188-008, Gray VP Files.

55. Gary Bryner, *Blue Skies, Green Politics: The Clean Air Act of 1990* (Washington, DC: CQ Quarterly Press, 1993).

56. Robert Hahn and Roger Noll, "Designing a Market for Tradable Emissions Permits," in *Reform of Environmental Regulation*, ed. Wesley Magat, 119–149 (Cambridge, MA: Ballinger, 1982); Robert Hahn and Roger Noll, "Barriers to Implementing Tradable Air Pollution Permits: Problems of Regulatory Interactions," *Yale Journal on Regulation* 1 (1983): 63–91.

57. S. E. Atkinson, "Marketable Pollution Permits and Acid Rain Externalities," *Canadian Journal of Economics* 16, no. 4 (1983): 704–722.

58. Division of Air Quality Control, *An Examination of Experience, Capabilities, and Attitudes Towards Emissions Trading in New England* (Boston: Massachusetts Department of Environmental Quality Engineering, 1986), folder, "New England ET—1986," Box CC, MLP.

59. Robert Hahn and Gordon Hester, "The Market for Bads: EPA's Experience with Emissions Trading," *Regulation* 11, no. 3 (1987): 48–53.

60. Roger Raufer and Stephen Feldman, *Acid Rain and Emissions Trading: Implementing a Market Approach to Pollution Control* (Totowa, NJ: Rowman & Littlefield, 1987).

61. Krupp's willingness to partner with industry has made him and EDF a continued source of fascination and opprobrium, one example of which provided the

biography given here. James Verini, "The Devil's Advocate," *New Republic*, September 24, 2007, accessed February 6, 2017, https://newrepublic.com/article/62836/the-devils-advocate.

62. John Fialka, "How a Republican Anti-Pollution Measure, Expanded by Democrats, Got Rooted in Europe and China," *Climatewire*, November 17, 2011, accessed January 6, 2017, http://www.eenews.net/stories/1059956562.

63. Fred Krupp, "New Environmentalism Factors in Economic Needs," *Wall Street Journal*, November 20, 1986.

64. Robert Stavins, "Harnessing Market Forces to Protect the Environment," *Environment* 31, no. 1 (1989): 4–35.

65. Peter Passell, "Economic Scene: Private Incentives as Pollution Curb," *New York Times*, October 19, 1988.

66. For instance, Republican pollster and Bush confidant Robert Teeter recommended that Bush direct environmental appeals to undecided women, for whom the issue was especially important and with whom Bush was polling poorly. Elsewhere, Teeter recommended that Bush emphasize environmental issues in San Francisco to chip away at Dukakis's substantial lead there. Robert Teeter, "California," 1988, folder, "California, 1988 (1)," Box 134, Mary Lunken Working Files, Individual States Files, Robert M. Teeter Papers, 1967–2004, Gerald R. Ford Library (RTP hereafter).

67. James Turner and Andrew Isenberg, *The Republican Reversal: Conservatives and the Environment from Nixon to Trump* (Cambridge, MA: Harvard University Press, 2018).

68. Philip Shabecoff, "Bush Tells Environmentalists He'll Listen to Them," *York Times*, December 1, 1988.

69. Turner and Isenberg, *The Republican Reversal*.

70. Landy, Roberts, and Thomas, *The Environmental Protection Agency*.

71. Landy, Roberts, and Thomas, *The Environmental Protection Agency*.

72. Michael Kaufman, "Bush Visit Today Gratifies Ottawa," *New York Times*, February 10, 1989.

73. Gray had managed the Task Force on Regulatory Relief that Bush chaired for Reagan and he continued to play a key role in the EPA's policymaking, including the writing of the Final Emissions Trading Policy as well as the contemplation of trading programs that the agency ultimately did not adopt, such as new standards for heavy truck engines. See, for example, John Daniel to Boyden Gray, March 10, 1982, Folder ID: 92043-005, Gray VP Files and C. Boyden Gray to Stephen Galeback, April 17, 1987, Folder ID: 15190-007, Gray VP Files.

74. Fialka, "How a Republican Anti-Pollution Measure, Expanded by Democrats, Got Rooted in Europe and China."

75. The EPA and the White House contracted the consultancy ICF Resources Incorporated to evaluate EDF's plan and make recommendations. Bruce Braine to Barry Elman, May 19, 1989, Folder ID: 45146-007, Jeffrey Holmstead Files, White House Counsel's Office, George H. W. Bush Presidential Library (JHF hereafter).

76. Daniel Dudek, "Emissions Trading: Environmental Perestroika or Flimflam?" *Electricity Journal* (November, 1989): 32–43.

77. Fred Krupp to Boyden Gray, June 5, 1989, Folder ID: 01412-02, Robert J. Portman Files, White House Counsel's Office, George H. W. Bush Presidential Library.

78. From the beginning, Krupp made it clear that EDF would only support Bush's proposal if it cut sulfur dioxide emissions in half. Fred Krupp to Boyden Gray, March 23, 1989, Folder ID: 45063-003, Gray President Files.

79. Bryner, *Blue Skies, Green Politics.*

80. Ozone is an allotrope of oxygen consisting of three oxygen molecules. Two of those molecules are bonded tightly together as an oxygen atom but the third oxygen molecule is loosely bonded and readily detaches to react with other things. In the stratosphere, ozone concentrates in a layer roughly ten to twenty miles from the earth's surface. There, the unstable compound reacts with ultraviolet light, dissipating the majority of those dangerous rays as heat. In the process, that unstable third oxygen molecule splits off to recombine with other oxygen atoms and make more ozone—a neat process frequently characterized as a perpetual reapplication of the earth's sunscreen. That same propensity to react with ultraviolet light also causes ozone to react with chlorofluorocarbons, a reaction that unfortunately does not produce a free oxygen molecule and thus works to wipe off the earth's sunscreen. Daniel Jacob's *Introduction to Atmospheric Chemistry* (Princeton, NJ: Princeton University Press, 1999).

81. The National Academy of Sciences and the National Cancer Institute conducted the studies that outlined the startling magnitude of the threat. The Rand Corporation conducted a study of possible responses for the EPA, but the agency did not intervene. Bureau of National Affairs, Inc., "Ozone Depletion, Skin Cancer Risk Greater than 1976 Prediction, NAS Says," *Environment Reporter* 10, no. 29 (November 16, 1979): 1521–1522.

82. The National Academy of Sciences and the National Cancer Institute conducted the studies that outlined the startling magnitude of the threat. Bureau of National Affairs, Inc., "Ozone Depletion, Skin Cancer Risk Greater than 1976 Prediction, NAS Says," *Environment Reporter* 10, no. 29 (November 16, 1979): 1521–1522; US Environmental Protection Agency, *Toxics Information Series: CFC's, Ozone, and Health* (Washington, DC, 1980).

83. Among other things, the National Association of Manufacturers lobbied against the United States' endorsement of a report on the ozone issue created by the Organisation for Economic Co-operation and Development in 1981. Daniel Cannon to Boyden Gray, March 26, 1981, Folder ID: 92043-004, Gray VP Files.

84. The Natural Resources Defense Council joined with the Environmental Defense Fund and other environmental organizations to campaign for a CFC ban throughout the 1980s. Alan Miller to Members of the National Clean Air Coalition, February 22, 1983, folder, "CFCs—Memoranda—NRDC et al.," Box 2, Series 2: Project Files, Acid Rain Subject Files (1979–1983), Sub-group 11.3 Toxic Chemicals Program—Projects, Washington, DC Office, Environmental Defense Fund Archives, Stony Brook University.

85. Susan Solomon, "The Discovery of the Ozone Hole," *Nature* 575 (2019): 46–47.

86. Economists at the EPA appear to have first considered the possibility of marketable CFC permits in 1977, spending the rest of Carter's administration considering

the legality and viability of such an approach. During Reagan's first term, two EPA economists published an account of how a tradable permit scheme would work. Andy Mark to Jim Janis, August 26, 1977, folder, "Marketable Permits, Box 47, DCP; Rob Rabin to Frans Kok, January 25, 1980, folder, "Marketable Permits, Box 47, DCP; Michael Shapiro and Ellen Warhit, "Marketable Permits: The Case of Chlorofluorocarbons," *Natural Resources Journal* 23, no. 5 (1983): 577–591.

87. The CFC production market was highly concentrated in the United States, with the two largest manufacturers (Du Pont and Allied Signal) accounting for 75 percent of all CFCs produced in 1986. Roughly 5,000 businesses used CFCs, raising fears that producers might benefit from production quotas. To prevent some manufacturers of CFCs from charging exorbitant prices for CFC rights, the United States imposed a tax on CFCs to soak up excess rents. Robert Hahn and Albert McGartland, "The Political Economy of Instrument Choice: An Examination of the U.S. Role in Implementing the Montreal Protocol," *Northwestern University Law Review* 83 (1989): 592–611.

88. CFC producers were allotted 100 percent of the 1986 baseline (based on market share) and then a decreasing percentage every year thereafter. Producers could only buy credits to produce 10 to 15 percent more than their apportionment. Tietenberg, "Ethical Influences on the Evolution of the US Tradable Permit Approach to Air Pollution Control."

89. Environment Defense Fund, "EDF Praises President's Proposal as Challenge to Congress to Enact Strong Acid Rain Bill," July 15, 1989, Folder ID: 45063-006, Gray Presidential Files.

90. Bush traded that strong intervention for less extensive controls on toxic emissions and urban smog. Samuel Hays, "The Politics of Clean Air," in *Explorations in Environmental History: Essays* by Samuel P. Hays, 219–312 (Pittsburgh: University of Pittsburgh Press, 1998).

91. 2.24 percent of SO_2 allowances were to be held back by the EPA every year for sale at auction (with returns from sales distributed to producers proportionate to their share of total allowances), guaranteeing liquidity in the market. Tietenberg, "Ethical Influences on the Evolution of the US Tradable Permit Approach to Air Pollution Control."

92. Hays, "The Politics of Clean Air."

93. Edison Electric Institute, "Meet the President's Emission Goals and Save $25 Billion," published in the *National Journal* on September 30 and October 7, 1989 and in *Roll Call* on October 2 and October 9, 1989, copy in Folder ID: 45063-006, Gray Presidential Files.

94. EEI made this argument in letters to the White House and in full page advertisements in Beltway publications. See, for example, Edison Electric Institute, "Meet the President's Emission Goals and Save $25 Billion."

95. Western coal interests were represented by the Alliance for Clean Energy, which fiercely resisted both technology requirements and proposals to have utilities across the country share the financial burden of reducing sulfur emissions in eastern states. See, for example, Alliance for Clean Energy, "Action Alert on Acid Rain Legislation," Folder ID: 45063-002, Gray Presidential Files.

96. Robert Stavins, "Lessons from the American Experiment with Market-Based Environmental Policies," Kennedy School of Government Faculty Research Working Paper Series RWP01-032, Working Paper No. 22.2002.

97. Turner and Isenberg, *The Republican Reversal.*

98. Boyden Gray to General Scowcroft, June 22, 1989, Folder ID: 45125-015, JHF. Emphasis in Original.

99. Jerry Jasinowski to John Sununu, October 26, 1989, Folder ID: 45125-017, JHF.

100. David Mason to Boyden Gray, March 2, 1990, Folder ID: 45058-001, Gray Presidential Files.

101. Though the Working Group represented the nation's largest corporations, they evidently saw a political utility in the imagery of trampled small businesses, at one point sending along a publication by the National Federation of Independent Businesses that imagined a new Clean Air Act imposing ruinous requirements on Main Street. "A Walk Down Maine Streets," included such examples of overreach as "Daniel Dedrick's Kennebunk Restaurant" being forced to install a containment unit for its charcoal grill. Attached to CAWG Comments, Folder ID: 45067-013, Gray Presidential Files.

102. CAWG Comments, Folder ID: 45067-013, Gray Presidential Files.

103. Policy positions and political importance conveyed in "Agenda for Meeting with the Clean Air Working Group," June 8, 1989, Folder ID: 45067-013, Gray Presidential Files.

104. Todd Gitlin, "Buying the Right to Pollute? What's Next?" *New York Times*, July 28, 1989.

105. See, for example, Dan Dudek to Max Baucus, October 24, 1989, Folder ID: 45063-003, Gray Presidential Files. In December 1989, Bush advisors deployed Krupp to personally reach out to Senators Heinz and Wirth (with whom Krupp had collaborated on *Project 88*) to ensure that they remained strong supporters of Bush's bill. Unsigned Memo, December 21, 1989, Folder ID: 45146-007, JHF.

106. EPA Office of Air and Radiation, August 2, 1989, Folder ID: 45063-006, Gray Presidential Files.

107. Bobbie Kilberg to David Demarest, August 2, 1989, Folder ID: 05302-022, Bobbie Kilberg Files, White House Office of Public Liaison, George H. W. Bush Presidential Library. Like EDF, the environmental organizations that did come out in favor of the bill insisted on a meaningful reduction in acid rain in exchange for their support. For instance, the president of the National Wildlife Foundation cited his testimony in favor of the bill in front of Congress to insist in a letter to Bush that nitrogen dioxide controls be beefed up. Jay Hair to George H. W. Bush, August 2, 1989, Folder ID: 45063-004, Gray Presidential Files.

108. Tietenberg, "Ethical Influences on the Evolution of the US Tradable Permit Approach to Air Pollution Control."

109. Kenneth Arrow et al. to Congressman Philip Sharp, October 4, 1989, Folder ID: 45063-003, Gray Presidential Files.

110. Martha Heese to John D. Dingell, September 26, 1989, Folder ID: 03689-025, Richard Schmalensee Files, Council of Economic Advisors, George H. W. Bush Presidential Library (RSF hereafter).

111. Dudek reported on his work with Sharp to Bush's advisors. Dan Dudek to John Schmitz, April 2, 1990, Folder ID: 45125-006, JHF.

112. Bryner, *Blue Skies, Green Politics.*

113. Landy, Roberts, and Thomas, *The Environmental Protection Agency.*

114. Providing an interesting insight into the relationship between EPA staff and environmental advocates in Congress, Bush advisors carefully avoided particulars in their implementation instructions to the EPA before the conference bill had been signed, warning any specific means of reducing costs would quickly be transmitted to congressional allies and explicitly disallowed in the final legislation. Michael Boskin to Governor Sununu, October 23, 1990, Folder ID: 08070-016, Michael Boskin Files, Council of Economic Advisors, George H. W. Bush Presidential Library (MBF hereafter).

115. Eileen Claussen interview with author, November 6, 2019.

116. "Utilities Soften Stance toward 'Pollution Rights," *Wall Street Journal,* April 10, 1991.

117. William Rosenberg interview with author, March 31, 2017.

118. Dan Dudek to Max Baucus, October 24, 1989, Folder ID: 45063-003, Gray Presidential Files. EDF reports emphasized that SO_2 trading would have "the serendipitous benefit of massive reductions in utility carbon dioxide emissions," resulting from increased energy efficiency as well as fuel switching. Environmental Defense Fund, "EDF Says Solving Acid Rain Will Reduce Greenhouse Heat: Report Says Market-Based Controls Have Dual Benefits," press release for "CO_2 and SO_2: Consistent Policy Making in a Greenhouse," January 11, 1990, Folder ID: 45125-013, JHF.

119. Abt provided technical research on subjects like "The Global Warming Implications of Increased Ethanol Use." Al McGartland to Michael Shelby and Alex Cristafaro, Folder ID: 45125-015, JHF. Gray provided talking points based on this research for a senator to "combat allegations made on the Senate floor this morning that the Administration is showing no leadership on global warming," as well as Bush's National Security Advisor to take to his international meetings on climate change. Respectively, Nancy Maloley to Boyden Gray et al., November 7, 1989, Folder ID: 45125-015, JHF; Boyden Gray to General Scowcroft, June 22, 1989, Folder ID: 45125-015, JHF.

120. Unsigned, December 21, 1989, Folder ID: 45146-007, JHF.

121. Draft of Boskin Speech to Acid Rain Advisory Committee, December 1990, Folder ID: 08061-065, MBF.

122. Boyden Gray to General Scowcroft, June 22, 1989, Folder ID: 45125-015, JHF.

123. Jim Tripp to Teresa Gorman, Bob Grady, and Ed Goldstein, July 3, 1991, Folder ID: 07654-023, Teresa Gorman Files, White House Office of Policy Development, George H.W. Bush Presidential Library.

124. "Environmental Perestroika: The Case for Incorporating Market Incentives in Environmental Management," 1991, attached to Allan Hubbard to Boyden Gray, December 10, 1991, Folder ID: 45126-003, JHF.

125. US Environmental Protection Agency Economic Incentives Task Force, "Economic Incentives: Options for Environmental Protection," 1991.

126. Terry Anderson and Donald Leal, *Free Market Environmentalism* (San Francisco: Pacific Research Institute for Public Policy, 1991).

127. In the case of the spotted owl, Bush's campaign excitedly described the controversy as a chance to "put together a coalition of the traditional Republicans with non-Republican blue collar voters," and carry Washington and Oregon in the 1992 election. The campaign considered "owls vs. jobs" such an opportunity that they conducted an 800- person telephone survey in July 1991 to get a better idea of the specific concerns of voters. Fred to Robert Teeter, August 31, 1991, folder, "Washington/Oregon, 1988–1992 (1)," Box 139, RTP; In a seminal essay on the hardening class lines revealed in this case, the environmental historian Richard White warned that environmentalists faced eroding support from working class communities for regulations that seemed to value charismatic animals over the humans who made their living close to the land. White vigorously (and correctly) insisted that this working-class backlash was a genuine grassroots reaction and not a case of corporate "astro-turfing." But the Bush administration's painstaking framing of "owls vs. jobs" as a campaign strategy might have given him pause as to whether it was environmentalists or their opponents who were really to blame for the stark owls versus jobs framing. Richard White, "So Are You an Environmentalist or Do You Work for a Living? Work and Nature," in *Uncommon Ground: Rethinking the Human Place in Nature*, edited by William Cronon, 171–185 (New York: W.W. Norton, 1995).

128. George H. W. Bush, "Memorandum on Recuing the Burden of Government Regulation," January 28, 1992. Digitized by the American Presidency Project, online at https://www.presidency.ucsb.edu/documents/memorandum-reducing-the-burden-government-regulation; David Rosenbaum and Keith Schneider, "Bush Is Extending Regulation Freeze as a Great Success," *New York Times*, April 29, 1992.

129. James Verini, "The Devil's Advocate," *New Republic*, September 24, 2007, accessed February 6, 2017, https://newrepublic.com/article/62836/the-devils-advocate.

130. Bush's advisors were strongly divided on the Rio approach. EPA Administrator Reilly pursued a strong United States commitment to reducing greenhouse gases but was eventually overruled by Chief of Staff John Sununu, who was skeptical about the problem of global warming and prevailed on Bush to take a cautious approach. Landy, Roberts, and Thomas, *The Environmental Protection Agency*.

131. "Text of Clinton Speech on Environment," *U.S. Newswire*, April 22, 1992. Cited in Ted Steinberg, "Can Capitalism Save the Planet?: On the Origins of Green Liberalism." *Radical History Review* 107 (2010): 7–24.

132. Richard Andrews, *Managing the Environment, Managing Ourselves: A History of American Environmental Policy*, 2nd ed. (New Haven, CT: Yale University Press, 2006).

133. Robert Stavins, "Lessons from the American Experiment with Market-Based Environmental Policies," Kennedy School of Government Faculty Research Working Paper Series RWP01-032, Working Paper No. 22.2002. Stavins and a group of other economists later found that far more savings came from railroad deregulation, which allowed eastern utilities access to low-sulfur western coal.

134. Gabriel Chan, Robert Stavins, Robert Stowe, and Richard Sweeny, "The SO_2 Allowance-Trading System and the Clean Air Act Amendments of 1990: Reflections on 20 Years of Policy Innovation," *National Tax Journal* 65, no. 2 (2012): 419–452.

135. Hays, "The Politics of Clean Air."

136. Barry Solomon and Russell Lee, "Emissions Trading and Environmental Justice," *Environment* 42, no. 8 (2000): 32–45.

137. Hays, "The Politics of Clean Air."

138. Solomon and Lee, "Emissions Trading and Environmental Justice."

139. Evan Ringquist, "Trading Equity for Efficiency in Environmental Protection? Environmental Justice Effects from the SO_2 Allowance Trading Program," *Social Science Quarterly* 92, no. 2 (2011): 297–323.

140. See, for example, Corbett Grainger and Thanicha Ruangmas, "Who Wins from Emissions Trading? Evidence from California," *Environmental and Resource Economics* (2017), https://doi.org/10.1007/s10640-017-0180-1; concerns from environmental justice groups about the risks of concentrating pollutants through emissions offsetting shaped recent debates about New York State's 2019 Climate Leadership and Community Protection Act.

141. Carol Browner, "30 Years of U.S. Environmental Protection," digitized and online at https://archive.epa.gov/epa/aboutepa/30-years-us-environmental-protection.html

142. Hays, "The Politics of Clean Air."

Epilogue

1. GDP gains calculated from 1970 to 2019 (the last year for which there are data) in 2010 dollars, https://data.worldbank.org/indicator/NY.GDP.MKTP.KD?locations=US; aggregate emission reductions from 1970 to 2019 (the last year for which there are data) https://gispub.epa.gov/air/trendsreport/2020/#home; air quality improvements from 1980 to 2019, https://www.epa.gov/air-trends/air-quality-national-summary. Estimates of monetary costs and benefits of improved air quality calculated from 1970 to 2020 in 2006 dollars. US Environmental Protection Agency, "The Benefits and Costs of the Clean Air Act, 1970 to 1990, October 1997." US Environmental Protection Agency, "The Benefits and Costs of the Clean Air Act from 1990 to 2020, April 2011."

2. International Governmental Panel on Climate Change, 2018 Report, digitized and online at https://www.ipcc.ch/sr15/chapter/chapter-3/.

3. Coral Davenport and Kendra Pierre-Louis, "U.S. Climate Report Warns of Damaged Environment and Shrinking Economy," *New York Times*, November 23, 2019.

4. Marshall Burke, W. Matthew Davis, and Noah Diffenbaugh, "Large Potential Reduction in Economic Damages under UN Mitigation Targets," *Nature* 557 (May 24, 2018): 549–607.

5. In a widely cited 2019 report, Morgan Stanley put the costs of meeting the targets of the 2015 Paris Agreement at $50 trillion. Morgan Stanley, "Decarbonisation: The Race to Zero Emissions," October 21, 2019.

6. Naomi Oreskes and Erik Conway, *Merchants of Doubt: How a Handful of Scientists Obscured the Truth on Issues from Tobacco Smoke to Global Warming* (London: Bloomsbury, 2010).

7. Arlie Hochschild, *Strangers in Their Own Land: Fear and Mourning on the American Right* (New York: New Press, 2016).

8. Richard Andrews, *Managing the Environment, Managing Ourselves: A History of American Environmental Policy*, 2nd ed. (New Haven, CT: Yale University Press, 2006).

9. Massachusetts v. Environmental Protection Agency, 549 U.S. 497 (2007).

10. James Turner and Andrew Isenberg, *The Republican Reversal: Conservatives and the Environment from Nixon to Trump* (Cambridge, MA: Harvard University Press, 2018).

11. Whitman v. American Trucking Associations, Inc. 531 U.S. 457 (2001).

12. Andrews, *Managing the Environment*.

13. Andrews, *Managing the Environment*.

14. Lisa Friedman, "E.P.A. Chief's $43,000 Phone Booth Broke the Law, Congressional Auditors Say," *New York Times*, April 16, 2018.

15. The Environmental Data and Governance Initiative (EDGI) was formed to scrape data from public portals after fears were raised that Pruitt and Trump would delete or pull down these vital public resources. The project evolved to collect oral histories from current and former staff to document the changes happening under the new administration. I have contributed to EDGI's interviewing work.

16. Lisa Friedman, "The Investigations That Led to Scott Pruitt's Resignation," *New York Times*, April 18, 2018.

17. Lisa Friedman, "E.P.A. Updates Plan to Limit Science Used in Environmental Rules," *New York Times*, March 4, 2020.

18. US EPA, "National Emission Standards for Hazardous Air Pollutants: Coal—and Oil-Fired Electric Utility Steam Generating Units—Reconsideration of Supplemental Finding and Residual Risk and Technology Review," *Code of Federal Regulations* 40 (April 16, 2020).

19. On the competition between states that also drives this shift, see Barry Rabe, *Statehouse and Greenhouse: The Emerging Politics of American Climate Change Policy* (Washington, DC: Brookings Institution Press, 2004).

20. See, for example, Natasha Chassagne, "Here's What the Coronavirus Pandemic Can Teach Us about Tackling Climate Change," *The Conversation*, March 26, 2020, https://theconversation.com/heres-what-the-coronavirus-pandemic-can-teach-us-about-tackling-climate-change-134399.

Bibliography

Archival Collections

Bates College, Edmund S. Muskie Archives and Special Collections Library
Edmund S. Muskie Papers
George H. W. Bush Presidential Library
C. Boyden Gray Files, Vice Presidential Records, Counsellor's Office
C. Boyden Gray Files, White House Counsel's Office
Jeffrey Holmstead Files, White House Counsel's Office
Michael Boskin Files, Council of Economic Advisors
Richard Schmalensee Files, Council of Economic Advisors
Gerald R. Ford Presidential Library
Edward C. Schmults Files: 1974–77
Edward C. Schmults Papers: 1973–77 (1978–81)
FG 6-16, Office of Management and Budget
FG 298, US Environmental Protection Agency
George Humphreys Files 1975–1977, Domestic Council
Glenn R. Schleede Files
L. William Seidman Files, 1974–77, Office of Economic Affairs
Robert M. Teeter Papers, 1967–2004
William Gorog Files, 1975–76, Office of Economic Affairs
Jimmy Carter Presidential Library
Charles L. Schultze's Subject Files, Staff Office—CEA
Domestic Policy Staff, Stuart Eizenstat Subject Files
Doug Costle Papers
Michael Levin Personal Collection
Michael Levin Papers
National Archives and Records Administration, Boston, Massachusetts.
Region 1 Regional Administrator, RG 412 Environmental Protection Agency
National Archives and Records Administration, College Park
Office of the Administrator, General Correspondence, 1971–1982, RG 412, Records of the
    Environmental Protection Agency
Office of the Administrator, Intra-Agency Memorandums, 1977–1983, RG 412, Records
    on the Environmental Protection Agency
National Archives and Records Administration, San Bruno
Region IX Enforcement Division, Hearing Officer's Records 1972–1976, P to S. (18), RG
    412 EPA
Richard Nixon Presidential Library
FG 6-17, Council on Environmental Quality
FG 298, US Environmental Protection Agency
Papers of Dr. Robert L. Sansom, 1972–74

White House Central Files, Staff Member and Office Files, John C. Whitaker Files
Ronald Reagan Presidential Library
Danny J. Boggs Files
Edwin L. Harper Files
FG 122, Environmental Protection Agency
Fred Fielding Files, 1981–1986
Stony Brook University
Khristine Hall, Sub-group II.1 Toxic Chemicals Program—Staff Files, Washington, DC
    Office, Environmental Defense Fund Archive,
Yale University
Board of Directors, 1970–1977, MS 1965, Accession 2013-M-064, Administrative,
Natural Resources Defense Council Records

Interviews

Becker, William. Interview by author. Personal phone interview. May 1, 2015.
Claussen, Eileen. Interview by author. Personal phone interview. November 6, 2019.
Clough, Kerrigan. Interview by author. Personal interview. Grayling, Michigan, July
    25, 2015.
Crocker, Thomas. Interview by author. Personal phone interview. May 1, 2015.
Crocker, Thomas. Interview by author. Personal phone interview. November 18, 2015.
Donovan, Deborah. Interview by author. Personal phone interview. September 2, 2015.
Drayton, William. Interview by author. Personal phone interview. October 23, 2019.
Gamse, Roy. Interview by author. Personal interview. Washington, DC, May 4, 2015.
Hawkins, David. Interview by author. Personal interview. New York, September 18, 2015.
Isber, Caroline. Interview by author. Personal phone interview. October 7, 2019.
Levin, Michael. Interview by author. Personal interview. Washington, DC, March
    16, 2015.
Levin, Michael. Interview by author. Personal interview. Washington, DC, May 7, 2015.
Loeb, Alan. Interview by author. Personal interview. Washington, DC, March 16, 2015.
Mannix, Brian. Interview with author. Personal interview. Washington, DC, May 5, 2015.
Morgenstern, Richard. Interview by author. Washington, DC, May 5, 2015.
Rosenberg, William. Interview by author. Personal phone interview. March 31, 2017.
Ruckelshaus, William. Interview by author. Personal phone interview. May 13, 2016.
Ward, Morris "Bud." Interview by author. Personal phone interview. April 24, 2015.
Whitaker, John C. Interview by Charles Wilkinson and Patty Limerick. Boulder, CO,
    November 19, 2003. Accessed February 24, 2016, http://centerwest.org/wp-content/
    uploads/2011/01/whitaker.pdf.
Wise, John. Interview by author. Personal phone interview. July 28, 2015.

Government Reports

Brookshire, David. "Method Development for Assessing Air Pollution Control Benefits."
    Washington, DC: US EPA, 1979.
Carlin, Alan. "History of Economic Research at the EPA." US EPA, National Center for
    Environment Economics, accessed December 9, 2015, http://yosemite.epa.gov/ee/epa/

eed.nsf/0000000000000000000000000000000000/2f68aa9ffb75364b8525779700781a24! OpenDocument.

Connecticut Department of Environmental Protection, Enforcement Project. *Economic Law Enforcement*, vol.1, *Overview*. Washington, DC: US Environmental Protection Agency, 1975.

National Research Council. *Risk Assessment in the Federal Government: Managing the Process*. Washington, DC: National Academies Press, 1983.

Secretary of Health, Education, and Welfare. *The Cost of Clean Air*. Washington, DC, 1969.

Subcommittee on Air and Water Pollution. *A Study of Pollution—Air, a Staff Report to the Committee on Public Works, United States Senate*. Washington, DC: 1963.

The World Bank. "GDP (current US$)." Accessed February 21, 2017, http://data. worldbank.org/indicator/NY.GDP.MKTP.CD.

United Nations. *Report of the United Nations Conference on the Human Environment, Stockholm, June 5–16, 1972*, A. Conf. 48, 14, Rev. 1, accessed December 20, 2016, http:// www.un-documents.net/aconf48-14r1.pdf.

US Environmental Protection Agency. "Air Quality National Summary." Accessed December 23, 2020. https://www.epa.gov/air-trends/air-quality-national-summary.

US Environmental Protection Agency. "Air Pollution Control; Recommendation for Alternative Emission Reduction Options within State Implementation Plans." *Federal Register* 44, no. 13 (January 18, 1979): 3740–3744.

US Environmental Protection Agency. *Brokering Emission Reduction Credits: A Handbook*. Washington, DC, 1981.

US Environmental Protection Agency. "Data Table of Ambient Air Levels, 1970–1999." Provided by Nick Magnus, US EPA Air Quality Standards, to author on November 18, 2015.

US Environmental Protection Agency, *Economic Incentives: Options for Environmental Protection*. 1991.

US Environmental Protection Agency. "Emissions Trading Policy Statement." *Federal Register* 47 (April 7, 1982): 15076.

US Environmental Protection Agency, "Emissions Trading Policy Statement," *Federal Register* 51, no. 233 (December 4, 1986): 43814.

US Environmental Protection Agency. *EPA Cumulative Bibliography, 1970–1976*. Washington, DC, 1976.

US Environmental Protection Agency. "National Primary and Secondary Ambient Air Quality Standards." *Federal Register* 36, no. 84 (April 30, 1971): 8186–8201.

US Environmental Protection Agency. "New Source Review in Non-Attainment Areas (Tradeoff Policy)," in *Environmental Protection Agency Transition Papers to Incoming Carter Administration on Areas of Agency Jurisdiction*, 1302–1303. Published in Bureau of National Affairs, *Environment Reporter* 7, no. 36 (January 7, 1977): 1288–1334.

US Environmental Protection Agency. "Non-Regulatory (Economic) Approaches to Environmental Programs," in *Environmental Protection Agency Transition Papers to Incoming Carter Administration on Areas of Agency Jurisdiction*, 1298–1299. Published in Bureau of National Affairs. *Environment Reporter* 7, no. 36 (January 7, 1977): 1288–1334.

US Environmental Protection Agency. "Photochemical Oxidants; Measurement of Ozone in the Atmosphere; Requirements for Preparation, Adoption, and Submittal of Implementation Plans." *Federal Register* 43, no. 121 (June 22, 1978): 26966.

US Environmental Protection Agency. "Notice of Proposed Standards for Sulfur Oxides, Particulate Matter, Carbon Monoxide, Photochemical Oxidants, Hydrocarbons, and Nitrogen Oxides." *Federal Register* 36, no. 21 (January 30, 1971): 1502–1515.

US Environmental Protection Agency. "Our Nation's Air." Accessed December 23, 2020. https://gispub.epa.gov/air/trendsreport/2020/#home.

US Environmental Protection Agency. *Profile of the Nonferrous Metals Industry.* Washington, DC, 1995.

US Environmental Protection Agency. "Revisions to the National Ambient Air Quality Standards for Photochemical Oxidants." *Federal Register* 44, no. 28 (February 8, 1979): 8205.

US Environmental Protection Agency. "Table of Historical CO NAAQS." Accessed November 18, 2015. https://www.epa.gov/co-pollution/table-historical-carbon-monoxide-co-national-ambient-air-quality-standards-naaqs.

US Environmental Protection Agency. *The Benefits and Costs of the Clean Air Act, 1970 to 1990.* Washington, DC, 1997.

US Environmental Protection Agency. *The Benefits and Costs of the Clean Air Act from 1990 to 2020,"* Final Report—Rev. A. Washington, DC, 2011.

US Environmental Protection Agency. *The Economics of Clean Air, Report of the Administrator of the Environmental Protection Agency to the Congress of the United States in Compliance with Public Law 90-148, The Clean Air Act, as Amended.* Washington, DC, 1971.

US Environmental Protection Agency. *Unfinished Business: A Comparative Assessment of Environmental Problems.* Washington, DC, February 1987.

US National Commission on Air Quality. *To Breathe Clean Air: Report of the National Commission on Air Quality.* Washington, DC, 1981.

US Public Health Service. *Proceedings—National Conference on Air Pollution, Washington, DC November 18–20, 1958.* Washington, DC, 1958.

US Public Health Service. *Guide to Research in Air Pollution for Projects Active in Calendar Year 1966.* Washington, DC, 1996.

US Surgeon General's Ad Hoc Task Group on Air Pollution Research Goals. *National Goals in Air Pollution Research.* Washington, DC: Public Health Service, 1960.

US Environmental Protection Agency. *Toxics Information Series: CFC's, Ozone, and Health.* Washington, DC, 1980.

Federal Register, Code of Federal Regulations, and Public Papers of the Presidents

Browner, Carol. "30 Years of U.S. Environmental Protection," April 22, 2000. Digitized and online at https://archive.epa.gov/epa/aboutepa/30-years-us-environmental-protection.html.

Executive Order 11821 of November 27, 1974, Inflation Impact Statements. http://www.presidency.ucsb.edu/ws/?pid=23905.

Executive Order 11949 of December 31, 1976, Economic Impact Statements. http://www.presidency.ucsb.edu/ws/?pid=23684.

Executive Order 12044 of March 23, 1978, Improving Government Regulations. http://www.presidency.ucsb.edu/ws/?pid=30539.

Executive Order 12291 of February 17, 1981, Federal Regulation, https://www.archives.gov/federal-register/codification/executive-order/12291.html.

Nixon, Richard. "Remarks on Signing the Clean Air Amendments of 1970," December 31, 1970.

Archived at the American Presidency Project, University of California, Santa Barbara, accessed February 24, 2016, http://www.presidency.ucsb.edu/ws/?pid=2874.

Nixon, Richard. "Special Message to the Congress About Reorganization Plans to Establish the Environmental Protection Agency and the National Oceanic and Atmospheric Administration, July 9, 1970, accessed February 26, 2016, http://www.presidency.ucsb.edu/ws/index.php?pid=2575&st=environmental+protection+agency&st1.

Nixon, Richard. "Statement About the National Environmental Policy Act of 1969," January 1, 1970. Archived at the American Presidency Project, University of California, Santa Barbara, accessed February 14, 2017, http://www.presidency.ucsb.edu/ws/?pid=2557.

Reagan, Ronald. Inaugural Address, January 20, 1981. Digitized as part of the American Presidency Project and online at https://www.presidency.ucsb.edu/documents/inaugural-address-11.

Reagan, Ronald. "Letter Accepting the Resignation of Anne M. Burford as Administrator of the Environmental Protection Agency." Archived at the American Presidency Project, University of California, Santa Barbara, accessed March 10, 2017, http://www.presidency.ucsb.edu/ws/index.php?pid=41033.

Annual Reports

Kennecott Copper Corporation. 1976 Annual Report.
Resources for the Future. *1953 Annual Report.*
Resources for the Future. *1954 Annual Report.*
Resources for the Future. *1955 Annual Report.*
Resources for the Future. *1956 Annual Report.*
Resources for the Future. *1957 Annual Report.*
Resources for the Future. *1958 Annual Report.*
Resources for the Future. *1959 Annual Report.*
Resources for the Future. *1960 Annual Report.*
Resources for the Future. *1961 Annual Report.*
Resources for the Future. *1962 Annual Report.*
Resources for the Future. *1963 Annual Report.*
Resources for the Future. *1964 Annual Report.*
Resources for the Future. *1965 Annual Report.*
Resources for the Future. *1966 Annual Report.*
Resources for the Future. *1967 Annual Report.*
Resources for the Future. *1968 Annual Report.*
Resources for the Future. *1969 Annual Report.*
Resources for the Future. *1970 Annual Report.*
Resources for the Future. *1971 Annual Report.*
Resources for the Future. *1972 Annual Report.*
Resources for the Future. *1973 Annual Report.*

Secondary Monographs and Articles

Ackerman, Frank and Lisa Heinzerling. *Priceless: On Knowing the Price of Everything and the Value of Nothing.* New York: New Press, 2004.

Anderson, Terry and Donald Leal. *Free Market Environmentalism.* San Francisco: Pacific Research Institute for Public Policy, 1991.

Andrews, Richard. "Economics and Environmental Decisions, Past and Present." In *Environmental Policy under Reagan's Executive Order: The Role of Benefit-Cost Analysis,* edited by V. Kerry Smith, 43–85. Chapel Hill: University of North Carolina Press, 1984.

Andrews, Richard. *Managing the Environment, Managing Ourselves: A History of American Environmental Policy.* 2nd ed. New Haven, CT: Yale University Press, 2006.

Atkinson, S. E. "Marketable Pollution Permits and Acid Rain Externalities." *Canadian Journal of Economics* 16, no. 4 (1983): 704–722.

Babich, Adam. "Citizen Suits: The Teeth in Public Participation." *Environmental Law Review* 25 no. 3 (1995): 10141–10151.

Balogh, Brian. *Chain Reaction: Expert Debate and Public Participation in American Commercial Nuclear Power, 1945–1975.* New York: Cambridge University Press, 1991.

Balogh, Brian . *The Associational State: American Governance in the Twentieth Century.* Philadelphia: University of Pennsylvania Press, 2015.

Beavers, Casey. "An Overview of Phosphate Mining and Reclamation in Florida." PhD diss., University of Florida, 2013.

Beckerman, W. and A. Markandya. "Pollution Control and Optimal Taxation: A Static Analysis." *Journal of Economics and Management* 1, no. 1 (1974): 43–52.

Berman, Elizabeth Popp. *Thinking Like an Economist: How Economics Became the Language of U.S. Public Policy.* Princeton, NJ: Princeton University Press, 2020.

Bernstein, Marver. "The Regulatory Process: A Framework for Analysis." *Law and Contemporary Problems* 26, no. 2 (1961): 329–346.

Biven, Carl. *Jimmy Carter's Economy: Policy in an Age of Limits.* Chapel Hill: University of North Carolina Press, 2002.

Black, Conrad. *Richard M. Nixon: A Life in Full.* New York: Public Affairs, 2007.

Blackmar, Elizabeth. "Peregrinations of the Free Rider: The Changing Logics of Collective Obligation." In *Transformations in American Legal History: Essays in Honor of Professor Morton J. Horowitz,* edited by Daniel Hamilton and Alfred Brophy, 267–297. Cambridge, MA: Harvard University Press, 2009.

Boulding, Kenneth. "Economics of the Coming Spaceship Earth," in *Environmental Quality in a Growing Economy,* edited by Henry Jarrett, 3–14. Baltimore, MD: Resources for the Future / Johns Hopkins University Press, 1966.

Britt, Douglas and James Fraser. "Adirondack Experimental Lake Liming Program." *Lake and Reservoir Management* 1, no. 1 (1984): 360–367.

Broughton, Edward. "The Bhopal Disaster and Its Aftermath: A Review." *Environmental Health: A Global Access Science Source* 4 (2005), accessed March 10, 2017 https://ehjournal.biomedcentral.com/articles/10.1186/1476-069X-4-6.

Bryner, Gary. *Blue Skies, Green Politics: The Clean Air Act of 1990.* Washington, DC: CQ Quarterly Press, 1993.

Burford, Anne M. and John Greenya. *Are You Tough Enough? An Insider's View of Washington Power Politics.* New York: McGraw-Hill, 1986.

Canedo, Eduardo. "The Rise of the Deregulation Movement in Modern America, 1957–1980." PhD diss., Columbia University, 2008.

Carpenter, Daniel. *Reputation and Power: Organizational Image and Pharmaceutical Regulation at the FDA*. Princeton, NJ: Princeton University Press, 2010.

Chan, Gabriel, Robert Stavins, Robert Stowe, and Richard Sweeny. "The SO2 Allowance-Trading System and the Clean Air Act Amendments of 1990: Reflections on 20 Years of Policy Innovation." *National Tax Journal* 65, no. 2 (2012): 419–452.

Carson, Rachel. *Silent Spring*. New York: Houghton Mifflin, 1962.

Coase, Ronald. "The Problem of Social Cost." *Journal of Law and Economics* 3 (1960): 1–44.

Committee on Air Pollution Controls. *Guide to Research in Air Pollution: Colleges, Universities, and Research Institutes*. 3rd ed. New York: Committee on Air Pollution Control, the American Society of Mechanical Engineers, 1956.

Conant, James and Peter Balint. *The Life Cycles of the Council on Environmental Quality and the Environmental Protection Agency, 1970–2035*. New York: Oxford University Press, 2016.

Conlan, Timothy. *New Federalism: Intergovernmental Reform from Nixon to Reagan*. Washington, DC: Brookings Institution, 1988.

Conley, Joe. "Environmentalism Contained: A History of Corporate Responses to the New Environmentalism." PhD diss., Princeton University, 2006.

Cowie, Jefferson. *Capital Moves: RCA's Seventy-Year Quest for Cheap Labor*. Ithaca, NY: Cornell University Press, 1999.

Crandall, Robert. "The Political Economy of Clean Air: Practical Constraints on White House Review." In *Environmental Policy under Reagan's Executive Order: The Role of Benefit-Cost Analysis*, edited by V. Kerry Smith, 205–225. Chapel Hill: University of North Carolina Press, 1984.

Crocker, Thomas. "Externalities, Property Rights, and Transactions Costs: An Empirical Study." *Journal of Law & Economics* 14, no. 2 (1971): 451–464.

Crocker, Thomas. "In Polk & Hillsborough Counties, Florida." *Bulletin of the Atomic Scientists* 21, no. 6 (1965): 17–19.

Crocker, Thomas. "The Structuring of Atmospheric Pollution Control Systems." In *The Economics of Air Pollution, A Symposium*, edited by Harold Wolozin, 61–86. New York: W. W. Norton, 1966.

Cross, Frank Jr. and Susan M. Hennigan. *National Directory of Environmental Impact Experts, Consultants, Regulatory Agencies*. Westport, CT: Technomic Publishing, 1974.

Dales, J. H. *Pollution, Property, & Prices: An Essay in Policy-Making and Economics*. Toronto: University of Toronto Press, 1968.

David, Paul A. and Peter Solar. "A Bicentenary Contribution to the History of the Cost of Living in America." *Research in Economic History* 2 (1977): 1–80.

Davidson, Kenneth, Leland Deck, and Christine Houle. "Assessing Public Opinions on Visibility Impairment due to Air Pollution: Summary Report." Washington, DC: Abt Associates, 2001.

Davis, Mike. "Melting Away." *The Nation*, October 24, 2005.

Decker, Jefferson. *The Other Rights Revolution: Conservative Lawyers and the Remaking of American Government*. New York: Oxford University Press, 2016.

Dewey, Scott. *Don't Breathe the Air: Air Pollution and U.S. Environmental Politics, 1945–1970*. College Station: Texas A&M University Press, 2000.

Dewey, Scott. "'Is This What We Came to Florida For?' Florida Women and the Fight against Air Pollution in the 1960s." *Florida Historical Quarterly* 77, no. 4 (1999): 503–531.

Disselhorst, Thomas. "Sierra Club v. Ruckelshaus: On a Clear Day . . ." *Ecology Law Quarterly* 4, no. 3 (1975): 739–780.

Douglas, M. and A. Wildavsky. *Risk and Culture*. Berkeley: University of California Press, 1982.

Drake, Brian. *Loving Nature, Fearing the State: Environmentalism and Antigovernment Politics before Reagan*. Seattle: University of Washington Press, 2013.

Drayton, William. "Getting Smarter about Regulation." *Harvard Business Review* 59, no. 4 (1981): 38–53.

Dudek, Daniel. "Emissions Trading: Environmental Perestroika or Flimflam?" *Electricity Journal* (November 1989): 32–43.

Dudek, Daniel and John Palmisano. "Emissions Trading: Why Is This Thoroughbred Hobbled?" *Columbia Journal of Environmental Law* 13 (1988): 217–255.

Eckstein, Otto. *Water-Resource Development: The Economics of Project Evaluation*. Cambridge, MA: Harvard University Press, 1961.

Edwards-Jones, Gareth. *Ecological Economics: An Introduction*. Malden, MA: Blackwell Science, 2000.

Esposito, John and Larry Silverman. *Vanishing Air: The Ralph Nader Study Group Report on Air Pollution*. New York: Grossman, 1970.

Fisher, Ann. "An Overview and Evaluation of EPA's Guidelines for Conducting Regulatory Impact Analyses." In *Environmental Policy under Reagan's Executive Order: The Role of Benefit-Cost Analysis*, edited by V. Kerry Smith, 99–118. Chapel Hill: University of North Carolina Press, 1984.

Flippen, J. Brooks. *Nixon and the Environment*. Albuquerque: University of New Mexico Press, 2000.

Fraas, Arthur. "Benefit-Cost Analysis for Environmental Regulation." In *Environmental Policy under Reagan's Executive Order: The Role of Benefit-Cost Analysis*, edited by V. Kerry Smith, 86–98. Chapel Hill: University of North Carolina Press, 1984.

Freeman, A. Myrick. "On Estimating Air Pollution Control Benefits from Land Value Studies." *Journal of Economics and Management* 1, no. 1 (1974): 74–83.

Freeman, A Myrick and Robert A. Haveman. "Clean Rhetoric and Dirty Water." *Public Interest* 28 (Summer 1972): 51–85.

Freeman, A. Myrick, Robert Haveman, and Allen Kneese. *The Economics of Environmental Policy*. New York: John Wiley, 1973.

Freeman, Jody and Charles D. Kolstad, eds. *Moving to Markets in Environmental Regulation: Lessons from Thirty Years of Experience*. New York: Oxford University Press, 2007.

Galbraith, John Kenneth. *The Affluent Society*. Boston: Houghton Mifflin Harcourt, 1958.

Gordon, H. Scott. "The Economic Theory of a Common-Property Resource: The Fishery." *Journal of Political Economy* 62, no. 2 (1954): 124–142.

Gorman, Hugh. *Redefining Efficiency: Pollution Concerns, Regulatory Mechanisms, and Technological Change in the U.S. Petroleum Industry*. Akron: University of Akron Press, 2001.

Gorman, Hugh and Barry Solomon. "The Origins and Practice of Emissions Trading." *Journal of Policy History* 14 no. 3 (2002): 293–320.

Gottlieb, Robert. *Forcing the Spring: The Transformation of the American Environmental Movement*. Washington, DC: Island Press, 1993.

Gómez-Baggethun, Erik, Rudolf de Groot, Pedro L. Lomas, and Carlos Montes. "The History of Ecosystem Services in Economic Theory and Practice: From Early Notions to Markets and Payment Schemes." *Ecological Economics* 69 (2010): 1209–1218.

Green, Mark and Beverly Moore. "Winter's Discontent: Market Failure and Consumer Welfare." *Yale Law Journal* (April 1973): 903–919.

Green, Mark and Ralph Nader. "Economic Regulation vs. Competition: Uncle Sam the Monopoly Man." *Yale Law Journal* 82, no. 5 (April 1973): 871–889.

Gregor, Howard. "Urban Pressures on California Land." *Journal of Land & Public Utility Economics* 33, no. 4 (November 1957): 311–325.

Griswold, S. Smith. "What Pollution Costs." *Bulletin of the Atomic Scientists* 21, no. 6 (1965): 12–16.

Grubb, W. Norton, Dale Whittington, and Michael Humphries. "The Ambiguities of Benefit-Cost Analysis: An Evaluation of Regulatory Impact Analyses Under Executive Order 12291." In *Environmental Policy under Reagan's Executive Order: The Role of Benefit-Cost Analysis*, edited by V. Kerry Smith, 121–164. Chapel Hill: University of North Carolina Press, 1984.

Hahn, Robert and Albert McGartland. "The Political Economy of Instrument Choice: An Examination of the U.S. Role in Implementing the Montreal Protocol." *Northwestern University Law Review* 83 (1989): 592–611.

Hahn, Robert and Gordon Hester. "Marketable Permits: Lessons for Theory and Practice." *Ecology Law Quarterly* 361 (1989): 361–406.

Hahn, Robert and Gordon Hester. "The Market for Bads: EPA's Experience with Emissions Trading." *Regulation* 11, no. 3 (1987): 48–53.

Hahn, Robert and Roger Noll. "Barriers to Implementing Tradable Air Pollution Permits: Problems of Regulatory Interactions." *Yale Journal on Regulation* 1 (1983): 63–91.

Hahn, Robert and Roger Noll. "Designing a Market for Tradable Emissions Permits." In *Reform of Environmental Regulation*, edited by Wesley Magat, 119–149. Cambridge: Ballinger, 1982.

Hamilton, Shane. *Trucking Country: The Road to America's Wal-Mart Economy*. Princeton, NJ: Princeton University Press, 2008.

Hardin, Garrett. "The Tragedy of the Commons." *Science* 162, no. 3859 (1968): 1243–1248.

Harvey, David. *A Brief History of Neoliberalism*. New York: Oxford University Press, 2005.

Hays, Samuel. *Beauty, Health, and Permanence: Environmental Politics in the United States, 1955–1985*. Cambridge: Cambridge University Press, 1987.

Hays, Samuel. "Political Choice in Regulatory Administration." In *Regulation in Perspective*, edited by Thomas McCraw, 124–154. Cambridge, MA: Harvard University Press, 1981.

Hays, Samuel. "The Politics of Clean Air." In *Explorations in Environmental History: Essays by Samuel P. Hays*, 219–312. Pittsburgh: University of Pittsburgh Press, 1998.

Hines, Lawrence. "Measurement of Recreation Benefits: A Reply." *Journal of Land & Public Utility Economics* 34, no. 4 (November 1958): 365–367.

Hoberg, George. *Pluralism by Design: Environmental Policy and the American Regulatory State*. New York: Praeger, 1992.

Hochschild, Arlie. *Strangers in Their Own Land: Fear and Mourning on the American Right*. New York: New Press, 2016.

Horowitz, Morton. *The Transformation of American Law, 1780–1860*. Cambridge, MA: Harvard University Press, 1979.

Huntington, Samuel. "The Marasmus of the ICC: The Commission, the Railroads, and the Public Interest." *Yale Law Journal*, 61, no. 4 (1952): 467–509.

Hurley, Andrew. *Environmental Inequalities: Class, Race, and Industrial Pollution in Gary, Indiana, 1945–1980*. Chapel Hill: University of North Carolina Press, 1995.

Jackson, Tim. *Prosperity without Growth: Economics for a Finite Planet*. London: Earthscan, 2009.

Jacobs, Meg. *Panic at the Pump: The Energy Crisis and the Transformation of American Politics in the 1970s*. New York: Hill and Wang, 2016.

Jones, Charles. "The Limits of Public Support: Air Pollution Agency Development." *Public Administration Review* 32, no. 5 (1972): 502–508.

Klyza, Christopher and David Sousa. *American Environmental Policy, 1990–2006: Beyond Gridlock*. Cambridge, MA: MIT Press, 2007.

Kneese, Allen and Charles Schultze. *Pollution, Prices, and Public Policy*. Washington, DC: Brookings Institution, 1975.

Kneese, Allen and F. Lee Brown. *The Southwest under Stress: National Resource Development Issues in a Regional Setting*. Baltimore: Johns Hopkins University Press for Resources for the Future, 1981.

Kolko, Gabriel. *Railroads and Regulation, 1877–1916*. Princeton, NJ: Princeton University Press, 1965.

Kosters, Marvin and Jeffrey Eisenach. "Is Regulatory Relief Enough?" *Regulation* 6 March/April (1982): 20–27.

Krippner, Gretta. *Capitalizing on Crisis: The Political Origins of the Rise of Finance*. Cambridge, MA: Harvard University Press, 2011.

Krutilla, John. "Conservation Reconsidered." *American Economic Review* 57, no. 4 (1967): 777–786.

Kula, Erhun. *History of Environmental Economic Thought*. London: Routledge, 1997.

Landy, Marc, Marc Roberts, and Stephen Thomas. *The Environmental Protection Agency: Asking the Wrong Questions*. New York: Oxford University Press, 1990.

Lash, Jonathan, Katherine Gillman, and David Sheridan. *A Season of Spoils: The Reagan Administration's Attack on the Environment*. New York: Pantheon, 1984.

Leopold, Aldo. *A Sand County Almanac: And Sketches Here and There*. New York: Oxford University Press, 1949.

Lifset, Robert. *Power on the Hudson: Storm King Mountain and The Emergence of Modern American Environmentalism*. Pittsburgh: University of Pittsburgh Press, 2014.

Liroff, Richard, *An Issue Report: Reforming Air Pollution Regulation: The Toil and Trouble of EPA's Bubble*. Washington, DC: Conservation Foundation, 1986.

Lytle, Mark. *The Gentle Subversive: Rachel Carson, Silent Spring, and the Rise of the Environmental Movement*. New York: Oxford University Press, 2007.

Markowitz, Gerald and David Rosner. *Lead Wars: The Politics of Science and the Fate of America's Children*. Berkeley: University of California Press, 2013.

Martineau, Robert and David Novello. *Clean Air Act Handbook*. Chicago: American Bar Association, 1997.

McCarthy, Tom. *Auto Mania: Cars, Consumers, and the Environment*. New Haven, CT: Yale University Press, 2007.

McCraw, Tom. *Prophets of Regulation*. Cambridge, MA: Harvard University Press, 1986.

Meckling, Jonas. *Carbon Coalitions: Business, Climate Politics, and the Rise of Emissions Trading*. Cambridge, MA: MIT Press, 2011.

Melnik, R. Shep, *Regulation and the Courts: The Case of the Clean Air Act*. New York: Brookings Institution Press, 1983.

Merchant, Carolyn. *The Death of Nature: Women, Ecology, and the Scientific Revolution*. San Francisco: Harper & Row, 1980.

Mintz, Joel. *Enforcement at the EPA: High Stakes and Hard Choices*. Austin: University of Texas Press, 2012.

Montrie, Chad. *Making a Living: Work and Environment in the United States*. Chapel Hill: University of North Carolina Press, 2008.

National Academy of Public Administration. *The Environment Goes to Market: The Implementation of Economic Incentives for Pollution Control*. Washington, DC: National Academy of Public Administration, 1994.

National Research Council. *Risk Assessment in the Federal Government: Managing the Process*. Washington, DC: National Academies Press, 1983.

Needham, Andrew. *Power Lines: Phoenix and the Making of the Modern Southwest*. Princeton, NJ: Princeton University Press, 2015.

Neves, Carol. *The Environment Goes to Market: The Implementation of Economic Incentives for Pollution Control*. Washington, DC: National Academy of Public Administration, 1994.

Norco, J. E. and R. K. Raufer, "Experience with an Emissions Trading Program," Presented at the 6th Annual Energy-Sources Technology Conference and Exhibition, Houston, Texas, January 1983, cited in Roger Raufer and Stephen Feldman, *Acid Rain and Emissions Trading: Implementing a Market Approach to Pollution Control*. Totowa, NJ: Rowman & Littlefield, 1987.

O'Connor, Martin, ed. *Is Capitalism Sustainable: Political Economy and Politics of Ecology*. New York: Guilford Press, 1994.

Oreskes, Naomi and Erik Conway. *Merchants of Doubt: How a Handful of Scientists Obscured the Truth on Issues from Tobacco Smoke to Global Warming*. London: Bloomsbury, 2010.

Orren, Karen and Stephen Skowronek. " 'Beyond the Iconography of Order: Notes for a "New Institutionalism.'" In *The Dynamics of American Politics*, edited by L. Dodd and C. Jillson, 311–330. Boulder, CO: Westview Press, 1994.

Phillips-Fein, Kim. *Invisible Hands: The Making of the Conservative Movement from the New Deal to Reagan*. New York: W.W. Norton, 2009.

Pigou, A. C. *The Economics of Welfare*. London: Macmillan, 1920.

Portney, Paul. "The Benefits and Costs of Regulatory Analysis." In *Environmental Policy under Reagan's Executive Order: The Role of Benefit-Cost Analysis*, edited by V. Kerry Smith, 226–240. Chapel Hill: University of North Carolina Press, 1984.

Prasad, Monica. *The Politics of Free Markets: The Rise of Neoliberal Policies in Britain, France, Germany, and the United States*. Chicago: University of Chicago Press, 2006.

Raufer, Roger and Stephen Feldman. *Acid Rain and Emissions Trading: Implementing a Market Approach to Pollution Control*. Totowa, NJ: Rowman & Littlefield, 1987.

Reich, Charles. "The New Property." *Public Interest* 3 (Spring 1966): 57–89.

Rome, Adam. *The Genius of Earth Day*. New York: Hill and Wang, 2013.

Rothman, Hal. *Saving the Planet: The American Response to the Environment in the Twentieth Century*. Chicago: Ivan R. Dee, 2000.

Rosencranz, Armin. "The ECE Convention of 1979 on Long-Range Transboundary Air Pollution." *American Journal of International Law* 75, no. 4 (1981): 975–982.

Rosner, David and Gerald Markowitz. *Deadly Dust: Silicosis and the Politics of Occupational Disease in Twentieth-Century America*. Princeton, NJ: Princeton University Press, 1991.

Rosner, David and Gerald Markowitz. *Lead Wars: The Politics of Science and the Fate of America's Children*. Berkeley: University of California Press, 2013.

Ruckelshaus, William. "Science, Risk, and Public Policy." *Science* 221, no. 4615 (1983): 1026–1028.

Sabin, Paul. "'Everything Has a Price': Jimmy Carter and the Struggle for Balance in Federal Regulatory Policy." *Journal of Policy History* 28, no. 1 (2016): 1–47.

Sabin, Paul. *The Bet: Paul Ehrlich, Julian Simon, and Our Gamble over Earth's Future*. New Haven, CT: Yale University Press, 2013.

Samuelson, Paul. "The Pure Theory of Public Expenditure." *Review of Economics and Statistics*, 36, no. 4 (1954): 387–389.

Schumacher, E. F. *Small Is Beautiful: A Study of Economics as if People Mattered*. London: Blond and Briggs, 1973.

Sellers, Christopher. *Crabgrass Crucible: Suburban Nature and the Rise of Environmentalism in Twentieth-Century America*. Chapel Hill: University of North Carolina Press, 2012.

Shapiro, Michael and Ellen Warhit. "Marketable Permits: The Case of Chlorofluorocarbons." *Natural Resources Journal* 23, no. 5 (1983): 577–591.

Snyder, Lynne. "'The Death-Dealing Smog over Donora, Pennsylvania': Industrial Air Pollution, Public Health, and Federal Policy, 1915–1963." PhD diss., University of Pennsylvania, 1994.

Solomon, Barry and Russell Lee. "Emissions Trading and Environmental Justice," *Environment* 42, no. 8 (2000): 32–45.

Spash, Clive. *Greenhouse Economics: Value and Ethics*. London: Routledge, 2002.

Spash, Clive. "The Brave New World of Carbon Trading." *New Political Economy* 15, no. 2 (2010): 169–195.

Stavins, Robert. "Harnessing Market Forces to Protect the Environment." *Environment* 31, no. 1 (1989): 4–35.

Stavins, Robert. "Lessons from the American Experiment with Market-Based Environmental Policies." Kennedy School of Government Faculty Research Working Paper Series RWP01-032, Working Paper No. 22.2002.

Stedman, Daniel. *Masters of the Universe: Hayek, Friedman, and the Birth of Neoliberal Politics*. Princeton, NJ: Princeton University Press, 2012.

Stein, Judith. *Pivotal Decade: How the United States Traded Factories for Finance in the Seventies*. New Haven, CT: Yale University Press, 2010.

Steinberg, Ted. "Can Capitalism Save the Planet?: On the Origins of Green Liberalism." *Radical History Review* 107 (2010): 7–24,

Stern, Nicolas. *Stern Review on the Economics of Climate Change*. London: Government Economic Service, 2006, accessed February 16, 2017, http://webarchive. nationalarchives.gov.uk/+/http://www.hm-treasury.gov.uk/sternreview_index.htm.

Stigler, George. "The Theory of Economic Regulation." *Bell Journal of Economics and Management Science* 2, no. 1 (1971): 3–21.

Stradling, David. *Smokestacks and Progressives: Environmentalists, Engineers, and Air Quality in America, 1881–1951*. Baltimore: Johns Hopkins University Press, 1999.

Tarr, Joel. *The Search for the Ultimate Sink: Urban Pollution in Historical Perspective*. Akron, OH: University of Akron Press, 1996.

Tietenberg, Tom. "Ethical Influences on the Evolution of the US Tradable Permit Approach to Air Pollution Control." *Ecological Economics* 24 (1998): 241–257.

Train, Russell, *Politics, Pollution, and Pandas: An Environmental Memoir*. Washington, DC: Island Press, 2003.

Turner, James and Andrew Isenberg. *The Republican Reversal: Conservatives and the Environment from Nixon to Trump*. Cambridge, MA: Harvard University Press, 2018.

Unknown Author. "National Conference on Air Pollution." *Public Health Reports* 78, no. 5 (1963): 423–429.

Unknown Author. "New PHS Divisions in Reorganization." *Public Health Reports* 75, no. 10 (1960): 924.

Vogel, David. *Fluctuating Fortunes: The Political Power of Business in America.* New York: Basic Books, 1989.

Vogel, Sarah. *Is It Safe? BPA and the Struggle to Define the Safety of Chemicals.* Berkeley: University of California Press, 2012.

Ward, Elliot. "The Los Angeles Affliction: Suggestions for a Cure." *Public Interest* 38 (Winter 1975): 119–128.

Waterhouse, Benjamin. *Lobbying America: The Politics of Business from Nixon to NAFTA.* Princeton, NJ: Princeton University Press, 2014.

White, Lawrence J. "The Auto Pollution Muddle." *Public Interest* 32 (Summer 1973): 97–112.

White, Richard. "So Are You an Environmentalist or Do You Work for a Living?: Work and Nature." In *Uncommon Ground: Rethinking the Human Place in Nature,* edited by William Cronon, 171–185. New York: W.W. Norton, 1995.

Wildavsky, Aaron. *Speaking Truth to Power: The Art and Craft of Policy Analysis.* Boston: Little, Brown, 1979.

Wilentz, Sean. *The Age of Reagan: A History, 1974–2008* (New York: Harper Collins, 2008.

Yaver, Miranda. "When Do Agencies Have Agency? Bureaucratic Noncompliance and Dynamic Lawmaking in United States Statutory Law, 1973–2010." PhD diss., Columbia University, 2015.

Index